THE ENGLISH
DRAMATIC CRITICS

THE ENGLISH
DRAMATIC CRITICS

AN ANTHOLOGY
1660-1932

Assembled by
JAMES AGATE

A DRAMABOOK

HILL AND WANG · NEW YORK

Published by arrangements with The Literary Executors
of the late James Agate
Library of Congress Catalog Card Number: 58-11370
Manufactured in the United States of America

CONTENTS

v

ACKNOWLEDGEMENTS

I WISH to acknowledge the courtesy of my fellow-critics for facilities in using the extracts appearing in this book under their names: Messrs. Max Beerbohm, Ivor Brown, Ashley Dukes, St. John Ervine, J. T. Grein, Desmond MacCarthy, Allan Monkhouse, Charles Morgan, R. Crompton Rhodes, George Bernard Shaw, Arthur Symons; and also of the following publishers of the books whose titles are given in brackets: Chapman & Hall (*The Contemporary Theatre*, 1925); Cobden-Sanderson (*Masques and Phases*); Columbia University Press (*Theatrical Criticism in London to* 1795); Constable & Co. (*Our Theatres in the Nineties* and *The Manchester Stage*); Elkin Mathews (*Eleonora Duse*); Greening & Co. (*Dramatic Criticism*); William Heinemann (*Around Theatres*); Methuen & Co. (*Drama and Life*); Routledge & Sons (*The Journal of a London Playgoer*); Walter Scott (*Dramatic Essays* and *The Theatrical World*). As indicated in the text, dramatic criticisms have been selected from the following periodicals, the proprietors of which are also thanked: " The Birmingham Post "; " The Manchester Guardian "; " The New Statesman "; " The Observer "; " The Saturday Review "; " The Sunday Times "; " The Theatre Arts Monthly "; " The Times "; " The Week-End Review."

NOTE

As I was reading one day about the salvaging of gold lost in the bowels of some sunken steamer, it occurred to me that English dramatic criticism contains much of buried treasure which ought to be recovered. It was then that I began to play with the idea of an anthology, meaning of course the bits which pleased *me* best. On reflection, this seemed hardly fair, for it is unlikely that there will ever again be an anthology of this kind. Such a one, then, must be as good and comprehensive as I could make it, having regard to everybody's taste.

It seemed an easy thing to do, since I vaguely remembered a statement by William Archer that Leigh Hunt was the first English dramatic critic of importance, subsequent to whom it seemed that my own reading and recollection would suffice. For form's sake Archer's statement had to be tested, and a month was sufficient to prove two things—first, that our erudite mentor had for once failed in erudition, and second, that research is a job for somebody having no other business.

Then the publication in America of Professor Charles Harold Gray's *Theatrical Criticism in London to* 1795 came to the rescue, and I gratefully acknowledge the Professor's expert guidance about this period, guidance without which this book could not have appeared for another ten years ! I am all the more grateful in that the British Museum had chosen this particular moment for the sequestration of its newspapers prior to their removal to Hendon.

For the period from 1795 to the present day I have relied upon my previous browsing in the subject. Readers will appreciate that an anthology is not an encyclopædia. Let me state that no attempt has been made at a history of the English stage or its players in the light of critical writings, since that also must have been encyclopædic. I have merely collected a

number of pieces the re-reading of which is calculated to afford
delight. Their point of unity is that they are with very few
exceptions the work of accredited dramatic critics in the
modern sense of that term, and not of historians like Genest,
preface-writers like Dryden, pamphleteers like Downes and
Collier, memoir-writers like Cibber and Doran.

I have now to decide whether to come to the 'osses or expand
this note into an elaborate essay on the function of dramatic
criticism. I choose the former, because the reader must
be impatient to run his eye over my proud and prancing
exhibits, and because there is not one of my collaborators who
could not do or have done the essay better.

Confiding this decision to Mr. Max Beerbohm I receive the
reply : You must string the pearls ! "

I have strung them, and with invisible thread.

J. A.

LONDON.
July 1932.

THE
ENGLISH DRAMATIC CRITICS
(1660–1932)

AN ANTHOLOGY

RICHARD FLECKNOE

(*d.* 1678 ?)

HOW THE EARLY ACTORS TRANSFORMED THEM-SELVES INTO THEIR PARTS

IT was the happiness of the Actors of those times to have such Poets as these [1] to instruct them, and to write for them ; and no less of those Poets to have such docile and excellent Actors to Act their Playes, as a Field and Burbidge [2] ; of whom we may say, that he was a delightful Proteus, so wholly transforming himself into his Part, and putting off himself with his Cloathes, as he never (not so much as in the Tyring-house) assum'd himself again until the Play was done : there being as much difference between him and one of our common Actors, as between a Ballad-singer who onely mouths it, and an excellent singer, who knows all his Graces, and can artfully vary and modulate his Voice, even to know how much breath he is to give to every syllable. He had all the parts of an excellent Orator, (animating his words with speaking, and Speech with Action) his Auditors being never more delighted then [*sic*]

---

[1] The poets referred to were Shakespeare, Ben Jonson, Beaumont, Fletcher, and Suckling.

[2] i.e. Richard Burbage.

when he spoke nor more sorry then [*sic*] when he held his peace ; yet even then, he was an excellent Actor still, never failing in his Part when he had done speaking ; but with his looks and gesture, maintaining it still unto the heighth, he imagining Age quod agis, onely spoke to him ; so as those who call him a Player do him wrong, no man being less idle then [*sic*] he, whose whole life is nothing else but action ; with only this difference from other mens, that as what is but a Play to them, is his Business : so their business is but a play to him.
—*Discourse of the English Stage.*

SIR RICHARD STEELE

(1672–1729)

MRS. BARRY, MRS. BRACEGIRDLE, AND DOGGETT IN *LOVE FOR LOVE*

Will's Coffee-House, April 8. [1709].

ON Thursday night was acted, for the benefit of Mr. Betterton, the celebrated comedy called *Love for Love*. Those excellent players, Mrs. Barry, Mrs. Bracegirdle, and Mr. Doggett, though not at present concerned in the house, acted on that occasion. There has not been known so great a concourse of persons of distinction as at that time ; the stage itself was covered with gentlemen and ladies, and when the curtain was drawn, it discovered even there a very splendid audience. This unusual encouragement, which was given to a play for the advantage of so great an actor, gives an undeniable instance, that the true relish for manly entertainments and rational pleasures is not wholly lost. All the parts were acted to perfection ; the actors were careful of their carriage, and no one was guilty of the affectation to insert witticisms of his own ; but a due respect was had to the audience, for encouraging this accomplished player. It is not now doubted but plays will revive, and take their place in the opinion of persons of wit and merit, notwithstanding their late apostacy in favour of dress and sound. This place is very much altered since Mr. Dryden frequented it ; where you used to see songs, epigrams, and satires, in the hands of every man you met, you have now only a pack of cards ; and instead of the cavils about the turn of the expression, the elegance of the style, and the like, the learned now dispute only about the truth of the game. But however the company is altered, all have shown a great respect for Mr. Betterton : and the very gaming part of this house have been so much touched with a sense of the uncertainty of human

3

affairs, which alter with themselves every moment, that in this gentleman they pitied Marc Antony of Rome, Hamlet of Denmark, Mithridates of Pontus, Theodosius of Greece, and Henry the Eighth of England. It is well known, he has been in the condition of each of those illustrious personages for several hours together, and behaved himself in those high stations, in all the changes of the scene, with suitable dignity. For these reasons, we intend to repeat this late favour to him on a proper occasion, lest he, who can instruct us so well in personating feigned sorrow, should be lost to us by suffering under real ones. The town is at present in very great expectation of seeing a comedy now in rehearsal, which is the twenty-fifth production of my honoured friend Mr. Thomas D'Urfey ; who, besides his great abilities in the dramatic, has a peculiar talent in the lyric way of writing, and that with a manner wholly new and unknown to the antient Greeks and Romans, wherein he is but faintly imitated in the translations of the modern Italian Operas.

—From *The Tatler* (No. 1).

STEELE ON THE DEATH OF BETTERTON

From my own Apartment. May 2. [1710].

HAVING received notice, that the famous actor Mr. Betterton was to be interred this evening in the cloisters near Westminster-abbey, I was resolved to walk thither, and see the last office done to a man whom I had always very much admired, and from whose action I had received more strong impressions of what is great and noble in human nature, than from the arguments of the most solid philosophers, or the descriptions of the most charming poets I had read. As the rude and untaught multitude are no way wrought upon more effectually, than by seeing public punishments and executions ; so men of letters and education feel their humanity most forcibly exercised, when they attend the obsequies of men who had arrived at any perfection in liberal accomplishments. Theatrical action is to be esteemed as such, except it be objected, that we cannot call that an art which cannot be attained by art. Voice, stature, motion, and other gifts, must be very bountifully bestowed by nature, or labour and industry will but push the unhappy endeavourer in that way, the further off his wishes.

Such an actor as Mr. Betterton ought to be recorded with the same respect as Roscius among the Romans. The greatest orator has thought fit to quote his judgement, and celebrate his life. Roscius was the example to all that would form themselves into proper and winning behaviour. His action was so well adapted to the sentiments he expressed, that the Youth of Rome thought they wanted only to be virtuous, to be as graceful in their appearance as Roscius. The imagination took a lively impression of what was great and good ; and they, who never thought of setting up for the art of imitation, became themselves inimitable characters.

There is no human invention so aptly calculated for the forming a free-born people as that of a theatre. Tully reports, that the celebrated player of whom I am speaking, used frequently to say, ' The perfection of an actor is only to become what he is doing.' Young men, who are too inattentive to receive lectures, are irresistibly taken with performances. Hence it is, that I extremely lament the little relish the gentry of this nation have, at present, for the just and noble representations in some of our tragedies. The operas, which are of late introduced, can leave no trace behind them that can be of service beyond the present moment. To sing, and to dance, are accomplishments very few have any thoughts of practising ; but to speak justly, and move gracefully, is what every man thinks he does perform, or wished he did.

—From *The Tatler* (No. 167).

STEELE ON WILKS AND CIBBER

Sheer-lane, June 7, [1710].

THE town grows so very empty, that the greater number of my gay characters are fled out of my sight into the country. My beaux are now shepherds, and my belles wood-nymphs. They are lolling over rivulets, and covered with shades, while we who remain in town, hurry through the dust about impertinences, without knowing the happiness of leisure and retirement. To add to this calamity, even the actors are going

5

to desert us for a season, and we shall not shortly have so much as a land-scape or a frost-scene to refresh ourselves with in the midst of our fatigues. This may not, perhaps, be so sensible a loss to any other as to me ; for I confess it is one of my greatest delights to sit unobserved and unknown in the gallery, and entertain myself either with what is personated on the stage, or observe what appearances present themselves in the audience. If there were no other good consequence in a play-house, than that so many persons of different ranks and conditions are placed there in their most pleasing aspects, that prospect only would be very far from being below the pleasure of a wise man. There is not one person you can see, in whom, if you look with an inclination to be pleased, you may not behold something worthy or agreeable. Our thoughts are in our features ; and the visage of those in whom love, rage, anger, jealousy, or envy, have their frequent mansions, carries the traces of those passions wherever the amorous, the choleric, the jealous, or the envious, are pleased to make their appearance. However, the assembly at a play is usually made up of such as have a sense of some elegance in pleasure ; by which means the audience is gener-ally composed of those who have gentle affections, or at least of such as at that time are in the best humour you can ever find them. This has insensibly a good effect upon our spirits ; and the musical airs which are played to us, put the whole company into a participation of the same pleasure, and by consequence, for that time, equal in humour, in fortune, and in quality. Thus far we gain only by coming into an audience ; but if we find, added to this, the beauties of proper action, the force of eloquence, and the gaiety of well-placed lights and scenes, it is being happy, and seeing others happy, for two hours ; a duration of bliss not at all to be slighted by so short-lived a creature as man. Why then should not the duty of the player be had in much more esteem than it is at present ? If the merit of a performance be to be valued according to the talents which are necessary to it, the qualifications of a player should raise him much above the arts and ways of life which we call mercenary or mechanic. When we look round a full house and behold so few that can, though they set themselves out to show as much as the persons on the stage do, come up to what they would appear even in dumb show ; how much does the actor deserve our approbation, who adds to the advantage of looks and motions, the tone of the voice, the dignity, the humility, the sorrow, and the triumph, suitable to the character he personates !

It may possibly be imagined by severe men, that I am too frequent in the mention of the theatrical representations ; but who is not excessive in the discourse of what he extremely likes ? Eugenio can lead you to a gallery of fine pictures, which collection he is always increasing. Crassus, through woods and forests, to which he designs to add the neighbouring counties. These are great and noble instances of their magnificence. The players are my pictures, and their scenes my territories. By communicating the pleasure I take in them, it may in some measure add to men's gratifications this way ; as viewing the choice and wealth of Eugenio and Crassus augments the enjoyments of those whom they entertain, with a prospect of such possessions as would not otherwise fall within the reach of their fortunes.

It is a very good office one man does another, when he tells him the manner of his being pleased ; and I have often thought, that a comment upon the capacities of the players would very much improve the delight that way, and impart it to those who otherwise have no sense of it.

The first of the present stage are Wilks and Cibber, perfect actors in their different kinds. Wilks has a singular talent in representing the grace of nature : Cibber, the deformity in the affectation of them. Were I a writer of plays, I should never employ either of them in parts which had not their bent this way. This is seen in the inimitable strain and run of good humour which is kept up in the character of Wildair, and in the nice and delicate abuse of understanding in that of Sir Novelty. Cibber, in another light, hits exquisitely the flat civility of an affected gentleman-usher, and Wilks the easy frankness of a gentleman.

If you would observe the force of the same capacities in higher life, can any thing be more ingenuous than the behaviour of prince Harry, when his father checks him ? any thing more exasperating than that of Richard when he insults his superiors ? To beseech gracefully, to approach respectfully, to pity, to mourn, to love, are the places wherein Wilks may be made to shine with the utmost beauty. To rally pleasantly, to scorn artfully, to flatter, to ridicule, and to neglect, are what Cibber would perform with no less excellence.

When actors are considered with a view to their talents, it is not only the pleasure of that hour of action, which the spectators gain from their performance ; but the opposition of right and wrong on the stage, would have lost its force in the assistance of our judgements on other occasions. I have at present under my tutelage a young poet, who, I design, shall entertain the town the ensuing winter. And, as he does me the honour to let me see his comedy as he writes it, I shall endeavour to make the parts fit the genius of the several actors, as exactly as their habits can their bodies. And because the two I have mentioned are to perform the principal parts, I have prevailed with the house to let the *Careless Husband* be acted on Tuesday next, that my young author may have a view of a play, which is acted to perfection, both by them and all concerned in it ; as being born within the walls of the theatre, and written with an exact knowledge of the abilities of the performers. Mr. Wilks will do his best in this play, because it is for his own benefit : and Mr. Cibber, because he writ it. Besides which, all the great beauties we have left in town, or within call of it, will be present, because it is the last play this season. This opportunity will, I hope, inflame my pupil with such generous notions, from seeing this fair assembly as will be then present, that his play may be composed of sentiments and characters proper to be presented to such an audience. His drama at present has only the outlines drawn. There are, I find, to be in it all the reverend offices of life such as regard to parents, husbands, and honourable lovers, preserved with the utmost care ; and at the same time that agreeableness of behaviour, with the intermixture of pleasing passions which arise from innocence and virtue, interspersed in such a manner, as that to be charming and agreeable shall appear the natural consequence of being virtuous. This great end is one of those I propose to do in my censorship ; but if I find a thin house on an occasion when such a work is to be promoted, my pupil shall return to his commons at Oxford.

—From *The Tatler* (No. 182).

JOSEPH ADDISON

(1672–1719)

HIS FUN ABOUT THE ITALIAN OPERA

Tuesday, March 6, 1710–11.

AN opera may be allowed to be extravagantly lavish in its decorations, as its only design is to gratify the senses, and keep up an indolent attention in the audience. Common sense, however, requires that there should be nothing in the scenes and machines which may appear childish and absurd. How would the wits of King Charles's time have laughed, to have seen Nicolini exposed to a tempest in robes of ermine, and sailing in an open boat upon a sea of pasteboard? What a field of raillery would they have been led into, had they been entertained with painted dragons spitting wildfire, enchanted chariots drawn by Flanders mares, and real cascades in artificial landscapes? A little skill in criticism would inform us, that shadows and realities ought not to be mixed together in the same piece; and that the scenes which are designed as the representations of nature should be filled with resemblances, and not with the things themselves. If one would represent a wide champaign country filled with herds and flocks, it would be ridiculous to draw the country only upon the scenes, and to crowd several parts of the stage with sheep and oxen. This is joining together inconsistencies, and making the desecration partly real and partly imaginary. I would recommend what I have here said to the directors, as well as to the admirers of our modern opera.

As I was walking in the streets about a fortnight ago, I saw an ordinary fellow carrying a cage full of little birds upon his shoulder; and as I was wondering with myself what use he would put them to, he was met very luckily by an acquaintance who had the same curiosity. Upon his asking what he had upon his shoulder, he told him that he had been buying sparrows for the opera. "Sparrows for the opera!" says his friend, licking his lips; "what, are they to be roasted?"—"No, no," says the other, "they are to enter towards the end of the first act, and to fly about the stage."

This strange dialogue awakened my curiosity so far, that I immediately bought the opera, by which means I perceived that the sparrows were to act the part of singing birds in a delightful grove; though, upon a nearer inquiry, I found the sparrows put the same trick upon the audience that Sir Martin Mar-all[1] practised upon his mistress: for though they flew in sight, the music proceeded from a *consort* of flageolets and bird-calls, which were planted behind the scenes. At the same time I made this discovery, I found, by the discourse of the actors, that there were great designs on foot for the improvement of the opera; that it had been proposed to break down a part of the wall, and to surprise the audience with a party of a hundred horse; and that there was actually a project of bringing the New-river into the house, to be employed in jet-d'eaus and water-works. This project, as I have since heard, is postponed till the summer season; when it is thought the coolness that proceeds from fountains and cascades will be more acceptable and refreshing to people of quality. In the mean time, to find out a more agreeable entertainment for the winter-season, the opera of *Rinaldo* is filled with thunder and lightning, illuminations and fire-works; which the audience may look upon without catching cold, and indeed without much danger of being burnt; for there are several engines filled with water, and ready to play at a minute's warning, in case any such accident should happen. However, as I have a very great friendship for the owner of this theatre, I hope that he has been wise enough to insure his house before he would let this opera be acted in it.

It is no wonder, that those scenes should be very surprising, which were contrived by two poets of different nations, and raised by two magicians of different sexes. Armida, as we are told in the argument, was an Amazonian enchantress, and poor

[1] In the comedy by John Dryden, borrowed from Quinault's *Amant Indiscret* and the *Etourdi* of Molière.

Signior Cassani, as we learn from the persons represented, a Christian conjuror, Mago Christiano. I must confess I am very much puzzled to find how an Amazon should be versed in the black art, or how a good Christian, for such is the part of the magician, should deal with the devil.

To consider the poets after the conjurors, I shall give you a taste of the Italian from the first lines of his preface : " *Eccoli, benigno lettore, un parto di poche sere, che se ben nato di notte, non è però aborto di tenebre, ma si farà conoscere figilio d'Apollo con qualche raggio di Parnasso.*" " Behold, gentle reader, the birth of a few evenings, which though it be the offspring of the night, is not the abortive of darkness, but will make itself known to be the son of Apollo, with a certain ray of Parnassus." He afterwards proceeds to call Mynheer Handel the Orpheus of our age, and to acquaint us, in the same sublimity of style, that he composed this opera in a fortnight. Such are the wits to whose tastes we so ambitiously conform ourselves. The truth of it is, the finest writers among the modern Italians express themselves in such a florid form of words, and such tedious circumlocutions, as are used by none but pedants in our own country ; and at the same time fill their writings with such poor imaginations and conceits, as our youths are ashamed of before they have been two years at the university. Some may be apt to think that it is the difference of genius which produces this difference in the works of the two nations ; but to show there is nothing in this, if we look into the writings of the old Italians, such as Cicero and Virgil, we shall find that the English writers, in their way of thinking and expressing themselves, resemble those authors much more than the modern Italians pretend to do. And as for the poet himself, from whom the dreams of this opera [1] are taken, I must entirely agree with Monsieur Boileau, that one verse in Virgil is worth all the clinquant or tinsil of Tasso.

But to return to the sparrows. There have been so many flights of them let loose in this opera, that it is to be feared the house will never get rid of them ; and that in other plays they may make their entrance in very wrong and improper scenes, so as to be seen flying in a lady's bed-chamber, or perching

---

[1] *Rinaldo*, an opera, 8vo, 1711. The plan by Aaron Hill ; the Italian words by Sig. G. Rossi ; and the music by Handel.

upon a king's throne ; besides the inconveniences which the heads of the audience may sometimes suffer from them. I am credibly informed, that there was once a design of casting into an opera the story of Whittington and his Cat, and that in order to do it, there had been got together a great quantity of mice ; but Mr. Rich the proprietor of the play-house, very prudently considered that it would be impossible for the cat to kill them all ; and that, consequently, the princes of his stage might be as much infested with mice, as the prince of the island was before the cat's arrival upon it ; for which reason he would not permit it to be acted in his house. And indeed I cannot blame him : for, as he said very well upon that occasion, I do not hear that any of the performers in our opera pretend to equal the famous pied piper, who made all the mice of a great town in Germany follow his music, and by that means cleared the place of those little noxious animals.

Before I dismiss this paper, I must inform my reader, that I hear there is a treaty on foot with London and Wise,[1] who will be appointed gardeners of the playhouse, to furnish the opera of Rinaldo and Armida with an orange-grove ; and that, the next time it is acted, the singing-birds will be personated by tom-tits, the undertakers being resolved to spare neither pains nor money for the gratification of the audience.

—From *The Spectator* (No. 5).

ADDISON ON THE HISTORY OF THE ITALIAN OPERA

Wednesday, March 21, 1710–11.

IT is my design in this paper to deliver down to posterity a faithful account of the Italian opera, and of the gradual progress which it has made upon the English stage ; for there is no question but our great grand-children will be very curious to know the reason why their forefathers used to sit together like an audience of foreigners in their own country, and to hear whole plays acted before them in a tongue which they did not understand.

Arsinoe was the first opera that gave us a taste of Italian music.

---

[1] London and Wise were the Queen's gardeners at this time.

The great success this opera met with, produced some attempts of forming pieces upon Italian plans, which should give a more natural and reasonable entertainment than what can be met with in the elaborate trifles of that nation. This alarmed the poetasters and fiddlers of the town, who were used to deal in a more ordinary kind of ware ; and therefore laid down, an established rule, which is received as such to this day, " that nothing is capable of being well set to music, that is not nonsense."

This maxim was no sooner received, but we immediately fell to translating the Italian operas ; and as there was no great danger of hurting the sense of those extraordinary pieces, our authors would often make words of their own which were entirely foreign to the meaning of the passages they pretended to translate ; their chief care being to make the numbers of the English verse answer to those of the Italian, that both of them might go to the same tune. Thus the famous song in *Camilla* :

Barbara si t'intendo, etc.
Barbarous woman, yes, I know your meaning,

which expresses the resentments of an angry lover, was translated into that English lamentation,

Frail are a lover's hopes, etc.

And it was pleasant enough to see the most refined persons of the British nation dying away and languishing to notes that were filled with a spirit of rage and indignation. It happened also very frequently, where the sense was rightly translated, the necessary transposition of words, which were drawn out of the phrase of one tongue into that of another, made the music appear very absurd in one tongue that was very natural in the other. I remember an Italian verse that ran thus, word for word :

And turn'd my rage into pity ;

which the English for rhyme sake translated,

And into pity turn'd my rage.

By this means the soft notes that were adapted to pity in the Italian, fell upon the word rage in the English ; and the angry sounds that were turned to rage in the original, were made to express pity in the translation. It oftentimes happened likewise, that the finest notes in the air fell upon the most insignificant words in the sentence. I have known the word " and " pursued through the whole gamut ; have been entertained with many a melodious " the "; and have heard the most beautiful graces, quavers, and divisions bestowed upon " them," " for," and " from," to the eternal honour of our English particles.

The next step to our refinement was the introducing of Italian actors into our opera ; who sung their parts in their own language, at the same time that our countrymen performed theirs in our native tongue. The king or hero of the play generally spoke in Italian, and his slaves answered him in English. The lover frequently made his court, and gained the heart of his princess, in a language which she did not understand. One would have thought it very difficult to have carried on dialogues after this manner without an interpreter between the persons that conversed together ; but this was the state of the English stage for about three years.

At length the audience grew tired of understanding half the opera ; and therefore, to ease themselves entirely of the fatigue of thinking, have so ordered it at present, that the whole opera is performed in an unknown tongue. We no longer understand the language of our own stage ; insomuch that I have often been afraid, when I have seen our Italian performers chattering in the vehemence of action, that they have been calling us names, and abusing us among themselves ; but I hope, since we put such an entire confidence in them, they will not talk against us before our faces, though they may do it with the same safety as if it were behind our backs. In the mean time, I cannot forbear thinking how naturally an historian who writes two or three hundred years hence, and does not know the taste of his wise forefathers, will make the following reflection : " In the beginning of the eighteenth century, the Italian tongue was so well understood in England, that operas were acted on the public stage in that language."

One scarce knows how to be serious in the confutation of an absurdity that shows itself at the first sight. It does not want any great measure of sense to see the ridicule of this monstrous practice ; but what makes it the more astonishing, it is not the taste of the rabble, but of persons of the greatest politeness, which has established it.

If the Italians have a genius for music above the English, the English have a genius for other performances of a much higher nature, and capable of giving the mind a much nobler entertainment. Would one think it possible, at a time when an author lived that was able to write the Phaedra and Hippolitus, for a people to be so stupidly fond of the Italian opera, as scarce to give a third day's hearing to that admirable tragedy ? Music is certainly a very agreeable entertainment : but if it would take the entire possession of our ears ; if it would make us incapable of hearing sense ; if it would exclude arts that have a much greater tendency to the refinement of human nature ; I must confess I would allow it no better quarter than Plato has done, who banishes it out of his commonwealth.

At present our notions of music are so very uncertain, that we do not know what it is we like ; only, in general, we are transported with anything that is not English : so it be of a foreign growth, let it be Italian, French, or High Dutch, it is the same thing. In short, our English music is quite rooted out, and nothing yet planted in its stead.

—From *The Spectator* (No. 13).

"THE LONDON CHRONICLE"

(1757–1823)

THE CHARACTER OF FALSTAFF, AND A CUT SCENE

Covent Garden, Jan. 25, 1757.

WAS performed, the first Part of *Henry the Fourth*, written by Shakespear. The Plays of this Author must never be judged by the strict Rules of Dramatic Poetry, with which it is to be imagined, he was not acquainted ; and therefore to try him by what he did not know, would be trying him by a Kind of *ex post facto* Law ; Regularity of Design being introduced in this Country since the Decease of that great Genius. Mr. Hume, in his History of Great Britain, has given a pretty just Character of him, when he says, "A striking Peculiarity of Sentiment, adapted to a singular Character, he frequently hits as it were by Inspiration ; but a reasonable Propriety of Thought he cannot, for any Time, uphold " ; unless the Character of Falstaff be an Exception to this very sensible Writer's Opinion. For indeed the Character of Sir John no where flags, and he generally upholds a Propriety of Thought, if it be considered in regard to the Manners of the Speaker. Bullying, Cowardice, Vaunting, Detection, boasted Activity, and bodily Indolence, Profligacy, and Pretentions to Decorum form such a party-coloured Groupe as moves our Laughter irresistibly ; his Wit, and, on all Occasions, the Pleasantry of his Ideas, provoke us to laugh with him, and hinder the Knight's Character from sinking into Contempt ; and we love him, in Spight [*sic*] of his degrading Foibles, for his enlivened Humour and his companionable Qualities. It is somewhat surprizing that the Players have agreed to supersede one of the best Scenes in the Play, which is that between Falstaff and the Prince, where Sir John personates by Turns the King and his

17

Son, with such a Vein of Humour as perhaps would divert an Audience beyond any thing in the Comedy.

—From " The London Chronicle," Jan. 25–27, 1757.

"THE LONDON CHRONICLE" ON BARRY AS RICHARD III

Covent-Garden, 27 Jan., 1757.

W AS performed *Richard the Third*, altered from Shakespear by Colley Cibber. Mr. Garrick has been such an admirable Commentator on this Character, that it is needless to criticise it. However, as Mr. Barry appeared in it, for the first Time, this Night, we propose hereafter to enter into an Examination of it ; but chuse to defer this Matter till we have seen Mr. Barry once more ; not thinking it fair to determine his Merit in it till he performs it free from the Solicitude of a first Adventure.

Covent Garden, Jan. 29, 1757.

W AS repeated *Richard the Third*, by Mr. Barry. The Qualities which constitute Richard's Character are such as require a nice Discernment of Spirits, otherwise the Actor will be likely to fail in the distinguishing Singularities of this very complicated Hero. This, we imagine, is the Case in many Scenes, as this Actor performs them. The deep designing Villainy of Richard is generally converted into Rant in the Soliloquies, which are never agitated with the Passions, except where Joy transports him. They are mostly Situations of dark, cool, and deliberate Wickedness, and should be uttered with deep and grave Tones of Voice, and a gloomy Countenance. These two Requisites Nature has denied this Performer, tho' she has been very liberal to him in Qualifications for Love, Grief and enraged Tenderness. Accordingly, he does not seem to carry with him that covered Spirit of Enterprize, which is so peculiar a Mark of the Character. He is too turbulent in all the Scenes where he is alone ; and the Humour of Richard, which never should take off the Mark, is with him too free and open. Richard's Pleasantry never rises to Mirth ; it always proceeds from what the Poet calls the *mala mentis gaudia*, the wicked Pleasures of the Mind ; and it should therefore never become totally jocund, but should ever be a mixed Emotion of Joy and Malice. Where he jokes about his Score or two of Taylors, and finds himself a marvellous proper Man, there should be no Free Exultation, because his Mirth is ironical, and he is still sensible of his own Deformity ; and therefore he should smile and smile, and be a Villain. This Rule will hold all through, except in the triumphant Self-Congratulations of Ambition. The Love Scene, we apprehend, he entirely mistakes : Richard has a Tongue that can wheedle with the Devil, but not pour out the melting Harmony of Romeo. Richard indeed says afterwards, He truly loved ; but his Love was nothing more than Lust. Were he capable of having any real Regard for a Woman, he could never have recourse to Expressions of his Passion suitable to a Varanes ; and as he only intended to have her, but not keep her long, however he might smooth his Face in Smiles, his Words could not come from him like Flakes of feathered Snow that melted as they fell. In the Scenes of Hurry and Bustle Mr. Barry rises upon his Audience, but is sometimes apt to set out with his Voice strained to its utmost ; by which Means it becomes thin, and therefore does not carry with it sufficient Terror. Upon the whole, we think this Contest lies between Mr. Barry and Mr. Mossop. If the former could play the three first Acts as well as Mr. Mossop, he would excel his Antagonist : And if the latter were as quick and animated as Mr. Barry in the last two Acts, he would approach very near to Mr. Garrick.

—From " The London Chronicle," Jan. 29–Feb. 1, 1757.

HAMLET COMPARED WITH ITS ORIGINAL : WHERE SHAKESPEAR ERRED

Covent-Garden. Feb. 17, 1757.

THE Tragedy of *Hamlet*, written by Shakespear, was performed at this Theatre. This Play is formed upon the Story of Amlett in the Danish History of Saxo-Grammaticus. If the Reader has a Mind to see the Use Shakespear made of it, we refer him to Mrs. Lenox's Shakespear illustrated, where he will find the Passage translated to his Hand by a Friend of that Lady's. The story has a very romantic Air ; abounds with Improbabilities ; and is such altogether as would scarce have struck any Imagination but Shakespear's. Amlett, we are told, put on the Guise of Folly, rolled on the Ground, covered his Face with Filth, raked the Embers with his Hands, etc. How finely has Shakespear taken this Hint ! And what a dignified Mind has he presented to us in young Hamlet ? . . . The Ghost is entirely his own Invention ; nothing of this Sort being in the History : How nobly is that imaginary Personage introduced ! And what a Solemnity of Ideas the Poet has assigned him ! The Scene, in which young Hamlet first hears of his Father's Spirit, is not the most important, but is as finely conducted as any Passage in the Play. The young Prince's disjointed Manner of asking Questions, and the minute exactness of those Questions . . . Staid it long ? . . . Armed, say ye ? . . . Pale . . . or Red . . . and fixed his Eyes upon you ? etc. All these little Touches are agreeable to the Affections of the Mind, when we talk of a Person we love either absent or dead, and in the present Case they serve to alarm the Imagination, and to raise our Expectation of the Event. In the original Story the Catastrophe is full of Terror : Amlett, having made the Nobility drunk, set Fire to the Palace, and during the Confusion, goes to the Usurper's Apartment, and tells him that Amlett was then to revenge his Father's Death ; upon which the King jumping out of Bed, he was instantly put to Death, and Amlith [sic] was proclaimed King. The Historian concludes with this Remark. " O brave young Man, who covered more than human Wisdom under the Guise of a Natural, and not only secured his own Safety by that Artifice, but obtained the Means of completely revenging his Father ; and it is now left to every Body to judge which was greater, his Bravery or Wisdom." If Shakespear had not deviated from this Circumstance, he would perhaps have given the finest Scenes of Terror in the last Act that ever have been imagined : and then a Subject that opens so nobly would have been grand also in the Close. As the Play now stands, the Innocent, contrary to Tradition, falls with the Guilty ; like the Personage in *Tom Thumb*, all he boasts is, that he falls the last ; and the World is left to judge which is worst, the Fencing of the Actors, or the Folly of the Poet in introducing it.

—From " The London Chronicle," 15–17 Feb., 1757.

MRS. BEHN'S *THE ROVER* SHOCKS THE LADIES, AND DELIGHTS THE MEN

Covent-Garden. Feb. 22, 1757.

WAS performed *The Rover*, a Comedy, written by Mrs. Behn. There are two Plays under this Title by this Lady, one exhibited first in the year 1677, the other in 1681. Mr. Pope has passed a very just Censure on this Writer in the two following Lines :

> The Stage how losely does Astrea tread,
> Who fairly puts all Characters to Bed ?

In the Play before us there is a very remarkable Instance of this putting to Bed. One of the Personages of the Drama takes off his Breeches in the Sight of the Audience, whose Diversion is of a complicated Nature on the Occasion. The Ladies are first alarmed ; then the Men stare : The Women put up their Fans.—" My Lady Betty, what is the Man about ? "—" Lady Mary, sure he is not in earnest ! "—Then peep thro' their Fans—" Well, I vow, the He creature is taking off his odious Breeches—He-he—Po !—is that all ?—the " Man has Drawers on."—Then, like Mrs. Cadwallador in the new Farce—" Well, to be sure, I never saw any Thing in the Shape of it."—Mean-time, the Delight of the Male Part of the Audience is occasioned by the various Operations of this Phœnomenon [*sic*] on the Female Mind.—" This is rare Fun, d—n me—Jack, Tom, Bob, did you ever see any thing like this ?—Look at that Lady yonder—See, in the Stage Box—how she looks half-averted," etc., etc. It is Matter of Wonder that the Upper Gallery don't call for an Hornpipe, or, " Down with the Drawers," according to their usual Custom of insisting upon as much as they can get for their Money. But to be a little serious, it should be re-membered by all Managers that this Play was written in the dissolute Days of Charles the Second ; and that Decency at least is, or ought to be, demanded at present. Had this Play been acted at Edinburgh, the Alarm spread among the

Scottish Clergy would not be in the least surprizing, and their Invective against Stage-Plays would have been just and seasonable [1]; whereas, we are well informed, their Displeasure is now directed against a very moral Piece, subservient to the Purposes of Religion and Virtue : And we are glad that the Manager of Covent-Garden Theatre is shortly to make Amends to the Public, for the Revival of *The Rover*, by exhibiting on his Stage *The Tragedy of Douglas* [1]; of which the Reader may see a Character in Mr. Hume's Dedication prefixed to his *Four Dissertations*, lately published by Mr. Millar.

—From " The London Chronicle," 22–24 Feb., 1757.

" THE LONDON CHRONICLE " ON
THE TRAGEDY OF DOUGLAS

Covent-Garden. March 14, 1757.

WAS presented, for the first Time, a new Tragedy, intitled, *Douglas*, to a most numerous and splendid Audience. As this Author writes intirely on the Side of Morality, we cannot conceive why an inflammatory Spirit should have arose against him in his own Country. It may, however, be some Consolation to him, that from a British Audience he has met with the warmest Testimonials of Approbation, and that he has sent many of them home, if not better Men, at least very sensibly alive to the Loveliness of Virtue. We cannot, at present, pretend to give an exact Critique on this Piece, but a short History of our own Affections, while under his Operation, is in our Power, and that we beg Leave to offer to the Public. From the opening of the Play, we felt our Passions irresistably seized, and attached to the Subject : Mrs. Woffington, who begins it, breaks into a beautiful Pathos, at once poetical and simple : As the Story unfolds itself by Degrees the Interest grew stronger ; and upon the Introduction of Mr. Barry our Hopes and Fears were agreeably set at Variance. The Scene in which Mr. Sparks makes his first Appearance seemed to us

---

[1] The author of *Douglas* was John Home, a clergyman, who dared to write a play at a time when the Church was violently attacking the Stage. The production of the play resulted in one of the bitterest and most famous controversies in the old feud between the Pulpiteers and the Players.

admirably written, and very finely performed by the Player :
The pastoral Simplicity of his Language and the Purity of his
Manners were highly pleasing : Our Expectation is well
worked up, and Terror and Pity reign in every Breast, till by
due Degrees the Discovery is made, when a Tide of Joy breaks
in upon us.   There is likewise a great deal of Tenderness between the Mother and the Son when she discovers herself to
him ;   and Mr. Barry in the Passage, which succeeds this,
entertained his Auditors with some masterly Strokes of Acting.
The Catastrophe was likewise very affecting : Hope, Joy,
Terror, and Pity, which are the true Tragic Passions, were here
agitated to a very high Degree of Emotion.   Upon the whole,
the Character appeared to us well drawn ;   the Diction has an
easy Strength, no where too rich, generally expressive, often
impassioned and sometimes sublime.   Though the Fable
bears a Resemblance to that of Merope, yet the Circumstances
are sufficiently varied.   Mr. Barry acquitted himself well in
his Part ;   Mrs. Woffington convinced us, that she can touch
the tender Passions very feelingly, and Mr. Sparks rose greatly
above himself by descending, if we may be allowed the Antithesis, from the Fustian of Acting to the simple Workings of
Nature.   To conclude, we met with a very pathetic Entertainment this Night, and will venture to promise our Readers
the same pleasing Melancholy whenever they chuse to see
the *Tragedy of Douglas.*

—From " The London Chronicle," 12–15 March, 1757.

THE CRITIC ON A YOUNG ACTOR'S FIRST AND FIERY " TRYAL "

Drury-Lane.   Sept. 28, 1758.

A T Drury Lane, on Thursday the 28th of last month, was
performed the Tragedy of *Romeo and Juliet* ; the part of
Romeo by a young gentleman who never appeared upon any
stage before.   The humanity and good nature of the English
is in nothing, perhaps, more conspicuously evident, than in
their reception of a new performer upon the stage : for however
the whole audience in a body may be regarded in the light of
his Judge, every individual appears to be of his Counsel, by the

great anxiety they manifest for his success, and the care they take to lay hold of, and blazon, every little incident that can possibly redound to his advantage. It was amidst the universal acclamations of such an audience as this, that the above-mentioned young gentleman made his first entrance ; and perhaps there never came any object before the Publick, which seemed more eminently to deserve their support, or to stand in greater need of it. Modesty, they say, is the inseparable concomitant of Merit ; it is therefore no wonder that Mr. Fleetwood should possess a very considerable share of it. To say the truth, it for some time seemed totally to subdue all his other faculties : however, as his confusion wore off, it afterwards turn'd to his advantage by giving an irresistible air to every thing he said, and did, and by enforcing those letters of recommendation (as Addison calls them) which were written so legibly in his countenance.

As the character of Romeo is in itself one of the most amiable upon the English stage, so the idea, which one may be supposed to conceive of his figure from Shakespear's description of it, cannot be more aptly conveyed than by the appearance of our young Roscius. But as the two first acts require more of ease and grace, than any other qualities of a good actor, so in my opinion he shone less in those, than in any other parts of the performance. And here I must take the liberty, in a very particular manner, to recommend to him a close application to his Fencing and Dancing Masters. People of a middle stature are sometimes genteel by nature ; but persons inclinable to be remarkably tall, are almost all born in original aukwardness ; and it requires the greatest pains for a player so circumstanced, to correct his motions in such a manner as to avoid shocking the spectator. I cannot help observing in this place, that there is hardly one performer upon either theatre, that knows how to stand still, except Mr. Garrick.

In the third act he appeared to great advantage ; and not a little so in the first scene where he encounters that brutal ruffian Tibalt. His pronounciation of

> Tibalt, the reason that I have to love thee
> Doth much excuse the appertaining rage
> Of such a greeting, etc.

with what he afterwards says upon Tibalt's injurious answer, and in which more is meant than meets the ear, was extremely significant. But in the fifth scene with the Fryar, he was absolutely masterly. I must own he appeared to me to be a strong imitator of Mr. Garrick, but then his imitation was so exquisitely satisfactory, that it was rather a proof of his great powers, and observation to profit by so excellent an Original, than any want of sufficiency in himself.

The limits which I am prescribed will not suffer me to point out several excellencies, which I took notice of in the performance of this scene, as well as in that of the Garden upon his departure from his wife. But I cannot help taking notice, that there was something astonishingly wild and passionate, in his performing of that part of the scene in Fryar Lawrance's [*sic*] cell, where, starting from the ground, upon the old nurse's telling him the distress'd situation of Juliet, and with that particular circumstance of her calling upon Romeo, and then flinging herself down upon her bed : he crys—

> As if that name
> Shot from the deadly level of a gun
> Did murder her, Oh tell me, Fryar, tell me,
> In what part of this vile anatomy
> Doth my name lodge ? tell me, that I may sack
> The hateful mansion.

There was something remarkably pathetick, and tender too, in his taking leave of Juliet.

He does not appear again till the fifth act ; in the first scene of which he performed with great spirit ; nor did he fall short of any actor I ever saw in the surprize, and shock which he expressed at the news of his wife's death. But in the celebrated soliloquy, begining with " I do remember an apothecary," he fixed his eyes upon the ground, and seemed to be utterly at a loss what to do, either with himself or them. It must be owned, that so long a declamation is a fiery tryal for a young actor ; and of this the judicious manager seemed to be conscious, by curtailing the above-mentioned on the present occasion. But if Mr. Fleetwood failed, in this point, to answer the expectations of a critical inquisitor, it only looked like a piece of art to heighten that pleasure which he was pre-paring to give him in the subsequent catastrophe : and I will close this paper with venturing to affirm, without setting apart any particular instances, that the last scene of Romeo and Juliet was never performed with more tenderness, energy and justness, in every respect, since the first revival of that tragedy, nor more to the satisfaction of all the judicious part of the audience, than it was by Mr. Fleetwood the first night of his performance. And I am the bolder to make this assertion, as I am assured it agrees with the opinion of the best actor, and judge of acting, in the world ; whose great good-nature in instructing young performers, and encouraging them with his applause, can never be sufficiently commended.

It would be injustice to make an end of this essay without mentioning Miss Pritchard : that amiable young actress can never fail to please. And it would be the highest injury to his merit, not to own that Mr. Palmer performs the part of Mercutio in such a manner, as to leave the town no manner of reason to regret Mr. Woodward, at least in that character.

—From " The London Chronicle," 3–5 Oct., 1758.

" THE LONDON CHRONICLE " ON HOW MRS. CENTLIVRE KEPT *HER* SECRET

Drury-Lane. 30 *Sept.*, 1758.

At Drury-Lane on Saturday last (by desire) was acted *The Wonder : A Woman Keeps a Secret.*

Mrs. Centlivre, the honest woman who thought proper to scribble this comedy, was (as we may learn from the notes on Pope's *Dunciad*, in which poem she procured herself a station by some dirty rhymes that she squirted at the author and his friends) the wife of one of his Majesty's yeomen of the mouth, or table-deckers. How she came to have the good luck to get her plays acted, I own, I am at a loss to determine, unless it was by Court interest. However, of eight or ten dramatic pieces which she made a shift to glean up, there was not one but what was acted at the Theatre-Royal in Drury-Lane, and, if we may credit her epistles dedicatory, with a decent share of applause. Be that as it will, peace to their manes ! they are now all buried in oblivion, except three, viz. *The Wonder, The Busy Body,* and

The Bold Stroke for a Wife. And as the former of these pieces has of late engrossed a good deal of the public attention, I shall take the liberty in this place to enquire what it is ? and whence it came from ?

And first, as to " what it is," that, I think, is easily answered by saying, that it is an indifferent play inimitably acted. However, I can by no means agree to its being so very wretched a performance, as some people are pleased to represent it : and for this reason : a good plot is on all hands allowed to be the principal ingredient towards a good comedy ; now that of the Wonder is not only entertaining, but in some respects exquisitely beautiful. But when you have said thus much, you have said every thing ; for the language is contemptible to the last degree ; and the first act in particular so lame and ungraceful, that it is hardly to be borne.

As to " whence it came from," this question cannot be so readily answered, as the precedent. For Mrs. Centlivre was a gentlewoman who plundered snug, and took care not to drop a syllable, either in her Prologues, or Prefaces, which might serve the readers as a clue to lead them to the place where she pilfered her materials for her plays. Notwithstanding, I think it is pretty palpable, that the main design of this comedy, at least as far as it comes under the title of a Woman keeps a Secret, carries a Spanish air. It is pretty palpable, I say, that the character of Felix is immediately copied from *Don Garcia of Navarre, or the Jealous Prince,* an heroic comedy written by Molière. This piece was damned by the French ; and indeed it is no wonder, for heroic comedy is a species of the drama, so contradictory in itself, so dull, and so trifling, that, I think, it is impossible it should succeed any where. As for the amour between Squire Lissardo and Mesdames Flora and Inis, it may be, for ought I know, partly her own ; tho' I remember the instance about the crooked legs, and Mrs. Inis's pulling up her petticoats, in a scene of an Italian farce between Scapin, Marinnetta and Columbine. However, they serve a darling purpose of hers extremely well in the last act, by making two additional couples in the marriage-dance ; for in every one of her plays, this Lady has manifested the greatest abhorrence of celibacy, and the most tender regard for the procreation of the species, by providing all her men with wives, as far as her women go.

We all remember how poorly *The Wonder* succeeded at Covent-garden, when it was revived there three or four years ago, for some body's benefit, being chiefly, if not entirely supported by Shuter's mimickry in the character of the Scotch footman : And indeed the value it now bears, must principally be attributed to him, who, like Midas, turns every thing he touches into gold. But I beg pardon for engaging the reader so long on a subject which might have been treated in much fewer words, since the writing of this comedy is below censure, and the acting of it above praise.

—From " The London Chronicle," 7–10 Oct., 1758.

" THE LONDON CHRONICLE " ON CONGREVE'S WIT IN *LOVE FOR LOVE*

Covent-Garden. 11 *Oct.*, 1758.

YESTERDAY evening was performed at the above theatre, the comedy of *Love for Love*.

Were I to give my own opinion, I should say, that this is the best comedy either antient or modern, that ever was written to please upon the stage ; for while the most superficial judges admire it, it is impossible but the nicest, and most accurate, must approve.

It is written strictly up to the rules of the drama ; yet it has all that variety of characters and incidents, which is pleaded in their excuse by those who deviate from them. What fault then can we find in it ? Oh, says somebody, it has too much Wit. Well, that is a fault so seldom committed, I should think we might overlook it for once ; but even in this case we can only say of Congreve, what Addison has already said of Cowley,

He'd pleas'd us more if he had pleas'd us less.

and it must be confessed indeed that Congreve was richer in wit, I mean in wit of the true sterling kind, than any man whatsoever ; and in this particular he puts me in mind of a certain Dutch Jewess I once heard of, who had so many jewels that she stuck them in the heels of her shoes, for he has made all the personages in his comedies Wits, from the highest to the lowest ; and in particular the character of Jeremy, in this play, is one of the wittiest that ever was writ. But, I don't know how it is, he has still taken care never to violate Nature ; for tho' he has shewn her every where loaded with finery, it may be rather said to set her off to advantage, than disguise her ; since her acquaintance might distinguish her at first sight.

Nor is there any Writer that has marked his characters so strongly, or so highly finished them, as Congreve. He seems indeed to have given in to the notion that vicious persons are the proper representations for a comic writer to make : and I remember Voltaire mentions it as an instance of his consummate knowledge in human nature that he has made all his characters speak the language of honest men, but commit the actions of knaves. I will not say that he copied his manners from the Great among whom he lived.

It is with great pleasure that I take this opportunity of doing justice to the merit of Mr. Ross, who performs Valentine better, than I ever saw it done by any one else. Indeed, genteel comedy seems to be his *fort* : not that I would be thought to insinuate as if he had it not in his power to make himself considerable in any part which he thought proper to take pains with ; but he has so much of the gentleman about him in every respect, that he appears to more immediate advantage in those, because this appears more like himself.

Collins takes the superstitious, credulous old fool upon him, in the character of Foresight, with great justness ; and no body can see Shuter in the part of Ben, without being put in a good humour.

I am at a loss how to reconcile the little notice which is taken of this excellent play, by a certain manager, with the ideas which I have conceived of his judgment in other respects. Nor can I be of any other way of thinking, than that if *Love for Love* were represented on Drury-lane stage, the actor who made such a figure in the prologue to Britannia, might give a pleasure in the part of Ben, which would more than recompence for the loss of the ballad about a Soldier and a Sailor.

—From " The London Chronicle," 12–14 Oct., 1758.

"THE LONDON CHRONICLE" ON *THE PROVOKED WIFE*, AND *THE MILLERS*

Drury-Lane. 7 Oct., 1758.

A T Drury-Lane last Saturday evening was presented the *Provoked Wife*, a comedy, written by Sir John Vanbrugh.

How Van wants grace who seldom wants for art

is a line of Mr. Pope, in his *Imitation of Horace's Epistle to Augustus* : and it is verified in this comedy, where Sir John has displayed a most enchanting vein of wit and humour, but is so horridly deficient in what, I imagine, Mr. Pope means by the word *grace* that one can hardly help being angry with oneself for being so excessively pleased with him.

It is generally thought that Mrs. Cibber wants spirit in the character of Lady Brute ; but if she does, it is in my opinion rather an advantage to it, which would otherwise appear too licentious : and, when all is said and done, her ladyship, and my cousin Belinda (which part is performed with a great deal of life by Miss Haughton) are at best a couple of as willing tits as a man would desire to meet with : but as I do not apprehend characters of this kind are likely to do much mischief, I cannot help thinking that the author was wholly in the right rather to draw his women as he has done, than by giving them opposite manners, to have made them such unmeaning things as half our modern comedies are filled with. For instance, can any one think that Lady Brute would give half so much pleasure to the audience if instead of being a wanton, intriguing, witty wag (as Razor calls her) the author had copied her from Patient Grizel.

It is amazing to me that Mr. Garrick will *attempt* the part of Sir John Brute ; a part which he not only apparently *mistakes*, but in which he is absolutely prejudicial to the morals of his countrymen.

Q——[1] made him a Brute indeed, an ill-natured, surly swine of a fellow ; and I dare swear every body most heartily despised and detested him : But with Garrick it is quite a different case ; the knight is the greatest favourite in the play ;

---

[1] This refers to James Quin, *d.* 1766.

such a joyous agreeable wicked dog, that we never think we can have enough of his company ; and when he drinks confusion to all order, there is scarce a man in the house, I believe, who is not for that moment a reprobate in his heart. In truth he is so very much the entertainment of the audience, that, to speak in a phrase which Sir John Brute might be supposed to make use of himself, whenever he goes off the stage, we are like so many people sitting round a table after the wine and glasses are removed, till he comes on again.

The celebrated scene in which Sir John is brought before the Justice in his wife's cloaths, was at the first representation of this comedy quite different. He then came on in the habit of a Clergyman : but so indecent a freedom taken with that sacred order was very justly decried ; upon which the author altered it as it now stands, much for the better in every respect : and though I have borne a *little hard* upon Mr. Garrick in *other parts* of the character, in this scene it must be allowed that he is the finest caricatura of a fine lady that ever was represented.

Constant and Heartfree are very natural and spirited characters. But, without a joke, I do not think Mr. Havard well calculated to appear to advantage in either of them. The inimitable Mrs. Clive, though her person is greatly against her in this part, gives perfect satisfaction in the affected and impertinent Lady Fanciful, the hint of which character the author has taken from the French ; and it is the very same from whence Dryden had before translated his Melantha in *Marriage-à-la-mode* ; which has since been frittered into an execrable farce, called *The Frenchified Lady never in Paris*.

At this same theatre on Thursday evening last was introduced a new pantomime dance, called, *The Millers*, in which Signor Grimaldi made his first appearance upon the English stage.

Some people hold dancing to be below the dignity of a regular Theatre : but I can by no means subscribe to their opinion ; since one of the principal ends of every theatre is to delight, and every thing that can contribute to that purpose, under proper restrictions, has an undoubted right to a place there. I shall not affect to shew my learning, by adding, that the Ancients not only admitted Dancing, but thought it a necessary ornament in the performance of the most celebrated Tragedies.

The French for many years carried all before them in this kind of merit ; but of late the Italians seem to have got the start of them : and it must be allowed, that the latter are much better actors, which in the comic dance which now prevails almost every where, is infinitely more requisite, than those graceful postures and movements on which the French dancers, or the most part, pique themselves.

But in this case a vast deal depends on the Maître de Ballet : and whoever composed *The Millers*, I think, has shewn himself a man of genius ; the figure of the contra dance being pleasingly intricate, and the whole admirably well adapted to the music ; however, I cannot help observing that he has been indebted to Don Quixote : for when Seignor [*sic*] Grimaldi comes in asleep upon his ass, it is stole from under him, in the very same manner that Gines de Passamonte robs poor Sancho of his : and the same joy is testified by both parties on the recovery of the beloved brute.

Grimaldi is a man of great strength and agility ; he indeed treads the air. If he has any fault, he is rather too comical ; and from some feats which I have been a witness to his performing, at the King's theatre in the Hay-market, it is my opinion that those spectators will see him with most pleasure, who are least solicitous whether he breaks his neck or not.

—From " The London Chronicle," 14–17 Oct., 1758.

" THE LONDON CHRONICLE " ON *THE WAY OF THE WORLD*

Drury-Lane, Nov. 14, 1758.

YESTERDAY evening at the above theatre was presented *The Way of the World*, a comedy, which for poignancy of wit ; delicacy of humour ; regularity of conduct ; propriety of manners ; and continuity of character ; may (if ever work might) be reckoned a finished piece.

Mr. Congreve had too intimate an acquaintance with human nature not to know that the generality of mankind have a much greater share of vices, than virtues, in their composition ; and

32

it is the business of a comic poet to turn the most glaring side outward. To this we owe his Fainal and Mirabel : two parts, the justness of which, Mr. Havard and Mr. Palmer made us conscious of ; and yet all that can be said in their favour is that they are a couple of well-bred rascals. Mirabel indeed seems to be immoral upon principle ; his vices are shewn as an ornament to his character. Fainal is vicious, but in a grosser way.

It was at two characters in this comedy (Witwoud and Petulant) that Mr. Pope seems to have levelled these lines,

> Observe how seldom even the best succeed,
> Tell me if Congreve's fools be fools indeed ?

because the above-mentioned gentlemen happened to say as many good things as any in the piece. But if they cannot properly be called fools, in which light the author intended to shew them, they must certainly be called cox-combs, which are but a degree above them. And since the best things degenerated become the worst, why may we not say that an impertinent wit is the most disagreeable of fools.

Mr. O'Brien has a peculiar tone of voice very fit for doing justice to a part of this kind ; and the significancy of his looks and gestures add not a little to the pleasure of the spectators. However, the quickness of his parts does not seem to slacken his industry, and if he continues to mind his business, I think there is no doubt of his making a great actor.

It may not be universally known, perhaps, as he has not thought proper to give any intimation of the kind, that Mr. Congreve took the plot of his *Way of the World* from the French. Yet the most unobserving reader will easily perceive upon looking over the Amorous Widow, a comedy translated from Dancourt, by Mr. Betterton, that both those plays have taken their rise from the same original. However Mr. Congreve was too great a Genius to submit to a servile copy ; he has therefore by his refinement, additions, and alterations, given the thing quite a different air. How much superior is Lady Wishfor't to Lady Laycock ? The author has invented a language on purpose for her ; forged new manners, and in short left nothing wanting but what can only be given by such an actress as Mrs. Clive.   Lady Wishfor't is indeed a ridiculous character, but she shews a ridiculous woman of quality ; whereas all the actresses that have hitherto performed the part have dressed themselves like mad women, and acted in the strain of an old nurse.   A high fruze tower, a gaudy petticoat of one sort, and a gown of another, was sure to create a laugh ; but Mrs. Clive is not obliged to have recourse to any such pityful expedients.   Accordingly she dresses the part in the pink of the present mode, and makes more of it than any actress ever did.

There is a strong tincture of affectation in the character of Millemant ; which is so foreign to Mrs. Pritchard's disposition, one of whose chief beauties is ease, and a close attention to nature, that it is not strange if this part should appear less becoming upon her than many others.   Nothwithstanding which, her life and spirit is such, that, since Mrs. Woffington's retirement from the stage, I do not see any actress, besides herself, in any degree equal to it.   Mrs. Yates does the part of Marwood incomparably well, and gives us great reason to regret that we have not the pleasure of seeing her oftener.

This is the last play that Mr. Congreve ever writ ; and it is said, that the cold reception which it met with from the public, on its first appearance, was the reason why he would never write another ; but since that, they have acquired a juster notion of its value ; and it gave me great pleasure to see such a crouded pit and boxes last night.   Yates, in the character of Sir Wilful, hardly ever opened his mouth, but he set the house in a roar ; and from the great satisfaction they expressed at the whole performance, it is evident, that however fond the town may be of those fantastical representations (which old Cibber aptly enough compares to dram-drinking) it is evident I say that their tastes are not yet so vitiated, but they have still a relish for some wholesome entertainments.

To this play was added a pantomime entertainment, called, *Queen Mab*.   I have not yet seen this farce above seven and thirty times ; but as soon as I am able to find out the design of it, I shall communicate my thoughts upon that subject.

—From " The London Chronicle," 14–16 Nov., 1758.

DAVID GARRICK COMPARED WITH WOODWARD IN
THE BUSY BODY

IN my last I promised a parallel between Mr. Garrick and Mr. Woodward in the character of Marplot. As I have already given a delineation of the character, and the criterion, by which the performance of it should be judged, the question now before us will admit of an easy discussion. I shall arrange the remarks I have to make under the heads which are essentially necessary to be considered in an examination of a point of this nature.

THE EXTERNAL INSIGNIA OF THE CHARACTER

Mr. Woodward has about him some traces of youth ; he is loosely genteel in his person ; has the air of a gay, giddy, unthinking town coxcomb : though he does not altogether appear the fine gentleman (which by the way is unnecessary in this part) he does not seem mean, or unbred : his deportment is easy and debonaire, very well adapted to the strenuous idleness of Marplot ; and he is so capable of mingling a tincture of the simpleton, in all the parts where it is proper, that this character sat very easy upon him ; and in all situations it seemed to *come to him,* as the theatrical critics generally phrase it : not to mention that his dress was well chosen.

Mr. Garrick looks much too old for a ward ; has not that frankness in his mien, which is peculiar to his rival : he cannot assume the giddy and the undesigning : he seems on many occasions in the play to be more underbred, than is consistent with Marplot's circumstances ; and all through the piece we see him attempting *to go to the* character (to use another town phrase) while the discerning critic cannot help remarking that he ought to observe the advice of the poet, when he says,

> Leave such to trifle with more grace and ease,
> Whom folly pleases and whose Follies please.

THE COUNTENANCE

In this Mr. Woodward was perfectly happy for the character in question. He appeared innocent of an idea, till some present object excited it, and even then it seemed but a kind of half-conception, which however served him as a will-o'-the-wisp to lead him on blundering, as it were, into sense, but ever mistaking his path, and running into absurdity. In this however he seemed to have no harm, but, on the contrary, strong appearances of the characteristick (*sic*) goodness of Marplot. He does mischief so innocently, that we all forgive him from our hearts ; and, whenever he goes wrong, they who suffer by it see plainly that his meddling disposition carries its atonement along with it. His looks are busy, but foolishly so ; and he is like the Absent Man in this point, that while a crowd of circumstances are about him claiming his attention, he is attached to a single point, namely his eagerness to know every thing that he may be of service to his friends, and, on that account, he very naturally is regardless of all other consequences.

Mr. Garrick's face is strongly marked with great sensibility ; it ever has the pale cast of thought ; the traces of care are rather too legible ; every look of his seems to carry with it a degree of cunning, and of sharp discernment : he has sometimes the curiosity of the Double Dealer, rather than that of Marplot, and when he would appear undesigning, is it not something of a counterfeit thoughtfulness, which seems to gleam, but faintly, over features generally fixed in habitual intenseness of thought ? In short, Mr. Garrick cannot look undesigning ; nor can his curiosity be thought to have its source in a total inattention to his own affairs, and the good-natured principle of helping others. It looked, to me, as if he had a sly intention to mar the projects of his friends, and, when the mischief is done, he assures them that

" He has a great regard for them, and meant them well,— But—a,—things have so fallen out, that a—but to be sure he never loved any body so well in his life."

VOICE

Mr. Woodward, as we have observed of Bullock and Pack, has a comical shrillness in his powers of elocution, that, when he pleases, sounds unthinking, and always inspirits every scene, where absurdity and whimsical distress are concerned.

Mr. Garrick's voice is remarkably distinct, articulate, and sensible, and every tone of it sounds as if it were influenced by a thinking mind. His modulation, which is very fine in most characters, is here too regularly and significantly harmonious for a silly, empty, giddy, frolicksome fellow ; and, like his looks, it seems to be the effect of an understanding that attends with accuracy to its own ideas :

> . . . His soul
> Still sits at squat, and peeps not from its hole.

Genius

In this Mr. Woodward is not by any means deficient : He has imagined so many characters with propriety, that it would be injustice to deny him a considerable portion of the *Vis comica*.

But in genius Mr. Garrick has not his equal. His imagination is generally correct, and always lively : it paints things to him in warm and strong colourings ; and thence it results that he often makes beautiful impressions on his audience. He generally perceives, to use an expression of Dr. Akenside's, *the finest attitudes of things*. But Genius cannot do every thing : it cannot create imagery. It can command the whole intellectual train ; it can awaken passions in its own breast, and convey their operation to others : but it cannot give a new face ; it cannot recall the days of youth ; wear out the visible lines of thought ; put another eye in the head ; nor form, for the purpose of one night, the organs of speech over again. It has performed wonders in Mr. Garrick, and with the help of chalk and charcoal makes him a Lear or an Abel Drugger. But with such assistances Marplot would be grotesque ; and upon the whole, he is not by nature fitted for this character, which he has chosen, in my opinion, very injudiciously.

The Execution

Mr. Woodward is equal throughout the part ; ever giddy, good-natur'd, boyish and unthinking. Curiosity and a desire to serve his friends are always uppermost, and go hand in hand.

In Mr. Garrick, the character appears variegated and inconsistent. Curiosity seems to be the predominant, nay the only
passion, and he is too intensely busy in almost every scene ;
occasionally he tips the audience the wink ; " Now for it,
says he, you shall see a bit of mischief." He is so
violently in earnest to see the monkey, that any body of
common sense, who knew the danger, would take care he
should not ; whereas Woodward is at first foolishly and
giddily bent upon it, but then he very soon desists, and you
see him look over his shoulder with his head averted from the
company, boyishly enjoying the thoughts of a peep at Pug,
and concealing his design from every one, insomuch that he is
the readiest in his vacant manner to quit the room : this is the
very nature of curiosity ; in order to gain its end, it appears
undesigning. Then Woodward returns in the highest glee to
take a view of Monkey, and when the china is thrown down,
he does not stand aghast as if he had seen a ghost : no snivelling ;
no whimpering ; in his countenance you read a joy that his
friend is escaped, and a confusion for the danger he has in-
curred ; and, to cover the whole, he briskly and pleasantly
tells how Pug flew into his face, etc. When Mr. Garrick gets
behind Miss Macklin to evade a cudgelling, he stands laughing
at the old fellow with the pleasantry of Ranger ; when he
draws his sword in the last act, his fencing attitude, and whole
manner, put us in mind of Don John : it is the same trick over
again : in another scene we have a touch of Abel Drugger, and
when he is eating an orange, instead of the gay, the vacant, and
the careless genteel young man, one would swear he is copying
Shuter in Squire Richard. These contrarieties are surprising
in Mr. Garrick, as on all other occasions he acts uniformly
upon one plan ; and, for the most part, upon true principles.
To conclude, throughout the whole character of Marplot, he is
so motley, that he seemed to me like Harlequin making up a
pound of snuff with a pinch from every body's box, Rapee and
Spanish, etc., jumbled together ; or like a miser, mentioned by
Fielding, who was happy when he picked his own pocket of a
guinea, and with joy locked it up in his bureau.

P.S.—It were injustice not to mention that in the scene
where Marplot attempts to bully the old man, Mr. Garrick

acts then like himself, and has the advantage over his antagonist : The circumstance of running about from door to door to alarm the neighbourhood by using the different knockers, might as well have been reserved for a pantomime. In Woodward's absence it might have been of service : I must add, in Mr. Garrick's just praise, that this is the first part in comedy, in which, I think, he has fallen very short of himself.

—From " The London Chronicle," 19–21 Dec., 1758.

OLIVER GOLDSMITH

(1728–1774)

REMARKS ON OUR THEATRES

OUR theatres are now opened, and all Grub-street is pre-paring its advice to the managers ; we shall undoubtedly hear learned disquisitions on the structure of one actor's legs, and another's eyebrows. We shall be told much of enuncia-tions, tones, and attitudes, and shall have our lightest pleasures commented upon by didactic dulness. We shall, it is feared, be told, that Garrick is a fine actor ; but then, as a manager, so avaricious ! That Palmer is a most surprising genius, and Holland likely to do well in a particular cast of character. We shall have them giving Shuter instructions to amuse us by rule, and deploring over the ruins of desolated majesty at Covent-Garden. As I love to be advising too, for advice is easily given, and bears a shew of wisdom and superiority, I must be per-mitted to offer a few observations upon our theatres and actors, without, on this trivial occasion, throwing my thoughts into the formality of method.

There is something in the deportment of all our players infinitely more stiff and formal than among the actors of other nations. Their action sits uneasy upon them ; for as the English use very little gesture in ordinary conversation, our English-bred actors are obliged to supply stage gestures by their imagination alone. A French comedian finds proper models of action in every company and in every coffee-house he enters. An Englishman is obliged to take his models from the stage itself ; he is obliged to imitate nature from an imitation of nature. I know of no set of men more likely to be improved by travelling than those of the theatrical profession. The inhabitants of the continent are less reserved than here ; they may be seen through upon a first acquaintance ; such are the proper models to draw from ; they are at once striking, and are found in great abundance.

Though it would be inexcusable in a comedian to add any thing of his own to the poet's dialogue, yet, as to action, he is entirely at liberty. By this, he may shew the fertility of his genius, the poignancy of his humour, and the exactness of his judgment ; we scarcely see a coxcomb or a fool in common life that has not some peculiar oddity in his action. These peculiarities it is not in the power of words to represent, and depend solely upon the actor. They give a relish to the humour of the poet, and make the appearance of nature more illusive ; the Italians, it is true, mask some characters, and endeavour to preserve the peculiar humour by the make of the mask ; but I have seen others still preserve a great fund of humour in the face without a mask ; one actor, particularly, by a squint which he threw into some characters of low life, assumed a look of infinite solidity. This, though upon reflection we might condemn, yet, immediately upon representation, we could not avoid being pleased with. To illustrate what I have been saying by the plays I have of late gone to see : in *The Miser*, which was played a few nights ago at Covent-garden. Lovegold appears through the whole in circumstances of exaggerated avarice ; all the player's action, therefore, should conspire with the poet's design, and represent him as an epitome of penury. The French comedian, in this character, in the midst of one of his most violent passions, while he appears in an ungovernable rage, feels the demon of avarice still upon him, and stoops down to pick up a pin, which he quilts into the flap of his coat-pocket with great assiduity. Two candles are lighted up for his wedding ; he flies, and turns one of them into the socket ; it is, however, lighted up again ; he then steals to it, and privately crams it into his pocket. *The Mock Doctor* was lately played at the other house. Here again the comedian had an opportunity of heightening the ridicule by action. The French player sits in a chair with a high back, and then begins to shew away by talking nonsense, which he would have thought Latin by those who he knows do not understand a syllable of the matter. At last he grows enthusiastic, enjoys the admiration of the company, tosses his

legs and arms about, and, in the midst of his raptures and
vociferation, he and the chair fall back together. All this
appears dull enough in the recital ; but the gravity of Cato
could not stand it in the representation. In short, there is
hardly a character in comedy, to which a player of any real
humour might not add strokes of vivacity that could not fail of
applause. But, instead of this, we too often see our fine gentlemen do nothing through a whole part, but strut and open their
snuff-box ; our pretty fellows sit indecently with their legs
across, and our clowns pull up their breeches. These, if once,
or even twice, repeated, might do well enough ; but to see
them served up in every scene, argues the actor almost as
barren as the character he would expose.

The magnificence of our theatres is far superior to any others
in Europe, where plays only are acted. The great care our
performers take in painting for a part, their exactness in all the
minutiæ of dress, and other little scenical proprieties, have been
taken notice of by Ricoboni, a gentleman of Italy, who
travelled Europe with no other design but to remark upon the
stage ; but there are several improprieties still continued, or
lately come into fashion. As, for instance, spreading a carpet
punctually at the beginning of the death-scene, in order to
prevent our actors from spoiling their clothes ; this immediately apprises us of the tragedy to follow ; for laying the
cloth is not a more sure indication of dinner than laying the
carpet of bloody work at Drury-lane. Our little pages also
with unmeaning faces, that bear up the train of a weeping
princess, and our awkward lords in waiting, take off much from
her distress. Mutes of every kind divide our attention, and
lessen our sensibility : but here it is entirely ridiculous, as we
see them seriously employed in doing nothing. If we must have
dirty-shirted guards upon the theatres, they should be taught
to keep their eyes fixed on the actors, and not roll them round
upon the audience, as if they were ogling the boxes.

Beauty, methinks, seems a requisite qualification in an actress.
This seems scrupulously observed elsewhere, and for my part
I could wish to see it observed at home. I can never conceive
an hero dying for love of a lady totally destitute of beauty. I
must think the part unnatural, for I cannot bear to hear him

call that face angelic, when even paint cannot hide its wrinkles.
I must condemn him of stupidity, and the person whom I can
accuse for want of taste will seldom become the object of my
affections or admiration. But if this be a defect, what must be
the entire perversion of scenical decorum, when for instance we
see an actress, that might act the Wapping Landlady without
a bolster, pining in the character of Jane Shore, and while
unwieldy with fat endeavouring to convince the audience that
she is dying with hunger !

For the future, then, I could wish that the parts of the young
or beautiful were given to performers of suitable figures ; for I
must own, I could rather see the stage filled with agreeable
objects, though they might sometimes bungle a little, than see
it crowded with withered or mis-shapen figures, be their
emphasis, as I think it is called, ever so proper. The first may
have the awkward appearance of new-raised troops ; but in
viewing the last I cannot avoid the mortification of fancying
myself placed in an hospital of invalids.

—From *The Bee* (No. 1), 6 Oct., 1759.

OLIVER GOLDSMITH'S STUDY OF MLLE. CLAIRON

MADEMOISELLE CLAIRON, a celebrated actress at Paris,
seems to me the most perfect female figure I have ever
seen upon any stage. Not, perhaps, that Nature has been more
liberal of personal beauty to her, than to be seen upon our
theatres at home. There are actresses here who have as much
of what connoisseurs call statuary grace, by which is meant
elegance unconnected with motion, as she ; but they all fall
infinitely short of her, when the soul comes to give expression
to the limbs, and animates every feature.

Her first appearance is excessively engaging ; she never
comes in staring round upon the company, as if she intended to
count the benefits of the house, or at least to see, as well as be
seen. Her eyes are always, at first, intently fixed upon the
persons of the drama, and she lifts them by degrees, with
enchanting diffidence, upon the spectators. Her first speech,
or at least the first part of it, is delivered with scarcely any
motion of the arm ; her hands and her tongue never set out

together ; but the one prepares us for the other. She sometimes begins with a mute eloquent attitude ; but never goes forward all at once with hands, eyes, head, and voice. This observation, though it may appear of no importance, should certainly be adverted to ; nor do I see any one performer (Garrick only excepted) among us, that is not in this particular apt to offend. By this simple beginning she gives herself a power of rising in the passion of the scene. As she proceeds, every gesture, every look acquires new violence, till at last transported, she fills the whole vehemence of the part, and all the idea of the poet.

Her hands are not alternately stretched out, and then drawn in again, as with the singing-women at Sadler's Wells ; they are employed with graceful variety, and every moment please with new and unexpected eloquence. Add to this, that their motion is generally from the shoulder ; she never flourishes her hands while the upper part of her arm is motionless, nor has she the ridiculous appearance, as if her elbows were pinned to her hips.

But of all the cautions to be given to our rising actresses, I would particularly recommend it to them never to take notice of the audience, upon any occasion whatsoever ; let the spectators applaud never so loudly, their praises should pass, except at the end of the epilogue, with seeming inattention. I can never pardon a lady on the stage who, when she draws the admiration of the whole audience, turns about to make them a low courtesy for their applause. Such a figure no longer resembles Belvidera, but at once drops into Mrs. Cibber. Suppose a sober tradesman, who once a year takes his shilling's worth at Drury-lane, in order to be delighted with the figure of a queen, the queen of Sheba for instance, or any other queen : this honest man has no other idea of the great but from their superior pride and impertinence ; suppose such a man placed among the spectators, the first figure that appears on the stage is the queen herself, curtseying and cringing to all the company ; how can he fancy her the haughty favourite of King Solomon the wise, who appears actually more submissive than the wife of his bosom. We are all tradesmen of a nicer relish in this respect, and such conduct must disgust every spectator who loves to have the illusion of nature strong upon him.

Yet, while I recommend to our actresses a skilful attention to gesture, I would not have them study it in the looking-glass. This, without some precaution, will render their action formal ; by too great an intimacy with this they become stiff and affected. People seldom improve, when they have no other model but themselves to copy after. I remember to have known a notable performer of the other sex, who made great use of this flattering monitor, and yet was one of the stiffest figures I ever saw. I am told his apartment was hung round with looking-glass, that he might see his person twenty times reflected upon entering the room ; and I will make bold to say, he saw twenty very ugly fellows whenever he did so.

—From *The Bee* (No. 2), 13 Oct., 1759.

"THE THEATRICAL REVIEW"

(1763)

ITS CRITICAL EXAMEN OF GARRICK'S ABILITIES AS AN ACTOR

To these (i.e. the superior genius and understanding of Mr. Garrick) it is that we are indebted for the entertainment we receive from the variety of character he represents ; a round, far more extensive, than is recorded in history of any other performer. In less judicious ages, actors have been extolled for the greatness of their merit, though their superiority consisted in nothing more than a single character. In more refined ones, he has been thought sufficiently great, who was excellent in five or six tragedy or comedy parts, (for they seldom extend to both) tolerable in a few others, and barely sufferable in the remainder. Alleyn was a great actor ; but we have no absolute certainty of his eminence but in comedy—Mohun and Hart were chiefly confined to the buskin—Nokes and Leigh to the sock—Betterton indeed rises much higher ; he was eminent in almost every cast of tragedy, and highly excellent in comedy, but not at all in the low and *outré* of the *vis comica*—Booth shone superior to all in the majestic and dignified walks of Melpomene, but was by no means considerable in the humorous paths of Thalia.—Wilks in the airy and genteel, and Cibber in the insignificant and ludicrous, of the latter, were incomparable ; but nothing but their names alone could tolerate their appearance in the former. We need not descend to later times ; let the judicious reader compare these instances (drawn, we hope, with candour and impartiality) with the extensive powers of our modern Roscius, and then decree the palm where he shall think it most equitably due.

From a general view of Mr. Garrick, let us proceed to some few particulars. In many parts of Tragedy by his judgment in conceiving, and his talents in executing, he never fails exciting similar feelings in the breasts of his audience. In that picturesque display, in *Hamlet*, of the poor parade of vestimental mourning, compared to the genuine grief of an affected heart, who can hear him without sympathy repeat

But I have that within *which* passeth *shew.*

In the scene with Lady Ann, in *Richard*, with what masterly judgment and surprising powers, with what a well dissembled passion, does he work the lady to a firm belief of his sincerity ! —When the ghost of Banquo rises, how repeatedly astonishing his transition, from the placidly merry, to the tremendously horrific !

Though Mr. Garrick's merit in Tragedy is very apparent, we are nevertheless inclined to think that Comedy is his more peculiar *fort*.—The manner of his playing his Bayes he entirely struck out himself ; and in our opinion it is a test of much judgment, infinite vivacity, ready invention, and every other quality which composes the genuine Vis Comica. In Benedic [*sic*] he has given us the highest specimen of the sprightly and the Humourous—In Kitely of the Jealous—In Chalkstone of the persevering Debauchee—And in a variety of other parts almost every character within the compass of the comic muse.

But it is not to be understood that we think Mr. Garrick utterly exempt from faults ; no—there are some few which we propose to enumerate. It gives us pain to see him sometimes exert a sort of Theatrical parade in Tragedy to catch the eyes and applause of the multitude. He too frequently uses a sort of hesitating stammering, when there is no natural obstacle to occasion it, meerly to strike a seeming shew of something out of nothing. A great objection has been raised by the critics to the propriety of Mr. Garrick's pauses—

" There are," says Aaron Hill, " rests and pauses, as well as breaks, both in speech and action, which are not only natural and proper in themselves, but infinitely beautiful in the spectator's eye."

That the generality of this great performer's pauses come within this description is most certainly true ; however we must admit that we have seen him make use of them where judgment could not warrant the adoption ; sometimes as a trap for applause where he could reasonably expect none ; sometimes indeed they have been occasioned by the too great length of a period, where he would have rendered himself absolutely inarticulate, had he endeavoured implicitly to conform to exact propriety ; though thus much may be said, that, in this case, some degree of knowledge is required in a speaker, in pausing where the sense is the least affected, and that as seldom as his breath will permit.—He is, every now and then, too stiff and prolix in his recitation : We have more particularly observed it in the narrative, colloquial, and imprecative parts, which require a degree of volubility, to distinguish them from the declamatory and imperative. We think an attention to this hint would greatly heighten the effect of that dire and heart piercing imprecation in *Lear*, which if uttered as a momentary impetuous effect of the passion, with little more than intelligible volubility, would never fail striking an audience in the most sensible and affecting degree.

If Mr. Garrick has any particular defect as a comedian, 'tis barely this, and from which few actors are exempt ; namely, an occasional compliance with the viciated taste of too many of the audience, in introducing the outré, for the sake of a laugh, where the author never intended it. The first is that of boxing in Abel Drugger : This character, as drawn by Johnson [*sic*], is that of a most credulous, timid, pusilanimous wretch ; the Broughtonian attitudes, into which Mr. Garrick throws himself, are utterly inconsistent with the part ; and consequently the weakness of those who are pleased with, and applaud it, is obviously manifest.

The next instance is Scrub ; We can see no cause for Mr. Garrick's affecting almost throughout this character a voice scarcely audible, and a deportment as if in expectation of the chastisement of his master whenever he is called to only the performance of his duty : nor can we assign any other reason for this peculiar method of exhibiting Scrub, but, that as the expectation of the people was raised by so great a performer's undertaking the part, there appeared to him a necessity of deviating from the manner of others, however characteristic, least [*sic*] the public should deem him a copy.

Upon a review of the whole, we will venture to affirm, that *impartial* JUSTICE *must* pronounce MR. GARRICK as the *First* of his PROFESSION : and that the *amazing* BLAZE of his EXCELLENCIES, greatly *obscures*, if not totally *eclipses* his DEFECTS.
—From " The Theatrical Review or Annals of the Drama," 1763.

JAMES BOSWELL

(1740–1795)

ON THE PROFESSION OF A PLAYER

Omnis Aristippum decuit color et status et res.—Hor.

THAT the profession of a player was anciently held sometimes as contemptible, and sometimes as odious, is known
to all who are acquainted with the history of mankind ; but
the causes of this are also known. Stage-playing being originally nothing better than coarse and rustic buffoonery, when
Thespis or such as Thespis exhibited their performances in a
cart, it could not fail to be contemptible ; and when the idea
of contempt is once annexed to a profession it is not easily
removed—hence it was that the business of stage-playing was
appropriated to slaves or to the meanest of the people. That
the profession was odious, there is no wonder ; since the
ancient comedy was a barefaced attack upon living characters,
who were brought upon the stage and exposed to public scorn.
In more modern times wherever the Christian religion was
established, players were looked upon with a most unfavourable
eye, because their shews tended to keep alive the fictions of
heathenish idolatry ; and however much later times may have
improved in liberality of sentiments, it must be acknowledged,
that their prejudices against the profession of a player have
continued much longer than could have been expected. The
effects have remained after the causes have ceased ; and
because players had once been obnoxious for having fomented
paganism, they were obnoxious still, when paganism was no
longer an object of attention : the human mind continued its
aversion to them, as a man, who has been tossed at sea, feels
himself agitated long after he is upon land, or as the foolish
person mentioned by Mr. Locke, who being accustomed to

51

strike the hours in imitation of a neighbouring clock, continued to strike after the clock was removed.

But the present age beholds the profession of a player in a proper light, and treats it accordingly. We now see that it ought to be ranked amongst the learned professions : for the truth is, that in order to be a good player, there is required a greater share of genius, knowledge, and accomplishments, than for any one profession whatever ; for this reason, that the profession of a player comprehends the whole system of human life.—*quicquid agunt homines*. When I talk thus, I talk of an universal player ; and surely in order to be that, in any degree of perfection, all that I have now mentioned is necessary. For any one of what are commonly called the three learned professions, viz. law, physic, and divinity, there is, no doubt, required much knowledge and much address, or many accomplishments. But the player must have a share of the requisites of each of these classes of men, because he must alternately represent an individual characteristical of each. Mr. Dryden's fine satirical lines on the duke of Buckingham,

> And in the space of one revolving moon,
> Is poet, statesman, fidler and buffoon,

may with a little variation be seriously applied to the universal player : for he must in the space of a moon be lawyer, divine, and physician, with all the other characters or discriminations of the human species, which have been formed in society. In Mr. Samuel Johnson's noble prologue, at the opening of Drury-lane theatre, it is said of Shakespeare—

> Each change of many coloured life he drew.

The same may be said of a player, who animates the paintings of Shakespeare. We who live at present, have an opportunity of observing a wonderful example of what I have now set forth. Mr. Garrick exhibits in his own person such a variety of characters, with such propriety and excellence as not only to catch the immediate applause of the multitude, but to be the delight and admiration of the judicious, enlightened and philosophical spectators : as was said of Terence,

> *Primores populi arripuit populumque tributim.*

When I maintain that learning is necessary to a player, who is to represent a man of learning, I do not mean that he is to be understood to have as much learning as may be annexed to the character which he represents. Thus, in order to appear well upon the stage, as a lawyer, a physician, or a divine, it certainly is not necessary to have a deep knowledge, either of law, physick or divinity ; yet it is necessary to have so much knowledge as to enter into the general scope of the character, and have a just perception of the different expressions : not to mention that without some knowledge of the science belonging to each character, it is impossible fully to see the blunders and absurdities, arising from ignorance, petulance and conceit, which often constitute the ridicule of the part, and appear unmeaning and insipid, if not set off by the player with due intelligence and poignancy.

It may, therefore, be fairly maintained that the more knowledge a player has, the more will he excel in his profession ; and so true is this, that superior judges of theatrical excellence can discern improvements even in the performance of Mr. Garrick, upon seeing him again in characters where they had once imagined it impossible for him to be greater : for Mr. Garrick is by study and observation continually adding to his stock of science, and enriching his mind with new ideas, towards which his late travels through a good part of Europe have no doubt very much contributed, and the fertility of his own lively fancy is always producing fresh thoughts.

But not only are learning and science necessary for an universal player ; he must also have all the genteel accomplishments—he must be an *elegans formarum spectator*—he must have elevation and tenderness of sentiment, dignity and ease of deportment—he must even have a knowledge of the weaknesses, the follies, the aukwardness, and rusticity of human life. Let us recollect Mr. Garrick in Hamlet and Abel Drugger, Lear and Sharp, Henry the fourth and Ranger, and the truth of what has now been observed will appear at one view. I grant that to be an universal player a man must be born with extraordinary talents and must employ unwearied pains ; and even that these should have their effect, a long course of practice is necessary, and every year will bring a greater degree of excellence. But the requisites for an universal player must be found in a greater or less degree, in every player who would hope to excel in his profession ; so that the more knowledge that he acquires in the department, or, to use the stage phrase, the *walk*, for which nature has intended him, the more will he be distinguished, and without a competent share of knowledge, it will be in vain for him to tread the stage.

We may indeed be told that we have had many players, whose names it would be invidious to mention, who though brought from the dregs of the populace, and grossly ignorant, have set the audience in a roar, and exhibited low comic characters, with much truth, as well as in a diverting manner. As to this it must be observed, that knowledge is not to be circumscribed to what we learn in books and schools ; a great variety of it is picked up in the practice of life ; and however ignorant low comedians may have been in a relative sense, it may be affirmed that none of them, who have excelled, have been destitute of discernment and observation in the sphere in which they have moved ; so that they cannot be said to have been ignorant of their *own subjects*, if that term may be here used. I would however beg leave to differ from the philosophers of old, who, when treating of the duties of men in their several stations, and comparing them to players, say, that " there is no matter what part is assigned to a performer, whether that of a king or a peasant "—The question is—has he done his part well ? For though there is no doubt that he who performs the part of a peasant well, is better than he who performs the part of a king ill, yet a player is entitled to a greater degree of praise in proportion as he represents a lesser or greater character, and also in proportion to the variety of characters which he represents.

—From " The London Magazine," 1770.

FRANCIS GENTLEMAN

(1728–1784)

DAVID GARRICK AND OTHER CONTEMPORARIES IN *MACBETH*

To delineate *Macbeth* is not easy ; the author seems like Prometheus, to have made a man of his own, but to have stolen his animation rather from Hell than Heaven : by the account we hear of him, previous to his entrance, magnanimity and courage appear conspicuous in his conduct ; yet, no sooner does he present himself, but with all the weakness of unpractised youth, he receives a strong impression from old women's prognostications ; and with all the aptness of a studied villain suggests the most pernicious practices, which from that moment, with a very few slight intervals, take entire possession of his heart ; from his future proceedings, we perceive him more actuated by jealous apprehensions than sound policy, more influenced by rage and desperation, than any degree of natural resolution ; credulous, impatient, vindictive ; ambitious without a spark of honour ; cruel without a gleam of pity—in short, as compleat a tool for ministers of temptation to work upon, as ever fancy formed, and too disgraceful for nature to admit amongst her works.

However, considered in the view of theatrical action, there is not one personage to be found in our English drama which more strongly impresses an audience, which requires more judgment and greater power to do him justice ; many passages are intricate, some heavy, but for the greater part, powerfully impassioned ; the mental agitation he is thrown into, requires expression peculiarly forcible, of action, look, and utterance, even so far as to make the hearts of spectators shrink, and to thrill their blood ; indeed, every assistance from externals is given the actor, such as daggers, bloody hands, ghosts, etc., but these must be treated judiciously, or the effect, as we have sometimes seen it, may take a ludicrous turn.

Through all the soliloquies of anxious reflections in the first act ; amidst the pangs of guilty apprehensions, and pungent remorse, in the second ; through all the distracted terror of the third ; all the impetuous curiosity of the fourth, and all the desperation of the fifth, Mr. GARRICK shews uniform, unabating excellence ; scarce a look, motion, or tone, but takes possession of our faculties, and leads them to a just sensibility.

As SHAKESPEARE rises above himself in many places, so does this his greatest and best commentator, who not only presents his beauties to the imagination, but brings them home feelingly to the heart : among a thousand other instances of almost necromantic merit, let us turn our recollection only to a few in the character of Macbeth ; who ever saw the *immortal actor* start at, and trace the imaginary dagger previous to Duncan's murder, without embodying, by sympathy, unsubstantial air into the alarming shape of such a weapon ? Who ever heard the low, but piercing notes of his voice when the *deed is done*, repeating those inimitable passages which mention the sleeping grooms, and murder of sleep, without feeling a vibration of the nerves ? Who ever saw the guilty distraction of features he assumes on Banquo's appearance at the feast, without sacrificing reason to real apprehension from a mimic ghost ; who has heard his speech, after receiving his death wound, uttered with the utmost agony of body and mind, but trembles at the idea of future punishment, and almost pities the expiring wretch, though stained with crimes of the deepest die ?

Theatrical performance to most spectators appears a mechanical disposition of limbs, and a parotted [*sic*] mode of speech ; so indeed it really is too often, but intrinsic merit soars far beyond such narrow, barren limits, she traces nature through her various windings, dives into her deepest recesses, and snatches ten thousand beauties which plodding method can never display ; the dullest comprehension may be taught to enter on this side or that ; to stand on a particular board ; to raise the voice here, and fall it there ; but unless motion and utterance are regulated by a cultivated knowledge of life, and self-born intelligent feelings, no greater degree of excellence can be attained than unaffecting propriety ; like a fair field whose native fertility of soil produces a beauteous luxuriant crop of spontaneous vegitation, which art can only regulate, not enrich ; Mr. GARRICK's matchless genius not only captivates our sportive senses, but also furnishes high relished substantial food for our minds to strengthen by.

Mr. QUIN, whose sole merit in tragedy was declamation, or brutal pride, was undescribably cumbersome in *Macbeth* ; his face, which had no possible variation from its natural grace, except sternness and festivity, could not be expected to exhibit the acute sensations of this character ; his figure, was void of the essential spirit, and his voice far too monotonous for the transitions which so frequently occur ; yet, wonderful to be told, he played it several years with considerable applause.

Mr. SHERIDAN shewed more variety of acting, in this part than any other, and made an astonishing good use of his limited powers ; without any exaggeration of compliment to that gentleman, we must place him in a very reputable degree of competition with Mr. GARRICK, in the dagger scene ; and at the same time confess a doubt, whether any performer ever spoke the words, " *this is a sorry sight*," better—as to the third, fourth, and fifth acts, his meaning well, was all we could ever perceive to recommend him.

Mr. BARRY, as a capital actor—indeed a very capital one in his proper cast, made, in our comprehension, but a lukewarm affair of Macbeth, his amorous harmony of features and voice, could but faintly, if at all, describe passions incident to a tyrant in such circumstances as he is placed ; his commanding figure, and other requisites, preserved him from being insipid, though far beneath himself.

Mr. POWELL—light lie the ashes of the respectable dead—was beyond doubt, partially received in this tragedy ; the requisite force of expression, and a proper disposition of features, were wanting ; after the murder, his feelings dwindled into a kind of boyish whimpering, and his countenance rather described bodily than mental pain ; in the third act, he seemed unequal to the arduous task of describing extreme horror, and in the fifth, Macbeth's weight of desperation bore him down ; even the soliloquies appeared too sententiously heavy for his expression ; as his playing the part was certainly matter of choice, we are sorry he ever mistook his own abilities so much, notwithstanding he met with public indulgence ; a compliment, in some measure, due even to the failings of a performer, who displayed so much intrinsic merit as he did on more suitable occasions.

Mr. HOLLAND, that industrious, useful, laborious, imitative actor, idolized his great instructor too much to be any thing original ; in Macbeth we deem him particularly unhappy ; aiming to be great, he frequently lost all trace of character : untunably stiff in all his declamation ; mechanical in action ; ungracious in attitude ; affected in feeling ; unharmonious in tones ; irregular in emphasis ; and wild in passion ; yet having an agreeable person, significant aspect, and powerful voice, he often pleased his audience, and kept attention awake, while judgment was obliged to slumber, or seek safety in silence, from popular prejudice.

Among many theatrical circumstances much to be lamented, is that terrible necessity which forces Mr. SMITH into an undertaking so opposite to every one of his requisites, except figure ; we are confident his good sense agrees with us, that saddling him with the part is an imposition upon that good nature and integrity which stimulate him to work through thick and thin, for the support of Covent-Garden house.

Macduff is a part of no great action, except on discovery of the King's murder, and the fourth act scene ; Messrs. RYAN and HAVARD both did him great justice, yet we must be of opinion that Mr. REDDISH depicts him with superior strength and beauty : his feelings are manly, yet tender ; spirited without excess ; and to us convey whatever an author intended, or an audience can wish.

Banquo's chief merit is as a ghost ; here Mr. Ross made the most striking, picturesque appearance we have ever seen, and with peculiar grace even beautified horror : All the rest of the men in this play are unworthy notice.

Lady Macbeth, as to the detestable composition of her character, has been sufficiently animadverted on, therefore little more is necessary than to observe, that though there does not appear much call for capital merit, yet several first-rate actresses have made but a languid figure in representing her.

Notwithstanding Mrs. WOFFINGTON was extremely well received, and really did the part as well as her deplorable tragedy voice would admit ; we must place Mrs. PRITCHARD foremost ; who made a very just distinction in the scene where Banquo's ghost appears, between reproving Macbeth's behaviour with passion, or the anxiety of apprehension, lest he should betray his guilt ; this latter method she happily pursued, and here, as well as in the sleeping scene, gained manifest superiority. Mrs. YATES, at present, comes nearest the point of praise, but certainly displays no very conspicuous merit in the character ; and to mention Mrs. BARRY would be to injure her, as it certainly does not at all coincide with her capabilities.

The witches we should take no notice of, but for a supposed amendment in speaking and dressing those characters at Covent-Garden ; as beings out of the course of nature, SHAKESPEARE furnished them with a peculiarity of style ; why then should we not suppose he meant a peculiarity of deportment and utterance ? He certainly did, as much as for Caliban ; a languid propriety of natural expression destroys in them pleasing and characteristic oddity—as to dressing them in the Sybillic taste, it makes them rather Roman than Scots witches, and sacrifices established national ideas, at the shrine of false decorum, for did appearance, ugly features, and advanced age, dub any female a witch in the times of credulity ; even now, a very disagreeable woman, bent with age, and wrapped in filthiness, is stigmatized with that title, though not so seriously, north of the Tweed ; nay, Macbeth himself stiles them *filthy* hags, most certainly alluding to personal appearance. If an alteration of dress is to take place in this play, we could wish the characters were dressed in habits of the times, which would be pleasing, and, we apprehend is necessary.

Macbeth, for its boldness of sentiment, strength of versification, variety of passions and preternatural beings, deserves to be esteemed a first rate tragedy, containing a number of beauties never exceeded, with many blemishes very censurable; dangerous in representation, as has been said, to weak minds ; unintelligible to moderate conceptions in several places, upon perusal ; therefore chiefly calculated for sound understanding, and established resolution of principles, either on the stage or in the study.

—From *The Dramatic Censor*. By Francis Gentleman, 1770.

HENRY BATE

(1745-1824)

DAVID GARRICK AS LEAR

Drury Lane.

MR. GARRICK last night repeated his capital representation
of Lear, and in consequence thereof drew together a most
crouded audience, principally composed of the first people of
distinction, who seem resolved to let no opportunity escape
them of enjoying the remainder of his inimitable performances.
However difficult it may be to prevail upon the absentees to
admit it, yet it will be readily confessed by those who were
fortunate enough to be present last night, that he never appeared so great in the character before.

The curse at the close of the first act,—his phrenetic appeal
to heaven at the end of the second on Regan's ingratitude,
were two such enthusiastic scenes of human exertion, that they
caused a kind of momentary petrefaction thro' the house, which
he soon dissolved as universally into tears.—Even the unfeeling
Regan and Gonneril, forgetful of their characteristic cruelty,
played thro' the whole of their parts with aching bosoms and
streaming eyes.—In a word, we never saw before so exquisite
a theatrical performance, or one so loudly and universally
applauded.

—From " The Morning Post." 22 May, 1776.

MRS. YATES AS JANE SHORE

Covent-Garden.

THE tragedy of *Jane Shore* was represented at this Theatre
last night, when Mrs. Yates, on account of the indisposi-
tion of Mrs. Hartley, performed the part of Jane Shore. The
idea of seeing Mrs. Barry and Mrs. Yates together, for the first
time, drew an immense house, though the representation did

not answer the general expectation. The Rival Tragic Queens seemed alarmed at the conscious idea of each other's superiority; and, in consequence thereof, played each of them considerably [below] par.—Indeed, Mrs. Yates's figure is grown rather too plump, and *majestic*, for the delicate Jane Shore; and Mrs. Barry never charmed us in the extravagant Alicia. The former, in stooping to Gloster, made a slip, and was under the necessity of saluting the boards *a tergo*; however, as a graceful attitude is ever admired by an English audience, we did not wonder to find this exceedingly applauded. Her white sattin festooned dress, trimmed with silver, was in every respect ill suited to the character.—Mr. Lewis was too impetuous, and inarticulate in Hastings. Mr. Ross might pass well enough for a guttling citizen, and consequently was a fit subject for the Royal Edward to honour with the order of cuckoldom.

—From " The Morning Post," 11 Feb., 1778.

THOMAS HOLCROFT

(1745–1809)

MRS. SIDDONS AND HER RÔLES

AGREEABLE to our promise of last month, we shall here attempt some sketches of the theatrical talents of Mrs. Siddons, and since rigid impartiality is, or should be, the essence of criticism, we are happy to observe the public so uniform in their admiration of her, lest we should otherwise have been suspected of writing a panegyric, instead of delivering the pure dictates of unbiassed judgement.

It is a reiterated assertion among such as affect to despise what they call the mob, that the public are occasionally seized with a kind of mania, and run in crowds while the frenzy lasts, predetermined to praise what they cannot comprehend. But this accusation is only true in part. The small talk of society it is true, is always imitative : it affirms, but does not investigate ; it sees, admires, and commends, not as reason, but, as fashion prescribes. It is the tongue of understanding however that gives the tone to the affirmations of folly, and whoever looks round, will easily perceive, that every man, in gradation, forms his opinions upon some one above him, whose judgement he has often experienced to be better than his own, and which he has therefore very rationally learnt to revere. Fools cannot bestow reputation ; they are themselves depised, and their remarks, when false, would be heard only to be ridiculed. Whence we may conclude when the praise is universal, the merit is real, and that those people who affect to contemn what the world approves, have either erected a false standard of taste for themselves, or contradict for the sake of being singular. If this be true, as we are persuaded it is, the annals of the Theatre do not afford an instance of more universal approbation, consequently none of greater merit, than Mrs. Siddons. Garrick himself did not exceed, if he equalled her, in awaking public curiosity. When he first appeared the Theatres were small, if compared to the present, yet it is a known fact that the boxes have been all engaged every night, for a fortnight or more in advance, on those nights when it was supposed she would play, and this for a continuance, while the other parts of the house have as continually overflowed ; nor is this avidity in the least abated. Let us endeavour by developing her excellencies to account for these extraordinary marks of public favour.

There never perhaps was a better stage figure seen than Mrs. Siddons. Her height is above the middle size ; she is not at all inclined to the embonpoint, yet sufficiently muscular, to prevent all appearances of asperity, or acute angles in the varieties of action, or the display of attitude ; the symmetry of her person is captivating ; her face is peculiarly happy, by having a strength of features without the least propensity to coarseness or vulgarity ; on the contrary, it is so well harmonized when quiescent, and so expressive when impassioned, that most people think her more beautiful than she is. So great too is the flexibility of her countenance, that it takes the instantaneous transitions of passion, with such variety and effect, as never to tire the eye. Her voice is remarkably plaintive, yet capable of all that firmness and exertion which the intrepidity of fortitude, or the impulse of sudden rage demand. Her eye is large and marking, and her brow capable of contracting to disdain, or dilating with the emotions of sympathy or pity ; her memory is tenacious, and her articulation clear, distinct, and penetrating.

That nature might not be partially bountiful, she has endowed her with a quickness of conception and a strength of understanding, equal to the proper use of such extraordinary gifts. So entirely is she mistress of herself, so collected, and so determined in her gestures, tone, and manner, that she seldom errs like other actors, because she doubts her powers or comprehension : she studies her Author attentively, conceives justly, and describes with a firm consciousness of propriety ; she is sparing in her action, because nature, (at least English nature), does not act much, but it is proper, picturesque, graceful, and dignified ; it arises immediately from the sentiments and feelings, and is not seen to prepare itself before it begins. No studied trick or start can be predicted, no forced tremulation, where the vacancy of the eye declares the absence of passion, can be seen ; no laborious strainings at false climax, in which the tired voice reiterates one high tone beyond which it cannot reach, can be heard ; no artificial heaving of the breasts, so disgusting when the affectation is perceptible ; none of those arts, by which the actress is seen, and not the character, can be found in Mrs. Siddons. So natural are her gradations and transitions, so classical and correct her speech and deportment, and so exceedingly affecting and pathetical are her voice, form, and features, that there is no conveying an idea of the pleasure she communicates by words. She must be seen to be admired. What is still more delightful, she is an original ; she copies no one living or dead, but acts from nature and herself.

This is general praise ; let us take a more particular view of her powers in some of those characters in which she has so repeatedly charmed the town.

Her first appearance was in Isabella in *The Fatal Marriage*, a play in which one of our greatest poets has produced some of his most happy effusions. There is not perhaps in the range of dramatic writing a more difficult character to support with justice than that of Isabella. Her settled melancholy for the loss of Biron, her distressful poverty, her sorrows at the cruelty of her incensed father-in-law, her maternal fears, and her reluctant acceptance of Villeroy, may be represented by abilities inferior to those of Mrs. Siddons, though not with that fullness of effect ; but the intervals of sanity and distraction that succeed, are so various, so numerous, and perplexed, that nothing but the utmost efforts of genius and of art can exhibit Isabella in all her thousand horrors. Any thing below excellence must be contemptible, and therefore it is with great justice that the critics have pronounced this to be her chef d'œuvre. Great talents are always most conspicuous where great obstacles are to be surmounted.

If there be any who still affect to doubt the superiority of Mrs. Siddons, who still affirm, they remember to have seen some one more excellent, let them examine her Isabella, let them behold her looking at Biron in disguise, let them listen to her soliloquy when he leaves her, let them hear her repeat

> What's to be done ?—for something must be done—
> Two husbands ! yet not one ! by both enjoy'd,
> And yet a wife to neither ! hold my brain.—

And again,

> I am contented to be miserable
> But not in this way,—etc.

Let them observe during her progressions to madness, with what distinct shades sanity and reason are depicted, let them behold her frenzy increase till she attempts to stab her husband, let them watch the inexpressible anguish of her looks, while she clings to his body when dead, let them view her in her last agonies give her laugh of horror, for having at last escaped from such inhuman persecutors and insupportable miseries, and then while their passions are warm, let them declare who is her equal.

In *Jane Shore* the same regard to propriety, to character, situation, and sentiment is preserved. We have heard it affirmed, that she mistakes the first part of this character, that she is too full of grief, and exhibits too strong a picture of melancholy, but this was evidently a hasty and ill formed criticism. Gloster and Lord Hastings before she appears describe her fully.

> *L. Hast.* I am to move your highness in behalf,
> Of Shore's unhappy wife.
> *Glost.*   Say you of Shore.
> *L. Hast.* Once a bright star that held her place on high,
> The first and fairest of our English dames,
> While royal Edward held the sovereign rule,
> Now sunk in grief and pining in despair ;
> Her waning form no longer shall incite,
> Envy in woman, or desire in man ;
> She never sees the sun but thro' her tears,
> And wakes to sigh the live long night away.
>   *Glost.* Marry the times are badly chang'd with her
> From Edward's days to these : then all was jollity,
> Feasting and mirth, light wantonness and laughter ;
> Piping and playing, minstrelsy and masquing,
> Till life fled from us like an idle dream,
> A shew of mummery without a meaning.

This quotation will prove how attentively Mrs. Siddons had studied her Author, when she gave rise to the above ill judged decision, and every sentence in her first scene is a confirmation that she was right. The whole character is indeed little more than a penitentiary repetition of past crimes, as the source of present misfortunes, till the fourth act, in which Jane Shore is tempted by Gloster to betray King Edward's children, and we never beheld Mrs. Siddons in this scene, without increasing admiration. From her performance of Isabella and Belvidera, we were convinced how powerfully she could inspire pity and terror, but her Grecian daughter and Jane Shore, convinced every beholder how perfectly she was mistress of the sublime as well as of the pathetic. Never were gratitude, patriotism, and disregard of partial selfish feelings better conceived or better expressed, than by Mrs. Siddons, after Gloster has told her that Hastings opposes those who wish to deprive the orphan prince of the crown, when she exclaims—

> *J. Sh.* Does he ! does Hastings !
> *Glost.*   Ay Hastings,
> *J. Sh.* Reward him for the noble deed just Heaven,
> For this one action guard him and distinguish him
> With signal mercies and with great deliverance,
> Save him from wrong adversity and shame,
> Let never fading honours flourish round him
> And consecrate his name even to time's end ;
> Let him know nothing else but good on earth,
> And everlasting blessedness hereafter.

She does not as we have seen others, stay to cast a look of contempt at Gloster, her whole soul is intent upon the generosity of Hastings, and her affection for her prince ; all other sensations are so totally absorbed, and these are poured forth in such a rapture of dignified enthusiasm, that the spectator forgets while she is speaking, the danger she incurs. There never was a Gloster but must appear insignificant by the side of Mrs. Siddons, notwithstanding all his threats, while she says

> Oh ! that my tongue had every grace of speech,
> Great and commanding as the breath of kings ;
> Sweet as the poet's numbers and prevailing
> As soft persuasion to a lovesick maid,
> That I had art and eloquence divine,
> To pay my duty to my master's ashes,
> And plead till death the cause of injured innocence.

Her fortitude if possible increases, and becomes equal to the strongest exertions of the strongest mind, after Gloster's denunciation of vengeance, when she thus devotes herself to misery, rather than abandon her gratitude and loyalty.

> Let me be branded for the public scorn,
> Turn'd forth and driven to wander like a vagabond ;
> Be friendless and forsaken, seek my bread
> Upon the barren, wild, and desolate waste,
> Feed on my sighs, and drink my falling tears,
> Ee'r I consent to teach my lips injustice,
> Or wrong the orphan who has none to save him.

Her resignation is so perfect, so determined, and so sublime, her tone of voice so firm, yet free from rant, her action so unconsciously noble, and her deportment so void of all ostentatious self applause, perceptible either in the player as speaking well, or the woman as acting with superiority, that we think we behold absolute perfection, both in the actress and the character. It is not the declamation of study, the display of attitudes, or the stride of assumed dignity by which we are charmed, but those exact and forcible expressions of feeling that stamp reality on fiction, and make it no longer an imitation but a truth.

And here we cannot but recommend to those gentlemen who do at present, or hope hereafter to perform Hastings, (as well as those young ladies, who shall make similar attempts on Jane Shore,) to observe with the utmost degree of assiduity, by what means Mrs. Siddons excels in this scene. Did they so do, we surely should no longer see Hastings in a scene, equal, if not superior, with respect to writing and theatrical advantages, depend alone on the strength of his voice for applause ; we should then see these performers emulative only to give a superior energy of fortitude instead of vociferation. We should no longer consider them as Actors, but as Heroes, when they say,

> On this foundation will I build my fame,
> And emulate the Greek and Roman name,
> Think England's peace bought cheaply with my blood,
> And die with pleasure for my country's good.

We read in the papers that a deputation had been sent to Mrs. Siddons, requesting her to speak in a more enfeebled tone in the last scene of *Jane Shore*. Whether such deputation was or was not sent, is not our business to enquire ; but as there is some justice in the criticism, we shall, for the entertainment of our Reader's curiosity, examine how far it is practicable in stage exhibition. That a woman emaciated with extreme hunger and in the agonies of death, should be able to speak so loud, we can readily allow to be almost impossible, and so it is that she should speak so much, or that she should continue to traverse the streets so immediately before she dies. But these seem rather to be among the necessary defects of imitation, in which fiction is obliged to allow its inferiority to fact, and in which the Poet and the Performer are at least to be excused if not justified, than of that kind that criticism by discovering, may reform. Had Jane Shore been shewn on the stage as feeble and helpless as she actually was, when expiring for want of food, her words must have been few, her actions none, and her voice not audible ; but the Poet wanted to express her thoughts, and the Actress to be heard ; to effect which, some improbabilities are perhaps inevitable. We will grant, however, that the weaker the voice, the more natural is the Player, provided she be entirely heard ; but this is the first consideration, and to this every other must give place.

In *The Grecian Daughter* Mrs. Siddons displays the nobler passions in a still more eminent degree : the characteristic virtues of Euphrasia are fortitude and filial piety, and of these she gives the strongest and most permanent picture. To cite every passage in which she is excellent, would be endless ; but there are two in which she rises so much above expectation, that not to note them would be unjust. The first is when she supposes her father murdered by Philotas.

> And dost thou then, inhuman that thou art,
> Advise a wretch like me to know repose ?
> This is my last abode—these caves, these rocks,
> Shall ring for ever with Euphrasia's wrongs :
> All Sicily shall hear me—Yonder deep
> Shall echo back an injured daughter's cause.
> Here will I dwell, and rave, and shriek, and give
> These scattered locks to all the passing winds ;
> Call on Evander lost, and pouring curses,
> And cruel Gods and cruel stars invoking,
> Stand on the cliff in madness and despair.

In the recitation of this speech, Mrs. Siddons is so perfectly what she describes, she raves and shrieks in accents so piercing and so loud, that the Spectator supplies all the other circumstances : he imagines all Sicily actually hears her, and that he sees her standing on the cliff in madness and despair !

The other is in the fourth act, where Dionysius requires her to draw off her husband Phocion and his powers from the siege ; to which she replies,

> Think'st thou then
> So meanly of my Phocion ? Dost thou deem him
> Poorly wound up to a mere fit of valour
> To melt away in a weak woman's tear ?
> *Oh thou dost little know him.*

Her manner of saying *Oh thou dost little know him*, conveys so consummate an idea of an elevated mind, that every one who hears her is persuaded she is perfectly capable in real life of acting the part she here only personates, and they admire the woman even more than the actress. When we say every one, we would be understood to mean every one of those who are themselves susceptible of the like sentiments.

We shall pass over her agitation while she fears Philotas has at last betrayed her father, and the manner of her stabbing the tyrant, as we must many more beauties, and make a few observations on her in *The Fair Penitent*.

Nothing, perhaps, gives more permanent satisfaction from Poet, Painter, or Player, than when they perfectly assume the *manners* of the persons they represent ; and in this Mrs. Siddons is particularly happy. Her look, her step, her gestures, vary with the character. In Isabella her behaviour is meekness and resignation to unmerited misfortunes ; in *Jane Shore* lowliness and contrition for past offences ; in *The Grecian Daughter* that true dignity which a conscious strength of mind and rectitude of action naturally inspires, is every where prevalent ; and in Calista that haughty affectation of being above controul, which a deviation from virtue ever produces in a great but proud mind. She walks with greater precipitation, her gestures are more frequent and more violent, her eyes are restless and suspicious, pride and shame are struggling for superiority, and guilt is in the contraction of her brow. We think however, that in her scene with Horatio in the third act, the night we saw her, she fell into an error by no means usual with her ; she discovered too much rage in the first part of the scene, and thus formed an anticlimax : but perhaps this was casual. Her general performance of the part is superlative, and the speech where she stabs herself is above description terrible in the utterance. It is immediately after the entrance of Horatio, who comes to tell her of her father's death.

> And dost thou bear me yet, thou patient earth ?
> Dost thou not labour with thy murd'rous weight ?
> And you ye glittering heav'nly host of stars,
> Hide your fair heads in clouds or I shall blast you ;
> For I am all contagion, death, and ruin,
> And nature sickens at me.—Rest thou world,
> This Parricide shall be thy plague no more,
> Thus—thus I set thee free.

So perfect is her conception of the infamy of her crime and the horror of its consequences, and such is her detestation of herself and of the ruin she has induced, that we think it impossible for an innocent female to behold her agony, without feeling an additional dread of the like sin ; or if she had begun to cherish vicious inclinations, not to be terrified from putting them in act. It is no hyperbole to say we congratulate the nation on the happy effects that are likely, at least for a time, to follow from its being so much the fashion among those of high rank to attend the performances of Mrs. Siddons. That they were degenerating into that laxity of manners which ridicules the idea of conjugal obligations, and the dictates of self denial, is too notorious to be disputed ; there is now, we hope, a probability that they may be roused from their lethargy.

We cannot close this account of her characters without noticing the affecting and capital stile in which she plays the mad scene in Belvidera, and of this nothing can be a better proof, than when in the midst of her phrenzy, she breaks out into a laugh, we see the audience always burst into tears. The reality of her madness must be thoroughly impressed upon the mind, before laughter can incite a sensation so different as that of weeping. The manner likewise of her pronouncing the exclamation oh ! in all passages where the passions are violently agitated, is one of her most marking beauties, and peculiar to herself. Let us conclude with a few general observations, which may point out to others the errors they are liable to, and the excellencies it is their duty to emulate.

We have before spoken of the attention which Mrs. Siddons pays to the manners, and we repeat the observation, to shew the necessity of this intention by its effects. All who excel as Artists, Poets, or Critics pay the strictest regard to consistency, and the production of a whole. Whoever neglects or slightly regards this, is in continual danger of offending. The idea of a whole must extend itself as carefully to each distinct part of a performance, as to the work collectively. Incongruities give disgust in a proportionate degree as they deviate from truth and reality. The Actor who at his entrance is seen to stare about, or even to take what he may suppose an unobserved peep, that he may examine how many of his acquaintance he can discover in the pitt and boxes, loses sight not only of character but of respect, and deserves a severe reprehension. Yet this is done at our theatres every night with an astonishing assurance. Whatever reminds the Spectator that he is at the playhouse, and that Rosincraus [sic] and Guildenstern are not the school-fellows of Hamlet, but two silly youngsters who have taken up the profession of an actor, because they are idle, and not because they are ambitious, brings to his remembrance several disagreeable circumstances all at once, and inspires him with a portion of contempt for Messieurs Rosincraus and Guildenstern, of which were they aware, they would certainly behave with more propriety and caution. Nor is this censure aimed at or confined to individuals ; the fault is so common, that there are but very few who are not sometimes guilty of it. This evil is of the same species with that of the Actors personal jokes and laughter on the stage among each other, concerning which we spoke in our last number : and of these we must say, in the language of Adam Overdo,[1] " It is time to take enormity by the forehead and brand it." Another very common and very great stage error is, the inattention with which Actors

[1] See Ben Jonson's *Bartholomew Fair*.

are apt to treat not only the general business of the play, but the very characters with whom they are speaking. If a letter be to be thrown down on the ground, the Actor scorns to lower his dignity so far as to stoop and take it up again ; the scene-man must enter to do such common drudgery ; no matter that it contains secrets of the utmost importance, and that the person he represents could not possibly be so careless about things on which his happiness or even life may depend. If a duel be to be fought, the hat is thrown away, for the sake of shewing, as we suppose, with what a grace it may be done, and not because men always throw away their hats when they fight duels ; and when some good-natured friend comes to part them, they disdain as much to pick up a hat as a letter, chusing rather to walk a few miles bareheaded. And here we may farther remark, that the sight of a drawn sword has very little or no effect on the countenance of a player ; death is rather a serious concern when it makes such *near* approaches, to all people else ; but as the property-man keeps neither three-edged nor two-edged swords in his possession, but a set of blunt, harmless weapons, that scorn with any force of arm to penetrate as far as the skin, the actor very logically concludes, it would be a folly to shew fear since he is certain there is no danger. He is likewise apt to discover an equal degree of contempt concerning the purport of the dialogue. It is none of his business to notice what other people say, if he, in Othello's phrase, do but " know his cue without the prompter." *That* is, what he is to watch for, and not to give any signs of anxiety or concern, at the reasons, threats, or promises of a person, who like him, is only come there to say his lesson. The proverb says, " every dog has his day," and again, " he that sharply chides is the most ready to pardon," both of which we often see verified on the stage, where each actor takes his turn to make a speech, and be *very* angry, and then—to hold his tongue, and be *very* cool. And thus the alternate buckets come and go ; the empty one descends, while the full one is wound up. The different passions that might be supposed once to have taken place in the minds, and been apparent in the countenances of the Roman mob, when Antony harangued over the dead body of Cæsar, are nothing to a player ; he neither knows, nor wants to know any thing about such matters. He is certain Cæsar's legacies will never descend to him or his heirs ; he never saw the Tiber, nor was he ever in the walks, the private arbors, or the new planted orchards, that Antony talks of : *he stands there to speak his part.* If, indeed, he can make his friends in the gallery laugh at the quaintness of his dress, or the drollery of his grimace, while Antony is deploring the fate of his mighty master, that is a deed worthy his ambition, but as for the real manner in which it may be conjectured the plebeians of Rome actually behaved on that occasion, it is a thing he never once thought of.

We have spoken thus ironically of glaring, though common improprieties, that the Reader may recollect, with the greater degree of force, the precision and accuracy of good performers, and especially of Mrs. Siddons. Her eyes never wander, her passions are as active while she is silent as when she is speaking, she is not Belvidera this moment, and Mrs. Siddons the next, but she is Belvidera always. She does not stab herself, as if she were sheathing her scissars in heroics. She does not continually make her exit with a strut or expire with a groan ; but her manner varies with her situation. She conjures up the ghost of the character she personates, beholds it with the piercing eye of strong imagination, and embodies the phantom.

—From " The English Review," 1783.

JOHN TAYLOR

(1757–1832)

MRS. SIDDONS APPEARS AS LADY MACBETH

Mrs. Siddons last night . . . appeared for the first time in the character of Lady Macbeth. . . . Throughout the first and second acts Mrs. Siddons never exhibited such chaste, such accomplished acting. There being little or no declamation, our ears were not wounded with the repetition of the *lark's shrill note*, or the blundering distribution of a vitiated emphasis ; the total absence of the pathetic prevented that perpetual shaking of the head and tossing of the chin, which we have before remarked as her principal defects in that line of acting, and the violent exertion of her arms, which shocks the critical spectator in Belvidera and Calista was suited to the masculine ferocity of the heroine in this drama.

Mrs. Siddons was at first much agitated ; in the scenes with Macbeth immediately before and after the murder of Duncan she was admirably expressive of the genuine sense and spirit of the author ; but in the banquet scene in the third act, her abilities did not shine to so much lustre. In several passages of the dialogue, she adopted too much the *familiar* manner, approaching to the *comic* ; this may be called her *epilogue* style in which she has already experienced an entire failure. In this scene an exception must be made to her rebuke of Macbeth (though even that had not the powerful effect we might have expected from Mrs. Siddons) and the congé to her guests, which last was delivered with inimitable grace.

In the taper scene she was defective ; her enunciation was too confined . . . the faces she made were horrid and even ugly, without being strictly just or expressive. She appeared in three several dresses. The first was handsome and neatly elegant : the second rich and splendid, but somewhat *panto-*

mimical, and the last one of the least becoming, to speak no worse of it, of any she ever wore upon the stage. Lady Macbeth is supposed to be *asleep* and not *mad* ; so that custom itself cannot be alledged as a justification for her appearing in *white sattin*.

—From " The Morning Post," February 3, 1785.

JOHN TAYLOR ON MRS. SIDDONS'S STRANGE DRESS FOR ROSALIND

Mrs. Siddons in Rosalind. The attempts of performers to excite the public curiosity and to engage the attention of the town to their benefits should always be considered at least as inoffensive if not laudable, and therefore should be exempted from the ordinary strictness of critical remark. Every actor is privileged on such an occasion to put himself before his friends in as ridiculous a situation as he thinks proper ; and it is not only permitted to reverse the sexes, but to commit every other violence against propriety that is at the same time consistent with the *utmost latitude* of decorum and subservient to the interest of the performer. In this point of view the attempt on Saturday of Mrs. Siddons should pass in silence ; but as the town has been taught to expect some novelty in the entertainment which they have heretofore received from the performances of this admired actress, a candid examination of her talents for the line of acting which she has recently engaged in, is a duty which we owe to the public.

With the sincerity and decision which it is always our aim to preserve in our criticisms we must pronounce Mrs. Siddons from the specimen she gave on Saturday night, utterly void of that humour which is the soul of Comedy. She shewed in various parts of the character she undertook much taste and feeling ; but she pleased only in the sentimental passages. Her *entrées* and her walk (or rather strut) on the stage, were those of Lady Macbeth or Belvidera, not of the volatile and sprightly Rosalind. Too close an attention to emphasis, and to a frittering refinement with a quaint sinking of her voice, rendered her utterance occasionally inaudible ; and the shake and declination of her head were the only indications of gaiety and humour.

Mrs. Siddons, however, received very great applause ; and who would not shew their judgment in applauding so great, so eminent an actress ? But she was acting Comedy ; she was delivering some of the most witty conceits of Shakespeare.— Did the audience laugh ? Were they diverted ? No. They were too much wrapped up in admiration at the extraordinary refinement of the actress : applause they gave in abundance ; but reserved their laughter for Mrs. Wrighten.

If in this impartial consideration of Mrs. Siddons's capabilities for comedy we may be allowed to advert to more minute affairs, we must observe that her dress was the most un-accountable we ever witnessed upon the stage. It was not that of either man or woman. Her Hussar boots with a gardener's apron and petticoat behind, gave her a most equivocal appearance, which rendered Orlando's stupidity astonishing, in not making a premature discovery of his mis-tress. What caused Mrs. Siddons to innovate upon the former representations of this character in the article of dress we cannot guess ; but we are certain that she could not appear to less advantage in any other habiliment whatever.

—From " The Morning Post," 2 May, 1785.

"THE DEVIL'S POCKET-BOOK"

(1786)

FIERY CRITICISMS OF RYDER, MRS. SIDDONS, KEMBLE, AND BENSLEY

Drury Lane.

ON Wednesday evening the celebrated Roscius of Ireland, Mr. Ryder, made his first appearance in the character of Sir John Falstaff : accustomed as the human mind is to the pressure of disappointment, not even a failure on the part of so reputed a comedian, in a character that has long been considered as the *ne plus ultra* of his powers, could effect any violent astonishment. There is an old saying of the Prince of Condé's, "No man can appear a hero to his own valet de chambre"; which implies, that the weaknesses of our nature are too perceptible to an intimate companion, to admit that he can have full credit for perfection. Had Mr. Ryder's efforts been confined to this kingdom, we are clearly of opinion, that the voice of temerity would not have presumed to compare his representation of the humourous knight, with the high-finished portraits of the late inimitable HENDERSON. The contracted state of RYDER's understanding is evident in all those new and tender discriminations which HENDERSON was wont to touch with the magic pencil of delicacy and truth. He succeeded best in the broad strokes of humour, where the vulgarity of the sensualist destroys the feelings of the gentleman ; and seemed more intent to catch the unmeaning thunder of the motley gods, by an unlicensed action, than to lay the cornerstone of an endless reputation, by a chaste adherence to the author, and a due obedience to the mandates of excellence.

That RYDER possesses great capability for the walks of low comedy, no man should dispute : we have seen his performance of Scapin with uncommon pleasure ; his mimickry was well-timed, and its execution remarkably characteristic ; but when, either from the impulse of his folly, or the dictates of the Manager he assumes the personification of a gentleman, it must prove such an injury to his consequence as a comedian, as no act can expiate, and no time efface : the muscles of his countenance tacitly bid defiance to the assumption of any appearance of gentility ; his voice is unharmonious, his face vulgar, and his person altogether bears that indelible stamp of meanness with which niggard Nature has signalized her poorest works, in the hours of her ill-humour and narrow economy.

We cannot close these strictures on Mr. RYDER, without regretting that his competitors at Drury-Lane Theatre should be so mean and scandalous, as to seize every opportunity of decrying his merits in the most public and illiberal manner.

On the same evening, the lethargic managers of Old Drury were so far roused from their usual torpidity, as to bring forward DODSLEY's bloody Tragedy of *Cleone* : the SIDDONS performed the heroine, and a most horrible performance it was; but this allusion is not meant as a wound to her theatric dignity ; for she was, if possible, super-eminently terrible. Though we by no means wish to detract from Mrs. SIDDONS's well-earned character, as the first female tragedian of the age, we cannot admit that she is on a footing of equality, even as a tragic actress, with Mrs. CRAWFORD, when the last-mentioned lady was in the zenith of her glory, ere she permitted the arrows of sensuality to murder her honest fame : the different sources from whence these different rivals draw their excellencies, must ever render their performances strikingly unlike, however near they may both approach to perfection ; Mrs. SIDDONS is manifestly the child of ART ; her best positions convey strongly the idea of having been previously studied ; they do not seem to arise out of the circumstance of the moment. The most confirmed ideot of the Theatre, who has seen her exhibit but three different characters, can tell, by the extension of one arm, when to expect an *Ah !* and by the brandishing of the other, when to expect an *Oh !* The same gestures accompany her mad exertions in all parts ; and it does not signify a rush whether the heroine of the piece is an Eastern Princess, or a private gentlewoman. But the labours of a

CRAWFORD were once far different ; for she was, literally, the child of NATURE. When she opened her mouth, it was to issue language that spoke instantly to the heart ; and the most inhuman miscreant in society could not behold her in a state of assumed anguish, without yielding, involuntarily, the tear of sensibility as a tribute to her sublime merit.

Mr. KEMBLE sustained the part of SIFROY, as Mr. KEMBLE sustains every other ; his conceptions were nearly just ; his action crampt, and disagreeable ; and his voice weak, coarse and inefficient ; Mr. BENSLEY's GLANVILLE only operated to awaken those sentiments in the mind, which will occur when we are consigned to the mortification of seeing and hearing him performing, namely, sentiments of amazement, that a man so weakly gifted and repulsive in almost every faculty that is necessary to the completion of an actor, should have had interest and effrontery sufficient to appear before a rational audience : it may be a compliment to the charity of the nation, that such a man is permitted to perform ; but it likewise conveys an aukward implication, that a British audience can be insulted with impunity.

Before a second representation of this tragedy takes place, we seriously recommend it to the Managers to pay a due share of respect to the dignity of their tragic heroes and heroines : it was a shame, on Saturday evening, to behold such a group of lofty and noble personages, strutting about the stage, in the cast-off habiliments of departed greatness ; and so un-appropriate were the dresses to the characters, that they appeared more like an assemblage of mad beggars at a Venetian carnival, than the first-rate performers in the elder theatre of the metropolis.

—From *The Devil's Pocket-Book*, No. III.

LEIGH HUNT

(1784-1859)

ON MR. POPE—" A ROBUSTIOUS FELLOW, WHO TEARS A PASSION TO TATTERS "

WHEN I place Mr. Pope immediately after Mrs. Siddons, everybody will see I do not criticise the actors according to their rank. But it is for the sake of contrast. If we have just had an example of almost perfect tragedy, we have now an instance of every fault that can make it not only imperfect but disgusting. Mr. Pope has not one requisite to an actor but a good voice, and this he uses so unmercifully on all occasions that its value is lost, and he contrives to turn it into a defect. His face is as hard, as immovable, and as void of meaning as an oak wainscot ; his eyes, which should endeavour to throw some meaning into his vociferous declamation, he generally contrives to keep almost shut ; and what would make another actor merely serious is enough to put him in a passion. In short, when Shakespeare wrote his description of " a robustious fellow, who tears a passion to tatters," one would suppose that he had been shown, by some supernatural means, the future race of actors, as Macbeth had a prophetic view of Banquo's race, and that the robustious phantom was Mr. Pope. Here is an actor, then, without face, expression, or delivery, and yet this complication of negative qualities finds means to be clapped in the theatre and panegyrised in the newspapers. This inconsistency must be explained. As to the newspapers, and their praise of this gentleman, I do not wish to repeat all the prevailing stories. Who does not know their corruptions ? There is, however, an infallible method of obtaining a clap from the galleries, and there is an art known at the theatre by the name of *clap-trapping*, which Mr. Pope has shown great wisdom in studying. It consists in nothing more than in gradually raising the voice as the speech draws to a conclusion, making an alarming outcry on the last four or five lines, or suddenly dropping them into a tremulous but energetic undertone, and with a vigorous jerk of the right arm rushing off the stage. All this astonishes the galleries ; they are persuaded it must be something very fine, because it is so important and so unintelligible, and they clap for the sake of their own reputation.

One might be apt to wonder at Mr. Pope's total want of various expression, when his merit as an artist is considered. It should seem that the same imitative observation, which gives so natural an elegance to his portraits on canvas, should enliven and adorn his portraits on the stage : that the same elegant conception which enables him to throw grace into the attitudes and meaning into the eyes of others, should inspire his action with variety and his looks with intelligence.

It is in the acknowledgment of gesture and attitude, but more particularly in the variation of countenance, in the adaption of look to feeling, that the actor is best known. Mr. Pope, in his general style, has but two gestures, which follow each other in monotonous alternation, like the jerks of a toy-shop harlequin : one is a mere extension of the arms, and is used on all occasions of candour, of acknowledgment, of remonstrance, and of explanation ; the other, for occasions of vehemence or of grandeur, is an elevation of the arms, like the gesture of Raphael's *St. Paul preaching at Athens*, an action which becomes the more absurd on common occasions, from its real sublimity. If Mr. Pope, however, is confined to two expressions in his gesture, he has but two expressions in his look : a flat indifference, which is used on all sober occasions, and an angry frown, which is used on all impassioned ones. With these two looks he undertakes to represent all the passions, gentle as well as violent ; he is like a quack who, with a phial in each hand, undertakes to perform every possible wonder, while the only thing to be wondered at is his cheating the mob. The best character he performs is Othello, because he performs it in a mask : for when an actor's face is not exactly seen, an audience is content to supply by its own imagination the want of expression, just as in reading a book we figure to ourselves the countenance of the persons interested. But when we are presented with the real countenance, we are disappointed if our imagination is not assisted in its turn ; the picture presented to our eyes should animate the picture presented to our mind ; if either of them differ, or if the former is less lively than the latter, a sensation of discord is produced, and destroys the effect of nature, which is always harmonious.

The pain we feel at bad acting seems, indeed, to be entirely the result of a want of harmony. We are pleased when the actor's external action corresponds with the action of his mind, when his eye answers his heart, when all we see is the animated picture of all we feel : we are displeased whenever the passion and the expression are at variance, when the countenance does not become a second language to the dialogue, when moderate tones express vehement emotions and when vehement tones express moderate emotions, when, in short, Mr. Pope is not Rolla or Romeo but Mr. Pope. A musician who tells us that he is going to play a melancholy movement, and then dashes his harp or his piano in a fury, cannot disappoint us more than this actor, when he raises from language merely sorrowful an expression of boisterous passion. The character of Hotspur has been reckoned a proper one for Mr. Pope, because it is loud and violent ; these are good reasons certainly, and we would rather hear him in Hotspur than in Hamlet, for noise, like any other enjoyment, is delightful in its proper season only. But to act Hotspur well is a mark of no great talent ; of all expressions, violence is the most easily affected, because the conception of violence has no sensation of restraint, it has no feelings to hide or to repress, and no niceties of action to study. The gentler passions give us leisure to examine them, we can follow every variation of feeling and every change of expression ; but here we have leisure for nothing ; everything is rapid and confused ; we are in the condition of a man who should attempt to count the spokes of a wheel in a chariot-race.

Mr. Pope, in short, may be considered as an example of the little value of a good voice unaccompanied with expression, while Mr. Kemble is a proof how much may be done by an expressive countenance and manner with the worst voice in the world.

But perhaps as I can say nothing of Mr. Pope as a tragic actor, I may be expected to say something of him as a comic one, for he does act in comedy. Any one, however, who examines this double gift, will discover that to act in comedy and to be a comic actor are two very different things. Mr. Kemble performs in comedy, but who will call Mr. Kemble a comic actor ? Who will reckon up the comic actors, and say, " We have Bannister, and Lewis, and Munden, and Kemble ? " If Mr. Pope acts in sentimental comedy, what is called sentimental comedy is nothing more than a mixture of tragedy and comedy, or, if Dr. Johnson's definition is to be allowed, it is sometimes entire tragedy, for he calls tragedy " a dramatic representation of a serious action." There may be very often a serious character in humorous comedies, such as a sober merchant, a careful father, or one of those useless useful friends who serve as a kind of foil to a gay hero ; but the actor who performs these characters never excites our livelier feelings or our mirth, and therefore cannot be called a comic actor. Lord Townley, for instance, in *The Provoked Husband*, is merely a tragic character who has stepped into comedy : Mr. Kemble represents Lord Townley with much gravity and stateliness ; yet nobody in the pit ever said at seeing this character, " Really that is very comic ! " It is necessary to a comic actor that he should be able to excite our laughter, or at least our smiles ; but Mr. Pope never excites either, at any rate not designedly. It is for this reason that he has been placed among the tragedians, and that Mr. Charles Kemble, Mr. Henry Johnston, Mr. Murray, and Mr. Siddons will be placed among them too. All these gentlemen might undoubtedly be called comic actors, as Robin Hood's companion, who was seven feet high, was called Little John ; or we might say such a man was as comic as Mr. Kemble or Mr. Henry Johnston, just as we say such a thing is as smooth as a file. But upon plain subjects I would rather be plain spoken.

—From *Dramatic Essays*. By Leigh Hunt.

ON MR. MATHEWS'S COMIC RÔLES

THOSE comedians are infinitely mistaken who imagine that mere buffoonery or face-making is a surer method of attaining public favour than chastened and natural humour. A monstrous grin, that defies all description or simile, may raise a more noisy laughter, but as I have before observed, the merest pantomime clown will raise a still noisier : laughter does not always express the most satisfied enjoyment, and there is something in the ease and artlessness of true humour that obtains a more lasting though a more gradual applause : it is like a rational lover, who allows confidence and extravagant mirth to catch a woman's eye first, but wins his way ultimately from the very want of qualities which please merely to fatigue. While such an actor, therefore, as Dowton will attempt buffoon-eries in which he neither can nor ought to succeed, it is no small credit to Mr. Mathews that he has the judgment to avoid in general what he really can exhibit with the greater effect. This is the proper pride of an actor who has a greater respect for the opinion of the boxes than of the galleries ; this is the laudable ambition that would rather be praised by those who are worthy of respect themselves than by a clamorous mob who, in fact, applaud their own likeness in the vulgarity and nonsense so boisterously admired.

Such a judgment is the more praiseworthy in Mr. Mathews, as his principal excellence is the representation of officious valets and humorous old men, two species of character that with most actors are merely buffoons in livery and buffoons with walking-sticks. His attention to correctness, however, by no means lessens his vivacity, but it is the vivacity of the world, not of the stage ; it seems rather his nature than his art, and though I dare say all actors have their hours of disquiet, and perhaps more than most men, yet he has not the air of one who elevates his sensations the moment he enters the stage and drops them the instant he departs. It is a very common and a very injurious fault with actors to come before the audience with a manner expressive of beginning a task ; they adjust their neck-cloths and hats as if they had dressed in a hurry, look about them as much as to say, " What sort of a house have I got this evening ? " and commence their speeches in a tone of patient weariness, as if they contemplated the future labours of the evening. This is a frequent error with Mr. H. Johnston, and a most peculiar one with Mr. C. Kemble, who often seems to have just arrived from a fatiguing walk. Mr. Mathews makes his appearance neither with this indifference on the one hand, nor on the other with that laboured mirth which seems to have been lashed into action like a top, and which goes down like a top at regular intervals. If, therefore, he does not amaze like many inferior actors with sudden bursts of broad merriment, he is more equable and consistent in his humour, and inspires his audience with a more constant spirit of cheerfulness. Such a cheerfulness is the most desirable effect in every comic performer, and this feeling is one of the sensations which render us more truly pleased with comedy than with farce : it is more agreeable to reason, because it leaves room for thinking ; it is removed from violence, which always carries a degree of pain into the more exquisite pleasures : it is more like the happiness that we may attain in real life, and therefore more fitted to dispose us to an enjoyment of our feelings.

The principal fault in the general style of Mr. Mathews is a redundancy of bodily motion approaching to restlessness, which I have sometimes thought to have been a kind of nervousness impatient of public observation ; but I think he has repressed this considerably within these few months, and if it be owing to want of confidence, the stage is not a place to increase any of the more bashful feelings. This fault, however, like Mr. Kemble's stiffness in Penruddock, becomes a beauty in his performance of the restless *Lying Valet*, and of Risk in *Love Laughs at Locksmiths*, who are both in a perpetual bustle of cheating and contrivance. Possibly it may be the frequency of his performance in characters of intrigue that originally led him to indulge it, for there is yet another character, that of the intriguing servant in the farce of *Catch him who Can*, in which he is at full liberty to indulge it. In this servant he gives a specimen of that admirable power of mimicry, in which he rivals Mr. Bannister. I believe there were many in the theatre who had much difficulty to recognise him in his transformation into the Frenchman, and for alteration of manner, tone, and pronunciation, it certainly was not inferior to the most finished deceptions of that great comedian. As this kind of deception, indeed, depends chiefly upon a disguise of the voice, one would imagine it ought not to be very difficult to an actor, one of whose first powers should be a flexibility of tone ; but this flexibility becomes valuable on our stage for its rarity, for it is curious enough to observe that we have not a single tragedian or female performer who can at all disguise the voice, and of all our comedians, who really ought to excel in this point, Mr. Bannister and Mr. Mathews seem the only two who can thus escape from themselves with any artifice : many of the comic actors, as Munden, Simmons, Blanchard, Liston, Johnstone, Wewitzer, and particularly Fawcett, seem blessed with such honest throats as to be incapable of the slightest deception.

The old age of Mr. Mathews is like the rest of his excellencies, perfectly unaffected and correct ; the appearance of years he manages so well, that many of his admirers, who have never seen him off the stage, insist that he is an elderly man, and the reason of this deception is evident : most of our comedians in their representation of age either make no alteration of their voice, and, like antiquarian cheats, palm a walking-stick or a hat upon us for something very ancient, or sink into so un-natural an imbecility that they are apt on occasion to forget their tottering knees and bent shoulders, and like Vertumnus, in the poet, are young and old in the turn of a minute. Mathews never appears to wish to be old ; time seems to have come to him, not he to time, and as he never, where he can avoid it, makes that show of feebleness which the vanity of age always would avoid, so he never forgets that general appearance of years, which the natural feebleness of age could not help. Our old men of the stage are in general of one unvarying age in all their various characters, as in the case of Munden, for instance, who, though he imitates the appearance of a hearty old gentleman with much nature, is seldom a jot the older or younger than his usual antiquity, whatever the author might have led us to imagine. The two characters of Don Manuel in *She would and She would not* and of Old Philpot in *The Citizen* are sufficient examples of the ease with which Mr. Mathews alters his years and of the general excellencies of his old age.

In the former piece he is a naturally cheerful old man, whose humour depends much on the humour of others, and who is overcome alternately with gaiety and with despair, as he finds himself treated by those about him. The voice of Mr. Mathews, were we to shut our eyes, would be enough to convince us of his age in this character, and of his disposition too ; there is something in it unaccountably petty and confined, while at the same time it appears to make an effort of strength and jollity ; and when his false pitch of spirits meets with a sudden downfall, nothing can be more natural than the total dissolution of his powers of voice, or the restless despondency with which he yields himself to a hundred imaginary miseries. When his spirits are raised again and his excessive joy gradually over-comes itself by its own violence, the second exertion of his fatigued talkativeness and of his excessive laughter reduces him to mere impotence ; he sinks into his chair ; and in the last weariness of a weak mind and body, cannot still refrain from the natural loquacity of old age, but in the intervals of op-pressed feeling attempts to speak when he has not only nothing to say, but when it is perfectly painful to him to utter a word. In this character, therefore, Mr. Mathews exhibits all the gradations of the strength and weakness of declining years ; in that of Philpot, he settles himself into a confirmed and un-resisting old age : his feeble attitudes, his voice, his minutest actions, are perfectly monotonous, as become a money-getting dotard, whose soul is absorbed in one mean object : his limbs contracted together are expressive of the selfish closeness of the miser, and in his very tone of utterance, so sparing of its strength and so inward, he seems to retire into himself.

From the general performances, however, of Mr. Mathews, I had been induced to consider him as an actor of habits rather than of passions ; and as the present essay originally stood, I had classed him in a rank much inferior to Bannister and Dow-ton. But one of his late performances raised his genius so highly in my estimation, that I cancelled the original para-graph on purpose to do justice to his Sir Fretful Plagiary in *The Critic*, to a performance which has proved his knowledge of the human heart, has given its true spirit to one of the most original characters of the first wit of our age, and has even persuaded the ancient dramatic connoisseurs to summon up the claps of former-times : nay, some of the old gentlemen, in the important intervals of snuff, went so far as to declare that the actor approached Parsons [1] himself. We are generally satisfied when an actor can express a single feeling with strength of countenance ; but to express two at once, and to give them at the same time a powerful distinctness, belongs to the perfection of his art. Nothing can be more admirable than the look of Mr. Mathews when the severe criticism is detailed by his malicious acquaintance. While he affects a pleasantry of countenance, he cannot help betraying his rage in his eyes, in that feature which always displays our most predominant feelings ; if he draws the air to and fro through his teeth, as if he was perfectly assured of his own pleasant feelings, he convinces everybody by his tremulous and restless limbs that he is in absolute torture ; if the lower part of his face expands into a painful smile, the upper part contracts into a glaring frown which contradicts the ineffectual good humour beneath ; everything in his face becomes rigid, confused, and uneasy ; it is a mixture of oil and vinegar, in which the acid predominates ; it is anger putting on a mask that is only the more hideous in proportion as it is more fantastic. The sudden drop of his smile into a deep and bitter indignation, when he can endure sarcasm no longer, completes this impassioned picture of Sir Fretful ; but lest his indignation should swell into mere tragedy, Mr. Mathews accompanies it with all the touches of familiar vexation : while he is venting his rage in vehement expressions, he accompanies his more emphatic words with a closing thrust of his buttons, which he fastens and unfastens up and down his coat ; and when his obnoxious friend approaches his snuff-box to take a pinch, he claps down the lid and turns violently off with a most malicious mockery of grin. These are the performances and the characters which are the true fame of actors and dramatists. If our farcical performers and farcical writers could reach this refined satire, ridicule would vanish before them, like breath from a polished knife.

—From *Dramatic Essays*.

[1] William Parsons (died 1795) was an admirable actor of old men in comedy. He was the original Sir Fretful Plagiary.

LEIGH HUNT ON THE DEATH OF ELLISTON

July 10, 1831.

WE have to lament, with all the lovers of genuine comedy and fervid animal spirits, the death of our old favourite Elliston, who was carried off last Friday by apoplexy—a death not peculiar, as many suppose, to the sluggish and over-fed, but too common to those who have lived a life of excitement, and drawn much upon sanguine heads. Elliston was of no spare class of men either : he seems to have eaten and drunk stoutly enough, perhaps too much for one who had so much to do, and whose faculties were half made up of sanguineness. We believe the wonder is that he lasted so long, especially as he had had severe attacks of illness on and off for a good many years, some of them of a mortal aspect. We remember hearing a long time back that his hands had become useless with palsy ; he recovered that shock, gesticulated as much as ever, and not long since had another attack. He recovered again, appeared on the stage as if nothing had happened, and was meditating, we believe, new characters, when he was taken off. A man of a less vital order would have been killed long ago. But the mystery of life, in some people, seems to carry itself on in spite of obstacles. They have more of the *life* of life in them than others. This is what is understood by the familiar but no less mysterious term, animal spirits. We have a theory respecting the cause of it, with which we will not trouble the reader. All we shall say is, that we take a man's parentage to have a great deal more to do with it than his education.

The death of a comic actor is felt more than that of a trage-dian. He has sympathised more with us in our every-day feelings, and has given us more amusement. Death with a tragedian seems all in the way of business. Tragedians have been dying all their lives. They are a " grave " people. But it seems a hard thing upon the comic actor to quench his airi-ness and vivacity—to stop him in his happy career—to make us think of him, on the sudden, with solemnity—and to miss him for ever. We could have " better spared a better man." It is something like losing a merry child. We have not got used to the gravity. Mrs. Siddons, the other day, was missed far less than Elliston will be. She had withdrawn, it is true, for some time ; but her life was, in a manner, always withdrawn. She lived with the tragic pall round her. Kemble was missed by those who had been used to him ; but he was missed rather as a picture than a man. There is something of this in the popularity of Charles Kemble ; but as the picture is of a more gallant and agreeable kind, none of the family will have been so cordially lamented as he will be when he dies—next century : for we suppose he does not mean even to grow old for these forty years.

Mr. Elliston was the best comedian, in the highest sense of the word, that we have seen. Others equalled him in some particular points ; Lewis surpassed him in airiness ; but there was no gentleman comedian who comprised so many qualities of his art as he did, or who could diverge so well into those parts of tragedy which find a connecting link with the graver powers of the comedian in their gracefulness and humanity. He was the best Wildair, the best Archer, the best Aranza ; and carrying the seriousness of Aranza a little further, or making him a *tragic gentleman* instead of a comic, he became the best Mortimer, and even the best Macbeth, of any performer who excelled in comedy. When Charles Kemble acts comedy, he gives you the idea of an actor who has come out of the chivalrous part of tragedy. It is grace and show that are most natural to him—the ideal of mediocrity. Elliston being naturally a comedian, and comedy of the highest class demanding a greater sympathy with actual flesh and blood, his tragedy, though less graceful than Charles Kemble's, was more natural and cordial. He suffered and was shaken more. The other, in his greatest grief, is but like the statue of some Apollo Belvedere vivified, frowning in beauty, and making a grace of his sorrow. The god remains impassive to ordinary suffering. Elliston's features were nothing nearly so handsome or so finely cut as the other's, but they were more sensitive and intelligent. He had nothing of the poetry of tragedy ; the other has the form of it ; but Elliston, in Macbeth, could give you something of the weak and sanguine and misgiving usurper ; and in

Mortimer, in the *Iron Chest*, he has moved the audience to tears. It ought not to be forgotten that he restored that character to the stage when John Kemble had killed it with his frigidity.

The tragedy of this accomplished actor was, however, only an elongation, or drawing out, of the graver and more sensitive part of his comedy. It was in comedy that he was the master. When Kean appeared and extinguished Kemble, Elliston seems prudently to have put out his tragic lamp. In comedy, after the death of Lewis, he remained without a rival. He had three distinguished excellencies—dry humour, gentlemanly mirth, and fervid gallantry. His features were a little too round, and his person latterly became a great deal too much so. But we speak of him in his best days. His face, in one respect, was of that rare order which is peculiarly fitted for the expression of enjoyment : it laughed with the eyes as well as mouth. His eyes, which were not large, grew smaller when he was merry, and twinkled with glee and archness ; his smile was full of enjoyment, and yet the moment he shook his head with a satirical deprecation, or dropped the expression of his face into an inuendo, nothing could be drier or more angular than his mouth. There was a generosity in his style, both in its greater and smaller points. He understood all the little pretended or avowed arts of a gentleman, when he was conversing or complimenting, or making love—everything which implied the necessity of attention to the other person, and a just, and as it were, mutual consciousness of the graces of life. His manners had the true *minuet dance* spirit of gentility—the knowledge how to give and take, with a certain recognition of the merits on either side, even in the midst of raillery. And then his voice was remarkable for its union of the manly with the melodious ; and as a lover nobody approached him. Certainly nobody approached a woman as he did. It was the reverse of that preposterous style of *touch and avoid,*—that embracing at arm's length, and hinting of a mutual touch on the shoulders—by which the ladies and gentlemen of the stage think fit to distinguish themselves from the characters they perform, and even the Pollys and Macheaths propitiate our good opinion. Elliston made out that it was no shame to love a woman, and no shame in her to return his passion. He took her hand, he cherished it against his bosom, he watched the moving of her countenance, he made the space less and less between them, and as he at length burst out into some exclamation of " Charming ! " or " Lovely ! " his voice trembled, not with the weakness, but with the strength and fervour of its emotion. All the love on the stage, since this, (with the exception of Macready's domestic tenderness) is not worth two pence, and fit only to beget waiters.

July 14, 1831.

In calling to mind the pleasant hours that had been given us by the talents of the late Mr. Elliston, we forgot to mention his defects. In tragedy, for want of a strong sympathy with the serious, he sometimes got into a commonplace turbulence, and at others put on an affected solemnity, and he was in the habit of *hawing* between his words. The longer he was a manager, the worse this habit became. He was not naturally inclined to the authoritative ; but having once commenced it in order to give weight to his levity, he seems to have carried about the habit with him, to maintain his importance. Unfortunately, he fancied that he was never more natural than on these occasions. He said once, at the table of a friend of ours, clapping himself on the knee, and breathing with his usual fervour, " Nature-*aw*, sir, is everything-*aw* : I-*aw* am always-*aw* natural-*aw*."

Theodore Hook had a ludicrous story of his calling upon Elliston at the Surrey Theatre, and having some conversation with him in the midst of his managerial occupations. In the course of their dialogue, Elliston would start in a grand manner from the subject, and give some direction to his underlings. He called for two of them successively in the following manner :

ELLISTON (turning suddenly to the right, and breathing with all his fervour). " Night watchman ! " (Enter night watchman, and has a word or two spoken to him by the manager.)

ELLISTON (scarcely having resumed the discourse, and turning suddenly as before). " *Other* night watchman ! " (Enter other night watchman, and is spoken to in like manner. The histrionic sovereign then resumes his discourse with Mr. Hook, with tranquil dignity.)

We had an hour's conversation with him once at Drury Lane, during which, in answer to some observation we made respecting the quantity of business he had to get through, he told us that he had formed himself " on the model of the Grand Pensionary De Witt." Coming with him out of the theatre, we noticed the present portico in Brydges Street, which had just been added to the front, and said that it seemed to have started up like magic. " Yes, sir," said he, " energy is the thing. I no sooner said it than it was done—it was a *Bonaparte blow*."

There was real energy, however, in all this, and the right animal spirits, as well as an innocent pedantry : nor did it hinder him from being the delightful comedian we have described. He could not have been it had he not been pleased with himself, and a little superfluous self-complacency off the stage was to be pardoned him. A successful actor would be a phenomenon of modesty if he were not one of the vainest of men. Nobody gets such applause as he does, and in such an intoxicating way, except a conqueror entering a city.

We must not forget to mention that Elliston's *homely* tragedy was excellent. He has rivalled Bannister in the performance of the Brazier in *John Bull* ; and his Sheva in the comedy of *The Jew* was admired to the last for its pathetic delicacy. Upon the whole, as the gallant of genuine comedy, and an accomplished actor of all work, he has left nobody to compare with him. He was as far superior to the gentlemen comedians now going, as Kean was superior to him in tragedy.

—From *Dramatic Essays*.

CHARLES LAMB

(1775–1834)

ON THE ACTING OF MUNDEN

Not many nights ago, I had come home from seeing this extraordinary performer in *Cockletop* ; and when I retired to my pillow, his whimsical image still stuck by me, in a manner as to threaten sleep. In vain I tried to divest myself of it, by conjuring up the most opposite occasions. I resolved to be serious. I raised up the gravest topics of life ; private misery, public calamity. All would not do—

> There the antic sate
> Mocking our state . . .

his queer visnomy—his bewildering costume—all the strange things which he had raked together—his serpentine rod, swagging about in his pocket—Cleopatra's tear, and the rest of his relics—O'Keefe's wild farce, and *his* wilder commentary—till the passion of laughter, like grief in excess, relieved itself by its own weight, inviting the sleep which in the first instance it had driven away.

But I was not to escape so easily. No sooner did I fall into slumbers, than the same image, only more perplexing, assailed me in the shape of dreams. Not one Munden, but five hundred, were dancing before me, like the faces which, whether you will or no, come when you have been taking opium—all the strange combinations, which this strangest of all strange mortals ever shot his proper countenance into, from the day he came commissioned to dry up the tears of the town for the loss of the now almost forgotten Edwin. O for the power of the pencil to have fixed them when I awoke ! A season or two since there was exhibited a Hogarth gallery. I do not see why there should not be a Munden gallery. In richness and variety, the latter would not fall far short of the former.

There is one face of Farley, one face of Knight, one (but what a one it is !) of Liston ; but Munden has none that you can properly pin down, and call *his*. When you think he has exhausted his battery of looks, in unaccountable warfare with your gravity, suddenly he sprouts out an entirely new set of features, like Hydra. He is not one, but legion : not so much a comedian, as a company. If his name could be multiplied like his countenance, it might fill a playbill. He, and he alone, literally *makes faces* ; applied to any other person, the phrase is a mere figure, denoting certain modifications of the human countenance. Out of some invisible wardrobe he dips for faces, as his friend Suett used for wigs, and fetches them out as easily. I should not be surprised to see him some day put out the head of a river-horse ; or come forth a pewitt, or lapwing, some feathered metamorphosis.

I have seen this gifted actor in Sir Christopher Curry—in old Dornton—diffuse a glow of sentiment which has made the pulse of a crowded theatre beat like that of one man ; when he has come in aid of the pulpit, doing good to the moral heart of a people. I have seen some faint approaches to this sort of excellence in other players. But in the grand grotesque of farce, Munden stands out as single and unaccompanied as Hogarth. Hogarth, strange to tell, had no followers. The school of Munden began, and must end, with himself.

Can any man *wonder*, like him ? can any man *see ghosts*, like him ? or *fight with his own shadow*—" SESSA "—as he does in that strangely-neglected thing, the *Cobbler of Preston*—where his alternations from the Cobbler to the Magnifico, and from the Magnifico to the Cobbler, keep the brain of the spectator in as wild a ferment as if some Arabian Night were being acted before him. Who like him can throw, or ever attempted to throw, a preternatural interest over the commonest daily-life objects ? A table, or a joint-stool, in his conception, rises into a dignity equivalent to Cassiopeia's chair. It is invested with constellatory importance. You could not speak of it with more deference, if it were mounted into the firmament. A beggar in the hands of Michael Angelo, says Fuseli, rose the

Patriarch of Poverty. So the gusto of Munden antiquates and ennobles what it touches. His pots and his ladles are as grand and primal as the seething-pots and hooks seen in old prophetic vision. A tub of butter, contemplated by him, amounts to a Platonic idea. He understands a leg of mutton in its quiddity. He stands wondering, amid the commonplace materials of life, like primæval man with the sun and stars about him.

—From *The Essays of Elia.*

WILLIAM HAZLITT

(1778–1830)

ON EDMUND KEAN'S RICHARD

M R. KEAN'S manner of acting this part has one peculiar advantage ; it is entirely his own, without any traces of imitation of any other actor. He stands upon his own ground, and he stands firm upon it. Almost every scene had the stamp and freshness of nature. The excellences and defects of his performance were in general the same as those which he discovered in Shylock ; though, as the character of Richard is the most difficult, so we think he displayed most power in it. It is possible to form a higher conception of this character (we do not mean from seeing other actors, but from reading Shakespear) than that given by this very admirable tragedian ; but we cannot imagine any character represented with greater distinctness and precision, more perfectly *articulated* in every part. Perhaps, indeed, there is too much of this ; for we sometimes thought he failed, even from an exuberance of talent, and dissipated the impression of the character by the variety of his resources. To be perfect, it should have a little more solidity, depth, sustained, and impassioned feeling, with somewhat less brilliancy, with fewer glancing lights, pointed transitions, and pantomimic evolutions.

The Richard of Shakespear is towering and lofty, as well as aspiring ; equally impetuous and commanding ; haughty, violent, and subtle ; bold and treacherous ; confident in his strength, as well as in his cunning ; raised high by his birth, and higher by his genius and his crimes ; a royal usurper, a princely hypocrite, a tyrant, and a murderer of the House of Plantagenet.

> But I was born so high ;
> Our airy buildeth in the cedar's top,
> And dallies with the wind, and scorns the sun.

The idea conveyed in these lines (which are omitted in the miserable medley acted for *Richard III*) is never lost sight of by Shakespear, and should not be out of the actor's mind for a moment. The restless and sanguinary Richard is not a man striving to be great, but to be greater than he is ; conscious of his strength of will, his powers of intellect, his daring courage, his elevated station, and making use of these advantages, as giving him both the means and the pretext to commit unheard-of crimes, and to shield himself from remorse and infamy.

If Mr. Kean does not completely succeed in concentrating all the lines of the character, as drawn by Shakespear, he gives an animation, vigour, and relief to the part, which we have never seen surpassed. He is more refined than Cooke ; more bold, varied, and original than Kemble, in the same character. In some parts, however, we thought him deficient in dignity ; and particularly in the scenes of state business, there was not a sufficient air of artificial authority. The fine assumption of condescending superiority, after he is made king—" Stand all apart—Cousin of Buckingham," &c. was not given with the effect which it might have received. There was also at times, a sort of tip-toe elevation, an enthusiastic rapture in his expectations of obtaining the crown, instead of a gloating expression of sullen delight, as if he already clutched the bauble, and held it within his grasp. This was the precise expression which Mr. Kean gave with so much effect to the part where he says, that he already feels

The golden rigol bind his brows.

In one who *dares* so much, there is little indeed to blame. The only two things which appeared to us decidedly objectionable, were the sudden letting down of his voice when he says of Hastings, " chop off his head," and the action of putting his hands behind him, in listening to Buckingham's account of his reception by the citizens. His courtship scene with Lady Anne was an admirable exhibition of smooth and smiling villainy. The progress of wily adulation, of encroaching humility, was finely marked throughout by the action, voice, and eye. He seemed, like the first tempter, to approach his prey, certain of the event, and as if success had smoothed the way before him. We remember Mr. Cooke's manner of representing this scene was more violent, hurried, and full of anxious uncertainty. This, though more natural in general, was, we think, less in character. Richard should woo not as a lover, but as an actor—to shew his mental superiority, and power to make others the playthings of his will. Mr. Kean's attitude in leaning against the side of the stage before he comes forward in this scene, was one of the most graceful and striking we remember to have seen. It would have done for Titian to paint. The opening scene in which Richard descants on his own deformity, was conceived with perfect truth and character, and delivered in a fine and varied tone of natural recitation. Mr. Kean did equal justice to the beautiful description of the camps the night before the battle, though, in consequence of his hoarseness, he was obliged to repeat the whole passage in an under-key.[1] His manner of bidding his friends good night, and his pausing with the point of his sword, drawn slowly backward and forward on the ground, before he retires to his tent, received shouts of applause. He gave to all the busy scenes of the play the greatest animation and effect. He filled every part of the stage. The concluding scene, in which he is killed by Richmond, was the most brilliant. He fought like one drunk with wounds : and the attitude in which he stands with his hands stretched out, after his sword is taken from him, had a preternatural and terrific grandeur, as if his will could not be disarmed, and the very phantoms of his despair had a withering power.

—From " The Morning Chronicle," 15 Feb., 1814 ; and reprinted in Hazlitt's *Collected Works*, 1903.

WILLIAM HAZLITT ON THE ART OF MRS. SIDDONS

PLAYERS should be immortal, if their own wishes or ours could make them so ; but they are not. They not only die like other people, but like other people they cease to be young, and are no longer themselves, even while living. Their health, strength, beauty, voice, fails them ; nor can they,

[1] The defects in the upper tones of Mr. Kean's voice were hardly perceptible in his performance of Shylock, and were at first attributed to hoarseness. (W. H.)

without these advantages, perform the same feats, or command the same applause that they did when possessed of them. It is the common lot : players are only *not* exempt from it. Mrs. Siddons retired once from the stage : why should she return to it again ? She cannot retire from it twice with dignity ; and yet it is to be wished that she should do all things with dignity. Any loss of reputation to her, is a loss to the world. Has she not had enough of glory ? The homage she has received is greater than that which is paid to Queens. The enthusiasm she excited had something idolatrous about it ; she was regarded less with admiration than with wonder, as if a being of a superior order had dropped from another sphere to awe the world with the majesty of her appearance. She raised Tragedy to the skies, or brought it down from thence. It was something above nature. We can conceive of nothing grander. She embodied to our imagination the fables of mythology, of the heroic and deified mortals of elder time. She was not less than a goddess, or than a prophetess inspired by the gods. Power was seated on her brow, passion emanated from her breast as from a shrine. She was Tragedy personified. She was the stateliest ornament of the public mind. She was not only the idol of the people, she not only hushed the tumultuous shouts of the pit in breathless expectation, and quenched the blaze of surrounding beauty in silent tears, but to the retired and lonely student, through long years of solitude, her face has shone as if an eye had appeared from heaven ; her name has been as if a voice had opened the chambers of the human heart, or as if a trumpet had awakened the sleeping and the dead. To have seen Mrs. Siddons, was an event in every one's life ; and does she think we have forgot her ? Or would she remind us of herself by shewing us what *she was not* ? Or is she to continue on the stage to the very last, till all her grace and all her grandeur gone, shall leave behind them only a melancholy blank ? Or is she merely to be played off as " the baby of a girl " for a few nights ?—" Rather than so," come, Genius of Gil Blas, thou that didst inspire him in an evil hour to perform his promise to the Archbishop of Grenada, " and champion us to the utterance " of what we think on this occasion.

It is said that the Princess Charlotte has expressed a desire to see Mrs. Siddons in her best parts, and this, it is said, is a thing highly desirable. We do not know that the Princess has expressed any such wish, and we shall suppose that she has not, because we do not think it altogether a reasonable one. If the Princess Charlotte had expressed a wish to see Mr. Garrick, this would have been a thing highly desirable, but it would have been impossible ; or if she had desired to see Mrs. Siddons *in her best days*, it would have been equally so ; and yet without this, we do not think it desirable that she should see her at all. It is said to be desirable that a Princess should have a taste for the Fine Arts, and that this is best promoted by seeing the highest models of perfection. But it is of the first importance for Princes to acquire a taste for what is reasonable ; and the second thing which it is desirable they should acquire, is a deference to public opinion : and we think neither of these objects likely to be promoted in the way proposed. If it was reasonable that Mrs. Siddons should retire from the stage three years ago, certainly those reasons have not diminished since, nor do we think Mrs. Siddons would consult what is due to her powers or her fame, in commencing a new career. If it is only intended that she should act a few nights in the presence of a particular person, this might be done as well in private. To all other applications she should answer—" Leave me to my repose."

Mrs. Siddons always spoke as slow as she ought : she now speaks slower than she did. " The line too labours, and the words move slow." The machinery of the voice seems too ponderous for the power that wields it. There is too long a pause between each sentence, and between each word in each sentence. There is too much preparation. The stage waits for her. In the sleeping scene, she produced a different impression from what we expected. It was more laboured, and less natural. In coming on formerly, her eyes were open, but the sense was shut. She was like a person bewildered, and unconscious of what she did. She moved her lips involuntarily; all her gestures were involuntary and mechanical. At present she acts the part more with a view to effect. She repeats the action when she says, " I tell you he cannot rise from his grave," with both hands sawing the air, in the style of parliamentary oratory, the worst of all others. There was none of this weight or energy in the way she did the scene the first time we saw her, twenty years ago. She glided on and off the stage almost like an apparition. In the close of the banquet scene, Mrs. Siddons condescended to an imitation which we were sorry for. She said, " Go, go," in the hurried familiar tone of common life, in the manner of Mr. Kean, and without any of that sustained and graceful spirit of conciliation towards her guests, which used to characterise her mode of doing it. Lastly, if Mrs. Siddons has to leave the stage again, Mr. Horace Twiss will write another farewell address for her : if she continues on it, we shall have to criticise her performances. We know which of these two evils we shall think the greatest.

Too much praise cannot be given to Mr. Kemble's performance of Macbeth. He was " himself again," and more than himself. His action was decided, his voice audible. His tones had occasionally indeed a learned quaintness, like the colouring of Poussin ; but the effect of the whole was fine. His action in delivering the speech, " Tomorrow and to-morrow," was particularly striking and expressive, as if he had stumbled by an accident on fate, and was baffled by the impenetrable obscurity of the future.—In that prodigious prosing paper, the Times, which seems to be written as well as printed by a steam-engine, Mr. Kemble is compared to the ruin of a magnificent temple, in which the divinity still resides. This is not the case. The temple is unimpaired ; but the divinity is sometimes from home.

—From " The Examiner," 16 June, 1816 ; and reprinted in Hazlitt's *Collected Works*.

WILLIAM HAZLITT ON KEAN'S LEAR

WE need not say how much our expectations had been previously excited to see Mr. Kean in this character, and we are sorry to be obliged to add, that they were very considerably disappointed. We had hoped to witness something of the same effect produced upon an audience that Garrick is reported to have done in the part, which made Dr. Johnson resolve never to see him repeat it—the impression was so terrific and overwhelming. If we should make the same rash vow never to see Mr. Kean's Lear again, it would not be from the intensity and excess, but from the deficiency and desultoriness of the interest excited. To give some idea of the manner in which this character might, and ought to be, made to seize upon the feelings of an audience, we have heard it mentioned that once, when Garrick was in the middle of the mad-scene, his crown of straw came off, which circumstance, though it would have been fatal to a common actor, did not produce the smallest interruption, or even notice in the house. On another occasion, while he was kneeling to repeat the curse, the first row in the pit stood up in order to see him better ; the second row, not willing to lose the precious moments by remonstrating, stood up too ; and so, by a tacit movement, the entire pit rose to hear the withering imprecation, while the whole passed in such cautious silence, that you might have heard a pin drop. John Kemble (that old campaigner) was also very great in the curse : so we have heard, from very good authorities ; and we put implicit faith in them.—What led us to look for the greatest things from Mr. Kean in the present instance, was his own opinion, on which we have a strong reliance. It was always his favourite part. We have understood he has been heard to say, that " he was very much obliged to the London audiences for the good opinion they had hitherto expressed of him, but that when they came to see him over the dead body of Cordelia, they would have quite a different notion of the matter." As it happens, they have not yet had an opportunity of seeing him over the dead body of Cordelia : for, after all, our versatile Manager has acted Tate's Lear instead of Shakespear's [1] ; and it was suggested, that perhaps Mr. Kean played the whole ill *out of spite*, as he could not have it his own way—a hint to which we lent a willing ear, for we would rather think Mr. Kean the most spiteful man, than not the best actor, in the world ! The impression, however, made on our minds was, that, instead of its being his master-piece, he was to seek in many parts of the character ;—that the general conception was often perverse, or feeble ; and that there were only two or three places where

[1] Nahum Tate altered *King Lear*, making Cordelia survive and marry Edgar. This version held the stage until 1840.

he could be said to electrify the house. It is altogether inferior to his Othello. Yet, if he had even played it equal to that, all we could have said of Mr. Kean would have been that he was a very wonderful man ;—and such we certainly think him as it is. Into the bursts, and starts, and torrent of the passion in Othello, this excellent actor appeared to have flung himself completely : there was all the fitful fever of the blood, the jealous madness of the brain : his heart seemed to bleed with anguish, while his tongue dropped broken, imperfect accents of woe ; but there is something (we don't know how) in the gigantic, outspread sorrows of Lear, that seems to elude his grasp, and baffle his attempts at comprehension. The passion in Othello pours along, so to speak, like a river, torments itself in restless eddies, or is hurled from its dizzy height, like a sounding cataract. That in Lear is more like a sea, swelling, chafing, raging, without bound, without hope, without beacon, or anchor. Torn from the hold of his affections and fixed purposes, he floats a mighty wreck in the wide world of sorrows. Othello's causes of complaint are more distinct and pointed, and he has a desperate, a maddening remedy for them in his revenge. But Lear's injuries are without provocation, and admit of no alleviation or atonement. They are strange, bewildering, overwhelming : they wrench asunder, and stun the whole frame : they " accumulate horrors on horror's head," and yet leave the mind impotent of resources, cut off, proscribed, anathematised from the common hope of good to itself, or ill to others—amazed at its own situation, but unable to avert it, scarce daring to look at, or to weep over it. The action of the mind, however, under this load of disabling circumstances, is brought out in the play in the most masterly and triumphant manner : it staggers under them, but it does not yield. The character is cemented of human strength and human weaknesses (the firmer for the mixture) :—abandoned of fortune, of nature, of reason, and without any energy of purpose, or power of action left,—with the grounds of all hope and comfort failing under it,—but sustained, reared to a majestic height out of the yawning abyss, by the force of the affections, the imagination, and the cords of the human heart—it stands a proud monument, in the gap of nature, over barbarous cruelty and filial ingratitude. We had thought that Mr. Kean would take possession of this time-worn, venerable figure, " that has out-lasted a thousand storms, a thousand winters," and, like the gods of old, when their oracles were about to speak, shake it with present inspiration :—that he would set up a living copy of it on the stage : but he failed, either from insurmountable difficulties, or from his own sense of the magnitude of the under-taking. There are pieces of ancient granite that turn the edge of any modern chisel : so perhaps the genius of no living actor can be expected to cope with Lear. Mr. Kean chipped off a bit of the character here and there : but he did not pierce the solid substance, nor move the entire mass.—Indeed, he did not go the right way about it. He was too violent at first, and too tame afterwards. He sunk from unmixed rage to mere dotage. Thus (to leave this general description, and come to particulars) he made the well-known curse a piece of downright rant. He " tore it to tatters, to very rags," and made it, from beginning to end, an explosion of ungovernable physical rage, without solemnity, or elevation. Here it is ; and let the reader judge for himself whether it should be so served.

> Hear, Nature, hear ; dear goddess, hear a father !
> Suspend thy purpose, if thou didst intend
> To make this creature fruitful :
> Into her womb convey sterility,
> Dry up in her the organs of increase,
> And from her derogate body never spring
> A babe to honour her ! If she must teem,
> Create her child of spleen, that it may live,
> And be a thwart disnatur'd torment to her :
> Let it stamp wrinkles in her brow of youth,
> With cadent tears fret channels in her cheeks ;
> Turn all her mother's pains and benefits
> To laughter and contempt ; that she may feel,
> How sharper than a serpent's tooth it is
> To have a thankless child.

Now this should not certainly be spoken in a fit of drunken choler, without any " compunctious visitings of nature," with-out any relentings of tenderness, as if it was a mere speech of hate, directed against a person to whom he had the most rooted and unalterable aversion. The very bitterness of the impre-cations is prompted by, and turns upon, an allusion to the fondest recollections : it is an excess of indignation, but that indignation, from the depth of its source, conjures up the dearest images of love : it is from these that the brimming cup of anguish overflows ; and the voice, in going over them, should falter, and be choked with other feelings besides anger. The curse in Lear should not be *scolded*, but recited as a Hymn to the Penates ! Lear is not a Timon. From the action and attitude into which Mr. Kean put himself to repeat this passage, we had augured a different result. He threw himself on his knees ; lifted up his arms like withered stumps ; threw his head quite back, and in that position, as if severed from all that held him to society, breathed a heart-struck prayer, like the figure of a man obtruncated !—It was the only moment worthy of himself, and of the character.

In the former part of the scene, where Lear, in answer to the cool didactic reasoning of Gonerill, asks, " Are you our daughter ? " &c., Mr. Kean, we thought, failed from a contrary defect. The suppression of passion should not amount to immobility : that intensity of feeling of which the slightest intimation is supposed to convey everything, should not seem to convey nothing. There is a difference between ordinary familiarity and the *sublime* of familiarity. The mind may be staggered by a blow too great for it to bear, and may not recover itself for a moment or two ; but this state of suspense of its faculties, " like a phantasma, or a hideous dream," should not assume the appearance of indifference, or *still-life*. We do not think Mr. Kean kept this distinction (though it is one in which he is often very happy) sufficiently marked in the foregoing question to his daughter, nor in the speech which follows immediately after, as a confirmation of the same sentiment of incredulity and surprise.

> Does any here know me ? This is not Lear :
> Does Lear walk thus ? speak thus ? where are his eyes ?
> Either his notion weakens, his discernings
> Are lethargied—Ha ! waking—'tis not so ;
> Who is it that can tell me who I am ?
> Lear's shadow ? I would learn ; for by the marks
> Of sovereignty, of knowledge, and of reason,
> I should be false persuaded I had daughters.
> Your name, fair gentlewoman ?—

These fearful interrogatories, which stand ready to start away on the brink of madness, should not certainly be asked like a common question, nor a dry sarcasm. If Mr. Kean did not speak them so, we beg his pardon.—In what comes after this, in the apostrophe to Ingratitude, in the sudden call for his horses, in the defence of the character of his train as " men of choice and rarest parts," and in the recurrence to Cordelia's " most small fault," there are plenty of stops to play upon, all the varieties of agony, of anger and impatience, of asserted dignity and tender regret—Mr. Kean struck but two notes all through, the highest and the lowest.

This scene of Lear with Gonerill, in the first act, is only to be paralleled by the doubly terrific one between him and Regan and Gonerill in the second act. To call it a decided failure would be saying what we do not think : to call it a splendid success would be saying so no less. Mr. Kean did not appear to us to set his back fairly to his task, or to trust implicitly to his author, but to be trying experiments upon the audience, and waiting to see the result. We never saw this daring actor want confidence before, but he seemed to cower and hesitate before the public eye in the present instance, and be looking out for the effect of what he did, while he was doing it. In the ironical remonstrance to Regan, for example :

> Dear daughter, I confess that I am old—
> Age is unnecessary, &c.

he might be said to be waiting for the report of the House to know how long he should bend his knee in mimic reverence, how far he should sink his voice into the tones of feebleness, despondency, and mendicancy. But, if ever, it was upon *this* occasion that he ought to have raised himself above criticism, and sat enthroned (in the towering contemplations of his own mind) with Genius and Nature. They alone (and not the critic's eye, nor the tumultuous voices of the pit) are the true judges of Lear ! If he had trusted only to these, his own counsellors and bosom friends, we see no limit to the effect he might have produced. But he did not give any particular effect to the exclamation—

> ——" Beloved Regan,
> Thy sister's naught : oh, Regan, she hath tied
> Sharp-tooth'd unkindness, like a vulture here : "

nor to the assurance that he will not return to her again—

> Never, Regan :
> She hath abated me of half my train,
> Look'd black upon me ; struck me with her tongue,
> Most serpent-like, upon the very heart.
> All the stored vengeances of heaven fall
> On her ingrateful top !

nor to the description of his two daughters' looks—

> ——Her eyes are fierce ; but thine
> Do comfort, and not burn :

nor to that last sublime appeal to the heavens on seeing Gonerill approach—

> Oh, heav'ns !
> If you do love old men, if your sweet sway
> Hallow obedience, if yourselves are old,
> Make it your cause, send down, and take my part.
> Art not asham'd to look upon this beard ?
> Oh, Regan, will you take her by the hand ?

One would think there are tones, and looks, and gestures, answerable to these words, to thrill and harrow up the thoughts, to " appal the guilty, and make mad the free," or that might " create a soul under the ribs of death ! " But we did not see, or hear them. It was Mr. Kean's business to furnish them : it would have been ours to feel them, if he had ! It is not enough that Lear's crosses and perplexities are expressed by single strokes. There should be an agglomeration of horrors, closing him in like a phalanx. His speech should be thick with the fulness of his agony. His face should, as it were, encrust and stiffen into amazement at his multiplied afflictions. A single image of ruin is nothing—there should be a growing desolation all around him. His wrongs should seem enlarged tenfold through the solid atmosphere of his despair—his thoughts should be vast and lucid, like the sun when he declines—He should be " a huge dumb heap " of woe ! The most that Mr. Kean did was to make some single hits here and there ; but these did not tell, because they were separated from the main body and movement of the passion. They might be compared to interlineations of the character, rather than parts of the text.

In the sudden reiteration of the epithet—"*fiery* quality of the Duke," applied to Cornwall by Gloucester, at which his jealousy blazes out to extravagance, we thought Mr. Kean feeble and indecisive : but in breaking away at the conclusion of the scene, " I will do such things : what they are, yet I know not ; but they shall be the terrors of the earth "—he made one of those tremendous bursts of energy and grandeur, which shed a redeeming glory round every character he plays.

Mr. Kean's performance of the remainder of the character, when the king's intellects begin to fail him, and are, at last, quite disordered, was curious and quaint, rather than impressive or natural. There appeared a degree of perversity in all this—a determination to give the passages in a way in which nobody else would give them, and in which nobody else would expect them to be given. But singularity is not always excellence. Why, for instance, should our actor lower his voice in the soliloquy in the third act, " Blow winds, and crack your cheeks," &c. in which the tumult of Lear's thoughts, and the extravagance of his expressions, seem almost contending with the violence of the storm ? We can conceive no reason but that it was contrary to the practice of most actors hitherto. Mr. Rae's manner of mouthing the passage would have been " more germane to the matter." In asking his companion—

> How dost, my boy ? Art cold ?
> I'm cold myself——

there was a shrinking of the frame, and a chill glance of the eye, like the shivering of an ague-fit : but no other feeling surmounted the physical expression. On meeting with Edgar, as Mad Tom, Lear wildly exclaims, with infinite beauty and pathos, " Didst thou give all to thy daughters, and art thou come to this ? " And again, presently after, he repeats, " What, have his daughters brought him to this pass ? Couldst thou save nothing ? Didst thou give 'em all ? "—questions which imply a strong possession, the eager indulgence of a favourite idea which has just struck his heated fancy ; but which Mr. Kean pronounced in a feeble, sceptical, querulous under-tone, as if wanting information as to some ordinary occasion of insignificant distress. We do not admire these cross-readings of a work like *Lear*. They may be very well when the actor's ingenuity, however paradoxical, is more amusing than the author's sense : but it is not so in this case. From some such miscalculation, or desire of finding out a clue to the character, other than " was set down " for him, Mr. Kean did not display his usual resources and felicitous spirit in these terrific scenes :—he drivelled, and looked vacant, and moved his lips, so as not to be heard, and did nothing, and appeared, at times, as if he would quite forget himself. The pauses were too long ; the indications of remote meaning were too significant to be well understood. The spectator was big with expectation of seeing some extraordinary means employed: but the general result did not correspond to the waste of preparation. In a subsequent part, Mr. Kean did not give to the reply of Lear, " Aye, every inch a king ! "—the same vehemence and emphasis that Mr. Booth did ; and in this he was justified : for, in the text, it is an exclamation of indignant irony, not of conscious superiority ; and he immediately adds with deep disdain, to prove the nothingness of his pretensions—

> When I do stare, see how the subject quakes.

Almost the only passage in which Mr. Kean obtained his usual heartfelt tribute, was in his interview with Cordelia, after he awakes from sleep, and has been restored to his senses.

> Pray, do not mock me :
> I am a very foolish fond old man,
> Fourscore and upward ; and to deal plainly,
> I fear, I am not in my perfect mind.
> Methinks, I should know you, and know this man ;
> Yet I am doubtful ; for I'm mainly ignorant
> What place this is ; and all the skill I have
> Remembers not these garments ; nay, I know not
> Where I did lodge last night. *Do not laugh at me,*
> *For, as I am a man, I think this lady*
> *To be my child Cordelia.*
>   *Cordelia.* And so I am ; I am.

In uttering the last words, Mr. Kean staggered faintly into Cordelia's arms, and his sobs of tenderness, and his ecstasy of joy commingled, drew streaming tears from the brightest eyes,

> Which sacred pity had engender'd there.

Mr. Rae was very effective in the part of Edgar, and was received with very great applause. If this gentleman could rein in a certain " false gallop " in his voice and gait, he would be a most respectable addition, from the spirit and impressiveness of his declamation, to the general strength of any theatre, and we heartily congratulate him on his return to Drury-lane.— Mrs. West made an interesting representative of Cordelia. In all parts of plaintive tenderness, she is an excellent actress. We could have spared the love-scenes—and one of her lovers, Mr. Hamblin. Mr. Holland was great in Gloster. In short, what is he not great in, that requires a great deal of sturdy prosing, an " honest, sonsy, bawzont face," and a lamentably broken-down, hale, wholesome, hearty voice, that seems " incapable of its own distress ? " We like his jovial, well-meaning way of going about his parts. We can afford, out of his good cheer, and lively aspect, and his manner of bestriding the stage, to be made melancholy by him at any time, without being a bit the worse for it. Mr. Dowton's Kent was not at all good : it was a downright discarded serving-man. Mr. Russel, in the absence of the Fool, played the zany in the Steward. The tragedy was, in general, got up better than we expected.

—From " The London Magazine," June 1820 ; and reprinted in Hazlitt's *Collected Works*.

"THE THEATRICAL LOOKER-ON"

(1822–1823)

ON MR. GRIMALDI

WE class ourselves among that species of human being
denominated "odd," and consequently it is not on
every occasion we can expect to find adherents to our notions
of men and things ; but as that does not give us a moment's
concern, we speak as we feel—and now for an instance.—To
our particular fancies the subject of this article is the first of
living actors.—We make no exception as to the line of character
in which he appears, but confine ourselves simply to the opinion
we have formed of his complete identification with nature.
We do not consider that the most accomplished tragedian of
the day can produce any finer effect, or portray a more
faithful picture, than is exhibited by GRIMALDI in his death, in
the serious pantomime of *Ko and Zoa*, where art is totally lost
sight of, and the agonies of the dying Indian alone present
themselves to the eye ;—and in comic pantomime GRIMALDI
has been the evergreen as long as our memory serves ; nor do
we consider it heresy to class his *Clown* " high in the world's
estate." To us the very name of pantomime is delightful—
we can never forget the impression it first made on our young
imagination, the fascination of which has grown up with us ;—
and, after all, what are the tricks, the bustle, the chicanery,
the *tout ensemble* of art, practised by the *Clown* (and such a
Clown as GRIMALDI) but a too faithful portraiture of all that is
passing in life !

The pantomimes of *Ko and Zoa* and of *Don Juan* have afforded
very considerable satisfaction during the last week, but the
grand reserve, on the part of those who agree with the saying
that " the end of life's a laugh," was made for Friday, when a
regular Harlequinade, entitled *Harlequin and the Three Wishes*,

was ushered forth with two sheets of Mr. KNOTT's best type—and we are delighted in recording that the house was crowded to excess, and the piece met with so favourable a reception as to induce the Manager to obtain its repetition on Monday. We literally roared at GRIMALDI, and although his SON for activity cannot be surpassed—although PAYNE is a very adroit and clever *Harlequin*—COLLIER a famous *Pantaloon*—and Miss WORGMAN sufficiently nimble in *Columbine*—yet give us JOE for ever and a day—his laugh is a comedy of itself—his action is the very summit of grace, yet ridicule as well—and his eye speaks more than his tongue could.—To say that the reception of himself and colleagues was flattering in the extreme, is quite unnecessary—from the rise to the fall of the curtain, one incessant laugh shook the sides of the Theatre—it was, as MILTON finely expresses it,—

Laughter holding both his sides ;

and we thank our stars we were of the number—and had we pitched by any accident on that waistband which would have confined our merriment, we should have discarded it with great contempt from our wardrobe for ever.

—From " The Theatrical Looker-on," No. XVI.   Birmingham, 1823.

JOHN FORSTER

(1812–1876)

MACREADY AS HAMLET

MR. MACREADY's Hamlet is a noble and a beautiful performance.[1] It is infinitely finer than it used to be, more subtle and various, multiplied and deepened in its lights and shadows, with its sudden and brilliant effects harmonised to the expression of profound feeling, lofty yet gentle, the grandest sustainment of imagination and sensibility we have ever witnessed on the stage. We considered Mr. Macready highly successful in this character before seeing him last Wednesday, yet he illustrated then what it is to study Shakespeare with a love unwearied by success. But genius may well be its own rival, for it has no other. We venture to think, without a shade of misgiving, that this performance was the noblest approach that the *stage* can present to Hamlet, as he exists in the wonderful creativeness of Shakespeare's fancy. Vivid delineations of moments of passion, we have seen equally fine, fragments of possibly superior beauty in the acting of the late Mr. Kean—but never such a grasp of thought, never such a sustained exhibition of single, profound, and enduring passion, cast in the yielding and varying mould of imagination. Mr. Macready was indeed the princely and heart-broken philosopher, the irresolute avenger, the friend of Horatio, the lover of Ophelia.

Hamlet is more than this, it is true ; but we must recollect the palpable intervention of the stage. Mr. Macready cannot exhibit that which " passeth show." We try in vain to conceive of an actor that should present with effect the exact Hamlet of Shakespeare. There is that in it, considered deeply in the closet, with which eye, and tone, and gesture have

[1] Drury Lane, October 7, 1835.

nothing to do. Supposing we had an actor who could subdue all sense of his art, could consent to sacrifice all dramatic point, all scenic effect, all brilliant antitheses of action,—who, with grace, wit, chivalrous and princely bearing, profound intellect, and a high faculty of imagination, could yet merge all these in a struggle of sensibility, of weakness, and of melancholy, and bear them with him about the stage, " like sweet bells jangled, out of tune and harsh,"—suppose such an actor upon the stage, who, with these accomplishments, chooses to show them only in such a struggle, using them unconsciously, and to himself not to others—who abstracts himself from the audience, the actors, and the theatre, and, wrapped in a veil of subtle intellectual refinement, only, as it were, reflects aloud,—supposing, we say, all this, which might alone serve the realisation of the book Hamlet, of his solitary musings, his silent thoughts, his " light-and-noise-abhorring ruminations," we are more than half-inclined to think that his audience might fancy he had little business where he was, and take to hissing the pointless and unprecise performance. We do not say they would be wrong. The necessities of his art limit the sway of the actor. It is evident to us that Mr. Macready has as true and profound a sense of the character of Hamlet as it would be possible to entertain, and that where he sacrifices anything of this, he is only surrendering to his art as much as is necessary to secure its own triumph. He is the Hamlet of our fancies reconciled to our waking thoughts. For this we pardon an occasional over-display of the resources of his art, such as Hamlet might never have indulged.

The impassioned and heart-breaking sorrow with which Mr. Macready opened the play in the first soliloquy was a noble foundation for the entire structure of the character. This quick and passionate sensibility he never lost sight of, whether under the influence of supernatural visiting, or goaded by the desire of earthly vengeance. If Mr. Macready's performance had suddenly closed in the soliloquy of " Oh ! what a rogue and peasant slave am I," at the words—

> Bloody, bawdy villain !
> Remorseless, treacherous, lecherous, KINDLESS villain !

we should have needed no better assurance of the power of his
genius to cope with this wonderful character. Where he
tempers this quick sensibility during his intercourse with
Horatio, with Rosencrantz and Guildenstern, and with
Ophelia, by the gentleness of the scholar, the schoolfellow, the
friend and the lover, we feel the apologies that are due for the
weaknesses and inconsistencies of Hamlet. In all this Mr.
Macready, as it seemed to us, touched the highest point of
perfection. His affection for Horatio and his reliance on his
judgment were marked and exclusive, and throughout excellently sustained—in the third act more especially, during
the progress of the Play-scene, and at last in the agonies of his
death, when his care is chiefly for him. In his intercourse with
Rosencrantz and Guildenstern, Mr. Macready happily kept up
the quiet demeanour of conscious detection, of cool observance
yet friendly familiarity, hitting one of the very nicest points in
Hamlet, without the intrusion of any violence or severe abrupt-
ness. We shall never forget the tone with which he broke into
" What a piece of work is a man ! " so earnest in its faith, and so
passionate in its sorrow. Here is the true Hamlet. No wonder the shock of this outraged sense of good should drive him
nearly mad. " 'That ever he was born to set it right ! " No
wonder his purpose failed by " thinking too precisely on the
event ! " No wonder that, even with his motive and his cue
for action, he should remain indolent and undecided, " un-
pregnant of his cause and can do nothing "—excess of thought
absorbing his faculty of action. If ever this was expressed on
the stage, it was expressed by Mr. Macready. If ever the
subtle madness of Hamlet, which is not madness, and yet not
an assumption, which might rather stand for the over-subtle
workings of the intellect, for the awful though quiet action of
the *sources* of wit and madness, passing through the brain alone,
and witnessed only in changes of metaphysical emotion, and in
the dejected ruins of a noble presence and universal accomplishment, " blasted by ecstasy "—if ever this was presented
upon the stage, it was presented by this great actor. His scene
with Ophelia was truly exquisite. It was the realisation of
Mr. Lamb's opinion, that the scene is " a profound artifice of
love, to alienate Ophelia by affected discourtesies, so to prepare

her mind for the breaking off of that loving intercourse, which can no longer find a place amidst business so serious as that which he has to do." It was indeed not alienation, but distraction purely, and such it made itself felt by her—not anger, but grief assuming the appearance of anger—love awkwardly counterfeiting hate, " as sweet countenances when they try to frown."

In the scene with the Ghost, Mr. Macready still sustained the burthen of this surpassing character. Nothing could be more true than his restless walk up and down on the platform before the terrible appearance, or than the solemn and awful effect of his adjuration afterwards. He sinks before that preternatural visitation. The burst of human energy he gives way to, when his friends endeavour to oppose him, was, as a momentary wild relief, and in the bold and awful contrast into which it throws the " Go on, I'll follow thee," extremely grand and effective. The variety, the power, and the brilliant animation of the play-scene were daring and fine to the last degree. His manner of turning from Horatio, as he hears the approaching footsteps of the King—" They are coming to the play, I must be idle,"—his quick and salient walk up and down the front of the stage, waving his handkerchief as if in idle and gay indifference,[1] but ill concealing, at that instant, the sense of an approaching triumph—was one of those things Shakespeare himself would have done had he acted Hamlet. The whole scene was masterly ; its bitterness fearful—" your Majesty and we that have free souls, it touches *us* not ! "—and its energy quite appalling. Mr. Macready made us feel, what is literally the case with Hamlet, that his power exhausts itself here. His attitude as the King hurries off, was a noble commentary on that subtle purpose of Shakespeare. As he stands there, in the flushed excitement of a triumph, we feel that he is satisfied with the discovery alone. It was an earnest to Horatio and to all, that that confirmation of his suspicions was all he sought, that the success of his experiment was his greatest aim, and that to *act* upon it was as far from his thoughts as ever. In the same exquisite apprehensiveness of Shakespeare

[1] This was the action which Forrest, the American actor, hissed. He called it a *pas de mouchoir*. (William Archer.)

was the loud bullying of himself, to thrust down the thought which would at once have disabled his act, as he rushed to stab through the arras,—and his fine, breathless change of tone, as he rushes back with " Is it the King ? " This scene, and his conduct to his mother throughout, was marked by profound discrimination.

If we might hazard an objection to a performance so truly great as this, it would be to the delivery of the celebrated Soliloquy on Death, as too quiet and deliberate, and to the reception and intercourse with the players, as not sufficiently familiar. Why did not Mr. Macready recognise them cordially, at least his " old friend,"—for does not Hamlet shake hands with his schoolfellows before the players enter, and assign as his reason, " lest my extent to the players, which, I tell you, must show fairly outward, should more appear like entertainment than yours ? " He has his reason for this familiarity, as he has reasons for all he does, and for all he does not do.

This praise of ours, which we have meant to be as enthusiastic as it is sincere, we have yet felt to be inadequate to the occasion. We conclude as we began by characterising Mr. Macready's performance of Hamlet as the most perfect achievement of the modern stage—in depth, in originality, in truth, in beauty, and in grandeur of sustainment. Its expression is altogether equal to its conception.[1]

—From " The Examiner," 11 Oct., 1835 ; and reprinted in *Dramatic Essays*, 1896.

JOHN FORSTER ON MACREADY'S PRODUCTION OF *KING LEAR*

WHAT we ventured to anticipate when Mr. Macready assumed the management of Covent Garden Theatre,[2] has been every way realised. But the last of his well-directed efforts to vindicate the higher objects and uses of the drama,

[1] Macready's own note on this performance is, " Acted Hamlet, to judge by the continued interest and the uniform success of all the striking passages, better than I ever played it before. Forster . . . thought it, as a whole, the best he had ever seen." (William Archer.)

[2] Macready became lessee of Covent Garden, September 30, 1837. *King Lear* was produced January 25, 1838, and was acted ten times that season. (William Archer.)

has proved the most brilliant and the most successful. He has restored to the stage Shakespeare's true *Lear*, banished from it, by impudent ignorance, for upwards of a hundred and fifty years.

A person of the name of Boteler has the infamous repute of having recommended to a notorious poet laureate, Mr. Nahum Tate, the " new modelling " of *Lear*. " I found the whole," quoth Mr. Tate, addressing the aforesaid Boteler in his dedication, " to answer your account of it ; a heap of jewels unstrung and unpolished, yet so dazzling in their disorder, that I soon perceived I had seized a treasure." And accordingly to work set Nahum, very busily indeed ; strung the jewels and polished them with a vengeance ; omitted the grandest things, the Fool among them, polished all that remained into commonplace ; interlarded love-scenes ; sent Cordelia into a comfortable cave with her lover, to dry her clothes and get warm, while her distracted and houseless old father was still left wandering without, amid all the pelting of the pitiless storm ; and finally rewarded the poor old man in his turn, and repaid him for all his suffering, by giving him back again his gilt robes and tinsel sceptre !

Betterton was the last great actor who played Lear before the commission of this outrage. His performances of it between the years 1663 and 1671, are recorded to have been the greatest efforts of his genius.[1] Ten years after the latter date Mr. Tate published his disgusting version, and this was adopted successively by Boheme, Quin, Booth, Barry, Garrick, Henderson, Kemble, Kean. Mr. Macready has now, to his lasting honour, restored the text of Shakespeare, and we shall be glad to hear of the actor foolhardy enough to attempt another restoration of the text of Tate ! Mr. Macready's success has banished that disgrace from the stage for ever.

The Fool in the tragedy of *Lear* is one of the most wonderful creations of Shakespeare's genius. The picture of his quick and pregnant sarcasm, of his loving devotion, of his acute sensibility, of his despairing mirth, of his heartbroken silence—

---

[1] These statements regarding Betterton and King Lear are somewhat imaginative—at least they are not the certainties which they are made to appear. (William Archer.)

contrasted with the rigid sublimity of Lear's suffering, with the huge desolation of Lear's sorrow, with the vast and outspread image of Lear's madness—is the noblest thought that ever entered into the mind and heart of man. Nor is it a noble thought alone. Three crowded audiences in Covent Garden Theatre have now proved by something better than even the deepest attention that it is for action—for representation : that it is necessary to an audience as tears are to an overcharged heart ; and necessary to Lear himself as the recollection of his kingdom, or as the worn and faded garments of his power. We predicted some years since that this would be felt, and we have the better right to repeat it now. We take leave again to say that Shakespeare would have as soon consented to the banishment of Lear from the tragedy, as to the banishment of his Fool. We may fancy him, while planning his immortal work, feeling suddenly, with an instinct of divinest genius, that its gigantic sorrows could never be presented on the stage without a suffering too frightful, a sublimity too remote, a grandeur too terrible—unless relieved by quiet pathos, and in some way brought home to the apprehensions of the audience by homely and familiar illustration. At such a moment that Fool rose to his mind, and not till then could he have contemplated his marvellous work in the greatness and beauty of its final completion.

The Fool in *Lear* is the solitary instance of such a character, in all the writings of Shakespeare, being identified with the pathos and passion of the scene. He is interwoven with Lear —he is the link that still associates him with Cordelia's love, and the presence of the regal state he has surrendered. The rage of the wolf Goneril is first stirred by a report that her favourite gentleman had been struck by her father " for chiding of his fool "—and the first impatient questions we hear from the dethroned old man are " Where's my knave—my fool ? Go you and call my fool hither."—" Where's my fool ? ho ! I think the world's asleep."—" But where's my fool ? I have not seen him this two days."—" Go you and call hither my fool." All which prepare us for that affecting answer stammered forth at last by the Knight in attendance—" Since my young Lady's going into France, sir, the fool hath much pined away." Mr. Macready's manner of turning off at this with an expression of half impatience, half ill-repressed emotion— "No more of that—*I have noted it well*"—was inexpressibly touching. We saw him, in the secret corner of his heart, still clinging to the memory of her who used to be his best object, the argument of his praise, balm of his age, "most best, most dearest." And in the same noble and affecting spirit was his manner of fondling the Fool when he sees him first, and asks him with earnest care—"How now, my pretty knave? *How dost thou?*" Can there be a doubt, after this, that his love for the Fool is associated with Cordelia, who had been kind to the poor boy, and for the loss of whom he pines away? And are we not even then prepared for the sublime pathos of the close, when Lear, bending over the dead body of all he had left to love upon the earth, connects with her the memory of that other gentle, faithful, and loving being who had passed from his side—unites, in that moment of final agony, the two hearts that had been broken in his service—and exclaims—"And my poor fool is hanged!"

Mr. Macready's Lear, remarkable before for a masterly completeness of conception, is heightened by this introduction of the Fool to a surprising degree. It accords exactly with the view he seeks to present of Lear's character.[1] The passages we have named, for instance, had even received illustration in the first scene, where something beyond the turbulent greatness or royal impatience of Lear had been presented—something to redeem him from his treatment of Cordelia. The bewildered pause giving his "father's heart" away—the hurry yet hesitation of his manner as he orders France to be called—"Who stirs? Call Burgundy"—had told us at once how much consideration he needed, how much pity, of how little of himself he was indeed the master, how crushing and irrepressible was the strength of his sharp impatience. We saw no material change in his style of playing the first great scene with Goneril, which fills the stage with true and appalling touches of nature. In that scene he ascends indeed with the heights of

[1] Yet Macready was so nervous about the restoration of the Fool that he almost decided to cut him out after all. The part was acted by a lady, Miss Priscilla Horton. (William Archer.)

Lear's passion ; through all its changes of agony, of anger, of impatience, of turbulent assertion, of despair, and mighty grief ; till on his knees, with arms upraised and head thrown back, the tremendous curse bursts from him amid heaving and reluctant throes of suffering and anguish. The great scene of the second act had also its old passages of power and beauty—his self-persuading utterance of " hysterica passio "—his anxious and fearful tenderness to Regan—the elevated grandeur of his appeal to the Heavens—his terribly suppressed efforts, his pauses, his reluctant pangs of passion, in the speech " I will not trouble thee, my child "—and surpassing the whole, as we think, in deep simplicity as well as agony of pathos, that noble conception of shame as he *hides his face* on the arm of Goneril and says—

> I'll go with thee—
> Thy fifty yet doth double five and twenty,
> And thou art twice her love !

The Fool's presence then enabled him to give an effect, un-attempted before, to those little words which close the scene, when, in the effort of bewildering passion with which he strives to burst through the phalanx of amazed horrors that have closed him round, he feels that his intellect is shaking, and suddenly exclaims, " O, Fool ! I shall go mad ! " This is better than hitting the forehead and ranting out a self-reproach.

But the presence of the Fool in the storm-scene ! The reader must witness this to judge its power, and observe the deep impression with which it affects the audience. Every resource that the art of the painter and the mechanist can afford is called in aid in this scene—every illustration is thrown on it of which the great actor of Lear is capable—but these are nothing to that simple presence of the Fool ! He has changed his character there. So long as hope existed he had sought by his hectic merriment and sarcasm to win Lear back to love and reason—but that half of his work is now over, and all that remains for him is to soothe and lessen the certainty of the worst. Kent asks who is with Lear in the storm, and is answered—

> None but the *Fool*, who labours to outjest
> His heart-struck injuries !

When all his attempts have failed, either to soothe or outjest these injuries, he sings, in the shivering cold, about the necessity of " going to bed at noon." He leaves the stage to die in his youth, and we hear of him no more till we hear the sublime touch of pathos over the dead body of the hanged Cordelia.

The finest passage of Mr. Macready's scenes upon the heath is his remembrance of the " poor naked wretches," wherein a new world seems indeed to have broken upon his mind. Other parts of these scenes wanted more of tumultuous extravagance, more of a preternatural cast of wildness. We should always be made to feel something beyond physical distress predominant here. The colloquy with Mad Tom, however, was touching in the last degree—and so were the two last scenes, the recognition of Cordelia and the death, which elicited from the audience the truest and best of all tributes to their beauty and pathos. Mr. Macready's representation of the father at the end, broken down to his last despairing struggle, his heart swelling gradually upwards till it bursts in its closing sigh, completed the only perfect picture that we have had of Lear since the age of Betterton.

—From " The Examiner," 4 Feb., 1838 ; and reprinted in *Dramatic Essays*, 1896.

GEORGE HENRY LEWES

(1817–1878)

WAS MACREADY A GREAT ACTOR?

THE greatest—incomparably so—of all living tragedians concluded his farewell performances at the Haymarket, on Monday last,[1] amidst the frantic bravos of a loving and regretting public. Although his farewell to the public will be bidden on the occasion of his benefit (fixed for the 26th instant), yet we may say that on Monday last he bade farewell to the stage. He has left it for ever. His career as an Actor is closed. We may select his niche in the Pantheon. The Actor is dead, and can no longer strut his brief hour on the stage. The curtain drops—the house empties—the lights are extinguished —silence, cold and cheerless, succeeds to the loud acclamations which made the vaulted roof reverberate erewhile—the Tragedian is washing the paint off his face, and in another hour will be in the retired privacy of his quiet happy home ! The mask is laid aside—and for ever.

Considering Macready, then, as dead—as I am bound to consider him in a theatrical sense—I will try to answer the question which my children and their friends are sure to ask me some day when I am running down *their* idolised tragedian, and try to spoil their pleasures by cheapening their " dear delightful Mr. ——," and assuring them I had seen " Edmund Kean and Macready in that part,"—the question, namely, " Was Macready a great Actor ? " " *To say nothing but good of the dead*," is a maxim for which I have always felt but a mediocre respect, mainly, perhaps, because the medal bears on the reverse side, " *To say nothing but evil of the living*." While a statesman or an artist lives, envy and all uncharitableness assail

---

[1] February 3, 1851. Macready's last appearance on the stage took place at Drury Lane, 26 Feb. 1851, when he played Macbeth.

him ; no sooner does the bell toll for his funeral than those who yesterday were foremost to assail, now become elegiac in their grief and hyperbolic in their eulogium. It has always seemed to me that the contrary would be the more generous as well as the more advantageous method. When blame ceases to give pain I see no reason why it should be spared ; when adverse criticism can " instruct the public " and yet not hurt an artist's fortunes, then is the time for the critic to speak without reservation—*then* let us have the truth in all its energy !

Do not suppose this to be a preface to an " attack " upon the fine actor who has just quitted the scene. My purpose is far from polemical. I merely wish, in the way of conversation, to jot down such hints towards an appreciation of his talent as have occurred to me ; and as, with all my admiration, I must still qualify the praise by advancing objections which thorough-going admirers will pronounce heresies, I claim, at the outset, the right of saying of the dead all the evil I think, and not of garlanding the tomb with artificial flowers.

It is a question often mooted in private, whether Macready was a *great* actor, or only an intelligent actor, or (for this, too, is not unfrequently said) an intrinsically bad actor. The last opinion is uttered by some staunch admirers of Kemble and Young, and by those critics who, looking at the drama as an *imitation of Nature*, dwell upon the exaggerations and other false colours wherewith Macready paints, and proclaim him, consequently, a bad artist. Now, in discussing a subject like the present, it is imperative that we understand the *point of view* from which we both look at it.

I am impressed with the conviction that the majority mistakes Art for an *imitation* of Nature. It is no such thing. Art is *representation*. This is why too close an approach to Reality in Art is shocking ; why coloured statues are less agreeable—except to the vulgarest minds—than the colourless marble.

Without pausing to expound that principle, I beg the reader will, for the present at least, take my word for its accuracy, that I may be able to place him at my point of view. Taking Art as a Representative rather than as an Imitative process (including imitation only as one of its *means* of representation), I say that the test of an actor's genius is not " fidelity to Nature," but simply and purely his power of exciting emotions in you respondent to the situation—ideal when that is ideal, passionate when that is passionate, familiar when that is familiar, prosaic when that is prosaic. A bad actor mouths familiar prose as if it were the loftiest verse ; but a good actor (such as Bouffé or Charles Mathews), if he were to play ideal characters with the same familiarity and close adherence to Nature as that which makes his performance of familiar parts charming, would equally sin against the laws of Art.

Let me go some distance back for an illustration. In Greek tragedy, acting, as we understand it, was impossible. Addressing an audience of thirty thousand (I give you the number on the authority of Plato), all of whom, like true democrats, insisted on hearing and seeing, the unassisted voice and the unaided proportions of the actor would of course have been useless. A contrivance considerably raised and amplified the man's stature, while his voice was assisted by a bronze mask with a round hole at the mouth, through which the actor spoke as through a speaking-trumpet. Now I ask you to place yourself upon stilts and shout " To be or not to be," through a speaking-trumpet, and *then* answer me whether acting were possible under *such* conditions !

This mask gives me the image I am in want of to convey my meaning. The Latin word *persona* is derived from thence, and *dramatis personæ* may be translated " *The masks through which the actors speak.*" Whether the actor dons a veritable mask of bronze, or whether he throws it aside and makes a mask of his own face, he is still only personating, *i.e.* speaking through a mask, *i.e.* representing. The Greeks had twenty-six different classes of masks, and bestowed immense pains on them. " There be actors that I have seen play, and heard some applaud too," who had but *one* invariable mask—and that a bad one—for every part. *Ma non ragioniam di lor !*

Taking, then, the masks as types of the various characters an actor has to play (to *personate*, as we correctly say), you see at once what a very different thing it was for the Greek actor to go to some antique Nathan and choose his mask, and for the modern who has to invent and make up his own mask with his own limited materials ! Many actors, nay, the vast majority, do still go to some Nathan's and borrow a *traditional* mask ; just as many poetasters go to the common fund for images, similes, rhymes and rhythms, or as politicians re-issue the old and well-worn currency of sophisms, facts, and paralogisms. So few men can compose their own masks.

To compose a mask, or, if you like it, to personate a character, there are three fundamental requisite conditions, which I will call—1. *Conceptual Intelligence* ; 2. *Representative Intelligence* ; 3. *Physical Advantages*. The first condition is requisite to *understand* the character ; the two last are requisite in different degrees to *represent* the character. High poetic culture, knowledge of human nature, sympathy with elemental states of passion, and all that we understand by a fine intellect, will assist the actor in his *study* of the character, but it will do no more. The finest intellect in the world would not enable a man to play Hamlet or Othello finely. Shakespeare himself couldn't do it ; but wisely cast himself (Oh ! the lesson to actor-managers !) as the Ghost. There are other requisites besides conception. There is the second requisite (what I have called representative intelligence), under which may be included the intelligent observation and reproduction of *typical* gestures, looks, tones—the mimetic power of imitating peculiarities. This requisite is possessed by actors oftener than the first. Without fine intellect it makes respectable actors ; carried to a certain degree and accompanied with certain physical advantages it makes remarkable actors, especially in the comic line. The third requisite, which I have named physical advantages, includes person, deportment, voice, and physical power. Too little consideration is devoted to that, yet it is enough of itself to make or mar an actor. All the intellect in the world, all the representative intelligence in the world, could not enable a man with a weak voice, limited in its compass, unless compensated by some peculiar effects in tone, to perform Othello, Macbeth, Shylock, etc., with success. Whereas a noble presence, a fine voice, and a moderate degree of representative intelligence, with no appreciable amount of conceptual intelligence, have sufficed to draw the town ere now, and make even critics believe a great actor has appeared.

Having thus briefly indicated what I conceive to be the

leading principles in the philosophy of acting, I proceed to apply them to Macready ; and first say that, inasmuch as he possesses in an unusual degree the three requisites laid down, he must be classed among the *great* actors. His conceptual intelligence every one will acknowledge. Even those to whom his peculiarities are offensive admit that he is a man of intellect, of culture. But I do not go along with those who exalt his intellect into greatness. I am not aware of any manifestation of greatness he has given. His conception always betrays care and thought, and never betrays foolishness. On the other hand, I never received any light from him to clear up an obscurity ; my knowledge of Shakespeare is little increased by his performances. I cannot point to any one single trace of illumination—such as Edmund Kean used to flash out. This may be my fault ; but I am here recording individual impressions, and I say that Macready's knowledge of Shakespeare and his art, unquestionable though it be, does not prove to me the greatness of intellect which his ardent admirers assume for him. The intelligence most shown by Macready is that which I have named representative intelligence, and which he possesses in a remarkable degree. Certain peculiarities and defects prevent his representing the high, heroic, passionate characters ; but nothing can surpass his representation of some others ; and connecting this representative intelligence with his physical advantages, we see how he can execute what he conceives, and thus become an actor. His voice—one primary requisite of an actor—is a fine one, powerful, extensive in compass, and containing tones that thrill, and tones that weep. His person is good, and his face very expressive. So that give him a character within his proper range and he will be great in it ; and even the greatest actors can only perform certain characters for which their representative intelligence and physical organisation fit them.

" I wish I had not seen Macready in *Macbeth*. I saw him in Werner, and came away with such an impression of his power that I regret having seen his Macbeth, which completely destroys my notion of him." That was the phrase I heard the other day at dinner, and it seemed to me a good text for a criticism on Macready ; for if the real test of an actor be that he raises emotions in you respondent to the situation, then assuredly does Macready stand this test whenever the situation be *not* of a grand, abstract, ideal nature. The anguish of a weak, timid, prostrate mind he can represent with a sorrowing pathos, as great as Kean in the heroic agony of Othello ; and in all the touching *domesticities* of tragedy he is unrivalled. But he fails in the characters which demand impassioned grandeur, and a certain *largo* of execution. His Macbeth and Othello have fine touches, but they are essentially unheroic—their passion is fretful and irritable, instead of being broad, vehement, overwhelming. His Hamlet is too morbid, irritable, and lachrymose. Lear is his finest Shakespearian character— because the fretfulness and impatience of the old man come within the range of Macready's representative powers, of which the terrible curse may be regarded as the climax. King John, Richard II, Iago, and Cassius are also splendid performances ; in each of them we trace the same characteristic appeal to the actor's peculiar powers. Although you can see him in no part without feeling that an artist is before you, yet if you think of him as a great actor, it is as Werner, Lear, Virginius, Richelieu, King John, Richard II, Iago—not as Othello, Macbeth, Hamlet, Coriolanus. Nor is this any ground of objection. Every actor is by nature fitted for certain characters, and unfitted for others. I believe Macready to be radically unfitted for ideal characters—for the display of broad elemental passions—for the representation of grandeur, moral or physical; and I believe him peculiarly fitted for the irritable, the tender, and the domestic ; he can depict rage better than passion, anguish better than mental agony, misery better than despair, tenderness better than the abandonment of love. But the things he can do he does surpassingly well ; and for this, also, I must call him a great actor.

The tricks and mannerisms which others copy, and which objectors suffer to outweigh all other qualities, I need waste no words on here. He was great in spite of them, as Kean was in spite of his.

Summing up these remarks into a compact sentence, I answer the question put by my imaginary questioners thus : "Yes, Macready *was* a great actor. Though not a man of genius, he was a man of intellect, of culture, of representative talent, with decided physical advantages, capable of depicting a wide range of unheroic characters with truth and power, an ornament to his profession, the pride of his friends, and the favourite of the public. He gained his position when Kean and Young were on the stage ; when they left it he stood alone. His departure left a blank. There was no successor ; none capable of bending the bow of Ulysses."

Before I conclude this incomplete notice let me, in extenuation of what may seem severity, observe that I have throughout criticised according to an abstract standard of the Art, and not according to the present condition of the stage. I might easily and conscientiously have written a panegyric ; but there would not have been half the real compliment in it there is in the foregoing attempt at philosophic analysis, though blame may have been " precipitated " by the analysis. True, very true, the adage, " Art is difficult, Criticism easy " ; but there is something far easier than Criticism, and that is panegyric !

—From " The Leader," 8 Feb., 1851 ; and reprinted in *Dramatic Essays*, 1896.

GEORGE HENRY LEWES ON THE PHÈDRE OF RACHEL

RACHEL was the panther of the stage ; with a panther's terrible beauty and undulating grace she moved and stood, glared and sprang. There always seemed something not human about her. She seemed made of different clay from her fellows—beautiful but not lovable. Those who never saw Edmund Kean may form a very good conception of him if they have seen Rachel. She was very much as a woman what he was as a man. If he was a lion, she was a panther.

Her range, like Kean's, was very limited, but her expression was perfect within that range. Scorn, triumph, rage, lust and merciless malignity she could represent in symbols of irresistible power ; but she had little tenderness, no womanly caressing softness, no gaiety, no heartiness. She was so graceful and so powerful that her air of dignity was incomparable ; but somehow you always felt in her presence an indefinable suggestion of latent wickedness. By the side of Pasta she would have appeared like a beautiful devil beside a queenly woman : with more intellect, more incisive and impressive power, but with less soul, less diffusive and subduing influence.

In her early days nothing more exquisite could be heard than her elocution—it was musical and artistically graduated to the fluctuations of meaning. Her thrilling voice, flexible, penetrating, and grave, responded with the precision of a keyed instrument. Her thin, nervous frame vibrated with emotion. Her face, which would have been common, had it not been aflame with genius, was capable of intense expression. Her gestures were so fluent and graceful that merely to see her would have been a rare delight. The ideal tragedies of Racine, which ignorant Englishmen call "cold," were, by her interpretation, shown to be instinct with passion and dramatic effect. But this was only in her early days. Later in her career she grew careless ; played her parts as if only in a hurry to get through them, flashing out now and then with tremendous power, just to show what she could do ; and resembling Kean in the sacrifice of the character to a few points. She, whose elocution had been incomparable, so delicately shaded were its various refinements and so sustained its music, came at last to gabble, and to mash up her rhythm till the verses were often unintelligible and generally ineffective. After the gabble she paused upon some well-known point, and flung upon it all the emphasis of her power. In what I have to say of her, I shall speak only of her acting in its better days, for it is that to which memory naturally recurs.

The finest of her performances was of Phèdre. Nothing I have ever seen surpassed this picture of a soul torn by the conflicts of incestuous passion and struggling conscience ; the unutterable mournfulness of her look and tone as she recognised the guilt of her desires, yet felt herself so possessed by them that escape was impossible, are things never to be forgotten. What a picture she was as she entered ! You felt that she was wasting away under the fire within, that she was standing on the verge of the grave with pallid face, hot eyes, emaciated frame—an awful ghastly apparition. The slow deep mournful toning of her apostrophe to the sun, especially that close—

Soleil ! je te viens voir pour la dernière fois—

produced a thrill which vibrates still in memory. The whole of the opening scene, with one exception, was inexpressibly affecting and intensely true. As an ideal representation of real emotion, it belonged to the highest art. The remorseful lines—

> Grâces au ciel, mes mains ne sont point criminelles :
> Plût aux dieux que mon cœur fût innocent comme elles—

were charged with pathos. And how finely expressed was the hurrying horror with, as it were, a shiver between each phrase, transient yet vividly indicated, when she confessed her guilt ;—

> Tu vas ouïr le comble des horreurs . . .
> J'aime . . . à ce nom fatal, je tremble, je frissonne . . .

(and her whole frame here quivered)

> J'aime . . .
> *Œnone.*—Qui ?
> *Phèdre.*—Tu connais ce fils de l'Amazone,
> Ce prince si longtemps par moi-même opprimé . . .
> *Œnone.*—Hippolyte ! Grands dieux !
> *Phèdre.*—C'est toi qui l'as nommé.

The one point in this scene to which I took exception was the mode of rendering the poet's meaning in this magnificent apostrophe, taken from Euripides, " C'est toi qui l'as nommé." She uttered it in a tone of sorrowing reproach which, as I conceive, is psychologically at variance with the character and the position. For Phèdre has kept her love a secret ; it is a horrible crime ; she cannot utter the name of Hippolyte because of her horror at the crime ; and not in sadness but in the sophistry of passion, she tries indignantly to throw on Œnone the guilt of naming that which should be unnameable.

In the second act, where Phèdre declares her passion to Hippolyte, Rachel was transcendent. She subtly contrived to indicate that her passion was a diseased passion, fiery and irresistible, yet odious to her and to him. She was marvellous in the abandonment to this onward-sweeping madness ; her manner was fierce and rapid, as if the thoughts were crowding on her brain in tumult, and she dared not pause to consider them ; and such was the amazing variety and compass of her expression that when she quitted the stage she left us quivering with an excitement comparable only to that produced by Kean in the third act of *Othello*. In the fourth act came the storm of rage, jealousy, and despair : it was lit up by wonderful flashes. Like Kean, she had a power of concentrating into a single phrase a world of intense feeling ; and even Kean himself could not have surpassed the terrific exclamation—

> Misérable ! et je vis !

Whoever saw Rachel play Phèdre may be pardoned if he doubt whether he will ever see such acting again.

Hermione, in *Andromaque*, was also another very fine part of hers, especially in the two great scenes with Pyrrhus. In the first, her withering sarcasm, calm, polished, implacable, was beyond description ; in the second she displayed her manifold resources in expressing rage, scorn, grief, and defiance. In her eyes charged with lightning, in her thin convulsive frame, in the spasms of her voice, changing from melodious clearness to a hoarseness that made us shudder, the demoniac element was felt. With touching and forlorn grace she revealed the secret of her heart in the lines :—

> Malgré le juste horreur que son crime me donne,
> Tant qu'il vivra craignez que je ne lui pardonne ;
> Doutez jusqu'à sa mort d'un courroux incertain :
> S'il ne meurt aujourd'hui *je puis l'aimer demain*.

In describing how she will avenge the insult to her beauty by slaying Pyrrhus—

> Je percerai le cœur que je n'ai pu toucher—

her wail was so piercing and so musical that the whole audience rose in a transport to applaud her ; and difficult as it was to prevent an anticlimax after such an effect, she crowned the scene with the exclamation of jealous threat when bidding him hasten to his mistress :—

> Va, cours ; mais crains encore d'y trouver Hermione.

The close was in the same high strain. The fine passionate speech in which she upbraids Orestes for having followed her orders and slain Pyrrhus (a speech which may be commended to those who fancy Racine is cold) was delivered as nobody but Rachel could deliver it.

Very noticeable it is that Rachel could not speak prose with even tolerable success ; deprived of the music of verse, and missing its *ictus*, she seemed quite incapable of managing the easy cadences of colloquial prose. The subtle influence of rhythm seemed to penetrate her, and gave a movement and animation to her delivery which was altogether wanting in her declamation of prose. Hence, among other reasons, the failure of her attempts in modern drama. As Kean was only truly great in Shakespeare and Massinger, Rachel was only truly herself in Racine and Corneille.

In the *Polyeucte* of Corneille she had one scene of incomparable grandeur, where, baptised in the blood of her martyred husband, she exclaims,—

> Son sang dont tes bourreaux viennent de me couvrir
> M'a dessillé les yeux, et me les vient d'ouvrir.
> Je vois, je sais, je crois !

The climbing exultation and radiant glory of the inspired convert, her face lighted with fervour, her whole frame trembling with the burden of overpowering thoughts, were fitly succeeded by the uplifting of her arms to heaven, while an expression of such fervent aspiration glowed in her features that she seemed a martyr welcoming the death which was the portal to eternal bliss. As an example of " face-acting " should be cited the very remarkable scene in *Les Horaces*, in which she stands silent during the long recital of her lover's death.

Rachel tried once or twice to play Molière. I did not see these attempts, which were pitilessly criticised by Jules Janin, but I am convinced that they were mistakes. She was wholly unsuited to comedy, unless it were comedy like that of Madame Girardin's Lady Tartufe, in which I thought her graceful, ladylike, and diabolical—very admirable in the way she thoroughly identified herself with the character, making its odiousness appear so thoroughly easy and unconscious that you almost doubted whether after all the woman were so odious. The manner in which Rachel walked to the fireplace, placed her gloves on the mantelpiece, and her right foot on the fender, as she began the great scene with her lover, was of itself a study. The sleek hypocrisy of the part was not exaggerated, nor was the cruel irony colder or crueller than seemed natural to such a woman ; it was like the occasional gleam of it in *Bajazet*, especially where Roxane is assured that Bajazet loves her still, and she replies, smiling with calm, bitter superiority—

Il y va de sa vie, au moins, que je le croie.

It would form an interesting question why actors so transcendent as Kean and Rachel should have been singularly limited in the range of characters they could play with effect— why, being confessedly great in a few difficult parts, they could not be even tolerable in many parts less difficult and demanding the same kind of talent. But as this is a question I am not prepared to answer, I content myself with calling attention to it.

—From *On Actors and the Art of Acting*. By George Henry Lewes, 1875.

LEWES ON LEMAÎTRE'S GREAT RÔLES

A MONG the few actors of exceptional genius who by reason of their very individuality defy classification, and provoke the most contradictory judgments, must be placed the singularly gifted Frédéric Lemaître. Those who have only seen him in the pitiable decay of his later years cannot easily understand the enthusiasm he excited in his prime ; but they will understand it, perhaps, if they reflect that because he was an actor of genius, and not an actor of talent, he necessarily lost his hold of audiences when age and reckless habits had destroyed the personal qualifications which had been the sources of his triumph.

There was always something offensive to good taste in Frédéric's acting—a note of vulgarity, partly owing to his daring animal spirits, but mainly owing, I suspect, to an innate vulgarity of nature. In his great moments he was great ; but he was seldom admirable throughout an entire scene, and never throughout an entire play. In his famous character of Robert Macaire the defects were scarcely felt, because the colossal buffoonery of that conception carried you at once into the region of hyperbole and Aristophanic fun which soared beyond the range of criticism. It disgusted or subdued you at once. In every sense of the word it was a creation. A common melodrama without novelty or point became in his hands a grandiose symbolical caricature ; and Robert Macaire became a type, just as Lord Dundreary has become one in our own day. The costume he invented for that part was in itself a magnificent effrontery. It struck the keynote ; and as the piece proceeded all was felt to be in harmony with that picture of ideal blackguardism. For the peculiarity of Robert Macaire is the union of a certain ideal grace and *bonhomie* with the most degraded ruffianism and hardness, as of a nobleman preserving some of the instincts and habits of his class amid the instincts and habits of the galleys and the pothouse. If he danced, it was not until he had first pulled on a pair of hyperbolically tattered kid gloves ; and while waltzing with incomparable elegance he could not resist picking the pocket of his fair partner. He sang, took snuff, philosophised, and jested with an air of native superiority, and yet made you feel that he was a hateful scoundrel all the while. You laughed at his impudence, you admired his ease and readiness, and yet you would have killed him like a rat. He was jovial, graceful, false, and cruel.

In Don César de Bazan there was another and a very different portrait of the picturesque blackguard. Here also was the union of grace and tatters, of elegance and low habits. The Spanish nobleman had stained his ermine, and dragged his honour through the wineshop and the brothel ; but he had never wholly lost himself, and had not perverted his original nature. It was difficult to conceive anything more disreputable and *débraillé* than this Don César when he first appeared, tipsy and moralising on the fact that he had " gambled with blackguards, who had cheated him like gentlemen." There was immense exaggeration, but it was the exaggeration of great scene-painting. Very shortly you perceived the real nature of the man underneath—the nature stained, not spoiled, by reckless dissipation ; and it was therefore no surprise when, as the play proceeded, the nobler elements of this nature asserted themselves, and Don César claimed respect.

But although Frédéric's performance of this part was in many respects incomparable, it had many serious defects. His love of " gagging " and his subordination of the scene to some particular effect were unpleasantly shown in that capital interview with the King, when his Majesty is discovered by Don César in his wife's apartment. He quite spoiled by vulgarity the effect of his retort when the King, not knowing him, gives himself out as Don César. " Vous êtes Don César de Bazan ? Eh bien ! alors je suis le Roi d'Espagne." He made it very comical, but it was farcical and inartistic ; and the stupid appeal to the vulgarest laughter of the audience in the grotesquely extravagant feather which danced in his hat was suited to a pantomime or burlesque, but very unsuited to the serious situation of the drama.

Very different was his acting in the prison scene, and especially noticeable was the rapid change from jovial conviviality over the wine cup to serious and dignified attention while the sentence of death was being passed on him. He stood with the napkin carelessly thrown over his arm, his hand lightly resting on one hip, and listened with grave calmness to the sentence ; at its conclusion he relapsed into the convivial mood, exclaiming, " Troisième couplet ! " as he resumed his song ; and you felt the irony of his gravity, felt the unutterable levity of his nature.

In pathos of a domestic kind, and in outbursts of passion, Lemaître was singularly affecting. When he played in *Paillasse*, *Trente Ans de la Vie d'un Joueur*, and *La Dame de St. Tropez*, he left indelible impressions of pathos and of lurid power ; but I must confess that I not only thought very little of his *Ruy Blas*, but always doubted whether his style of acting were not essentially unsuited to the poetic drama. He seemed to feel himself ill at ease, walking upon stilts. His expressions were conventional, and his gestures vehement and often common. As the lackey he was ignoble ; as the minister and lover his declamation was, to my thinking, cold and unimpassioned in its violence. This, however, was not the opinion of M. Victor Hugo, who, as a Frenchman and the author of the play, may be supposed to be a better judge than I am, and in fairness I will quote what he says in the appendix to his play :—" Quant à M. Frédéric Lemaître, qu'en dire ? Les acclamations enthousiastes de la foule le saississent à son entrée en scène [rather premature enthusiasm] et le suivent jusqu'après le dénouement. Rêveur et profond au premier acte, mélancolique au deuxième, grand, passionné, et sublime au troisième, il s'élève au cinquième à l'un de ses prodigieux effets tragiques du haut desquels l'acteur rayonnant domine tous les souvenirs de son art. Pour les vieillards c'est Lekain et Garrick mêlés dans un seul homme ; pour nous c'est l'action de Kean combinée avec l'émotion de Talma. Et puis, partout, à travers les éclairs éblouissants de son jeu, M. Frédéric a des larmes, de ces vraies larmes qui font pleurer les autres, de ces larmes dont parle Horace : *si vis me flere dolendum est primum ipsi tibi.*"

In answer to such a dithyramb as this I can only appeal to the recollections of those readers who have seen Frédéric play Ruy Blas. For myself I confess to have the smallest possible pleasure in a French actor when he is " profond et rêveur "; and that not only did I detect no tears in Frédéric's Ruy Blas, but his sublime tragic effects—what the French critics call " ses explosions "—left me wholly unmoved. Indeed, to speak of Lemaître as a rival of Kean or Rachel seems to me like comparing Eugène Sue with Victor Hugo—the gulf that separates prose from poetry yawns between them.

Lemaître was very handsome. He had a wonderful eye, with large orbit, a delicate and sensitive mouth, a fine nose, a bold jaw, a figure singularly graceful, and a voice penetrating and sympathetic. He had great animal spirits, great daring, great fancy, and great energy of animal passion. He always created his parts—that is to say, gave them a specific stamp of individuality ; and the creative activity of his imagination was seen in a hundred novel details. But as his physical powers decayed his acting became less and less effective ; for in losing the personal charm, it had no stage traditions to fall back upon. And the last time I saw him, which must be fourteen or fifteen years ago, he was rapidly degenerating ; every now and then a flash of the old fire would be visible, but the effects were vanishing and the defects increasing. An interesting letter which recently appeared in the " Pall Mall Gazette " gave a graphic account of this great actor in the last stages of his ruin. I should be sorry to see the man who had once swayed audiences with irresistible power reduced to the painful feebleness which this correspondent describes.

—From *On Actors and the Art of Acting*.

LEWES ON FECHTER AND RISTORI

IN contrast was [Fechter's] performance of Othello. It had no one good quality. False in conception, it was feeble in execution. He attempted to make the character natural, and made it vulgar. His idea of the character and of the play from first to last showed strange misconception. He departed openly from the plain language of the text, on points where there is no justification for the departure. Thus, Othello tells us he is " declined into the vale of years " ; Fechter makes him young. Othello is black—the very tragedy lies there ; the whole force of the contrast, the whole pathos and extenuation of his doubts of Desdemona, depend on this blackness. Fechter makes him a half-caste, whose mere appearance would excite no repulsion in any woman out of America. Othello is grave, dignified, a man accustomed to the weight of great responsibilities, and to the command of armies ; Fechter is unpleasantly familiar, paws Iago about like an over-demonstrative schoolboy ; shakes hands on the slightest provocation ; and bears himself like the hero of French *drame*, but not like a hero of tragedy.

In his edition of the play, Fechter urges two considerations. First, that Shakespeare is to be acted, not recited ; secondly, that *tradition* ought to be set aside. In both points he will find most people agreeing with him, but few willing to see any novelty in these positions. We, who remember Kean in *Othello*, may surely be excused if we believe that we have seen Othello *acted*, and so acted as there is little chance of our seeing it acted again ; the consequence of which is, that we look upon Fechter's representation as acting, indeed, but as very bad acting.

Then as to tradition, we are willing enough, nowadays, to give up all conventional business which does not justify itself ; but we are very far from supposing that, because Fechter's arrangement of the business is new, therefore it is justifiable or acceptable. In some respects it is good ; in the arrangement of the scene in the senate there was a very striking improvement, which gave a really natural air to the scene ; and some other scenical details show a decided faculty for stage arrangement. But in many others there is a blundering perversity and disregard of the obvious meaning of the text, which is only to be accounted for on the supposition that Fechter wished to make *Othello* a *drame* such as would suit the Porte St. Martin.

The principle has doubtless been the same as that which, in a less degree, and under happier inspiration, made the success of *Hamlet :* the desire to be natural—the aim at realism. But here the confusion between realism and vulgarism works like poison. It is not consistent with the nature of tragedy to obtrude the details of daily life. All that lounging on tables and lolling against chairs, which help to convey a sense of reality in the *drame*, are as unnatural in tragedy as it would be to place the " Sleeping Fawn " of Phidias on a comfortable feather-bed. When Fechter takes out his door-key to let himself into his house, and, on coming back, relocks the door and pockets the key, the *intention* is doubtless to give an air of reality ; the *effect* is to make us forget the " noble Moor," and to think of a sepoy. When he appears leaning on the shoulder of Iago (the great general and his ensign !), when he salutes the personages with graceful prettiness, when he kisses the hand of Desdemona, and when he employs that favourite gesticulation which reminds us but too forcibly of a *gamin* threatening to throw a stone, he is certainly *natural*,—but according to whose nature ?

In general, it may be said that, accomplished an actor as Fechter certainly is, he has allowed the acting-manager to gain the upper hand. In his desire to be effective by means of small details of " business," he has entirely frittered away the great effects of the drama. He has yet to learn the virtue of simplicity ; he has yet to learn that tragedy acts through the emotions, and not through the eye ; whatever distracts attention from the passion of the scene is fatal.

Thus, while his Hamlet satisfied the audience by being at once naturally conceived and effectively represented, his Othello left the audience perfectly cold, or interested only as by a curiosity, because it was unnaturally conceived and feebly executed. Had the execution been fine, the false conception would have been forgotten, or pardoned. Many a ranting Othello contrives to interest and to move his audience without any conception at all, simply uttering the language of Shakespeare with force, and following the traditional business. Shakespeare, if the personality of the actor be not too violently in contradiction with the text, carries effect in every scene ; we listen and are moved. But unhappily Fechter's personality is one wholly unsuited to such a character as Othello. This is evident from the first. My doubts began with the first act. In it Othello has little *to do*, but much *to be*. In this masterpiece of dramatic exposition the groundwork of the play is grandly laid out. It presents the hero as a great and trusted warrior, a simple, calm, open, reliant nature—a man admirable not only in his deeds, but in his lofty and heroic soul. Unless you get a sense of this, you are as puzzled at Desdemona's choice as Brabantio is. But it is inevitable that with such a personality as Fechter's you should feel none of this. He represents an affectionate but feeble young gentleman, whose position in the army must surely have been gained by " purchase." This is not the actor's fault. Even had he been calm and simple in his gestures, he could not have been dignified and impressive ; nature had emphatically said No to such an effect. Voice and bearing would have failed him had his conception been just. An unintelligent actor who is at the same time a superb animal, will be impressive in this act if he is simply quiet. If, for example, you compare Gustavus Brooke with Fechter, you will see this at once. Still more strikingly is this seen on a comparison of Edmund Kean with Fechter. Kean was undersized—very much smaller than Fechter ; and yet what a grand bearing he had ! what an impressive personality !

In the second act my doubts increased. The entrance of Othello, with the flame of victory in his eye, eager to clasp his young wife to his breast, and share with her his triumph and his joy, was an opportunity for being *natural* which Fechter wholly missed. Never was there a tamer meeting. Kean's tones, "O my fair warrior!" are still ringing in my ears, though a quarter of a century must have elapsed since I heard them; but I cannot recall Fechter's tones, heard only the other night. I only recall a vision of him holding his wife at most "proper" distance, kissing her hand, his tone free from all tremulous emotion, though he has to say—

> O my soul's joy!
> If after every tempest come such calms,
> May the winds blow till they have wakened death!
> If it were now to die
> 'Twere now to be most happy; for I fear
> My soul hath her content so absolute
> That not another comfort like to this
> Succeeds in unknown fate.

And from Desdemona he turns to the gentlemen of Cyprus, as affable and calm as if he had but just come home from a morning stroll. There was none of the emotion of the situation.

In the scene of the brawl we have the first indication of Othello's tremendous vehemence when roused. Fechter was loud, but he was not fierce.[1] It is characteristic of his whole performance in the passionate parts, that he goes up the stage and bids them

> Silence that *dreadful* bell, it frights the isle
> From her propriety,

with an accent of impatient irritability, as if he were angry at the bell's preventing his hearing what was to be said.

But little as the performance in these two acts came up to even my moderate expectations of Fechter's power to represent Othello, it was not until the third act that I finally pronounced judgment. That act is the test of a tragedian. If he cannot produce a great effect there, he need never seek elsewhere for an opportunity; the greatest will find in it occasion for all his powers, and the worst will hardly miss some effects. To think of what Edmund Kean was in this act! When shall we see again that lion-like power and lion-like grace—that dreadful culmination of wrath, alternating with bursts of agony—that

---

[1] Fuyant le naturel sans trouver la grandeur.

SAMSON: *L'Art Théatral.*

Oriental and yet most natural gesture, which even in its *naturalness* preserved a grand ideal propriety (for example, when his joined uplifted hands, the palms being upwards, were lowered upon his head, as if to keep his poor brain from bursting)—that exquisitely touching pathos, and that lurid flame of vengeance flashing from his eye? When shall we hear again those tones : " Not a jot, not a jot "—" Blood, Iago, blood,"—" But oh, the pity of it, Iago ! the pity of it " ? Certainly no one ever expected that Fechter, with his sympathetic temperament and soft voice, could approach the tragic grandeur of the elder Kean ; but neither could anyone who had heard that his Othello was " the talk of the town " have supposed that this third act would fail even to move the applause of an audience very ready to applaud.

In saying that he failed to arouse the audience, I am saying simply what I observed and felt. The causes of that failure may be open to discussion : the fact is irresistible ; and the causes seem to me clear enough. He is incapable of representing the torrent of passion, which by him is broken up into numerous petty waves : we see the glancing foam, breaking along many lines, instead of one omnipotent and roaring surf. He is loud—and weak ; irritable, not passionate. The wrath escapes in spirts, instead of flowing in one mighty tide ; and after each spirt he is calm, not shaken by the tremulous subsidence of passion. This lapse from the wildness of rage to the calmness of logical consideration or argumentative expostulation, this absence of gradation and *after-glow* of passion, I have already indicated as the error committed by Charles Kean and other tragedians ; it arises from their not identifying themselves with the feeling of the part.

To give what Bacon calls an " ostensive instance," let me refer to the opening of the fourth act. Othello, worked upon by Iago's horrible suggestions, is so shaken by wrath and grief that he falls down in a fit. Fechter, probably because he felt that he could not render the passion so as to make this natural, omits the scene, and opens the act with Iago soliloquising over his senseless victim. In spite of the awkward attitude in which Fechter is lying, those of the audience who are not familiar with the play imagine that Othello is *sleeping* ; and when he rises from the couch and begins to speak, he is indeed as calm and unaffected by the fit as if he had only been asleep.

Another source of weakness is the redundancy of gesture and the desire to make a number of points, instead of concentrating attention on the general effect. Thus, when he is roused to catch Iago by the throat, instead of an accumulation of threats, he jerks out a succession of various threats, looking *away* from Iago every now and then, and varying his gestures, so as to destroy all sense of climax.

If it is a fact—and I appeal to the audience as witnesses—that we do not feel deep pity for the noble Moor and do not sympathise with his irrational yet natural wrath, when Fechter plays the part, surely the reason can only be that the part is not represented *naturally*? Now much of this, I repeat, is the necessary consequence of his personality. He could not represent it naturally even if he conceived the part truly; and, as already intimated, the conception is not true. Certain points of the conception have been touched on; I will now specify two others. The unideal (consequently unnatural) representation may be illustrated by the manner in which he *proposes*, instead of ordering Cassio's death. Shakespeare's language is peremptory :—

> Within these three days let me hear thee say
> That Cassio's not alive.

The idea in his mind is simply that Cassio has deserved death. He does not trouble himself about the means; and surely never thinks of *murder*. A general who orders a soldier to be hung, or shot, without trial, is not a murderer. Yet Fechter *proposes* a murder, and proposes it with a sort of subdued hesitation, as if conscious of the crime. He thus completely bears out Rymer's sarcasm : " He sets Iago to the fighting part, to kill Cassio ; and chuses himself to murder the silly woman, his wife, that was like to make no resistance." [1]

The second illustration which may be noticed, is the perverse departure from the obvious meaning of the text, which, in his

[1] RYMER : *A Short View of Tragedy, its original excellency and corruption.* 1693. P. 93. This most amusing attack on Othello reads very often like sound criticism, when one has just witnessed the performances at the Princess's Theatre. (G. H. L.)

desire for originality and naturalness in the business, makes him destroy the whole art of Shakespeare's preparation, and makes the jealousy of Othello seem preposterous. One defect in the play which has been felt by all critics is the rapidity with which Othello is made to believe in his wife's guilt. Now, allowing for the rapidity which the compression necessary to dramatic art renders almost inevitable, I think Shakespeare has so exhibited the *growth* of the jealousy, that it is only on reflection that the audience becomes aware of the slight grounds on which the Moor is convinced. It is the actor's part to make the audience feel this growth—to make them go along with Othello, sympathising with him, and *believing* with him. Fechter deliberately disregards all the plain meaning of the text, and makes the conviction sudden and preposterous. It is one of his new arrangements that Othello, when the tempter begins his diabolical insinuation, shall be seated at a table reading and signing papers. When first I heard of this bit of " business," it struck me as admirable ; and indeed I think so still ; although the manner in which Fechter executes it is one of those lamentable examples in which the *dramatic* art is subordinated to serve *theatrical* effect.[1] That Othello should be seated over his papers, and should reply to Iago's questions while continuing his examination, and affixing his signature, is *natural* ; but it is not natural—that is, not true to the nature of Othello and the situation—for him to be dead to the dreadful import of Iago's artful suggestions. Let us hear Shakespeare.

Othello and Iago enter as Cassio takes leave of Desdemona ; whereupon Iago says, meaning to be heard, " Ha ! I like not that ! "

> *Othello.* What dost thou say ?
> *Iago.* Nothing, my lord : or if—I know not what.
> *Othello.* Was not that Cassio parted from my wife ?
> *Iago.* Cassio, my lord ? no sure, I cannot think it,
> That he would *steal away,* so *guilty-like,*
> Seeing *your coming.*
> *Othello.* I do believe 'twas he.
> *Des.* How now, my lord.

[1] Having now seen Salvini in Othello I conclude that this " business " was imitated from him—but Fechter failed to imitate the expression of emotion which renders such business significant. (G. H. L.)

I have been talking with a suitor here,
A man that languishes in your displeasure.
  Othello. Who is't you mean ?
  Des. Why your lieutenant Cassio ; good my lord,
If I have any grace or power to move you,
His present reconciliation take.
I prithee call him back.
  Othello. Went he hence now ?
  Des. Ay sooth ; so humbled
That he hath left part of his grief with me
To suffer with him. Good love, call him back.
  Othello. Not now, sweet Desdemona ; some other time.
  Des. But shall't be shortly ?
  Othello. The sooner, sweet, for you.
  Des. Shall't be to-night at supper ?
  Othello. No, not to-night.
  Des. To-morrow, dinner, then ?
  Othello. I shall not dine at home.

These short evasive sentences are subtly expressive of the state of Othello's mind ; but Fechter misrepresents them by making Othello free from all misgiving. He " toys with her curls," and treats her as a father might treat a child who was asking some favour which could not be granted yet which called for no explicit refusal. If the scene stood alone, I should read it differently ; but standing as it does between the two attempts of Iago to fill Othello's mind with suspicion, the meaning is plain enough. He has been made uneasy by Iago's remarks ; very naturally, his bearing towards his wife reveals that uneasiness. A *vague* feeling, which he dares not shape into a suspicion, disturbs him. She conquers him at last by her winning ways ; and he vows that he will deny her nothing.

If this be the state of mind in which the great scene begins, it is obviously a serious mistake in Fechter to sit down to his papers, perfectly calm, free from all idea whatever of what Iago has suggested ; and answering Iago's insidious questions as if he did not divine their import. So clearly does Othello divine their import, that it is *he,* and not Iago, who expresses in words their meaning. It is one of the artifices of Iago to make his victim draw every conclusion from premises which are put before him, so that, in the event of detection, he can say, " I said nothing, I made no accusation." All he does is to lead the thoughts of Othello to the conclusion desired. The scene thus begins :—

> *Iago.* My noble lord—
> *Othello.* What dost thou say, Iago ?
> *Iago.* Did Michael Cassio, when you wooed my lady,
> Know of your love ?

Now Iago perfectly well knew this, for he had heard Desdemona say so just the minute before.

> *Othello.* He did from first to last : Why dost thou ask ?
> *Iago.* But for the satisfaction of my thought ;
> *No further harm.*

Properly, Iago's answer should end at the word thought ; that is the answer to the question ; but he artfully adds the suggestion of harm, which falls like a spark on the inflammable mind of his victim, who eagerly asks, " Why of thy thought, Iago ? "

> *Iago.* I did not think he had been acquainted with her.
> *Othello.* Oh yes ; and went between us very oft.
> *Iago.* Indeed ?
> *Othello.* Indeed ? Ay, indeed : Discern'st thou aught in that ?
> Is he not honest ?
> *Iago.* Honest, my lord ?
> *Othello.* Honest ? ay, honest ?
> *Iago.* My lord, for aught I know.
> *Othello.* What dost thou think ?
> *Iago.* Think, my lord ?

It is difficult to comprehend how anyone should fail to interpret this dialogue, every word of which is an increase of the slowly growing suspicion. If the scene ended here, there might indeed be a defence set up for Fechter's notion that Othello should reply to the insinuation in a careless manner, " playing with his pen as he speaks " ; but no defence is permissible for one moment when we know how the scene proceeds.

> *Othello.* Think, my lord ? By heaven he echoes me !
> As if there were *some monster* in his thought
> *Too hideous* to be shown. Thou *dost mean something ;*
> I heard thee say but now, thou lik'dst not that
> When Cassio left my wife : what didst not like ?
> And when I told thee he was of my counsel
> In my whole course of wooing, thou cry'dst, Indeed ?

And didst contract and purse thy brow together,
As if thou then hadst shut up in thy brain
Some horrible conceit. If thou dost love me
Show me thy thought.

Fechter would perhaps urge that this language is not to be understood seriously, but as the banter of Othello at seeing Iago purse his brow and look mysterious about trifles. It is in this sense that he plays the part. But how widely he errs, and how seriously Othello is disturbed, may be read in his next speech :—

I know thou'rt full of love and honesty,
And weigh'st thy words before thou giv'st them breath,
Therefore these stops of thine *fright me the more ;*
For such things in a *false disloyal knave*
Are tricks of custom ; but in a man that's just
They're close denotements, working from the heart
That passion cannot rule.

Is this banter ? and when he bids Iago

Speak to me, as to thy thinkings,
As thou dost ruminate ; and *give thy worst of thoughts*
The worst of words,

it is impossible to suppose that his mind has not already shaped the worst suspicions which he wishes Iago to confirm.

Here, I affirm, the plain sense of Shakespeare is not only too clearly indicated to admit of the most ingenious reading in another sense, but any other reading would destroy the dramatic art with which the scene is conducted, because it would destroy those indications of the *growth* of the feeling, which feeling, being really founded on Iago's suggestions and the smallest possible external evidence, becomes preposterous when the evidence alone is appealed to. Now, Fechter so little understands this, as not only to miss such broadly marked indications, but to commit the absurdity of making Othello *suddenly* convinced, and by what ? by the *argument* of Iago, that Desdemona deceived her father, and may therefore deceive her husband ! But *that* argument (setting aside the notion of a character like Othello being moved by merely intellectual considerations) had already been forcibly presented to his mind by her father :—

> Look to her, Moor, have a quick eye to see
> She did deceive her father, and may thee.

Whereupon he replies, " My life upon her faith." And so he would reply to Iago, had not his mind already been filled with distrust. Fechter makes him careless, confident, unsuspicious, until Iago suggests her deception of her father, and then *at once* credulous and overcome. This may be the art of the Porte St. Martin, or the Variétés ; it is not the art of Shakespeare.

Ristori is universally spoken of as the rival of Rachel : many think her superior. The difference between them seems to me the difference between talent and genius, between a woman admirable in her art, and a woman creative in her art. Ristori has complete mastery of the mechanism of the stage, but is without the inspiration necessary for great acting. A more beautiful and graceful woman, with a more musical voice, has seldom appeared ; but it is with her acting as with her voice— the line which separates charm from profound emotion is never passed. When I saw her in Lady Macbeth my disappointment was extreme : none of the qualities of a great actress were manifested. But she completely conquered me in Medea ; and the conquest was all the more noticeable, because it triumphed over the impressions previously received from Robson's burlesque imitation. The exquisite grace of her attitudes, the mournful beauty of her voice, the flash of her wrath, and the air of supreme *distinction* which seems native to her, gave a charm to this performance which is unforgettable. No wonder that people were enthusiastic about an actress who could give them such refined pleasure ; and no wonder that few paused to be very critical of her deficiencies. I missed, it is true, the *something* which Rachel had : the sudden splendour of creative power, the burning-point of passion ; yet I confess that I then thought it possible she might prove a more consummate comedian than Rachel, though so manifestly inferior to her in great moments. That supposition was a profound mistake. I discovered it on seeing Adrienne

Lecouvreur the other night. The disappointment, not to say weariness, felt at this performance, caused me to recur to the disappointment felt at her Lady Macbeth : these performances marked a limit, and defined the range of her artistic power. In Adrienne there was still the lovely woman, with the air of distinction and the musical voice ; but except in the recitation of the pretty fable of the two pigeons, the passage from *Phèdre*, and the one look of dawning belief brightening into rapture, as she is reassured by her lover's explanation, there was nothing in the performance which was not thoroughly conventional. Nor was this the worst fault. In the lighter scenes she was not only conventional, but committed that common mistake of conventional actors, an incongruous *mixture* of effects.

Let me explain more particularly what is meant by the term conventional acting. When an actor feels a vivid sympathy with the passion, or humour, he is representing, he *personates*, *i.e.* speaks through the *persona* or character ; and for the moment *is* what he *represents*. He can do this only in proportion to the vividness of his sympathy, and the plasticity of his organisation, which enables him to give *expression* to what he feels ; there are certain physical limitations in every organisation which absolutely prevent adequate expression of what is in the mind ; and thus it is that a dramatist can rarely personate one of his own conceptions. But within the limits which are assigned by nature to every artist, the success of the personation will depend upon the vividness of the actor's sympathy, and his honest reliance on the truth of his own individual expression, in preference to the conventional expressions which may be accepted on the stage. This is the great actor, the creative artist. The conventional artist is one who either because he does not feel the vivid sympathy, or cannot express what he feels, or has not sufficient energy of self-reliance to trust frankly to his own expressions, cannot *be* the part, but tries to *act* it, and is thus necessarily driven to adopt those conventional means of expression with which the traditions of the stage abound. Instead of allowing a strong feeling to express itself through its natural signs, he seizes upon the conventional signs, either because in truth there is no strong feeling moving him, or because he is not artist enough to give it genuine expression ; his lips will curl, his brow wrinkle, his eyes be thrown up, his forehead be slapped, or he will grimace, rant, and " take the stage," in the style which has become traditional, but which was perhaps never seen off the stage ; and thus he runs through the gamut of sounds and signs which bear as remote an affinity to any real expressions, as the pantomimic conventions of ballet-dancers.

A similar contrast is observed in literature. As there are occasionally actors who *personate*—who give expression to a genuine feeling—so there are occasionally writers, not merely littérateurs, who give expression in words to the actual thought which is in their minds. The writer uses words which are conventional signs, but he uses them with a sincerity and directness of individual expression which makes them the genuine utterance of *his* thoughts and feelings ; the littérateur uses conventional phrases, but he uses them without the guiding instinct of individual expression ; he tries to express what others have expressed, not what is really in his own mind. With a certain skill, the littérateur becomes an acceptable workman ; but we never speak of him as a *writer*, never estimate him as a man of genius, unless he can make his own soul speak to us. The conventional language of poetry and passion, of dignity and drollery, may be more or less skilfully used by a writer of talent ; but he never delights us with those words which come from the heart, never thrills us with the simple touches of nature—those nothings which are immense, and which make writing memorable.

In saying that Ristori is a conventional actress, therefore, I mean that with great art she employs the traditional conventions of the stage, and reproduces the effects which others have produced, but does not deeply move us, because not herself deeply moved. Take away her beauty, grace, and voice, and she is an ordinary comedian ; whereas Schröder, Devrient, and Pasta were assuredly neither handsome nor imposing in physique ; and Rachel made a common Jewish physiognomy lovely by mere force of expression. In Medea Ristori was conventional and admirable. In Adrienne she was conventional and inartistic ; for while the character was not *personated*, but simulated, it was simulated by conventional signs drawn from a totally wrong source. The comedy was the comedy of a *soubrette* ; the playfulness had the *minauderie* of a frivolous woman, not the charm of a smile upon a serious face. It is a common mistake of conventional serious actors in comic scenes to imitate the " business " and manner of comic actors. The actor of serious style wishing to be funny thinks he must approach the low comedy style, and is often vulgar, always ineffective, by his very efforts at being effective. Ristori might have learned from Rachel that the lighter scenes of Adrienne could be charming without once touching on the " business " of the *soubrette* ; and play-goers who remember Helen Faucit, especially in parts like Rosalind (a glimpse of which was had the other night), will remember how perfectly that fine actress can represent the joyous playfulness of young animal spirits, without once ceasing to be poetical. The gaiety of a serious nature even in its excitement must always preserve a certain tone which distinguishes it from the mirth of unimpassioned natures : a certain ground-swell of emotion should be felt beneath. The manner may be light, but it should spring from a deep nature : it is the difference between the comedy of Shakespeare or Molière, even when most extravagant, and the comedy of Congreve or Scribe ; there may be a heartier laugh, but it has a more serious background. At any rate, the unity of effect which is demanded in all representation is greatly damaged when, as in the case of Adrienne represented by Ristori, instead of the playfulness of an impassioned woman, we have a patchwork of effects—a bit of a *soubrette* tacked on to a bit of the coquette, that again to a bit of the *ingénue*, and that to a tragic part. Ristori was not one woman in several moods, but several actresses playing several scenes.

Nevertheless, while insisting on her deficiencies, I must repeat the expression of my admiration for Ristori as a distinguished actress ; if not of the highest rank, she is very high, in virtue of her personal gifts, and the trained skill with which these gifts are applied. And her failures are instructive. The failures of distinguished artists are always fruitful in suggestion. The question naturally arises, why is her success so great in certain plays, and so dubious in Shakespeare or the drama ? It is of little use to say that Lady Macbeth and Adrienne are beyond her means ; that is only re-stating the fact ; can we not trace both success and failure to one source ? In what is called the ideal drama, constructed after the Greek type, she would be generally successful, because the simplicity of its motives and the artificiality of its structure, removing it from beyond the region of ordinary experience, demand from the actor a corresponding artificiality. Attitudes, draperies, gestures, tones, and elocution which would be incongruous in a drama approaching more nearly to the evolutions of ordinary experience, become, in the ideal drama, artistic modes of expression ; and it is in these that Ristori displays a fine selective instinct, and a rare felicity of organisation. All is artificial, but then all is congruous. A noble unity of impression is produced. We do not demand individual truth of character and passion ; the ideal sketch suffices. It is only on a smaller scale what was seen upon the Greek stage, where the immensity of the theatre absolutely interdicted all individualising; spectators were content with masks and attitudes where in the modern drama we demand the fluctuating physiognomy of passion, and the minute individualities of character.

When, however, the conventional actress descends from the ideal to the real drama, from the simple and general to the complex and individual in personation, she is at a disadvantage. Rachel could make this descent, as all will remember who saw her Adrienne or Lady Tartufe ; but then Rachel *personated*, she spoke through the character, she suffered her inward feelings to express themselves in outward signs ; she had not to cast about her for the outward signs which conventionally expressed such feelings. She had but a limited range ; there were few parts she could play ; but those few she personated, those she created. I do not think that Ristori could personate ; she would always seek the conventional signs of expression, although frequently using them with consummate skill.

—From *On Actors and the Art of Acting.*

HENRY MORLEY

(1822–1894)

SAMUEL PHELPS AT SADLER'S WELLS

September 22, 1860.

MR. PHELPS, who is now sole lessee of the theatre with which his name will be hereafter associated, fulfils at SADLER'S WELLS all those conditions which the Freiherr von Wolzogen considers necessary to the honest progress of the drama. He acts national plays in a house small enough to allow all to see, though few may appreciate, the subtlest and most delicate shades of expression proper to the art of the actor ; he has a company of performers trained and accustomed to support each other steadily, and peculiarly able to present each play as an effective whole. The unhallowed union of music with the drama, so deeply abhorred by Herr von Wolzogen, is not sanctioned at SADLER'S WELLS ; and while the stage is always well appointed, scenic display is made, even to a remarkable degree, expressive of poetical intention.

Mr. Phelps has opened the campaign with two plays of Shakespeare—*As You Like It* and *Coriolanus*. *Coriolanus* I have been to see, and here as ever the first mention is due to the whole truth and harmony of the representation. The actors are all in accord together ; and although the company includes few bright particular stars, yet each does justice to the dignity of his profession. Mr. Barrett is a genial and genuine Menenius Agrippa ; Mr. Hermann Vezin, a new member of the company, who, I believe, has earned honours as first tragedian in a transpontine house, is a discreet and serious Aufidius, who mars nothing by errors of commission, and errs only on the hopeful side by under-acting his part. The Roman mob, admirably grouped and disciplined, cannot easily be represented by a better first citizen than Mr. Lewis Ball.

The little part of the domestic friend and gossip of the women in the hero's household is spoken delightfully by Mrs. Marston. Miss Kate Saxon, an intelligent actress, who supplies one of the losses of the company, delivers with all due simplicity the few sentences that fall to her lot as the wife of Coriolanus, and expresses quietly by her stage-bearing the modest, faithful gentleness that follows, strong in love, the warrior's career. As the proud mother of the prouder son, Miss Atkinson also labours her best, but she does not achieve her best. When she desires with face and gesture to express scorn, it not seldom happens that she fails to suggest more than intensity of spite. For this reason her Volumnia is wanting in some of the dignity with which the character has been invested by the poet. It is a hard trial, no doubt, to measure the expression of a Roman mother's pride with the show of pride that a man can put into the part of Coriolanus. Pride, after all, is not a woman's passion, for what passes by the name is often vanity.

The pride of Coriolanus is heroic and is a man's pride, from which vanity is altogether absent. His own praises are irksome in his ears. That which he is, he is ; and it is little in his simple estimation of himself, for he esteems himself by what he feels the power of becoming. Upon comparisons between himself and the base multitude he never wastes a thought. It matters not at what level other men are content to dwell ; his mind abides on its own heights. Thus when Caius Marcius in the camp, beset with irksome praises that he is compelled to hear, is named Coriolanus, and there is added to this honour the exhortation " Bear the addition nobly ever," Mr. Phelps represents him stirred by the warning into a large sense of what is in his soul, and lifted upon tiptoe by his soaring thought. The same action gives grandeur to the words,

> I'd rather be their servant in my way
> Than sway with them in theirs,

and is afterwards more than once used, not ostentatiously, and never without giving the emphasis intended.

As in the action of the piece, that pomp of processions with the constant noise of drum and trumpet, which in the good old days of the drama formed a prominent part of the play, is

subdued, and made to follow instead of leading the march of
the poem, so in the action of Coriolanus himself it is remembered that heroic pride is self-contained. The passion least to
be concealed by it is impatience of subjection to the shifting
voices of the mob. The pride of Coriolanus is a virtue over-
grown, and is associated with the utmost purity and tenderness
of home affections ; next to his love of honour is his love of
home. The two qualities belong naturally to the same mind,
and in the end of this play we are left unable to determine which
feeling has prevailed. It is meant, doubtless, to be questionable whether love would have conquered had not the mother
made her son—as Mr. Phelps does not forget to mark very distinctly—flinch at such a pleading as,

> Say my request's unjust
> And spurn me back ; but, if it be not so,
> *Thou art not honest.*

The expulsion of Coriolanus from Rome is presented in a
capital stage-picture by the grouping of the mob, and here the
actor's reading of his part is marked very distinctly. He had
been wrung by the urgency of his friends and the commands
of his mother to attempt to flatter into quiet the excited mob.
The attempt to do this is presented with all signs of suppressed
passion, and impatient, yet in itself almost heroic, endurance
of what is really intense torture. When the tribune calls
Coriolanus traitor, he recoils as from a blow, and lets his wrath
have way. But when the mob raising their staves expel him
from the city, he mounts proudly the steps from which as from
his mental height he looks down on them, and he is lord of
himself, lord as he feels of Rome. With a sublimity of disdain
he retorts on them that " I banish you," which Edmund Kean
erred in delivering with an ungovernable passion.

The scenic effect of the view of Antium by the light of the
rising moon, when the banished Coriolanus haunts the door of
Aufidius, his deadly enemy, is contrived to give colour to the
poetry. But there is no scene in the play more impressive to
the eye than the succeeding picture of the muffled figure of
Coriolanus, seated by the glowing embers of the brazier that
represents his enemy's hearth. It is one of the omissions of

Mr. Vezin that he makes no sign whatever when the stranger-guest discloses his name, though he had vowed that

> Where I find him, were it
> At home, upon my brother's guard, even there,
> Against the hospitable canon, would I
> Wash my fierce hand in his heart.

If nothing more were to be done, hands tightly clenched at the hearing of the name, slowly relaxing till they are held out in friendship with the words

> O Marcius, Marcius,
> Each word thou hast spoke hath weeded from my heart
> A root of ancient envy,

would be better than absolute inaction.

I must not dwell much longer upon this performance. Let me add only that the meaning of the heroic close furnished by Shakespeare to the play is well brought out at SADLER'S WELLS. The lofty pride that when defied by Rome had defied Rome herself, and was to set a foot upon the neck of the world's ruler, had, after painful struggle, knelt at the voice of a mother, yielding nobly when to yield was dangerous, if not mortal. When Coriolanus has attained his greatest height, Aufidius, fallen to his lowest, has sunk into a dastardly chief of assassins. All hearts are thus secured for sympathy with the pride with which, as Mr. Phelps shows us, the hero resents the taunt of an enemy basely triumphant. His whole frame enlarges, and his hands press on the expanding breast, as he cries,

> Measureless liar, thou hast made my heart
> Too great for what contains it !

And so at last the loftiness of his disdain carries all sympathies with it when he whets the swords of the conspirators by telling them

> How, like an eagle in a dovecote, I
> Fluttered your Volscians in Corioli :
> Alone I did it.—Boy !

—From *The Journal of a London Playgoer*. By Henry Morley, 1866.

ON FECHTER'S OTHELLO

October 26, 1861.

THE dignity of the heroic Moor, who fetches "life and being from men of noble siege," Mr. Fechter appears in the first two acts of *Othello* willing rather than able to represent. At once, therefore, we have attention called especially to his quick impressionable character.

In the very first passage of special note—Othello's speech before the senators in answer to the charge of having taken Desdemona from her father—the quickness of emotion in Mr. Fechter's Othello is strongly marked. While Brabantio complains to the Duke, he looks like a man conscious of a good reply in store, which he is impatient to utter. He is eager to speak. He begins so instantly upon the Duke's question, "What, in your own part, can you say to this?" that Brabantio's interpolation, "Nothing, but this is so," comes as an interruption to be swept aside. And when he does utter the well-known speech, standing near to the table under the Doge's chair which has Brabantio and two or three senators about it, having confessed that he has "ta'en away this old man's daughter"—

> It is most true; true, I have married her;
> The very head and front of my offending
> Hath this extent, no more,—

he utters the "no more" as one violently repelling a foul imputation on his honour, with fierce gesture of advance towards the table. Upon this senators rise as if they almost expected an attack, and Othello gives the next eight or nine lines, "Rude am I in speech," etc., as a special apology called for by that show of violence—an apology given, with Mr. Fechter's French accent, in a tone that might seem, to a critic out of tune with the actor, oddly suggestive of a French politeness by no means in accord with the speaker's own estimate of his character. But we have no right to speak of it so lightly. The device is new and ingenious, it gives a lively break to the speech, and carries it to the end in true colloquial fashion. Shakespeare, however, meant dignity of expression here; and

whatever force his true interpreter would give to the " no more"
was not such as to make the court rise at Othello, or convert
his simple soldierly words in the following lines into a French
apology for his excitement, considered as a rudeness. The
subsequent description of the wooing is given with a colloquial
ease that is most clever and agreeable, though not at all
" unvarnished."

In the second act, Mr. Fechter's Othello first appears in
Cyprus less as the soldier than as the newly-married husband
who rejoins the bride from whom he was parted on the wedding
day. When, roused from his bridal bed, he enters to quell the
riot following Cassio's drunkenness, there is more dignity of
manner ; but the quick temper breaks into a tone of passion
almost petulant as he turns round upon the tolling of the alarm-
bell to cry, " Silence that dreadful bell ! "—rather as if its
noise had worried him, than as if there were any special
significance in the word " dreadful," related to the reason he
adds—as passionate men are not apt to do in the same breath
with a command—

> It frights the isle
> From her propriety.

But the scene is well sustained, and Mr. Fechter, in the first
two acts of *Othello*, though he wins no laurels, loses none.

I do not understand why, when Iago brings Othello to the
room where Cassio is taking leave of Desdemona, Othello
sees their parting with a spasm of emotion preceding Iago's
" Ha ! I like not that." There was no suspicion planted in
his mind, and the disturbance expressed is beyond what
should be excited by the sight of the disgraced Cassio, whom
yet he loves. Mr. Fechter, too, himself, goes on to prolong the
period of complete trust through much of the succeeding
colloquy, and is not disturbed by Iago's hints until he says,

> She did deceive her father, marrying you ;
> And when she seem'd to shake, and fear your looks,
> She loved them most.

Here our new actor represents Othello tortured with a deep,
nervous thoughtfulness. He stands aside with his eye fixed on

vacancy, as one reasoning out in contemplation the path shown him to the hell whither it leads. Few passages in Mr. Fechter's rendering of the part are more finely conceived than the manner of the sudden stop with a sense of bitter shame and humiliation followed by " Leave me, Iago," when Othello finds himself, having so far accepted the poison offered to his mind, impelled to say to his ancient, " Set. on thy wife to observe."

The soliloquy of Othello after Iago has left him Mr. Fechter delivers with admirable emphasis, and the manner of his address to Desdemona in the little scene next following, when he throws down her handkerchief, is in its distressful hardness perfectly expressed. As the passion grows the action becomes more wholly emotional, and Mr. Fechter shows the physical effect of mental suffering in convulsive twitchings and in-voluntary drawings of the corners of the mouth till all the teeth are bare. The epilepsy into which Shakespeare represents Othello as falling in the first scene of the fourth act, and which is now wisely restored, Mr. Fechter foreshadows by these signs of physical yielding to the mental torture. When Othello demands the handkerchief of Desdemona, the scene is enriched with some new touches of tenderness. His face is averted when she says, " It is not lost," and he turns suddenly with all his love and trust flowing back on him, to take her to his arms, when she repels him with the addition, " but what an' if it were ? " A like expression, only more prolonged, is given to the scene in Desdemona's chamber, where Emilia waits at the door. The " O Desdemona " is given as a cry of irrepressible tenderness, at which the lovers wind insensibly into each other's arms, and the following passage is spoken by Othello seated with Desdemona at his feet, her face between his hands, in tones of the old gentleness, that are to give place to a renewal of the fury.

The scene between Cassio and Bianca having been restored at the beginning of the fourth act, which opens upon Othello insensible with epilepsy, and so passes to what seems the strongest proof of Desdemona's guilt, the sense of pity becomes strengthened. The appeal is, by Mr. Fechter's rendering, more simply to pity for Othello than we suppose Shakespeare to have intended, but it is most effective, is made powerfully and with much success. The gentler sympathies of the whole audience are secured, and the fifth act therefore becomes very painful.

Here, too, Mr. Fechter has made noticeable innovations. The Bedchamber is elaborately set, and the bed, no longer in an alcove at the back, is a pompous structure at the side of the stage, with its back to the audience, so as to conceal the sleeping Desdemona, and raised on a dais with several steps so that it looks as portentous as a catafalque prepared for a great funeral pomp. Othello is in the room already ; and although one door is closed, open doors lead to the outer world, where operatic boatmen perform Desdemona's willow song, whereto he listens. That is a small effect unworthy of Shakespeare ; and the showy effects now got with a great bed are rather more melodramatic than Shakespearean. Othello bolts the door that leads from within the house, but the doors by which there may be entry from without are left wide open. The murder also is too ostentatiously a murder, morally and physically.

When in the last act Othello enters Desdemona's chamber to inflict upon his wife what he regards as the just penalty of her offence, because his soul shrinks from the contemplated act, he strengthens it by bidding it look not to the bloody deed, but to the reason justifying it.

> It is the cause, it is the cause, my soul !
> Let me not name it to you, ye chaste stars.

When Mr. Fechter spoke these lines holding a hand-glass like a hair-brush that he had deliberately gone to fetch from Desdemona's bed, and which he threw, after speaking a few lines in dudgeon, to the carpenter, I had not imagination strong enough to conceive what he meant. Probably, I thought, Desdemona's vanity is being symbolised as the cause of her fall—a very poor notion, but let it pass. Now Mr. Fechter's explanatory book shows me that here Othello looks at his face in the glass, and is telling his soul that his skin is the cause of his misfortunes ! It is his skin that he will not name to the chaste stars !

Othello is, as he should be, in his own eyes executing justice, and when stirred to passion cries—

> O perjur'd woman ! thou dost stone my heart,
> And make me call what I intend to do,
> A murder—which I thought a sacrifice.

The act, in Mr. Fechter's reading of it, is full of passion and emotion, and the audience is deeply stirred, but the effects in some respects belong rather to French melodrama than to English tragedy, and Mr. Fechter even closes his Othello with a melodramatic but false reading, by half-throttling Iago— whom he wounded before his sword was taken from him, whom he would not be suffered again to lay hold of with a dagger in his hand, and on whom in his last speech he is very far from spending thought. For it is then that he accuses himself only for one, whose hand,

> Like the base Judean,[1] threw a pearl away,
> Richer than all his tribe.

Instead of telling his tale of the circumcised dog whom he took by the throat and smote him—" thus," in contempt of himself mixed with a reminder of his old soldierly prowess, Mr. Fechter's Othello is pulling Iago about with uplifted dagger, and at the " thus "—to flash surprise—stabs not Iago but himself.

—From *The Journal of a London Playgoer.*

[1] The old reading.

JOSEPH KNIGHT

(1829–1907)

SIGNOR SALVINI AND OTHER PLAYERS OF OTHELLO

April 10, 1875.

No slight censure of modern English art is involved in the fact that the mention of the masterpieces of Shakespearian tragedy is apt to bring up recollections of foreign actors. Hamlet is at the present moment associated in public estimation with Mr. Irving. A year ago, however, the names it first recalled were those of Emil Devrient, Mr. Fechter, and M. Rouvière. Mdlle. Stella Colas has not during recent years been surpassed in Juliet, and since Mrs. Siddons, Signora Ristori is unapproached as Lady Macbeth. Within the last few years another character has been wrested from us, and Othello henceforward will be associated in the memory of playgoers with Signor Salvini. Othello has not been a favourite character with English exponents, happier always in presenting the sombre rage of Northern blood than the fierce and burning passion of the South. Those who remember Edmund Kean are few, and can speak only from distant recollections. Macready's Othello was the weakest of his Shakespearian performances. So weak was it, that men who, with the present writer, contemplated in it the most intellectual of tragedians for the first time, doubted whether his reputation was merited, and were scarcely disposed to see him in a second part. Neither Young nor Charles Kean has left many recollections as Othello. Mr. Phelps has played the part often, but it is far from the best of his tragic impersonations. It is strange, indeed, that the only man in days comparatively recent who has acquired any high reputation in Othello is one whose fame as an actor has since suffered eclipse. Before large theatres or other influences known to be prejudical to English art had done their work, Mr.

G. V. Brooke was an actor of promise, and his Othello still stands highest in the recollections of English playgoers.

In coming before the public then as Othello, Signor Salvini has to fear little competition, either actual or retrospective. So unlike anything that the present generation has seen is, however, his impersonation of the Moor, that opportunity is scarcely offered for comparison. It is splendid alike in its qualities and its defects, in virtues which raise it to something like supremacy in tragic art, and in defects powerful enough to mar its beauty, and leave the prevalent impression on the mind one not far from disappointment. Much as English actors may learn from the distinguished stranger who now comes among us, it will be an evil day for art when young actors begin to train themselves in the school of which he is the most illustrious exponent.

Few physical advantages are wanting to Signor Salvini. His frame is manly and robust, his stature tall, his face handsome and expressive, and his voice powerful. These gifts have, of course, been cultivated to the utmost ; the bearing is perfect in simplicity and nobility, the features are singularly mobile, and the music of the voice is as remarkable as its power.

Signor Salvini's conception of Othello is that we expect from a thoughtful, perceptive, and cultivated man. Othello with him is a barbarian, whose instincts, savage and passionate, are concealed behind a veneer of civilisation so thick that he is himself scarcely conscious he can be other than he appears. Friendly, loving, and courteous, he can, as Iago says :

> As tenderly be led by the nose
> As asses are.

When the poison of jealousy ferments in his blood, the strife between the animal nature and the civilising influences of custom is long and sharp. In the end the barbarian triumphs, the concluding scene, if not wholly savage, exhibiting mere glimpses of those restraints which in the third act, though rarely tested, remain dominant. The picture is exact of a noble animal turning piteously in the toils in which it has been enmeshed, and finding its efforts at escape serve only to render the position more desperate.

In dwelling upon some salient features in the interpretation, it is well to note the gradual conquest of the intellectual nature and its disappearance before the rising passion and fury.

To the counsel of the Duke, in the first act, Othello listens with dignified attention. As Brabantio enters, uttering exclamations concerning his daughter's loss, mixed with charges against Othello, the face of the Moor exhibits a variety of emotions, of which pity is the most conspicuous. His address to the senators is delivered with calm and sustained dignity, and with less aid of gesture than is common. The first revelation of his true nature occurs upon the appearance of Desdemona, whom he covers with a glance of indescribable tenderness. As she claims from the Duke permission to go with her husband to the wars his gaze becomes burning. Forgetful of all restraints, he approaches and almost folds her in his arms ; but awaking in time to recollections of the august presence in which he stands, he turns from her with a gesture of apology. The start with which he receives Brabantio's caution—

> Look to her, Moor ; have a quick eye to see ;
> She has deceived her father, and may thee—

shows not only his quickness in receiving a hint which, taken in conjunction with other matters, works afterwards " like madness in the brain," but his fiery and impetuous disposition.

His delivery of the speech in the second act, on rejoining Desdemona at Cyprus, is steeped in Southern voluptuousness, for which the words afford warrant, since words can scarcely depict more profound contentment or more burning love. The interruption of the brawl begotten of Cassio's drunkenness is noticeable only inasmuch as it exhibits Othello as the commander of men, and reveals the qualities which have raised a Moor to a position of trust in a republic so intolerant of strangers as that of Venice. A noteworthy touch of uxoriousness is found in the manner in which Othello, after limiting the punishment of Cassio to dismissal, grows more angered upon Desdemona's appearance :

> Look if my gentle love be not raised up !
> (*To* Cass.) I'll make thee an example.

Supreme beatitude is evinced in the look which accompanies the delivery in the next act of the well-known speech, " Excellent wretch," etc. The duel with Iago commences, and uneasiness is gradually communicated to the mind of Othello by the " leprous distilment " which Iago drops in his ear. Sitting at the table, Othello, at the first word, suspends his work, his attention becomes gradually close, until at the words, " Thou dost mean something," he rises from his chair, throwing down impatiently the pen he has been using. Few gestures are subsequently employed until the meaning of Iago's accusation is made plain. The slowness of his mind to drink in suspicion, and the manner in which presentiment of evil is transfigured into horror and rage, are the most striking and original characteristics of the interpretation. Iago's repetition of the charge previously brought against Desdemona of deceiving her father pains him, but communicates no downright mistrust, and the words, " Not a jot, not a jot " (*Punto, punto*) seem an attempt at self-encouragement. With uneasy steps he now paces about the room, drinking in the words of Iago, until slowly the foul accusation takes shape in his mind. Shortly and sharply, and with tones of authority, he bids his antient farewell. He would fain be alone and hide his struggles from all observation ; the injunction, " Set on thy wife to observe," comes as an afterthought. A brief episode of the loss by Desdemona of the handkerchief and its transfer to Iago separates the two portions of the duel. When with mind almost distracted he re-enters, he gazes gloomily back through the door which he holds open. Then follows the most impressive scene of the play. The famous farewell to his former occupation is delivered with much pathos. It is virtually a farewell also to his better self. When the voice of Iago breaks the thread of his reflections, the animal nature springs to assert itself. Seizing fiercely Iago by the throat, he crushes the cowering miscreant to the ground, and in the whirlwind of his passion lifts his foot to stamp the heel upon his head, it might even be to stamp out his brains. Recalled, however, to reason, he turns away, and with averted head he stretches out his hand, and penitently, yet with a species of loathing, raises the prostrate wretch from the ground. In this scene, the one profoundly electrical effect of the interpretation is reached. Quitting Iago, he sits at the very back of the stage, until as the tempter deals the poison in stronger doses, and speaks of Cassio's sleeping words, he comes again forward to kneel and swear a terrible revenge.

Little opportunity is offered in the fourth act. His ill-worn courtesy to Desdemona renders more marked the menace of his eye, in which burns a lurid light of resolution. The blow before the messengers from Venice is well given, and the speech, " She can turn, and turn," is spoken with suppressed passion and enforced politeness, strikingly contrasted. The speech, " Had it pleased Heaven," etc., is delivered at the back of the stage. It has pathos, though scarcely in an eminent degree. When the interview with Desdemona is over, Othello shakes savagely the money in his purse in the ear of Emilia, and departs throwing it at her feet with a fine expression of scorn and indignation.

Thus far, though there are points on which we have doubts, the merits of the impersonation so completely overpower its defects, we have not stayed to hint censure. In the concluding scenes of the last act the conquest of the civilised being by the barbarian is carried out at the sacrifice of Shakspeare's intentions and at that of Art. After delivering the speech, " It is the cause," slowly, the first lines being spoken close to the door by which he enters, Othello kisses his sleeping wife, then goes to the window, and stands with the lightning playing upon his face. Desdemona wakes, sees him, and approaches. His recoil, expressive partly of unwillingness to embrace one who has so foully wronged him, next of fear lest the sweet seductive influence of her caress might yet unman him, is fine. After the short dialogue of supplication on the one side, and refusal on the other, he seizes her by the hair of the head, and, dragging her on to the bed, strangles her with a ferocity that seems to take a delight in its office. The murder committed, Othello walks agitatedly backwards and forwards, not answering the cry of Emilia. When she tells him of the death of Roderigo by the hand of Cassio he starts, then relapses into a sullen fury of discontent. He remains motionless for a while, with eye glazing, as he learns how mightily he has been abused, then staggers forward with open mouth and with a countenance charged with tragic passion. The following words are delivered in a wild abandonment of grief, that in the end becomes inarticulate in utterance, and with an accompaniment of beating of his head with his hands which, according to English canons of art, is excessive. Suddenly the thought of the tempter comes to him. Crouching low like a wild beast, he prepares for a spring. A sword is in the girdle of one of the attendants. Upon this he seizes, and passes it with one thrust through the traitor's body. Staggering then to a seat, he commences, sitting and weeping, the final speech. Nearing the end, he rises, and at the supreme moment cuts his throat with a short scimitar, hacking and hewing with savage energy, and imitating the noise that escaping blood and air may together make when the windpipe is severed.

Nothing in art so terribly realistic as this death-scene has been attempted. It is directly opposed to Shakspeare, who makes Othello say :

> I took by the throat the circumcised dog,
> And smote him—thus.

A man does not take by the neck one whose throat he is going to cut, since he would cut his own fingers in so doing. He seizes one, on the contrary, into whose heart he is about to plunge a dagger. The word "smote" in Shakspeare is, indeed, sufficiently clear to leave no room for doubt or misconception. The effect on the audience is repellent to the last degree. This kind of death-scene needs only such slight and easily provided additions as the rupture of a bladder of blood, which the actor might place within reach, the exhibition of a bleeding throat, and a stream of blood serpenting upon the floor, to reach the limits of attainable realism. Tendencies in the direction of this kind of so-called art were seen in Signora Ristori, and marred her marvellously artistic impersonations. In the present case their effect is singularly detrimental to the artistic value of the performance. A movement in the same direction is, moreover, noticeable in other arts. When we instance the famous picture of Regnault, " An Execution in a Moorish Palace," the reader will at once see the parallel we draw. It is a different matter even to give realistic effects in pictures and to introduce them into Shakspearian tragedy. Aristotle's definition of Tragedy has never been surpassed. Its aim is to give the pleasure which arises from pity and terror through imitation—τὴν ἀπὸ ἐλέον καὶ φόβου διὰ μιμήσεως ἡδονὴν παρασκευάζειν. Terror is indeed the aim of all tragic art. When for this is substituted horror, and even common-place horror, the degradation of art has commenced. Here is the one blot upon an interpretation which otherwise would command our warmest admiration. We have left ourselves no space to dwell on the version presented, which differs, in some respects, from that ordinarily adopted, upon the general cast, or upon any other features of interest. It may be mentioned that the get-up of Signor Salvini is always admirable, the most striking appearance being that assumed in the second act, when he is dressed in chain armour, with a steel helmet and hauberk.

—From *Theatrical Notes.* By Joseph Knight, 1893.

KNIGHT ON THE COMÉDIE FRANÇAISE

A CURIOUS change of feeling, attributable doubtless to increased knowledge on the part of the public, is manifested by the reception accorded the Comédie Française on its second visit to England. When, in the evil day of Paris, the more prominent members of the company gave a series of performances in London, in which, owing to the paucity of their numbers, actors of highest mark sustained all *rôles* down to the most subordinate, a mere fraction of the public assembled to witness performances absolutely unequalled. It was not, indeed, until a movement for a complimentary banquet, the inception and execution of which belongs to the " Athenæum," had been set on foot that the playgoing world understood the opportunities of artistic enjoyment and education placed within its reach. Since the period of scarcely controllable excitement begotten of that movement most important facts connected with the Comédie Française have been dealt with in the English press, until the nature, construction, and value of the corporation are now understood as clearly as those of any other alien institution are ever understood in England. As a consequence fashion has taken the Comédie Française under its wing, and the eagerness and enthusiasm which are manifested are in excess of the occasion and have a false ring. Not a place was obtainable for the opening night, the entrance of those duly provided with seats was impeded by the exit of disappointed applicants, and those whose interest in the art is most keen found themselves thrust into positions in which it was all but impossible for them to frame an accurate judgment.

The opening performance consisted of two pieces of Molière and an act from Racine. A prologue by M. Jean Aicard, entitled " Molière à Shakspeare," was, however, first recited by M. Got, in presence of the entire company. This is a little rhetorical, as such addresses ordinarily are, and has less epigram than we are accustomed to find. It is, however, ingenious and well written, and was finely delivered.

Though the masterpiece of the comedy of Molière, the one play in which the dramatist puts into burning words his sense of his own wrongs and his weariness under the share allotted him of the burden of humanity—his *Hamlet*, in fact—*Le Misanthrope* is a difficult play wherewith to please an English audience. Without either action or situation, it seeks to interest by purely psychological processes, and exposes to vulgar gaze a nature which vulgar perceptions can never penetrate. It is painful, if edifying, to watch the efforts to force into drollery the biting phrases of Alceste, out of regard for a public which, hearing of Molière as a comic writer, waits for comic scenes. Still, thanks to the brilliant and tasteful dresses, which make the whole a faithful reproduction of seventeenth-century life, and to the exquisite delivery of the verse—and thanks also to the careful elaboration of character by actors such as MM. Delaunay and Coquelin and Madame Favart—the whole, if a little long, was pleasant to contemplate. M. Delaunay imparts to Alceste more fierceness and disdain than we are accustomed to associate with the character, and less feeling of defeat and sorrow. The title chosen by Molière justifies, and indeed may seem to necessitate this view. It is possible, however, to conceive of Alceste as one who is like the poet

> Dowered with the hate of hate, the scorn of scorn,
> The love of love.

His cynicism is but skin-deep, and that the mood which counsels his retreat into obscurity is ultimately to be changed seems apparent from the concluding lines of the play, addressed by Philinte, his one friend, to Eliante, whom, in a fashion not quite easy to reconcile with his passion for Célimène, Alceste regards as her possible successor :

> Allons, madame, allons employer toute chose,
> Pour rompre le dessein que son cœur se propose.

No such aspect is indicated by M. Delaunay, though it was suggested by his predecessor, M. Bressant. M. Coquelin was excellent as Oronte, and was the very marquis Molière loved to draw—the combination of aristocratic and ridiculous qualities at whom it was very easy and unsafe to laugh. Madame Favart gave with purest diction and with admirable acerbity the speeches of Arsinoé, and Mdlle. Broisat was natural and agreeable as Eliante. MM. Prudhon, Baillet, and Boucher presented with a fidelity worthy of the predecessor and namesake of the artist last named the young butterflies of the court—men whose duties did not extend beyond attending the *petit lever* of their monarch. Mdlle. Croizette alone, whose style leans towards the realistic, seemed scarcely suited to the part she played.

The second act of *Phèdre* is that in which, with writhings and convulsions of shame and passion, Phèdre owns to Hippolyte her fierce and incestuous love. No better part could be found for showing the intensity of which Mdlle. Sarah Bernhardt is possessor. Such experiments can seldom be satisfactory, since an artist ought, in fact, to rise by the slow and requisite gradations of the drama to the point at which her passion is evinced. In the present case no difficulty of the kind was encountered. From the moment she entered on the stage, carefully guarded and supported by Œnone, Mdlle. Bernhardt realised fully the passionate, febrile, and tortured woman. Her supple frame writhed beneath the influence of mental agony and restless desire, and her postures seemed chosen with admirable art for the purpose of blending the greatest possible amount of seduction with the utmost possible parade of penitence. This is, of course, the true reading, and the whole shame of Phèdre is due to her ill success. The key-note to her character is struck in a later act, the third, wherein she says :

> Il n'est plus temps : il sait mes ardeurs insensées,
> De l'austère pudeur les bornes sont passées.
> J'ai déclaré ma honte aux yeux de mon vainqueur,
> Et l'espoir malgré moi s'est glissé dans mon cœur.

While, accordingly, she exhausts herself in invective against herself for her crime, she is, in fact, in the very whirlwind of her passion studying, like a second Delilah,

> His virtue or weakness which way to assail.

Obvious as is this view, it is not always presented, the cause of absence being, perhaps, the weakness of the actress. In the present case it was fully revealed, and the picture of abject and lascivious appeal was terrible in its intensity. The performance proves that Mdlle. Bernhardt deserves her high reputation. M. Mounet-Sully was excellent, his acting being wholly free from the extravagance with which it is sometimes charged. Full advantage was taken of the one or two opportunities for the display of power which the act affords.
—From *Theatrical Notes.*

KNIGHT ON SARAH BERNHARDT IN *HERNANI*

THAT the performance of *Hernani* proved the greatest success of the season, so far as this has yet extended, is attributable to Mdlle. Bernhardt. The general representation had conspicuous merits. It is a treat of a high order to see the youth of Spain presented by those who wear the cloak and sword as though their shoulders and loins had been always familiar with them. It is a delight to find preserved an atmosphere of passion, voluptuousness, and romance into which enters no element or suggestion of every-day life. Excellent as are these things, something more is required to elevate the performance into grandeur. From the admirable to the sublime is a wide step. That the interval between the two was bridged is wholly attributable to Mdlle. Bernhardt. During the earlier acts there was nothing to suggest what was to follow. Looking admirably picturesque in a mediæval dress, with slashed sleeves, and frills round the neck which set off the lovely carriage of the head, Mdlle. Bernhardt took, as it seemed, but a moderate interest in the scenes before her. Hypercriticism might almost have suggested that her attitudes, supremely graceful as they seemed, were not quite unstudied, and that more fitful and uncertain moods should be shown by one who was the subject of accidents so strange and surprises so startling. Amends for all were made, however, in the fifth act, In this the languor and the ripe and passionate contentment of the woman when her long-deferred nuptials were at length brought about proved the prelude to one of those electrical displays of passion which, since the disappearance of Rachel, have been unknown upon the stage. It is impossible after once seeing them to recall the various changes by which the quick succeeding emotions were indicated. The bursts of wild, savage energy, the convulsive clasp in which she locks the living man whom she may not hold in life, the abject despair of her supplications, the sublime and desperate resolution with which she shares or anticipates her lover's fate, and the sweet, sad melody of her farewell and death, succeed each other with such swiftness that they are blended one with another, and the memory finds it difficult to disentangle them. Acting like this has, however, the impress of absolute genius, and the world needs have no doubt that it has the opportunity of contemplating such art as by its appearance marks an epoch. M. Worms, as Don Carlos, acts with remarkable dignity and force, and maintains a truly regal presence. M. Maubant gives due impressiveness to the character of Ruy Gomez, though he looks almost too stalwart for one whose weakness is a subject of constant allusion. M. Mounet-Sully has burning intensity and his expression is charged with the strongest emotion. He is not free, however, from rhodomontade. Other parts were well sustained, but no other character has sufficient importance to call for comment.

—From *Theatrical Notes*.

KNIGHT ON THE TRIUMPH OF BERNHARDT

THE value of the triumph obtained by the Comédie Française on its visit to London is, so far as the general body is concerned, diminished by the extreme popularity of one of the company. While a respectable amount of enthusiasm attends ordinary performances, those occasions on which Mdlle. Bernhardt appears create what is currently called a *furore*. It is easy to imagine a circumstance like this exercising a depressing influence upon a body of artists whose special aim is to supply an interpretation of dramatic work in which everything is subordinated to general effect, and no individual prominence, beyond what is incidental to the character of the piece performed, is sought for or allowed. This feeling is likely to be intensified when, on the strength of personal popularity and the need there is for her services, backed up, it may well be supposed, by feminine wilfulness and insubordination, the actress who thus stands forth from her fellows takes means still further to separate herself from them by giving outside performances at which they do not assist. That such feelings should assert themselves in the Comédie Française is natural and pardonable, if, indeed, it is not inevitable. None the less it is foolish. What in most members of the company is fine and highly cultivated talent is in Mdlle. Bernhardt genius. We are not disposed to plunge into the sea of troubles that awaits those who attempt a definition of the quality thus named. We content ourselves with a bare assertion that the powers of dramatic exposition possessed by this lady reach this point. The present generation, which possesses few and distant recollections of Rachel, the last actress of the highest order who belonged to the Comédie Française, attests, it may be too warmly, certainly with something of fanaticism, its delight in a class of acting which seemed to have been lost to the stage, and in so doing contributes to spoil what it so profoundly admires and enjoys. Prudential considerations are not likely to weigh with the public, nor can they be expected to do so. What the Comédie Française, if it consults its own interests, will do, and indeed does, is to take the gifts the gods provide, and maintain as long as it can a connection that may in time become impossible. Genius is an uncomfortable and unmanageable thing, and in its association with mediocrity or even with excellence it brings endless confusion and discord. The world seldom knows how to treat it, and still more seldom does it know how to treat itself. None the less it must be left to itself. It is impossible to chain it as a watch-dog to a kennel, or to shut it like domestic cattle in a pen. It is often inconvenient and ridiculous, resembling, as Baudelaire says of the poet, the albatross, the

> Prince des nuées
> Qui hante la tempête et se rit de l'archer ;
> Exilé sur le sol au milieu des huées,
> Ses ailes de géant l'empêchent de marcher.

These counsels are given with no intention to lecture the Comédie Française, which has shown full capacity to manage its own affairs, but because the matters dealt with have provoked complaints in English newspapers which have been copied into French journals, and there seems a chance that the visit to London, which financially and artistically is a conspicuous success, may prove the contrary as regards the harmony and even the well-being of the institution.

Of the pieces in which Mdlle. Bernhardt has yet appeared, *Phèdre* has produced the most profound effect. The admirable limpidity of diction of the actress gives to the verse of Racine its full value, and her electrical bursts of passion render the stronger scenes profoundly impressive. In the course of the five years during which Mdlle. Bernhardt has held possession of this *rôle* at the Théâtre Français, she has converted what at first was a fine and original conception into a finished and magnificent piece of acting. On the mingled elements of seduction and humiliation she exhibits in the second act we have dwelt. In contrast absolutely marvellous with these are the almost lurid gaze with which she contemplates the crime that puts the seal on her baseness, the shuddering horror with which she speaks of her appearance to answer in hell at the tribunal of her father for crimes before unheard of, and the remarkable self-conquest indicated in the closing scene, when the spirit seems by its energy to triumph over dissolution, and compel death itself to wait till the latest word of her dismal confession is made. In this character the interest of the play centres. It is pleasant to be able to speak highly of the Hippolyte of M. Mounet-Sully, the Aricie of Mdlle. Martin, which was excellent, and the Œnone, of Madame Provost-Pousin. The general interpretation is, indeed, highly to be commended.

Voltaire's tragedy of *Zaire* is better than its reputation. Its plot is interesting, the conflict in the bosom of the heroine, who, while loving passionately her Mohammedan captor, discovers she is a Lusignan, and is bound by creed, by family ties, and by family entreaties to reject him, leading to some very strong and original situations. In his " Lettre à M. de la Roque," Voltaire says : " *Zaire*, est la première pièce de théâtre dans laquelle j'aie osé m'abandonner à toute la sensibilité de mon cœur ; c'est la seule tragédie tendre que j'ai faite. Je croyais, dans l'âge même des passions les plus vives, que l'amour n'était point fait pour le théâtre tragique. Je ne regardais cette faiblesse que comme un défaut charmant qui avilissait l'art de Sophocle." In this case departure from rules led to results that were never obtained by their observance, and *Zaire* may dispute with any of Voltaire's dramas the right to rank as his masterpiece. The character of the heroine offers few opportunities for the display of tragic passion, and it is accordingly the more tender side of Mdlle. Bernhardt's art which is revealed. One or two magnificent outbursts showed the nervous power the actress possesses. The whole performance conveyed, however, a notion of fatigue and lassitude. M. Mounet-Sully as Orosmane presented an admirable picture. He is, according to English theories of art, wanting in the art of repose. M. Maubant as Lusignan looked well fitted to lead the Christian hosts to combat with the Pagans, but forgot, apparently, that his voice as well as his frame have been injured by long confinement, and that when he appears he is practically moribund. The Slave of M. Davrigny was magnificently made up ; a more sinister-looking figure never kept watch in a seraglio. Garrick played Lusignan in Aaron Hill's version of *Zaire*, which, under the title of " Zara," takes rank as the best of Hill's dramatic works. Mrs. Siddons subsequently appeared as the heroine. Bond, the first Lusignan at the production of *Zara* at Drury Lane, 12th January, 1736, fainted on the stage, was carried home, and died next morning. It is curious to find Reed taxing Hill with plagiarism from a playwright named Hudson, while Voltaire's share in the work passes unacknowledged or unknown.

In *Le Sphinx*, Mdlle. Bernhardt shared the honours of the performance with Mdlle. Croizette. The actress last named displayed remarkable passion in her original *rôle* of Blanche, and the scene of her death by the poison contained in the bezel of her ring was a marvellous piece of stage realism. Mdlle. Bernhardt meantime had little to do until the fourth act, when a burst of frenzy startled those who had before admired the perfection of her ordinary method. M. Worms as Savigny had a difficult part, in which he acquitted himself well. M. Maubant was the Admiral ; M. Febvre was well got up, and displayed his customary stolidity as Lord Astley ; and M. Coquelin *cadet* went dangerously near extravagance as Ulric the musician.

—From *Theatrical Notes*, 1893.

KNIGHT ON ALFRED DE MUSSET'S DRAMAS

IF the most popular portion of the *répertoire* of the Comédie Française is found in the drama of M. Victor Hugo, that of Alfred de Musset comes in general estimation immediately behind it. More interest indeed, of a kind, attaches to the performance of *Les Caprices de Marianne* or *On ne badine pas avec l'Amour* than to that of *Hernani* or *Ruy Blas*. Translations of the plays of M. Hugo are not unknown, and one or two of them have attained considerable popularity upon the stage. The comedies or the proverbs of Musset meanwhile defy the translator, and their representation calls for a class of acting of which our stage knows nothing. Not easy is it, indeed, to see, after the retirement of M. Delaunay, whenever that event may take place, how these works are to remain on the stage. M. Delaunay is the ideal of Valentin and Perdican, parts in which no other actor has shown a capacity to approach him. It will be a great misfortune if the works of Musset, which have a *cachet* as distinct as that of M. Hugo, or indeed of Shakspeare,

are driven from the stage for the want of interpreters. The representation of *Il ne faut jurer de Rien* is noteworthy for the excellent performances of M. Delaunay as Valentin and Mdlle. Madeleine Brohan as La Baronne, and for the complete failure of M. Got as L'Abbé. When, eight years ago, M. Got played L'Abbé, it was one of the best parts in his *répertoire*. It was difficult to estimate too highly the powers of an actor who filled up with art so consummate a character the mere outline of which was presented. Unfortunately the great actor is sometimes as vain as the small. Because he made much of a part M. Got seeks to make more, the result being that he completely overbalances himself, and that the performance is poor, and as an attempted impersonation contemptible. A village curé is often, doubtless, ridiculous enough. An abbé, however, who plays piquet with *la baronne*, even though he may undertake parish work and have appointments with the sacristan and the beadle, is not in the habit of wearing a preposterous hat and running about like a madman. Strange indeed is it to see a man such as M. Got, whose place is at the very top of his profession, fall into an error which springs ordinarily from the ill-regulated vanity and ambition of youth. M. Got's very eminence is, however, a reason why an exhibition like this should incur gravest condemnation. As La Baronne, Mdlle. Madeleine Brohan is perfect. Her dignity and repose of style are wholly suited to the part. M. Delaunay meanwhile, as Valentin, displays to highest advantage the animal spirits and conceit which are the foundation of the character, and steers entirely clear of the vulgarity to which a less delicate interpretation would lead. M. Thiron is a good Vanbuck and Mdlle. Reichemberg an agreeable Cécile.

As *Barberine* is not in the actual *répertoire* of the Comédie Française, and as *Le Chandelier* is, for obvious reasons, not likely to be given in England, the more dramatic works of Musset are exhausted, so far as the English stage is concerned, with the production of *On ne badine pas avec l'Amour*.

This favourite play is perhaps the most characteristic of Musset's dramas. In none other are tenderness and passion so strangely blended with mockery, in none other is the full value

shown of a method which unites an intensity almost Shakspearian to a heat of imaginative expression suggestive of Byron,
and a serious and cynical humour the direct bequest of Heine.
In the outset the play is as much a pastoral as the *Aminta*, the
Fidalma, the *Pastor Fido*, or any of the dramatic idyls of the
Italians. The end of all is death, however, and the motto of
the play might be taken from Shakspeare :

> Golden lads and girls all must,
> As chimney-sweepers, come to dust.

A difficult task is accomplished in presenting a piece of this
kind in a manner that shall produce no feeling of disenchant-
ment. More than this is done in the present instance. M.
Delaunay is the Perdican of the play, and his petulant wooing
of Rosette is perfect ; Mdlle. Croizette is a conceivable Camille,
and Mdlle. Reichemberg is an agreeable Rosette. It is,
however, strange to say, in the minor characters that the
triumph over difficulties is most remarkable. Nothing can well
be better than the presentation by M. Truffier of the *Chœur des
Jeunes Gens*, or that by M. Richard of the *Chœur des Vieillards*.
The two pedants and gourmands, Bridaine and Blasius, were
fairly depicted, and the Baron of M. Thiron and the Dame
Pluche of Madame Jouassain were excellent. A more attractive performance is not often seen on the stage.

—From *Theatrical Notes*.

LE BARBIER DE SÉVILLE, ANDROMAQUE, ETC.

THOUGH inferior in every respect to *Le Mariage de Figaro*,
Le Barbier de Séville of Beaumarchais is interesting, both
for its characterisation and for the merits of its dialogue.
Taking the accepted types of the drama of Molière and of
Regnard, Beaumarchais elevated Léandre and Eraste into
Almaviva, and Mascarille and Crispin into Figaro. That he
showed the commencement of that rebellion of the valet
against the ill-treatment and blows to which he had been
accustomed, which was one of the many indications of the
coming revolution, while his predecessors are silent concerning
it, must of course be attributed to the later period at which he

wrote. The hundred years which elapsed between the production of *L'Avare* and that of *Le Barbier de Séville* had witnessed little absolute change, but much preparation for change. The forces which were to result in upheaval had accumulated. What difference had arisen in the relation between master and servant is shown by comparing the language of Maître Jacques in *L'Avare* with that of Figaro in *Le Barbier de Séville*. " Passe encore pour mon maître," says the former, when he has been beaten by Harpagon, " il a quelque droit de me battre " ; while Figaro, acknowledging the existence of a similar state of things, but rebelling against it, avoids notice of his superiors : " Je me crus trop heureux d'en être oublié, persuadé qu'un grand nous fait assez de bien quand il ne nous fait pas de mal." For the rest the story is a pleasant if farcical imbroglio, with theatrical and original situations, which lost their freshness in subsequent days, but belong, so far as invention is concerned, to Beaumarchais ; the dialogue is admirably bright, and its animal spirits are irresistible. M. Coquelin's Figaro is unsurpassable. By physical gifts, as by training, M. Coquelin is specially qualified for this class of parts, of which he is the best living representative, and, indeed, the best representative the present generation has seen. M. Febvre's Le Comte was moderately satisfactory, and M. Coquelin *cadet's* Bazile had a thoroughly comic physiognomy. Mdlle. Barretta was Rosine, and M. Thiron Bartolo.

In *L'Avare* M. Got gave a representation of Harpagon altogether masterly. In the treatment of the passion of avarice Molière seems for once to have gone outside his usual bounds, and the scene in which Harpagon, when robbed, seizes upon himself as the imagined robber, and declares his wish to hang all mankind, is conceived and executed in a spirit not unlike that which influenced Marlowe when he wrote *The Jew of Malta*. Of the opportunities afforded him M. Got took full advantage, and the tragical side of the character, for such it may almost be called, received fine and most powerful interpretation. With M. Delaunay as Cléante, M. Worms as Valère, M. Thiron as Maître Jacques, M. Coquelin *cadet* as Laflèche, and Mdlle. Dinah Félix as Frosine, this play received a brilliant interpretation. The voice of Mdlle. Barretta, who played Elise, is still so affected by cold that its state amounts to a disqualification for the stage.

In *Le Dépit Amoureux*, which is played in two acts, Mdlle. Samary is a piquant Marinette, M. Coquelin *cadet* an amusing Gros-Rhéné, and M. Truffier a satisfactory Mascarille.

Leaving on one side the character of Hermione, in which Rachel obtained a brilliant success, Mdlle. Bernhardt took, in the revival of *Andromaque*, the subordinate and comparatively colourless character of Andromaque. In this she has little to do except to display the grief and desolation of a faithful consort mourning over her dead lord. At one point, however, when Pyrrhus makes the death of her son the penalty for the rejection of his suit, an opportunity is afforded of which the actress took instant advantage. Her recoil of horror, and the manner in which she flung herself at the feet of her conqueror, had the charm and power which characterise her acting at its best. That the entire performance had infinite grace and delicacy need scarcely be said. M. Mounet-Sully acted very finely as Oreste. He has excellent gifts, but yields to a temptation to abuse his magnificient voice. Mdlle. Dudley played with passion as Hermione, but allowed her method to be seen. She is a clever and thoughtful student, but has shown as yet no power to go out of herself. M. Sylvain's Pyrrhus merits a word of praise.

L'Etincelle of M. Pailleron, a piece of no special merit, deserves attention on account of the display of archness of Mdlle. Samary in a character half *ingénue*, half romp. M. Delaunay and Mdlle. Croizette play well the two lovers in whose breasts *l'étincelle* is lighted.

The performance of *Ruy Blas*, on which many expectations had been built, resulted in disappointment. At one or two points Mdlle. Bernhardt showed her full power, but her entire presentation is best described as graceful and picturesque. There is little for the actress to do except to express *ennui* at court life, and a strong yearning for love to break the monotony of an existence which is, in fact, imprisonment. When in the gallant courtier the queen finds the unknown worshipper whose silent homage has long been her one interest in life, she displays some of that languorous charm which is a valuable portion of her means in art ; when subsequently, on his revealing himself as the patriot whose chief aim is the salvation of his country, she yields to the impulses that beset and besiege her, and stoops and kisses him on the forehead, the contact, slight as it is, almost overmasters her, and supreme longing and utter incapacity to resist are shown with magic skill. At last, when the climax is reached, and she finds her lover at her feet, dying at what he takes to be her bidding, there is one burst of supreme passion, in which she clasps his head to her bosom, fondles it, and recoils shuddering from the lips already stiffening with death which she presses against her own. In these situations the acting was fine, and at the point last named magnificent. M. Mounet-Sully's Ruy Blas was a failure so complete it does not even call for criticism. While disapproving always of M. Mounet-Sully's method, we have seen in his acting proof of conception, and have found some of his outbursts impressive. In *Ruy Blas*, until the last act was reached, he was simply wearisome. His acting had not even the picturesqueness in which generally it has never failed. Ruy Blas among the grandees of the Spanish Court looked the lackey he was, and his rodomontades could never have secured him anything beyond personal chastisement. It is melancholy to contemplate a failure so complete. In the last act one or two powerful bursts elicited from the audience warm recognition, and proved the actor capable of an interpretation altogether different from that he gave. M. Coquelin's Don César was a singularly bright and virile performance, full of colour and displaying admirably the more imaginative side of M. Coquelin's talents. M. Febvre was an admirable Don Salluste. Most of the subordinate characters were well played, and many of the figures about the Spanish Court had striking individuality.

The performance of *Mercadet le Faiseur* left little to desire. M. Got, whose masterpiece it is, played the hero in a style quite unsurpassable, from a French standpoint. That the kind of alternate rebuke and cajolery he employed would prove effective with English creditors may be doubted. It is not, however, with English creditors he has to deal. It is, meanwhile, difficult to praise too highly the perfection of detail in his acting and the breadth of the general result. Excellent support was afforded him by M. Febvre, whose De la Brive was equally excellent in make-up and in acting, by M. Barré as Verdelin, M. Coquelin *cadet* as Violette, the lachrymose creditor, and M. Truffier as Justin. The claim of *Mercadet* to rank as a comic masterpiece becomes more evident with each successive representation.

With it was given *L'Eté de la Saint-Martin*, a clever little one-act piece of MM. Meilhac and Halévy, which has been previously seen in England, and was on this occasion very naturally and pleasantly played by MM. Thiron and Prudhon, and Mesdames Jouassain and Barretta.

—From *Theatrical Notes.*

CLEMENT SCOTT

(1841–1904)

HENRY IRVING'S HAMLET

Lyceum Theatre, 31 Oct., 1874.

"THE History of Hamlet," says an eloquent critic, "is like that of Macbeth, a story of moral poisoning." The subtle analysis of Goethe, the brilliant peroration of M. Taine, the scholarly criticisms of William Hazlitt, unanimously confirm this verdict. It is Goethe who tells us of the brilliant youth a lover of art, beloved by his father, enamoured of the purest and most confiding maiden, who has perceived—from the height of the throne to which he was born—nothing but the beauty, happiness, and grandeur, both of Nature and humanity. It is Goethe who paints for us the fall of misfortune upon this sensitive soul. M. Taine, with the passionate style and antithesis of his nation, whirls us along through all the stages of the moral disease, admitting the feigned madness, but insisting upon the ethical disturbance of Hamlet's mind, which, "as a door, whose hinges are twisted, swings and bangs with every wind."

William Hazlitt is so in love with the beauty of Shakespeare's picture, that he would not have the character acted. He says there is no play that suffers so much in being transferred to the Stage. He has seen Mr. Kean and Mr. Kemble ; but the English critic refuses to be satisfied. He cannot discover his ideal Hamlet. He wants someone to "think aloud." He insists that there should be no "talking at" the hearers, but that "there should be as much of the gentleman and scholar infused into the part, *and as little of the actor*" ! Such criticisms as these are of the highest value as guides to the consideration of the Hamlet of Henry Irving, and to the previous history of the actor who has determined to realise his highest intellectual effort in the exhibition of moral poison.

When we come to think of it, is it not true that the study, the experiences and the peculiar influence of Mr. Irving's art tend in the direction of such a Hamlet as was pictured by Goethe, William Hazlitt, and M. Taine? The actor who harrowed our feelings with the agonies of the conscience-stricken Mathias, conquering many prejudices by the power of his intelligence and the minute detail of his art ; the poet—for it was with the inspiration of a poet that the sorrows of Charles I. were realised—who expressed the exquisite influence of home life, the crushed heart on the discovery of a false friend, the distressing agony of an everlasting farewell ; the artistic dreamer, who, with consummate daring, thought an English audience could be appalled—and it nearly was—by the mental terrors of Eugene Aram . . . was not this the actor for an ideal Hamlet, was not this the adequate and faithful representative of the effects of moral poison ?

It was thus that Mr. Irving's admirers reasoned, when, considering his antecedents, they instinctively felt that his Hamlet would be the true one. They did not argue and discuss as Germans do ; they did not gesticulate and prate like Frenchmen ; but, like sturdy, honest Englishmen, resolute in their convictions, they crowded to the doors of the Lyceum Theatre at half-past three in the afternoon, prepared to struggle for a performance which would not close before midnight. Here were devotion, impulse, interest. If the drama was to die, the public resolved it should not perish without an heroic struggle for the rescue. If an honest ambition was paramount, it should not lack recognition. It was an audience which will long be remembered. Far more important than the interested occupiers of the stalls and boxes, was the sight of the unreserved portions of the house—the pit and gallery, containing as they did members of that class which is the best friend of the drama. The audience that assembled to welcome Mr. Irving was a great protest against the threatened decline of the drama in a country which is becoming more and more educated every day. And so, with all on the tip-toe of excitement, the curtain rose.

All present longed to see Hamlet. Bernardo and Marcellus,

the Ghost, the platform, the grim preliminaries, the prologue or introduction to the wonderful story, were, as usual, tolerated —nothing more. Away go the platform, the green lights, the softly-stepping spirit, the musical-voiced Horatio. The scene changes to a dazzling interior, broken in its artistic lines, and rich with architectural beauty ; the harps sound, the procession is commenced, the jewels, and crowns, and sceptres, dazzle, and at the end of the train comes Hamlet. Mark him well, though from this instant the eyes will never be removed from his absorbing figure. They may wander, but they will soon return. The story may interest, the characters may amuse, the incidents may vary, but from this moment the presence of Hamlet will dwarf all else in the tragedy. How is he dressed, and how does he look ? No imitation of the portrait of Sir Thomas Lawrence, no funereal velvet, no elaborate trappings, no Order of the Danish Elephant, no flaxen wig after the model of M. Fechter, no bugles, no stilted conventionality. We see before us a man and a prince, in thick robed silk and a jacket, or paletot, edged with fur ; a tall, imposing figure, so well dressed that nothing distracts the eye from the wonderful face ; a costume rich and simple, and relieved alone by a heavy chain of gold ; but, above and beyond all, a troubled, wearied face displaying the first effects of moral poison.

The black disordered hair is carelessly tossed about the forehead, but the fixed and rapt attention of the whole house is directed to the eyes of Hamlet : the eyes which denote the trouble—which tell of the distracted mind. Here are " the windy suspiration of forced breath," " the fruitful river in the eye," the " dejected 'haviour of the visage." So subtle is the actor's art, so intense is his application, and so daring his disregard of conventionality, that the first act ends with comparative disappointment. Those who have seen other Hamlets are aghast. Mr. Irving is missing his point, he is neglecting his opportunities. Betterton's face turned as white as his neckcloth, when he saw the Ghost. Garrick thrilled the house when he followed the spirit. Some cannot hear Mr. Irving, others find him indistinct. Many declare roundly he cannot read Shakespeare. There are others who generously observe that Hamlets are not judged by the first act ; but over all, disputants or enthusiasts, has already been thrown an indescribable spell. None can explain it ; but all are now spell-bound. The Hamlet is " thinking aloud," as Hazlitt wished. He is as much of the gentleman and scholar as possible, and " as little of the actor."

We in the audience see the mind of Hamlet. We care little what he does, how he walks, when he draws his sword. We can almost realise the workings of his brain. His soliloquies are not spoken down at the foot-lights to the audience. Hamlet is looking into a glass, into " his mind's eye, Horatio ! " His eyes are fixed apparently on nothing, though ever eloquent. He gazes on vacancy and communes with his conscience. Those only who have closely watched Hamlet through the first act could adequately express the impression made. But it has affected the whole audience—the Kemble lovers, the Kean admirers, and the Fechter rhapsodists. They do not know how it is, but they are spell-bound with the incomparable expression of moral poison.

The second act ends with nearly the same result. There is not an actor living who on attempting Hamlet has not made his points in the speech, " Oh ! what a rogue and peasant slave am I ! " But Mr. Irving's intention is not to make points, but to give a consistent reading of a Hamlet who " thinks aloud." For one instant he falls " a-cursing like a very drab, a scullion " ; but only to relapse into a deeper despair, into more profound thought. He is not acting, he is not splitting the ears of the groundlings ; he is an artist concealing his art ; he is talking to himself ; he is thinking aloud. Hamlet is suffering from moral poison, and the spell woven about the audience is more mysterious and incomprehensible in the second act than the first.

In the third act the artist triumphs. No more doubt, no more hesitation, no more discussion. If Hamlet is to be played like a scholar and a gentleman, and not like an actor, this is the Hamlet. The scene with Ophelia turns the scale, and the success is from this instant complete. But we must insist that it was not the triumph of an actor alone ; it was the realisation of all that the artist has been foreshadowing. Mr. Irving made no sudden and striking effect, as did Mr. Kean.

" Whatever nice faults might be found on this score," says Hazlitt, " they are amply redeemed by the manner of his coming back after he has gone to the extremity of the stage, from a pang of parting tenderness to press his lips to Ophelia's hand. It had an electrical effect on the house." Mr. Irving did not make his success by any theatrical *coup*, but by the expression of the pent-up agony of a harassed and disappointed man. According to Mr. Irving, the very sight of Ophelia is the keynote of the outburst of his moral disturbance. He loves this woman ; " forty thousand brothers " could not express his overwhelming passion, and think what might have happened if he had been allowed to love her, if his ambition had been realised. The more he looks at Ophelia, the more he curses the irony of fate. He is surrounded, overwhelmed, and crushed by trouble, annoyance, and spies.

They are watching him behind the arras. Ophelia is set on to assist their plot. They are driving him mad, though he is only feigning madness. What a position for a harassed creature to endure ! They are all against him. Hamlet alone in the world is born to " set it right." He is in the height and delirium of moral anguish. The distraction of the unhinged mind, swinging and banging about like a door ; the infinite love and tenderness of the man who longs to be soft and gentle to the woman he adores : the horror and hatred of being trapped, and watched, and spied upon were all expressed with consummate art. Every voice cheered, and the points Mr. Irving had lost as an actor were amply atoned for by his earnestness as an artist. Fortified with this genuine and heart-stirring applause, he rose to the occasion. He had been understood at last. To have broken down here would have been disheartening ; but he had triumphed.

The speech to the players was Mr. Irving's second success. He did not sit down and lecture. There was no affectation or princely priggishness in the scene at all. He did not give his ideas of art as a prince to an actor, but as an artist to an artist. Mr. Irving, to put it colloquially, buttonholed the First Player. He spoke to him confidentially, as one man to another. He stood up and took the actor into his confidence, with a half deferential smile, as much as to say, " I do not attempt to dictate to an artist, but still these are my views on art." But with all this there was a princely air, a kindly courtesy, and an exquisite expression of refinement which astonished the house as much from its daring as its truth. Mr. Irving was gaining ground with marvellous rapidity. His exquisite expression of friendship for Horatio was no less beautiful than his stifled passion for Ophelia. For the one he was the pure and constant friend, for the other the baffled lover.

Determined not to be conquered by his predecessors, he made a signal success in the play scene. He acted it with an impulsive energy beyond all praise. Point after point was made in a whirlwind of excitement. He lured, he tempted, he trapped the King, he drove out his wicked uncle conscience-stricken and baffled and with an hysterical yell of triumph he sank down, " the expectancy and rose of the fair state," in the very throne which ought to have been his, and which his rival had just vacated. It is difficult to describe the excitement occasioned by the acting in this scene. When the King had been frighted, the stage was cleared instantaneously. No one in the house knew how the people got off. All eyes were fixed on Hamlet and the King ; all were forgetting the real play and the mock play, following up every move of the antagonists, and from constant watching they were almost as exhausted as Hamlet was when he sank a conqueror into the neglected throne.

It was all over now. Hamlet had won. He would take the ghost's word for a thousand pounds. The clouds cleared from his brow. He was no longer in doubt or despair. He was the victor after this mental struggle. The effects of the moral poison had passed away, and he attacked Rosencrantz and Guildenstern in the Recorder scene with a sarcasm and a withering scorn which were among the results of a reaction after pent-up agony. But this tremendous act was even now not yet over. There was the closet-scene still to come—a scene which still further illustrates the daring defiance of theatrical tradition exhibited by Mr. Irving. If the Hamlet was to be a mental study it should be one to the last. The actor who could conquer prejudices so far, was bound to continue, and when the audience looked at the arras for the pictures, or round the necks of the actor and actress for the counterfeit presentment of two brothers, they found nothing.

Mr. Irving intended to conjure up the features of the dead King by a mental struggle, not by any practical or painted assistance. Speaking of David Garrick, Mr. Percy Fitzgerald says, " it was a pity he did not break through the stale old tradition of Hamlet's pulling out the two miniatures instead of the finer notion suggested by Davies of having them on the tapestry—*or the better idea still of seeing them with his mind's eye only.*"

It is this idea which Mr. Irving adopts, and with so striking a success that the audience could scarcely believe that they had for so many years been misled. It is unquestionably the correct view to take, and it can be done with the best possible effect. An act which was such an intellectual strain as this for both actor and audience could not fail to be felt. It was exhausting, overpowering. The play ought to have ended here. It was too much for one night.

The nervousness and paralysing excitement occasioned by such an evening made its mark on the actors. It was too great an effort. The fear of being shut out from a glass of beer before midnight frightened the audience, and there were a few minutes of doubt and anxiety. But art conquered, and the audience obeyed. Miss Isabel Bateman came on to play the mad scene of Ophelia, at the very moment when the house was longing for reaction, and was hungry to be free. She conquered at the most important instant of the evening, and she crushed down cruel scoffs by her true artistic impulse. It was a great sight to see the young lady—a true artist—sitting down, playing with the flowers, and acting the most difficult scene that was ever written, at a moment when it required the greatest discipline to keep peace. But Miss Bateman conquered, with the rest of the artists, mainly owing to the admirable taste and assistance of an audience loyal to, and appreciative of, art. Not all the heresies of Garrick, nor the sarcasms of Voltaire, would permit Mr. Bateman to remove, either the King's praying scene, or the churchyard ceremonies. Poor Mr. Swinbourne went through the first to a chorus of hammering and shouting from behind ; and Mr. Compton, as the

First gravedigger, had not time to remove his ten waistcoats. Still the audience, true to its purpose, never ventured to interfere. The strain upon the nervous system of Mr. Irving upon so important an occasion, the growing lateness of the hour, and the wealth of beauty in the play, prevented the success which will yet be obtained by Ophelia's mad scene, by Mr. Compton's acting of the Clown, or Gravedigger, and by Hamlet's churchyard passion. But let it not for a moment be supposed that Hamlet ended in an anti-climax. A fencing scene between Hamlet and Laertes, which would have rejoiced the heart of M. Angelo, and which will, owing to the practice and industry of both Mr. Irving and Mr. Leathes, make us forget the tradition of Charles Kean and Alfred Wigan in *The Corsican Brothers* ; to say nothing of the murder of the King by Hamlet, which, as regards impulse, determination, and effect, has never been equalled, put the final touches to this overwhelming work.

It may be that the intellectual manager will yet have to see how far *Hamlet* can be curtailed to suit this luxurious and selfish age. There are not many audiences which will relinquish their beer for the sake of art. This was a very special occasion. But the supreme moment for the audience had come when the curtain fell. If they had sacrificed their refreshment, waiting there, as many of them had done, since three o'clock in the afternoon, they had done something for art. They had, at least, deserved the pleasure of cheering the artist who had inspired them. It was no *succès d'estime*. The actor of the evening had, in the teeth of tradition, in the most unselfish manner, and in the most highly artistic fashion, convinced his hearers that William Hazlitt, the critic, was right. Here was the Hamlet who *thinks aloud* ; here was the scholar, and so little of the actor. So they threw crowns, and wreaths, and bouquets, at the artist, and the good people felt that this artistic assistance had come at a turning point in the history of English dramatic art. "A pensive air of sadness should sit reluctantly on his brow, but no appearance of fixed and sullen gloom. He is full of weakness and melancholy ; but there is no harshness in his nature. He is the most amiable of misanthropes." So wrote William Hazlitt of Hamlet. It might have been written to-day of Henry Irving. "I have acted Ophelia three times with my father ; and each time, in that beautiful scene where his madness and his love gush forth together, like a torrent swollen with storms, that bears a thousand blossoms on its troubled waters, I have experienced such deep emotion, as hardly to be able to speak. The letter and jewel cases I was tendering him, were wet with tears." So wrote Fanny Kemble of her father, Charles Kemble. The words might have been spoken of Henry Irving, whose scene with Ophelia will never be forgotten. This is not a critical essay on the distinguished merit of a most valuable performance, but a necessarily brief comment on the impressions registered by a remarkable evening at the play. Time will not allow one to linger as one might on the distinguished and loyal assistance of such artists and favourite actors as Mr. Thomas Mead, Mr. Chippendale, Mr. Swinbourne, and Miss Pauncefort. The effect of Mr. Mead's splendid elocution, and of Miss Pauncefort's facial agony cannot be overrated. It would be highly pleasant also to congratulate such genuine young enthusiasts of another and more modern school, as Mr. George Neville, Mr. Leathes, Mr. Beveridge, and Miss Isabel Bateman. But our efforts, without prejudice, have been devoted to the actor who will be valued by his fellows, and to a performance which will make its mark in the dramatic history of our time. The position of Mr. Irving, occasionally wavering and pleasantly hesitating in the balance, has now been firmly established. The Hamlet of Henry Irving is a noble contribution to dramatic art.

—*From " The Bells " to " King Arthur."* By Clement Scott, 1896.

CLEMENT SCOTT ON IRVING'S LOUIS XI

Lyceum Theatre. 9 *Mar.*, 1878.

THOSE who would stimulate the mind and sharpen the dramatic appetite with the anxious, clear-cut, and, in many respects, noble art-study that has happily resulted in the Louis XI of Mr. Henry Irving, may be earnestly recommended to judge the centre figure apart from its surrounding framework. A sensitive and fastidious age like ours, with its nervous horror of prolonged death-scenes on the stage, its hatred of intense expression, its shuddering opposition to that exquisitely fine realism at which the artist's ambition strains, its hunger for variety, and its distrust of concentration, in turning its back upon the kind of play an actor must use in order to exercise his highest gifts, virtually raises an opposition to the spirit of tragedy. The noblest expression of an actor's art can no more be confined in the limits of comedy, drama, or melodrama, than can a thoroughbred horse develop his powers in a court-yard or a paddock.

When an actor departs from the stereotyped lines of dramatic effect, and grapples boldly with psychological problems, he must remove his kid gloves, and put on his armour. He must pour out the sorrows of his heart as Lear, show the dauntless courage of Macbeth, express the absorbing passion of Othello, fight to the grim death as Richard, and fall like Julius Caesar, if he would concentrate the attention of his audience, not merely on a passing scene, an ingenious situation, or a theat-rical surprise, but on the conflicting passions of a great character. It is deliberately unfair to the actor to charge his account with the form of art in which psychological studies must be expressed on the stage. When people go to the play, and, after watching a masterly exposition of the varied passions of one of the giants of the world's history, delicate in its subtlety, sensitive in its irony, studied to the very finger nails ; when they see, in the space of a couple of hours, the con-centrated essence of a tremendous life-time, and then complain that Louis XI is a terribly long time dying, that the realism of death-throes is very painful, that they " don't like to have their feelings harrowed up," that they " don't go to the play to be made miserable," and so on, they merely mean that tragic expression has no interest for them, and they imply that, if they had their way, the art of acting should be deprived of its highest and most intense aim. The study of a character such as Louis XI, is surely not complete without elaborate detail, and the tragedian who would embody such a character must be judged by the quality of the task he undertakes.

No one pretends to put this play of *Louis XI* on a very am-bitious pedestal of literary exercise. Mr. Boucicault, under-standing the temper of his audience, has carefully relieved the

classical severity of Casimir Delavigne's work. He has turned
its course occasionally towards the lighter paths of the drama,
has given it scientific opportunities and chances for theatrical
effect ; and, though the actors in it are little assisted by
rhetorical flowers, dignity of language, and nobility of poetical
expression, still, at any rate, there is a very fair and suitable
frame-work for a character that might have been selected for
treatment by Shakespeare or Racine. It is the character of
Louis XI with which we have simply to deal. The immediate
predecessor of Richard the Third in history is as absorbing a
stage study. The very same year that the usurping King of
England was murdering young Edward V, and his brother,
in the Tower, the medical attendants of the dying King of
France, and murderer of Nemours, were pouring the warm
blood of infants into his exhausted veins. There were giants
in those fifteenth-century days, albeit they were wicked giants ;
and object to mere matters of detail as we will, no one can
follow the play of *Louis XI* without having the attraction
rivetted on the picturesque monster.

The actor triumphs when the force of his art obliterates the
surroundings of the scene. Mr. Boucicault has done what he
could to suit the French play to an English audience. Save
for a feeble and pointless first act, serving no purpose as a
prologue or introduction, the scenes as they stand give fair
opportunity for showing the cruelty in life and the agony in
death of the terrible King of France. We see him crafty in
trick, fawning in abasement, hypocritical in religion, and
terrified in his death agony. The author of the passing scenes
is assisted by decorative and scenic art. The richness of costume, the care of archæology, the beauty of scenery, the
sounds of soft music, the wail of the distant hymn, the pomp
of the religious ceremony—all serve their legitimate purpose.
But from the moment that the usher in the doorway calls aloud
" The King," scenery, crowds, tapestry, armour, drawbridge,
and portcullis, monkish chant, and rustic dance all go to the
background, and the actor is the prominent figure. This is as
it should be, and it is in this fact that the latest triumph of Mr.
Irving as a student and an artist is contained. There may be
differences of opinion, and justly so, upon this or that matter of

detail. Comparisons will be made with that lost and valued actor, who did so much for the English stage, and first centered our absorbed interest in this remarkable effort. There may be complaints of the actor's manner in minor and insignificant matters ; but such a study as this should be treated in a broad, manly, and comprehensive spirit, and it is not too much to say —and we say it without hesitation—that Charles Kean, were he alive, would, with that liberal and art-loving spirit that distinguished him, be the last man to grudge Mr. Irving his legitimate success, or to refuse him the genuine praise that must follow so comprehensive and so powerful a performance.

Nay, we go further, and draw, from the genuine and generous conduct of Mrs. Charles Kean in the matter of this revival, the inevitable conclusion that our lost actor would cordially have rejoiced to find that the traditions and dignity of the stage were upheld in so true and so laudable a spirit.

Let us return, then, to that moment when King Louis XI comes upon the scene, for from that instant every eye is firmly fixed upon the centre figure, and seldom after that the attention wanders from Mr. Irving. Pages of dialogue could not so well express the meaning of the man as does the actor's appearance. His thin, drawn, cruel face, his curious crafty eye, his uncertain voice, broken, petulant, and shrill, his restless manner, give the first idea of the character.

Mark, also, how a certain invincible determination tries to conquer the palpable signs of age. This is not a mere trick of limping, it is the very feebleness of senility. The thin shanks are old, the feet are old, the tread upon the floor is age itself. Throughout this long scene, containing the defiant threats of Charles the Bold, the actor's manner, voice, bearing, and attitude, change a dozen times. He never seems to be acting. The art is concealed. Touches of irritable passion are succeeded by quick, sharp strokes of irony, and comedy shows her face again and again. Before the King has been seen for ten minutes, all seem instinctively to understand his disposition. The cruelty is in the eye, the irresolution in his manner. He will bully one minute, and cringe another. He dares and threatens until grappled with, and then whines for pardon. He cheats his conscience, and endeavours to hide his cowardice with subterfuge—his tyranny with religion. He scratches nervously at his lower jaw when craftily considering how far he can go, and hypocritically pats the head of the Dauphin, of whose youth and popularity he is profoundly jealous. Amidst such remarkable detail, it is impossible to dwell long on much of the light and shade that so well illustrate the character ; but we may point to the attitude of the King when taking his throne and awaiting the deputation as a remarkable illustration of Mr. Irving's finished art.

Once more the idea of extreme age and feebleness is expressed in the relief of sitting. The figure falls limp into the throne. The jaw drops, a wearied expression comes over the features, and, without a word uttered, there is conveyed the depression attending formal ceremony. This is but one instance of many showing the sharp incision of the study, and it may be affirmed, without hesitation, that the first act in which the King appears is the most remarkable illustration Mr. Irving has given of his command of detail and absolute identification with the character assumed. Here, at any rate, old mannerisms disappear ; not that any actor has ever lived without mannerisms, but, down to this point, there is nothing to identify the actor with his part. It may seem ungracious to point out one instance of what looked like mistaken emphasis, or rather, over-accentuation, in such a remarkable scene ; but the keen interest it created must plead as an excuse.

The sudden breaking off from the suggestion of Nemours to the attitude of prayer at the sound of the " Angelus " was, perhaps, too marked an exhibition of outward hypocrisy. At this point, the mere mechanical movement of the lips, and assumed devotional spirit, would be sufficient without emphasis. The hypocrisy is conveyed in the attitude, and does not require accentuation. Without wishing to indulge in any comparison, we may remark that it was here that Charles Kean made his most marked effect. He did not mutter the prayer, as much as to say to the audience, " Don't you see I am praying ?—and how ridiculous is prayer at this moment ! "—the sudden change of manner conveyed all that was requisite. At this particular moment, and again in the prayer to the Virgin at the *prie-dieu*, there was just a suspicion of trying to do too much—a slight mistake in art which was proved by the laughter momentarily provoked—and there would be no justification for lingering on these slight matters were not the whole performance so instinct with truth and care. If the attention were not so completely rivetted that it followed every turn and twist of the actor's meaning, there would be less excuse for suggesting an alteration as simple as this. The second act of the play is one that most vividly sets forth the King's character, and is as such in many respects the most interesting ; but it should not necessarily detract from the more powerful situation gradually working up to the climax of the King's death.

The third act contains the well-known pilgrimage of the King to the Saint's shrine in the forest glade, and here the audience enjoys a moment's interlude of comedy relief. Excellently assisted by Mrs. Chippendale, as the rustic Martha, who, with a woman's tact, sees through the grim superstition of the tottering monarch, and promises him a hope of revived love and a dream of life for a hundred years, and gaining the support of Mr. Edmund Lyons, a quick judge of marked character, who plays the booby peasant doomed to say the wrong thing at awkward moments, Mr. Irving entered thoroughly and earnestly into the lighter scenes of the play. Showering the gold upon the heads of the rustic dancers, and sardonically grinning over a welcome conquest and a visionary promise of long life, the old King, still showing the possession of a tiger's power, gradually approaches the realms of a deeper tragedy.

Comedy by quiet and modulated steps is left behind with the scene where the monarch, with cat-like softness and studied deception, extracts from Marie the secret of her love for Nemours, and the fact of his presence in their midst. From that second the passion of the situation increases, and we gradually approach that moment when the Duke de Nemours, hidden by his father's friend behind the arras of the King's chamber, surprises his grim old enemy at his orisons, threatens him in the silence of the chamber, extracts from him a craven humiliation, and gives him, as a supreme revenge, his life.

In all this scene Mr. Irving had what is known as uphill work. Owing to a certain coarseness of treatment, and a rough, ill-disciplined form of elocution on the part of Mr. F. Tyars, who played Nemours, the scene certainly lacked harmony, and wanted finish. In a dramatic sense it is the finest moment of the play, but Mr. Irving struggled with the greatest difficulty against unsympathetic aid, and succeeded only by the most determined resolution. Sympathetic treatment was here essential. The better Nemours acted, the more terrible would have been the abject terror of the King. But, as it was, the want of appreciation shown by Mr. Tyars, his lack of heart, and his failure in delicate treatment, told seriously against the prostrate King, whose efforts had already been severely taxed. Away from Nemours, the King had been acting admirably. There was no want of unison in the scene of the confession, for the Confessor, François de Paule, was played by Mr. T. Mead with rugged earnestness and sound effect. There was no failure in colour when relieved from the presence of Nemours. The half-maddened King summoned his attendants, and in an agony of fear, despatched his guard after the retreating assassin. Far finer than the best scenes of his Richelieu, Mr. Irving here abandoned himself to the tempest of the situation, and the curtain fell upon applause, spontaneous, hearty and well-deserved.

The death-scene remained as the fitting conclusion to the history of this melancholy life, and whatever objections may be taken to death realism in the abstract, the passing hours of this bad great man, as illustrated on the stage, are eloquent with truth and vividly impressive as a clever study. The conscientious objections of such people as protest against the dark shadows of the valley of death being illustrated by art, deserve a certain respect ; and if it be granted that tragedy, the tragedy of such a life as that of Louis XI, is not to be robbed of its orthodox conclusion, then surely art more delicate has seldom been bestowed upon a painful subject. The death of Louis XI on the stage is no more reprehensive than the death of a hundred other heroes of tragedy ; and those who, distrusting tragedy, take this as an illustration, incur a grave responsibility. If the lives of all stage heroes are to pass away without pain, then the limits of art are circumscribed. Mr. Henry Irving had no such scruples. He attacked his task boldly, and he succeeded in being impressive without attempting to be morbid. He had to illustrate a double death—a death of weakness, and a death of reality. He had to describe a death-like want of animation, an interval of sleep, and the last grand struggle. Such a study cannot be too elaborate for those who believe in the power of art. So long as it was not shocking, it was within the bounds of art. A complete change had come over Louis XI when he tottered into the throne room to die. They had clothed him in his robes of regal office, given him crown and sceptre, and flattered his last moments with pomp and insignia.

He was a splendid mockery in the hour of death, a hideous example of the vanity of man's power. Clothe him as they would in crown and velvet, the inevitable must, in the end, prevail. These were the thoughts suggested by the acting of Mr. Irving. He was a melancholy wreck, a decorated effigy. There was something grand even in this dogged determination not to die ; but, fight as he would, King or not, it was death that gained the victory. The quick, horrible spasms, the pause of relief after them, the colourless eye, the twitching of the fingers, the nervous plucking of the regal robe, all told of the ghastly inevitable. A final spasm, and then came a torpor. To all beholders, the King was dead. The doctor felt his pulse and then his heart. The Dauphin, in the silence of the death-chamber, took his father's wasted hand. It fell inanimate. But then came the last spasm, the spasm of returning life, and, as the Dauphin placed upon his boyish brow the crown he was to wear, he felt upon his shoulders the clutch of the dead King's fingers. He lived for that moment of reproach. He lived to repent and forgive his enemies and when, with bated breath, the old formula was uttered, " Le roi est mort, vive le roi," all was silence and all was peace.

The stage management of the last scene was without reproach. This is an art too little recognised. Good at other points, the arrangement of the final passage was distinguished for its dignity, its impressive character, and its intense solemnity. The situation gathered strength as it went on. The revival of the King, and his check of the Dauphin's impetuosity, were excellent enough ; but from the moment that Marie summoned the courtiers to the fall of the curtain, there was not an instant where levity was possible.

And this is the secret of earnest stage work. So impressive, indeed, was the solemnity of the death-scene, that for some time the audience, demonstrative to a fault hitherto, refused to cheer, and it was only with this effort of reaction that Mr. Irving was called again and again before the curtain to thank those who so cordially thanked him, and to say many grateful words concerning the goodwill and encouragement of Mrs. Charles Kean. In discussing a success of this kind, it is impossible to dwell with proper force upon the minor assistance that helped to swell the actor's triumph.

There were certain blots on the general performance, no doubt, but such essential characters as the Dauphin and Oliver were sustained with earnest intelligence by Mr. Andrews and Mr. Archer. The female interest is weak enough, and Miss Virginia Francis did what she could with Marie ; but the best of the unrecognised aids, apart from the general tone of the stage arrangements, were the distant musical strains, no doubt perfected by Mr. Robert Stoepel. That far-off hymn to Heaven for the King's life, as he sat warming himself by the massive grate, is one of those suggestive and excellent effects which are so thorough, that they are not readily forgotten. Such touches as these give a gleam of poetry to scenes which seem to pass away, but, in reality, linger affectionately in the memory. They do so because they are true, and because it is true that the Louis XI of Mr. Henry Irving will be recognised as his most complete and scholarly study.

—*From " The Bells " to " King Arthur."*

CLEMENT SCOTT ON ELLEN TERRY'S NEW OLIVIA

Lyceum Theatre, 28 May 1885.

FOR seven years the Olivia of Miss Ellen Terry has been laid up in lavender, and the picture of a loving and lovable woman, with all her waywardness, trust, disappointment and anguish, is presented to us with an added sweetness and a deepening colour. The artist evidently has not put this admirable study of a true woman wholly out of her mind. She has not played the part for a long time on the stage, but she must often have thought of it. New ideas, fresh suggestions, innumerable delicate touches, never lost on the observant spectator, have been brought to bear on the new Olivia, who stands out as one of the most striking personalities—as fine in perspective as in outline, as tender in thought as it is in sentiment—that the modern stage has seen. In the first act of the play, Miss Ellen Terry has little more to do than strike the key-note of the poem. She has to show how Olivia is the fairest of the old Vicar's flock, the loveliest and most winsome of his many children, the loved companion of her brothers and sisters, her father's idol.

Dr. Primrose has a generous and loving heart. He mounts the youngsters on his knee or lifts them on his shoulder to look across the lovely country towards the lights of cruel London ; for his good wife he has a deep affection, consecrated by long years of trial ; he is beloved by his neighbours, cheerful to all those around him, but in Olivia, the favourite child, his whole heart is centered. " She came between me and my love for God, and I am punished for it at last," says the Vicar in his supreme anguish at the loss of her, so it became necessary to show, at the outset, the truth and depth of the affection that is to be so cruelly shattered. Thus Olivia becomes the sunshine of her father's house. When the villagers assemble to congratulate him on his silver wedding and to sing a carol under the Vicarage windows, when old Farmer Flamborough ventures to call and grumble at the fine airs of the Vicar's lady, it is Olivia with her sunny face and winning manner who seems to avert the storm arising on the domestic horizon.

But for all that, simple parson's daughter as she is, inexperienced in the world and its ways, she already shows how strong and absolute is the affectionate nature that is in her. She loves the young squire, not because he has a fine coat and winning manners, not because he is above her in social station, but because her nature leans towards some one who appears stronger in character and less dependent on love than herself. Squire Thornhill's very indifference fascinates her.

Olivia pretends to pet and pout when her Edward talks of

the fine ladies in London, she makes believe that she will dismiss her lord if he treats her so carelessly as he sometimes does ; but we who watch know full well that she would never let her lover stray far from her side, and would beckon him back, did he retreat only so far as the Vicarage hedge. It is this loving, this trusting nature, the depth of this heart, the mine of this woman's love as yet unexplored, that the old Vicar alone understands so well. Olivia's mother is occasionally inclined to resent her husband's determination to spoil the girl ; there is an occasional sneer upon her lips as the old clergyman makes his Livy his comforter and his friend.

But so it is. When the clouds of trouble gather on the old man's brow, when despair is settling down on the house, it is to Olivia that her father looks for help—not to his wife. In that still evening hour when the white-haired man gathers his family around him in the dying daylight, to learn what trouble has befallen him, it is Olivia who is at his knees kissing his hands, and looking up into his dear tear-stained eyes. We come to the second scene. Love, the master, has worked havoc in Olivia's heart. Gradually, but very delicately, Miss Terry shows how her father is forgotten for the sake of her lover. She hates Burchell because he dares to doubt the man she loves. She defends her Thornhill with a woman's desperation and a woman's unreason. He may have deceived other women, but he loves me ! That is her argument, and it is urged with brilliant petulance.

The second scene with Thornhill brings out some very subtle suggestions. It is as excellently played by Mr. Terriss as by Miss Terry. Both are goaded by destiny. For a moment she would hold back, and so would he. She cannot forget her father, nor he his honour. The man is not wholly reckless yet. There is a pause, but it is momentary. Selfishness prevails ; the strong man conquers, not the weak, but the loving woman ; and once she has given her promise, we know that she will not turn back. No father, no family, no religion, no remembrances can step between her and her determined spirit.

Then comes that exquisite scene when, at the twilight hour, Olivia distributes her little presents to the loved ones before she steals away from home to join the lover of her future life. The deep choking tones of Miss Terry's voice, her fine power of absolutely identifying herself with the situation, the real tears that course down her cheeks, the struggle to repress as much as to express, make this one of the most pathetic moments that modern art has illuminated and intensified.

It is powerful, but not morbid; it is terrible in its despair, but so true that the very grief it causes is satisfying and pleasant. Our deepest sympathies are aroused, our better feelings are stimulated. And so, when the Vicar is dreaming over the fire, when the mother is at her homely work and the rest are singing at the old harpsichord, Olivia steals from home, and her pale face is seen at the latticed window, kissing her farewell to the home she is to leave for ever.

It is, however, in the third act that Miss Terry's acting has most visibly improved. She has here emphasised the contrast between the happy married woman and the heart-broken, despairing dupe. The actress begins the scene with an excess of gaiety. If Thornhill's love has grown more cold, hers has gained in force and impetuosity. Her object now is to retain her lover by her side. Her short life with him has intensified her affection. She coquettes with him, she hangs close to his neck, she laughs, and is merry. At the thought of home and Christmas-time she becomes a child again. She kisses the leaves they have brought to her from the hedge at home, and ties them round her neck as if they were the most precious posy in the world. There is no joy like hers, no heart so light, no life so full of promise.

Suddenly, and without warning, comes the storm which is to wreck her life. Her lover tells her that he has deceived her. She is not his wife. The announcement at first stuns her. She cannot believe or understand. She beats her brains to get at the truth. The realisation of her situation is awful. Father, mother, home, friends, contempt, humiliation, crowd before her eyes like ghastly spectres; the love has suddenly changed to savage hate, and as Thornhill advances to comfort her she strikes him on the breast, and in that one word "Devil!" is summed up the unspeakable horror that afflicts her soul. But as yet the act is not nearly over. The most beautiful passages of it have yet to come, when her father returns to rescue the lamb that is on the road. Never before to our recollection on the stage has woman's grief been depicted with such infinite truth. Olivia has been beaten and so sorely bruised ; but in her father's arms she is safe.

The sobs that wring her heart are the true cure. In her old father's presence she is a child again. No mother in the world could give her greater comfort. She feels she is forgiven and at rest. She has passed through the purgatory trial and gained the paradise of love. Here, as far as art is concerned, the study, complex and beautiful as it is, must necessarily stop. For the purpose of the play Thornhill must be forgiven, and presumably Olivia must be reconciled to him, but we cannot bring our minds to believe that the reconciliation would be so sudden or the forgiveness so swift as this. We leave Olivia confronted with her father, and that is enough. The poem is complete at that point, and we want no more.

We cannot doubt that this study from the life will attract as much, if not more, attention than it did seven years ago. Such acting as is contained in the Olivia of Ellen Terry, as fine in conception as it is impressive in effect, is seen very rarely on the stage of any country.

Unquestionably also the play is made doubly interesting by the reading of the Vicar given by Mr. Henry Irving, a performance more carefully restrained and modulated, a study more innocent of trick and less disfigured by characteristics of marked style and individuality than anything he has attempted before. At the outset, it was feared that he had too quickly been fascinated by the sentiment of the story, that he drifted into pathos too suddenly, that he started the tears too soon, and did not call direct attention to the happy Vicar as he lived amongst his family and friends before the dark clouds settled on his household.

But this idea soon vanished, when it was seen how the actor, by many a subtle and suggested idea, had penetrated into the mind and nature of the venerable clergyman. It was his love for Olivia marked with so many happy touches, it was the desire to emphasise the fact that his whole life was bound up in this child, that gave so much interest to the first act, and lent such special importance to the subsequent scenes of affection which were evolved from it.

Mr. Irving's Vicar is a dignified, resigned, and most pathetic figure, who lingers on the mind long after the theatre is quitted. The scene of the announcement of Olivia's departure was as finely acted as it was boldly conceived. The grief that unnerves, distracts and unmans ; the sorrow that paralyses, were expressed with absolute truth and surprising force, and quite as admirable was the melting from almost ungovernable rage to the comparative calm of resignation. " Did I curse him ? " murmurs the old man, half-dazed and in a dream, and so in time his religion and his duty help the white-haired minister to bear the blow. " She came between me and my love for God ; I am punished for it at last." This is the one strong point on which Mr. Irving evidently leans. It is the resignation to the Divine will, shown all through, that gives such beauty and interest to Mr. Irving's fine study of paternal affection.

But, perhaps, the best idea that came into the actor's mind, and in effect the finest moment of his acting was in the scene where the Vicar comes to rescue his daughter. For a moment, troubled and travel-stained as he is, he breaks away from her, and remembers that he has a duty to perform. He loves the child surpassingly well, but he is her father, and she has erred. He has to summon up all his courage for a homily on her lost sense of duty. He nerves himself for what he conceives to be necessary, and begins, with tears starting in his eyes, to tell Olivia of her grievous fault. But the old man breaks down over the effort of forced calm ; the strain is too much for him ; all at once he melts, he casts aside the manner of the priest, and calling Olivia to his arms, becomes her loving father once more. The effect of this was instantaneous. The house was astonished and delighted. As regards acting, it was a moment of true inspiration, a masterpiece of invention.

The Squire Thornhill of Mr. William Terriss, excellent as it was seven years ago, has improved relatively as much as the Olivia of Miss Ellen Terry. The careless love of this young coxcomb, his innate vanity, his implied power over women, his charming and yet impudent air, gave to the young rake the very colour that was requisite. And we saw, notwithstanding all his villainy, that Thornhill had the making in him of a better man. This was most cleverly shown in the sulky horror with which Thornhill confesses his sin to Olivia, and the fierce reaction of rage with which he turns upon Burchell.

—From " The Bells " to " King Arthur."

W. T. ARNOLD

(1852–1904)

SARAH BERNHARDT AS PHÈDRE

THE audience which greeted Mme. Bernhardt in *Phèdre*
last night was probably not so numerous as that which
witnessed *Frou-Frou*, but it was an audience worth playing to.
It was only the *public d'élite* that could be expected to be very
anxious to witness a French classical tragedy, and from a
business point of view *Phèdre* will no doubt always be the least
successful of Mme. Bernhardt's performances. There is, to
speak frankly, an ineradicable prejudice against Corneille
and Racine in the minds of most Englishmen. There was once
an equally ineradicable prejudice entertained by Frenchmen
against Shakspere. But that day is past ; with educated
Frenchmen Shakspere is as much an article of faith as with
ourselves. The victory won by Shakspere has not, however,
been won by Corneille and Racine, and the English judgment
of them is often as *saugrenu* as was the current French opinion
of Milton or Shakspere a century ago. It is an honourable
mission for Mme. Bernhardt to make French tragedy better
known and better appreciated out of France, and her reputation
would suffer if she were to neglect a part in which she shows
so much new and surprising power as in that of *Phèdre*.
Manchester playgoers would hardly have seen all the capacities
of the actress if they had not seen her in the part which occupies
on the French stage the sort of position that the part of Lady
Macbeth does on our own. There was a fair sprinkling of men
in the house who had seen Rachel, and they of course would not
have been content without witnessing her successor in Rachel's
greatest part. The reception awarded to Mme. Bernhardt was
the best proof of her success. After the second act in particular
the applause was as enthusiastic as it was well deserved.

There is an interesting passage on Racine in a recent essay of Mr. Matthew Arnold. The passage illustrates, by the way, the supreme charm which Racine's verse possesses for French readers and listeners, and is worth quoting if only on that account :—" If Molière cannot make us insensible to the inherent defects of French dramatic poetry, still less can Corneille and Racine. Corneille has energy and nobility, Racine an often Virgilian sweetness and pathos. But while Molière in depth, penetrativeness, and powerful criticism of life, belongs to the same family as Sophocles and Shakspere, Corneille and Racine are quite of another order. We must not be misled by the excessive estimate of them among their own countrymen. I remember an answer of M. Sainte-Beuve, who always treated me with great kindness, and to whom I ventured to say that I could not think Lamartine a poet of very high importance. 'He was important to *us*,' answered M. Sainte-Beuve. In a far higher degree can a Frenchman say of Corneille and Racine, 'They were important to *us*.' Voltaire pronounces of them : ' These men taught our nation to think, to feel, and to express itself. *Ces hommes enseignèrent à la nation à penser, à sentir et à s'exprimer.*' They were thus the instructors and formers of a society in many respects the most civilised and consummate that the world has ever seen, and which certainly is not inclined to underrate its own advantages. How natural, then, that it should feel grateful to its formers and should extol them ! ' Tell your brother Rodolphe,' writes Joseph de Maistre from Russia to his daughter at home, ' to get on with his French poets ; let him have them by heart, the inimitable Racine above all ; never mind whether he understands him or not. I did not understand him when my mother used to come and sit on my bed, and repeat from him, and put me to sleep with her beautiful voice to the sound of this incomparable music. I knew hundreds of lines of him before I could read, and that is why my ears, having drunk in this ambrosia betimes, have never been able to endure common stuff since.' " Mr. Arnold is here arguing against the French estimate of Racine, which, however, is not perhaps in the case of the present generation so unqualified as he seems to think. For English readers it is necessary to state Racine's merits rather than his faults. His marvellous gift of style is indicated by Mr. Arnold's implied comparison between him and Virgil. Untrained English ears often fail to find beauty in Racine's Alexandrines, and it is indeed true that the music of Racine is not the music of Shakspere. But it is necessary to remember that the art of reading French verse rightly by no means of necessity goes along with an ordinary conversational knowledge of the language, and no one who heard Mme. Bernhardt, or even M. Train, last night could deny the sweetness of Racine's poetry. Moreover, the great tragic force and intensity of Racine's play came clearly out. The wit of man never devised a more extraordinary *tour de force* than the French classical tragedy. To take ancient subjects wholesale and present them on a modern stage to a modern audience, then to take a metre which only the perfection of art can keep from being sing-song and monotonous, and to expect poet and actor alike to express the whole gamut of passion as easily as in our own flexible and various blank verse—this was the task imposed upon Racine. That he should move with any power in such silver fetters is a wonderful thing, that he should write a great and moving tragedy under such conditions is the triumph of mind over matter. If we remember, too, that till Lekain made the change to the Greek and Roman dress, Greeks and Romans were represented in full French Court dress, wigs and all, the wonder will not be less. Racine has, it is true, borrowed freely for his tragedy. *Phèdre* is, of course, directly founded on the *Hippolytus* of Euripides, and Seneca has been freely drawn upon ; but the play is nevertheless fairly and honestly his own, as much as *Julius Cæsar* is Shakspere's own despite of Plutarch. The characters are clearly drawn—we do not altogether agree with Professor Morley's criticism that " dramatists of Racine's school never have painted character with a firm hand in clear and distinct touches "—and in the part of Phèdre in particular an actress will do as much as human nature can do if she extracts from Racine all his thought without seeking to introduce new ideas of her own.

Rachel and Ristori, for instance, are often praised for the clearness with which they represent the passion of Phèdre as one beyond her volition, and Phèdre herself as cursed by the cruel goddess. But if an actress does not represent these things, she does not represent the character at all. Racine's intention is plain enough ; the only question is, can the actress carry it out with sufficient subtlety and power ? The intensity of passion that breathes through the play, despite all the elaborate artificiality of its form, calls for a great actress to interpret it. But it is a matter of interpretation, not of creation. Mlle. Clairon, the great actress of the last century, has some remarks on Racine's text, which show that she understood with what care and study it should be handled. The words are, perhaps, worth quoting, if only for the purpose of recalling to mind one of the most perfect passages in Mme. Bernhardt's performance last night : " Phèdre a des remords : ils sont vrais, continuels ; l'exposé du premier acte, et sa mort au cinquième, le prouvent. Sa vertu surmonterait sans doute sa passion, si cette passion n'était produite que par l'égarement ordinaire des sens et de l'imagination ; mais la malheureuse Phèdre cède, en aimant, au pouvoir de Vénus. Une force supérieure l'emporte continuellement à faire, à dire ce que continuellement aussi sa vertu réprouve. Dans toute l'étendue du rôle ce combat doit être sensible aux yeux, à l'âme du specta- teur. Je m'étais prescrit, dans tout ce qui tient aux remords, une diction simple, des accents nobles et doux, des larmes abondantes, une physionomie profondément douloureuse ; et dans tout ce qui tient à l'amour, l'espèce d'ivresse, de délire que peut offrir une somnambule, conservant dans les bras du sommeil le souvenir du feu qui la consume en veillant. Je pris cette idée dans ces vers :—

> Dieux ! que ne suis-je assise à l'ombre des forêts !
> Quand pourrai-je, au travers d'une noble poussière,
> Suivre de l'œil un char fuyant dans la carrière ?
> . . . Insensée ! Où suis-je, et qu'ai-je dit ?
> Où laissé-je égarer mes vœux et mon esprit ?
> Je l'ai perdu. Les dieux m'en ont ravi l'usage.

We do not know how Mlle. Clairon said those verses, and it is melancholy to think that a hundred years hence no one will know how Mme. Bernhardt used to say them ; but Mlle. Clairon shows the right and sensitive way of dealing with Racine's poetry, and Mme. Bernhardt last night justified her

by a reading of the verses exactly in accordance with her suggestion. Could anything have been more deliciously poetical
than that kindling eager eye, the hand slowly stretched out,
and the finger pointing into space, as Phèdre sees before her
half in a dream the chariot " fuyant dans la carrière " ? It
is pleasant thus to connect the great actress of a century ago
with her young successor in the present.

The power of Racine's play is indicated not only by the
supreme position it holds in France, where every ambitious
débutante seeks to play in it, and the actress who can best expound its chief character is by general consent hailed the chief
tragic actress of France, but by the frequency with which it has
been played even in England. The performances of Rachel
and Ristori in the part are still well remembered in this country,
and when Mme. Bernhardt first played the part in London last
year she had to compete with an exacting tradition. Of
Ristori's performance we do not need to say much. Professor
Morley praised it at the time in hyperbolical terms, but the
French, though the actress was at one time exceedingly
popular in Paris, never regarded Phèdre as one of her best
parts, and would have smiled at Professor Morley's apparent
preference of her to Rachel.

The great Phèdre has hitherto been that of Rachel. It is
useless to dilate upon Rachel's tragic power. Her performance
alike in the second and in the fourth acts is declared by all
competent critics to have been all but perfection. The
doubtful question is rather whether she was capable of rendering the tenderness and the infinite piteousness of the hapless
woman as she rendered her transports of passion. We can
conceive Rachel as having been better than Mme. Bernhardt
in the denunciation of Œnone, and, indeed, M. Sarcey, in his
notice of the performance of *Phèdre* by the Comédie Française in
London last year, intimates that she was so ; but we should like
to know how Rachel said such passages as this :

> Œnone, il peut quitter cet orgueil qui te blesse ;
> Nourri dans les forêts, il en a la rudesse.
> Hippolyte, endurci par de sauvages lois,
> Entend parler d'amour pour la première fois :
> Peut-être sa surprise a causé son silence ;
> Et nos plaintes peut-être ont trop de violence.

The inexpressible tenderness with which those lines were sighed rather than spoken was all Mme. Bernhardt's own. This line again :

> Et l'espoir malgré moi s'est glissé dans mon cœur.

And this, when she has discovered the love of Hippolyte and Aricie, and contrasts their affection with her own guilty passion :

> Tous les jours se levaient clairs et sereins pour eux.

These were the passages which Mme. Bernhardt marked with the most personal and enduring charm, and in these we cannot believe that she has not surpassed her forerunners.

A performance of *Phèdre*, however, cannot rest on a few passages of infinite charm, and it is necessary to go through the play in a little more detail. In the first act the great scene is of course the revelation made by Phèdre to Œnone. The critical words are these :

> PHÈDRE.
> Tu connais ce fils de l'Amazone,
> Ce prince si longtemps par moi-même opprimé ?
>
> ŒNONE.
> Hippolyte ! grands dieux !
>
> PHÈDRE.
> C'est toi qui l'as nommé !

In reference to this passage G. H. Lewes made the following remarks on Rachel's performance : " The one point in this scene to which I took exception was the mode of rendering the poet's meaning in this magnificent apostrophe, taken from Euripides, ' C'est toi qui l'as nommé ! ' She uttered it in a tone of sorrowing reproach which, as I conceive, is psychologically at variance with the character and the position. For Phèdre has kept her love a secret ; it is a horrible crime ; she cannot utter the name of Hippolyte because of her horror at the crime ; and not in sadness but in the sophistry of passion she tries indignantly to throw on Œnone the guilt of naming that which should be unnameable." It is interesting that Mme. Bernhardt should have played the part exactly as the critic rightly indicates it should be played. She turned with the words upon the nurse, and then shrank back in her seat, crouching together as if she were seeking to hide herself from the nurse's gaze and stifle her own thoughts. In the long speech that followed, the great line—

C'est Vénus tout entière à sa proie attachée,

was delivered with terrible passion and force. In the second act Phèdre betrays herself to Hippolyte. Phèdre is half in a dream—"somnambule," to use Mlle. Clairon's phrase. She is overpowered by the intensity of the passion that burns her, and as she speaks to Hippolyte she draws nearer with wooing sweetness of speech and outstretched arms till she suddenly recalls herself to herself and shrinks back in sudden dread and horror. And then comes the long speech in which all restraints are broken through, sixty lines which have all to be delivered in a breath, ending with the frenzied wrenching of the sword from Hippolyte :

Au défaut de mon bras prête-moi ton épée ;
Donne !

Mlle. Clairon frankly avowed that she could never deliver that speech to her satisfaction, and it must be marvellously difficult. Mme. Bernhardt's extraordinary rapidity of diction helps her much, and her fevered frenzy of manner when she clutches at the sword is probably the right manner. We wish we could have called up the spirit of Mlle. Clairon and asked her what she thought of it ! In the fourth act, the scene where Phèdre suddenly turns upon the nurse was rendered with much power, though it ended perhaps with excessive violence. It would be superfluous to praise the pathos of the dying scene. It is not contested that Mme. Bernhardt knows how to die.

The general impression left by the performance was favourable in a high degree. Mme. Bernhardt shows the possession of the *grande tenue* necessary for classic tragedy, as well as of the airy manner of light comedy in such a play as *Frou-Frou*. The simple feminine side of the character was given as well as it could be given. The highly-impassioned scenes were on the whole first-rate, but here and there in the fourth act the voice was a little forced, and the manner lost a little in dignity. On the whole we are doubtful of the Comédie Française finding a successor to Mme. Bernhardt all in a moment.

Madame Devoyod was an admirable Œnone, sinister and unscrupulous as well as devoted. M. Sarcey says that she is the best Œnone he ever saw on the stage. M. Train was an agreeable surprise in Hippolyte. Not that his acting has made a bad impression in Manchester, but it was not supposed that the *jeune premier tragique* was in his line. He made up well, and his elocution was most excellent. He well deserved the recall he received—and he was the only performer who received that honour last night beside Mme. Bernhardt herself. M. Talbot must forgive us for quoting M. Sarcey on his Théramène. M. Sarcey is perhaps a little ill-natured, but he is very comical, and M. Talbot can afford to be laughed at for a performance of a part so out of his usual line as Théramène, as long as he gives us such a Michonnet as he gave us the other evening.

"Talbot jouait Théremène. Non, qui n'a pas vu Talbot dans Théramène n'a rien vu. Mon Dieu ! que j'ai regretté que nous ne fussions pas entre Parisiens ! Quelle bonne partie de rire nous eussions faite ! Ce diable de public anglais nous imposait ! Il fallait devant lui composer son visage, se retenir ! il était si sérieux lui-même ! il avait l'air de trouver cela si naturel ! Talbot recontant la mort de ce pauvre Hippolyte ! Quelle bonne figure de porteur d'eau il s'était faite ! et quelle déclamation ! C'étaient des sanglots, c'étaient des soupirs, c'étaient des notes graves qu'il tirait du fond de ses bottes, et tout au long des gémissements aigus qu'il prenait dans le haut de sa tête. Et des vers faux ! et des vers faux ! à faire frémir la nature ! Mais il ne semblait pas y prendre garde, tant il était absorbé par la douleur ! Il y avait dans la salle deux ou trois confrères en journalisme parisien. Nous n'osions pas nous regarder. Eh bien, mes amis, ces Anglais sont si parfaitement courtois, que cela a passé comme une lettre à la poste. Pas un muscle de leur visage n'a bougé, et quelques uns mêmes ont fait le geste d'applaudir. Ca, c'était un comble ! "

"Les Anglais" may be "parfaitement courtois," but we venture to think that his Manchester audience knows how to distinguish M. Talbot's Michonnet from his Théramène.

—From "The Manchester Guardian," 26 June, 1880 ; and reprinted in *The Manchester Stage : 1880-1900.*

WILLIAM ARCHER

(1856–1924)

ON GEORGE BERNARD SHAW'S *ARMS AND THE MAN*

No one with even a rudimentary knowledge of human nature will expect me to deal impartially with a play by Mr. George Bernard Shaw. "Jones write a book!" cried Smith, in the familiar anecdote—"Jones write a book! Impossible! Absurd! Why, *I knew his father*!" By the same cogent process of reasoning, I have long ago satisfied myself that Mr. Shaw cannot write a play. I had not the advantage of knowing his father (except through the filial reminiscences with which he now and then favours us), but—what is more fatal still—I know himself. He is not only my esteemed and religiously-studied colleague, but my old and intimate and valued friend. We have tried our best to quarrel many a time. We have said and done such things that would have sufficed to set up a dozen lifelong vendettas between normal and rightly-constituted people, but all without the slightest success, without engendering so much as a temporary coolness. Even now, when he has had the deplorable ill-taste to falsify my frequently and freely-expressed prediction by writing a successful play, which kept an audience hugely entertained from the rise to the fall of the curtain, I vow I cannot work up a healthy hatred for him. Of course I shall criticise it with prejudice, malice, and acerbity; but I have not the faintest hope of ruffling his temper or disturbing his self-complacency. The situation is really exasperating. If only I could induce him to cut me and scowl at me, like an ordinary human dramatist, there would be some chance of his writing better plays—or none at all. But one might as well attempt "to bully the Monument."

There is not the least doubt that *Arms and the Man* [1] is one of the most amusing entertainments at present before the public. It is quite as funny as *Charley's Aunt* or *The New Boy* ; we laughed at it wildly, hysterically ; and I exhort the reader to go and do likewise. But he must not expect a humdrum, rational, steady-going farce, like *Charley's Aunt*, bearing a well-understood conventional relation to real life. Let him rather look for a fantastic, psychological extravaganza, in which drama, farce, and Gilbertian irony keep flashing past the bewildered eye, as in a sort of merry-go-round, so quickly that one gives up the attempt to discriminate between them, and resigns oneself to indiscriminating laughter. The author (if he will pardon my dabbling in musical metaphor) is always jumping from key to key, without an attempt at modulation, and nine times out of ten he does not himself know what key he is writing in. Here, indeed, lies the whole truth. If one could think that Mr. Shaw had consciously and deliberately invented a new species of prose extravaganza, one could unreservedly applaud the invention, while begging him in future to apply it with a little more depth and delicacy. But I more than suspect that he conceives himself to have written a serious comedy, a reproduction of life as it really is, with men and women thinking, feeling, speaking, and acting as they really do think, feel, speak, and act. Instead of presenting an episode in the great war between the realms of Grünewald and Gerolstein, or in the historic conflict between Paphlagonia and Crim Tartary, he places his scene in the (more or less) real principality of Bulgaria, dates his action to the year and day (6th March 1886), and has been at immense pains to work in Bulgarian local colour in the dialogue, and to procure correct Bulgarian costumes and genuine Balkan scenery. It is an open secret, I believe, that Mr. Shaw held counsel on these matters with a Bulgarian Admiral,—a Bohemian Admiral would scarcely be more unexpected,—and that this gallant horse-marine gave him the hints as to the anti-saponaceous prejudices of the Bulgarians, their domestic architecture, their unfamiliarity with electric bells, and the mushroom growth of their aristocracy, which he has so religiously, and in some cases amusingly, utilised. But all this topographical pedantry proves, oddly enough, that " 'e dunno where 'e are." By attempting to fix his action down to the solid earth he simply emphasises its unreality. He is like the young man in *Pickwick*, who, having to write an essay on " Chinese Metaphysics," read up the articles " China " and " Metaphysics " in the Encyclopædia, and combined the two. Mr. Shaw went to his Admiral for " Bulgaria," and to his inner consciousness for " Psychology," and combined the two in an essay on " Bulgarian Psychology." Why confound the issues in this way, my dear G. B. S. ? Some critics have assumed, quite excusably, that the play was meant as a satire upon Bulgaria, and I should not be in the least surprised if it were to lead to a " diplomatic incident " like that which arose from the introduction of the Sultan in *Don Juan*. Of course you really know and care no more about Bulgaria than I do. Your satire is directed against humanity in general, and English humanity in particular. Your Saranoff and Bluntschli and Raïna and Louka have their prototypes, or rather their antitypes, not in the Balkan Principalities, but in that romantic valley which nestles between the cloud-capped summits of Hampstead and Sydenham. Why not confess as much by making your scene fantastic, and have done with it ?

Having now disentangled " Bulgaria " and " Psychology," I put the former article aside as irrelevant, and turn to the latter. Mr. Shaw is by nature and habit one of those philosophers who concentrate their attention upon the seamy side of the human mind. Against that practice, in itself, I have not a word to say. By all means let us see, examine, realise, remember, the seamy side. You will never find me using the word " cynic " as a term of moral reproach. But to say of a man that he is habitually and persistently cynical is undoubtedly to imply an artistic limitation. To look at nothing but the seamy side may be to see life steadily, but is not to see it whole. As an artist, Mr. Shaw suffers from this limitation ; and to this negative fault, if I may call it so, he superadds a positive vice of style. He not only dwells on the seamy side to the exclusion of all else, but he makes his characters turn their moral garments inside out and go about with the linings displayed, flaunting the seams and raw edges and stiffenings and paddings. Now this simply does not occur in real life, or only to a very limited extent ; and the artist who makes it his main method of character-presentation, at once converts his comedy into extravaganza. It is not Mr. Shaw's sole method, but he is far too much addicted to it. His first act is genuine fantastic comedy, sparkling and delightful. Here he has set himself to knock the stuffing, so to speak, out of war ; to contrast a romantic girl's ideal of battle and its heroic raptures, with the sordid reality as it appears to a professional soldier. He has evidently " documents " to go upon, and he has seized with inimitable humour upon the commonplace and ludicrous aspects of warfare. Of course Bluntschli's picture is not the whole truth any more than Raïna's, but it presents a real and important side of the matter, the side which chiefly appeals to Mr. Shaw's sceptical imagination. The great and serious artists—Tolstoi, Zola (for I am impenitent in my admiration for *La Débâcle*), Whitman in his *Specimen Days*, Stendhal (I am told) in *La Chartreuse de Parme*—give us both sides of the case, its prose and its poetry. Even Mr. Kipling, who also has his " documents," has found in them a thing or two beyond Mr. Shaw's ken. But for the nonce, and in its way, Mr. Shaw's persiflage is not only vastly amusing, but acceptable, apposite. So far good. At the end of the first act we do not quite know where the play is coming in, for it is obvious that even Mr. Shaw cannot go on through two more acts mowing down military ideals with volleys of chocolate-creams. But there are evident possibilities in this generous romantic girl and her genially cynical instructor in the art of war ; and we hope for the best. Observe that as yet we have not got upon the ground of general psychology, so to speak ; we have had nothing but a humorous analysis of one special phase of mental experience— the sensations of a soldier in battle and in flight. In the second act all is changed. Bluntschli, in whom the author practically speaks in his own person, without any effort at dramatisation, has almost disappeared from the scene, and the really dramatic effort commences in the characterisation of the Byronic swaggerer, Sergius Saranoff, and the working out of his relation to Raïna. At once Mr. Shaw's ease and lightness of touch desert him, and we find ourselves in Mr. Gilbert's Palace of Truth. The romantic girl is romantic no longer, but a deliberate humbug, without a single genuine or even self-deluding emotion in her bloodless frame. Sergius the Sublime has no sort of belief in his own sublimity, but sets to work before he has been ten minutes on the stage to analyse himself for the entertainment of the maid-servant, and enlarge on the difficulty of distinguishing between the six or seven Sergiuses whom he discovers in his composition. Petkoff and his wife are mere cheap grotesques both more or less under the influence of the Palace of Truth. The major-domo, under the same magic spell, affords a vehicle for some of the author's theories as to the evils engendered on both sides by the relation of master and servant. And the most wonderful character of all, perhaps, is the maid Louka, who seems to have wandered in from one of the obscurer of Mr. Meredith's novels, so keen is her perception, and so subtle her appreciation, of character and motive. All this crude and contorted psychology, too, is further dehumanised by Mr. Shaw's peculiar habit of straining all the red corpuscles out of the blood of his personages. They have nothing of human nature except its pettinesses; they are devoid alike of its spiritual and its sensual instincts. It is all very well for Mr. Shaw to be sceptical as to the reality of much of the emotion which passes by the name of love, and over which so much fuss is made both in fiction and in life. For my part, I quite agree with him that a great deal of foolish and useless unhappiness is caused by our habit of idealising and eternalising this emotion, under all circumstances and at all hazards. But it is one thing to argue that the exultations and agonies of love are apt to be morbid, factitious, deliberately exaggerated and overwrought, and quite another to represent life as if these exultations and agonies had no existence whatever. Here we have a girl who, in the course of some six hours, transfers her affections (save the mark!) from a man whom she thought she had adored for years, to one whom she has only once before set eyes on, and a young man who, in the same space of time, quarrels with the mistress about nothing at all, and, for no conceivable reason, makes up his mind to marry the maid. Such instantaneous *chassés-croisés* used to be common enough in Elizabethan drama, and are quite the order of the day in Gilbertian extravaganza. In any more serious form of modern drama they would be not only preposterous but nauseous.

It is impossible, in short, to accept the second and third acts of *Arms and the Man* as either " romantic comedy " or coherent farce. They are bright, clever, superficially cynical extravaganza. In the second act, there are some, not many, intervals of dullness ; but with the reappearance of Captain Bernard Bluntschli-Shaw the fun fully revives, and in the third act there are even some patches of comedy, in the author's finer vein. Pray do not suppose, moreover, from my dwelling on the pettiness and sordidness of motive which reign throughout, that the whole effect of the play is unpleasant. Mr. Shaw's cynicism is not in the least splenetic ; on the contrary, it is imperturbably good-humoured and almost amiable. And amid all his irresponsible nonsense, he has contrived, generally in defiance of all dramatic consistency, to drag in a great deal of incidental good sense. I begin positively to believe that he may one day write a serious and even an artistic play, if only he will repress his irrelevant whimsicality, try to clothe his character-conceptions in flesh and blood, and realise the difference between knowingness and knowledge.

The acting was good from first to last. Mr. Yorke Stephens seemed to have cultivated that ironic twist of his lip for the special purpose of creating the " chocolate-cream soldier " ; Mr. Bernard Gould played the " bounder " with humour and picturesqueness ; Miss Alma Murray lent her seriousness and charm (invaluable qualities both, as it happened) to the part of Raïna ; Miss Florence Farr made a memorable figure of the enigmatic Louka ; and Mr. Welch, Mrs. Charles Calvert, and Mr. Orlando Barnett were all as good as need be.

—From *The Theatrical World of* 1894. By Wm. Archer, 1895.

ON PINERO'S *THE NOTORIOUS MRS. EBBSMITH*

THE " St. James's Gazette," in an article headed " The Notorious Mr. Redford," [1] argues that because Mr. Pinero's new play at the Garrick has been licensed, the Censorship is not practically repressive to dramatic literature. Ingenuous " St. James's " ! Does it really imagine that if *The Notorious Mrs. Ebbsmith* [2] had been the work of an unknown writer, or, indeed, of any one but Mr. Pinero, it would have been licensed ? Not a bit of it. This admirable work, which even Mr. Clement Scott hails as " a tragedy which brings out in authorship and acting the very best that we have got in English art," would have been consigned to the limbo of still-born improprieties. As it is, we all know that *Mrs. Ebbsmith* escaped the veto by the skin of her " pretty white teeth." I speak simply from common report. I have no private information on the point, from Mr. Pinero or any one else. If I asked Mr. Pinero for the " true truth " of the matter, he would probably have to place me under a promise of secrecy ; for it is one of the pleasing traditions of Stable Yard, St. James's, to consider as " confidential " any communication it deigns to hold with its victims, and to put on airs of injury if its sayings or doings are allowed to leak out. I prefer, then, not to go to headquarters for information, but simply to challenge the Vehmgericht to deny that *The Notorious Mrs. Ebbsmith* was within an ace of being consigned to one of its oubliettes. Frankly, I could find it in my heart to wish that it had been. The time is pretty nearly ripe for the revolt that must come sooner or later—the storming of the secret, silent Bastille. But prudence eventually prevailed in Stable Yard, and the fight is postponed till further notice.

The new play is in all essentials a great advance on *The Second Mrs. Tanqueray*. Those critics who take the opposite view are in reality hankering after the more commonplace and melodramatic elements in the earlier play. In it we had

[1] The appointment of Mr. George Redford, a gentleman in the employ of the London and South Western Bank, to the office of Examiner of Plays, was announced immediately after the production of *The Notorious Mrs. Ebbsmith*. (W. A.)

[2] March 13–May 11 [1895]. On May 15, Miss Olga Nethersole succeeded Mrs. Patrick Campbell in the title-part, and the run was continued until June 14. (W. A.)

character precipitated by external coincidence ; here we have character working itself out entirely from within. Moreover, Mr. Pinero has here chosen a much more vital theme. Most of us can afford to take a very abstract interest in the theory of marriage with a demirep. We know in advance that it is a hazardous experiment—that the county people won't call, while the lady's former associates probably will. Thus *The Second Mrs. Tanqueray* is really little more than the portrait of Paula—a brilliant piece of work, but isolated, almost irrelevant. In *The Notorious Mrs. Ebbsmith*, on the other hand, Mr. Pinero goes straight for the universally relevant theme of marriage in general, and draws three characters in place of one. It is unfair to complain that his treatment of the theme is inconclusive. If it had been " conclusive," on one side or other, those who dissented would have dubbed Mr. Pinero a " faddist " and complained of being preached at. What he has conclusively shown is that, as society is at present constituted, it takes exceptional characters on both sides to make a free union any more successful than a marriage. This is not a very difficult point to prove ; but as a contribution to the philosophy of the subject, it is at least as valid as Mr. Grant Allen's contention that two people of perfect character may form an ideal union " without benefit of clergy," especially if one of the parties will have the good taste to die of typhoid before time has tested the strength of the bond.

The design of the play, then, is above reproach. It is technically by far the strongest thing our modern stage has to show. An expository character or two might perhaps be dispensed with, and an over-nicety of explanation as to the comings and goings of the personages might possibly have been avoided ; but these are the veriest trivialities. The main fact is that we have a drama consisting simply in the interaction of two characters, developing itself through four acts, without situations, revelations, starts, surprises, or picture-poster attractions of any sort, yet from first to last enthralling the attention and stimulating the intelligence. Stimulating, I say, not always satisfying ; for when we come to look into the characters we cannot but doubt whether Mr. Pinero has quite achieved what he seems to have intended. Lucas Cleeve is admirable—

the man of facile enthusiasms and discouragements, " possess-
ing ambition without patience, self-esteem without confidence"
—but Agnes Ebbsmith, however vividly and ably projected,
can scarcely pass muster as a well-observed type. Mr. Pinero
has not entered with sympathetic clairvoyance into the mental
history and habit—he has not even mastered the vocabulary,
the jargon, if you will—of the class of woman he sets out to
portray. I suspect him of holding " views " as to feminine
human nature in general ; and " views," like knotty window-
panes, are fatal to observation. In this he is by no means
alone. Nine-tenths of masculine woman-drawing is vitiated
by " views "—and, in these latter days, about nineteen-
twentieths of feminine woman-drawing. You may think it a
reckless paradox, but Ibsen seems to me one of the few modern
writers whose studies of feminine character are undistorted
by " views." He does not go to work syllogistically, saying to
himself, " All women are this, that, and the other thing ; my
heroine is a woman ; therefore she is this, that, and the other
thing." He looks straight at and through women, and draws
them in their infinite variety. Time was when he, too, held
views, and then he drew *his* Agnes, and other characters of that
order. They were beautiful in their time, but he has gone
far beyond them. Ten years hence we may perhaps be saying
the same of Mr. Pinero's Agnes.

She is the daughter, so she says, of a revolutionary Socialist,
atheist, and all the rest of it ; yet her whole habit of mind is
that of one who has been steeped from the outset in orthodoxy,
and has embraced heterodoxy in fear and trembling, with a
sense of strangeness and adventure. " In spite of father's
unbelief and mother's indifference," she says, " I was in my
heart as devout as any girl in a parsonage. . . . Whenever I
could escape from our stifling rooms at home, the air blew
away uncertainty and scepticism." We are told of no external
influence that made her regard her father's ideas as " strange,"
and think of his paganism as " scepticism." Mr. Pinero seems
to assume " devoutness " as a sort of universal instinct of the
childish, or at any rate of the woman-childish, heart, and to
conceive that this instinct alone would prevent the ideas of a
much-loved father from " soaking into " his daughter. Now,

as a matter of fact (I don't think Mr. Diggle himself would deny this), your ordinary child is instinctively an out-and-out pagan. The childish criticism of the universe is remorselessly rationalistic. It is religion, not irreligion, that a child requires to be taught. The father's agnosticism might not soak very deep into the child, and might be effectually counteracted by some other and more positive influence ; but we hear of nothing of the sort. It is even possible that, by some freak of atavism, like that which makes the daughter of Mr. Grant Allen's *Woman who Did* an incurable little snob and numskull, the atheist father and indifferent mother might produce a daughter with a constitutional bent towards mysticism, an innate genius for piety. But that is not Agnes's case. For fourteen years of her mature life she has been a pagan ; for six of them she has been an active propagandist ; she conceives herself to be still a pagan at the very moment when, by talking of " uncertainty and scepticism," " hope and faith," she shows that she regards religious belief as the normal and fundamental attitude of the human mind. Now, whether this be so or not, it is certainly the last thing that a woman like Agnes would admit or assume. Her spiritual history does not hang together. It is not probably constructed or possibly expressed. Mr. Pinero has failed to put himself in the position of what may be called a congenital pagan—a woman who from childhood has taken in rationalism at the pores of her skin, as most children take in Christianity. Yet that, for aught we can see or reasonably conjecture, is precisely Agnes's case. It seems to be Mr. Pinero's belief that " every woman is at heart a "— saint. The Bible incident, I take it, at the end of the third act, symbolises his " view " that no woman is strong enough to go through life without some supernatural refuge to fly to in time of need ; so that, even if she thinks she has cast her " hope and faith " into the fire, she will presently pluck them out again, though she sear her flesh in the attempt. Well, there are instances that favour that view, and I think there are instances against it. But though we may cite women who preach atheism to-day, and go to confession or to Thibet to-morrow, while they *are* secularists they stand at, and speak from, the secularist's point of view. Agnes Ebbsmith, on the other hand, even in expounding her heterodoxy, unconsciously adopts the standpoint and uses the language of orthodoxy.

Equally unrealised are her sociological doctrines. John Thorold, for instance, must have been a very strange Socialist if his daughter ever heard him talking about " division of wealth, and the rest of it." That is the language of the gentleman who writes to the " Times " to point out that, if all property were equally divided to-day, there would be rich men and poor men to-morrow, millionaires and paupers the day after. This Socialist daughter of a Socialist does not know the phraseology of her party. Again, her objections to marriage are curiously—shall I say empirical ? Because her father and mother and " most of our married friends " lived a cat-and-dog life, and because her own husband was a brute, she sets forth to preach Free Union as the panacea for a cantankerous world. It does not seem to enter her head that there are drawbacks to marriage even between people of reasonably good tempers, good hearts, and good manners. Of the economic, ethical, and sentimental commonplaces of attack upon marriage, which a woman in her position would be bound to have at her fingers' ends, she appears to know nothing. It is especially noteworthy that she ignores the question of children, as affecting the relation of the sexes. The world of her speculations is a childless world. A triangle, in her trigonometry, consists of two straight lines. Her struggle, too, against what she calls " passion," seems to me to show a misconception on Mr. Pinero's part of the type of woman with whom he is dealing—or rather a confusion of two distinct types. He thinks vaguely of rebellion against the primary conditions of sex as a general characteristic of the " new " or advanced woman. Now there are—or rather there have been, for the type is surely " going out "—women constitutionally inaccessible to passion, who resent it as a degrading servitude, and would fain make their individual limitation a law, or an ideal, for their fellow-women. But such women would be the last to enter on a free union. Married they may be—they may have taken on the yoke before they realised their own temperament, or they may have condescended to marriage for the sake of its social and economic advantages. But love, in the largest sense of the word, is as incomprehensible to them as passion. They do not want even the friendship or close companionship of a man. Their instinct is to make their own sex as nearly as possible self-sufficing. Why, then, should they incur all sorts of social disadvantages for the sake of a companionship which they do not require or desire ? And, in any case, Agnes is clearly not a creature of this brood. She is not naturally a passionless woman. She loves Lucas, in the fullest sense of the word, with a love that survives even her fuller insight into his character. Her aspiration towards a " colder, more temperate, more impassive companionship," is a merely intellectual vagary, and I venture to think that it springs from a misconception on Mr. Pinero's part. Newspaper moralists have so persistently prefixed the stereotypes " sexless " and " unsexed " to the " new woman " that he has been betrayed into grafting an inconsistent attribute upon his heroine's character. The real, or, at any rate, the characteristic, " new woman " accepts with something more than equanimity the destinies of her sex, and would certainly not ignore the possibility of motherhood in her rearrangement of the scheme of things. One could understand Agnes's position if her previous experience of marriage had given her such a horror of " passion " that she had resolved from the very outset to maintain her companionship with Lucas on a supersexual basis. But we are told in so many words that this is not the case. Her rebellion against passion is an afterthought, and surely an improbable one. It might pass as a whim of the moment, but such a whim should be the subject of a comedietta, not of a serious play.

Perhaps you think that, if these criticisms are justified, there is very little of Agnes left. But when you see the play you will discover that they are more verbal than essential—that in order to obviate them only a few changes of phraseology would be required, the main lines of the action, the fundamental processes of emotion, remaining unaltered. I, for my part, flatly dissent from that " view " of Mr. Pinero's, to which we owe the Bible incident and the pietistic end ; but, after all, he has a perfect right to hold and illustrate this view. For the rest, *The Notorious Mrs. Ebbsmith* seems to me the work of a born and highly accomplished dramatist, who goes right essentially and by instinct, and wrong superficially, for lack of special know-ledge. It should be quite possible to tell Agnes's story, up to the moment when she thrusts her hand into the fire, without altering a single incident or emotion, yet in such a way as to obviate all the above objections, which are founded upon phrases rather than facts. But here I must break off a dis-cussion which has already exceeded all bounds. I hope to resume it in another article, and to say something of the acting.

MRS. EBBSMITH AGAIN

AFTER pointing out, last week, what seem to me certain errors of observation in the character of Agnes Ebbsmith, I stated my belief that these errors are verbal rather than essential. It should be possible, I said, to tell Agnes's story, at any rate up to the end of the third act, without altering any incident or emotion, yet in such a way as to obviate all my criticisms. Let me now make the attempt ; repeating, how-ever, that my—what shall I call it ?—my exposition stops short at the Bible incident. To account for that, it would be necessary to introduce a new element into Agnes's previous history ; and that is against the rules of the game.

Well then—she is the daughter of a Socialist orator, has imbibed her father's religious and political ideas, and has seen, in her home life, the miseries of an ill-assorted marriage. Nevertheless, she marries early, to find herself her husband's sultana for one year and his servant for seven—at the end of which period he dies. Confirmed, by her personal ill-hap, in her allegiance to her father's ideas, she becomes an active propagandist of social democracy and female emancipation ; but losing her voice and being in the pinch of poverty, she takes to nursing as a means of livelihood, and in the course of her duties comes across Lucas Cleeve. All this is probable enough, and all this is precisely what Agnes relates of herself. It is not in the facts, but in her wording of them that the improbability comes in. She speaks of both free-thought and socialism, not as one to the manner born, but rather as one not yet acclimatised, and ignorant of technicalities and shibboleths. Lucas Cleeve (to return to the story) is in the hot fit of rebellion against marriage with a hard-natured worldly woman who despises him instead of bringing him the sympathy and appreciation for which his weak egoism craves. These qualities, together with a tender unworldliness, he finds in Agnes. Illness and distance make his old life and its ambitions and interests seem infinitely aloof from him, and he is quite ready to be infected by the enthusiasms of this stately creature, the antithesis in every respect of the wife who has wounded him. He loves in her a " ministering angel," and she a convert in him. So they cast in their lots together, and we find them in Venice. But now, as Lucas regains strength, and as the decisive moment approaches when he must break once for all with his traditions and his career, the habits of his caste reassert themselves, and he finds his enthusiasm for free union in the abstract, and for social democracy in the concrete, rapidly cooling. He still loves Agnes, but not as she longs to be loved. He loves her in spite of, not in and for, her ideas. She gradually comes to feel that her aspirations towards " plain living and high thinking," towards labour, and if need be martyrdom, for social emancipation and justice, are in his eyes little better than eccentricities of which she must be gradually cured. He would have her put on the gowns and the prejudices of his caste. She sees, with deep humiliation, that she holds him by his senses, not by his intellect ; that they are not fellow-workers in a great cause, not shining examples of a high ideal, but are simply living in vulgar vice, a rich young profligate and his mistress. On realising this, she tries to save her self-respect by raising their companionship to a purely intellectual and supersexual plane ; so that even this recrudescence of the innate puritanism of the English middle-classes becomes comprehensible enough if we take it, not as a general characteristic of the type of woman Mr. Pinero is portraying, but as resulting from the special circumstances of Agnes's case. At this juncture the Duke of St. Olpherts comes on the scene, a living embodiment of all those forces in Lucas's nature against which Agnes is carrying on a despairing battle. She knows that what seemed eccentric in Lucas's own eyes will appear grotesque and hateful when seen in the concave mirror of the Duke's scepticism. She seeks an encounter with the Duke so as to know and measure her adversary. To say that such a woman would not " Trafalgar Square " him in her own drawing-room is absurd. There is a great deal of human nature even in collectivists, and it would be a foolish affectation on her part to treat the Duke as though they met on the neutral territory of ordinary social intercourse. The verbal form of her " Trafalgar Squaring " may be open to criticism ; the fact is natural and even inevitable. Having gauged the Duke's strength, she sees that she must either give up the battle or fight him with his own weapons. To give it up would be not only to lose a convert and shatter a still fascinating dream, but to submit to the soiling of her life with a futile and degrading episode. It is tolerable, it may even be piquant, not to be a man's first love ; it is intolerably humiliating not to be his last. So she determines to fight the Duke—the World, the Flesh, and the Devil incarnate—with his own weapons. She has wit and beauty ; she will use them ! She puts off the " dowdy demagogue " and puts on the bewitching woman ; and hey presto ! Faust is at her feet again and Mephistopheles is apparently routed. And now, to her own surprise, she finds herself, for a moment, thrilling with the joy of triumph—and of surrender. " Her sex has found her out " ; she knows that it is no longer the convert she loves in Lucas, but the man ; and beneath her sense of treachery to her ideals, she is conscious of a tremulous delight. It was in this phase of the character that Mrs. Patrick Campbell's otherwise brilliant performance seemed to me to fall a little short. It may be that I am refining too much upon Mr. Pinero's conception, but I can certainly see nothing *in*consistent with a reading more subtle and at the same time more human than Mrs. Campbell's. The actress seemed to feel only the irony in Agnes's thoughts, not the genuine underlying joy. There was nothing but bitterness in her realisation that her " woman's one hour " had come; and that I cannot take to have been the author's meaning. It is true that Agnes had expected her hour to come in a very different shape ; but her sentiment on finding that it has taken her by surprise is surely not one of mere disgust and discontent. Mrs. Campbell seemed to me to ignore in effect, as she certainly delivered without conviction, that outburst of Agnes's in answer to the Duke's wish that Lucas were " a different sort of feller "—" Nothing matters now—not even that. He's mine. He would have died but for me. I gave him life. He is my child, my husband, my lover, my bread, my daylight—all— everything. Mine. Mine." Beautiful and fascinating as Mrs. Campbell undoubtedly was throughout, I could not but find a certain superficiality, hardness, almost shrewishness, in her treatment of the third act. Agnes's " hour," at any rate, is a very brief one. Lucas has not sense enough to realise her sacrifice. Finding her, as he thinks, " gowned " and in her right mind, he must needs take the opportunity to insult and exult over the ideals and aspirations which were to have been the bond of union between them ; and she sees that at best she has to face a second cycle of passion and satiety, like that of her first marriage. Then, putting him to the test with death in her heart, she finds him prepared for, and even hankering after, a squalid compromise, in which she, instead of making her life a proud and open protest against the slavery of marriage is to join the furtive horde of mercenary irregulars who smooth the way for the triumphant march of the hymeneal legion. At this her soul revolts ; and leaving behind her the four words, " My hour is over," she departs from the palace of her day-dream, which has become in her eyes a house of shame.

Have I kept my promise ? Frankly, I think so. I have told the story of a very true, very subtle, and very tragic play, a play which none but a master dramatist could have invented and composed ; and it is simply Mr. Pinero's play up to the last five minutes of the third act, with nothing added, and nothing essential left out. It is the play you can see every night at the Garrick Theatre, somewhat, but very slightly, obscured by a few unrealised phrases placed in Agnes's mouth. Mr. Pinero, I take it, is much in the position of (say) a clergy-man of great ability, insight, and literary power, who should undertake to write a novel of stage-life, having an actress for its heroine, with no more intimate knowledge of the stage, and its ways of thought and speech, than may be gained from a few casual visits to the Lyceum stalls. He might quite well draw a very true and fascinating woman, though an unconvincing actress ; and Agnes, in the same way, is a very true and fascinating woman, though an unconvincing Socialist and Secularist. I wish the play ended, as it might very well, at the point where my narrative leaves off. It is at this point that Mr. Pinero's preconceived "view" of feminine character intervenes, to my thinking, rather disastrously. I see no reason why Agnes should throw the Bible into the fire, no reason why she should pluck it out again. That seems to me the culmination of another play, another character-study. As for the great scene of the last act—the scene between Agnes and Sybil Cleeve—it is a daring and scathing piece of satire, but somewhat of a superfluity none the less. Agnes's acquiescence in Sybil's proposal simply takes my breath away. I can trace it only to a queer survival of the heroic-self-sacrifice superstition which inspired so many of the French sentimental dramas of twenty years ago. One might almost say of it, as Dr. Johnson said of the *Beggar's Opera :* " There is in it such a labefaction of all principles as may be injurious to morality."

Of Mrs. Patrick Campbell's performance I have already spoken. Mr. Hare's Duke of St. Olpherts is one of his most masterly studies. It has gained in firmness and precision since the first night, and is now a perfect impersonation. Both on the first night and when I saw the play again, Mr. Forbes-Robertson seemed to me a little too much bent on showing that he saw through Lucas Cleeve. He " gave him away " too frankly, especially in the third act. I could imagine a more plausible rendering of the character, but scarcely one that would be more effective from the point of view of the average audience.

And now, in conclusion, a word in Mr. Pinero's ear. He has written two profoundly interesting and admirable plays— plays which deserve to take rank with the best French and German work of the day—plays which those only can despise who make a virtue of despising the theatre as a whole. We are very grateful to him for what he has done, though he may perhaps think that some of us are tolerably successful in dissembling our gratitude. But when we put *The Notorious Mrs. Ebbsmith* beside *The Second Mrs. Tanqueray*, and try to generalise their characteristics, the first that strikes us is a certain depressing negativeness—I had almost said aridity. They are studies in failure—the failure of marriage, the failure of love, the failure of high idealisms, the failure of good intentions—with no glimpse of compensation, no loophole for hope, no message, no stimulus, no sustenance. They do not even " purge the heart with pity and terror." They leave us dry-eyed and fevered rather than moved and heart-stricken. In a word, they put us on a distinctly " lowering " spiritual regimen. Mr. Pinero, I am sure, will not suspect me of clamouring for " comic," or even sentimental, " relief." I am not clamouring for anything or complaining of anything. Only I should be sorry if Mr. Pinero suffered this purely negative outlook upon the world to become habitual. I plead for a little more atmosphere in his work, and a more inspiring tone of thought. I am the last to make pessimism an artistic crime ; but when pessimism becomes mannerism, it is certainly an artistic weakness.

—From *The Theatrical World of* 1895.

GEORGE BERNARD SHAW

(b. 1856)

DUSE AND BERNHARDT

Mr. William Archer's defence of the dramatic critics against Mr. Street's indictment of them for their indifference to acting appears to be falling through. Mr. Archer pleads that whereas Hazlitt and Leigh Hunt had frequent opportunities of comparing ambitious actors in famous parts, the modern dramatic critic spends his life in contemplating "good acting plays" without any real people in them, and performers who do not create or interpret characters, but simply lend their pretty or popular persons, for a consideration, to fill up the parts. Mr. Archer might have added another reason which applies to nearly all modern works : to wit, the operation of our copyright laws, whereby actors and actresses acquire the right not only to perform new plays but to prevent anyone else from performing them. Nevertheless we critics can now at last outdo Hazlitt and Leigh Hunt if we have a mind to ; for we have just had two Mrs. Ebbsmiths to compare, besides a fourth Fédora, and Duse and Sarah Bernhardt playing *La Dame aux Camélias* and Sudermann's *Heimat* against one another at Daly's Theatre and at Drury Lane. Clearly now or never is the time for a triumphant refutation of the grievance of the English actor against the English Press : namely, that hardly any critic knows enough about acting to be able to distinguish between an effective part and a well played one, or between the bag of tricks which every old hand carries and the stock of ideas and sense of character which distinguish the master-actor from the mere handy-man.

This week began with the relapse of Sarah Bernhardt into her old profession of serious actress. She played Magda in Sudermann's *Heimat*, and was promptly challenged by Duse in the same part at Drury Lane on Wednesday. The contrast between the two Magdas is as extreme as any contrast could possibly be between artists who have finished their twenty years' apprenticeship to the same profession under closely similar conditions. Madame Bernhardt has the charm of a jolly maturity, rather spoilt and petulant, perhaps, but always ready with a sunshine-through-the-clouds smile if only she is made much of. Her dresses and diamonds, if not exactly splendid, are at least splendacious ; her figure, far too scantily upholstered in the old days, is at its best ; and her complexion shews that she has not studied modern art in vain. Those charming roseate effects which French painters produce by giving flesh the pretty color of strawberries and cream, and painting the shadows pink and crimson, are cunningly reproduced by Madame Bernhardt in the living picture. She paints her ears crimson and allows them to peep enchantingly through a few loose braids of her auburn hair. Every dimple has its dab of pink ; and her finger-tips are so delicately incarnadined that you fancy they are transparent like her ears, and that the light is shining through their delicate blood-vessels. Her lips are like a newly painted pillar box ; her cheeks, right up to the languid lashes, have the bloom and surface of a peach ; she is beautiful with the beauty of her school, and entirely inhuman and incredible. But the incredibility is pardonable, because, though it is all the greatest nonsense, nobody believing in it, the actress herself least of all, it is so artful, so clever, so well recognized a part of the business, and carried off with such a genial air, that it is impossible not to accept it with good-humor. One feels when the heroine bursts on the scene, a dazzling vision of beauty, that instead of imposing on you, she adds to her own piquancy by looking you straight in the face, and saying, in effect : " Now who would ever suppose that I am a grandmother ? " That, of course, is irresistible ; and one is not sorry to have been coaxed to relax one's notions of the dignity of art when she gets to serious business and shews how ably she does her work. The coaxing suits well with the childishly egotistical character of her acting, which is not the art of making you think more highly or feel more deeply, but the art of making you admire her, pity her, champion her, weep with her, laugh at her jokes, follow her fortunes breathlessly, and applaud her wildly when the curtain falls. It is the art of finding out all your weaknesses and practising on them—cajoling you, harrowing you, exciting you—on the whole, fooling you. And it is always Sarah Bernhardt in her own capacity who does this to you. The dress, the title of the play, the order of the words may vary ; but the woman is always the same. She does not enter into the leading character : she substitutes herself for it.

All this is precisely what does not happen in the case of Duse, whose every part is a separate creation. When she comes on the stage, you are quite welcome to take your opera-glass and count whatever lines time and care have so far traced on her. They are the credentials of her humanity ; and she knows better than to obliterate that significant handwriting beneath a layer of peach-bloom from the chemist's. The shadows on her face are grey, not crimson ; her lips are sometimes nearly grey also ; there are neither dabs nor dimples ; her charm could never be imitated by a barmaid with unlimited pin money and a row of footlights before her instead of the handles of a beer-engine. The result is not so discouraging as the patrons of the bar might suppose. Wilkes, who squinted atrociously, boasted that he was only quarter of an hour behind the handsomest man in Europe : Duse is not in action five minutes before she is quarter of a century ahead of the handsomest woman in the world. I grant that Sarah's elaborate Monna Lisa smile, with the conscious droop of the eyelashes and the long carmined lips coyly disclosing the brilliant row of teeth, is effective of its kind—that it not only appeals to your susceptibilities, but positively jogs them. And it lasts quite a minute, sometimes longer. But Duse, with a tremor of the lip which you feel rather than see, and which lasts half an instant, touches you straight on the very heart ; and there is not a line in the face, or a cold tone in the grey shadow that does not give poignancy to that tremor. As to youth and age, who can associate purity and delicacy of emotion, and simplicity of expression, with the sordid craft that repels us in age ; or voluptuous appeal and egotistical self-insistence with the candor and generosity that attract us in youth ? Who ever thinks of Potiphar's wife as a young woman, or St Elizabeth of Hungary as an old one ? These associations are horribly unjust to age, and undeserved by youth : they belong of right to differences of character, not of years ; but they rule our imaginations ; and the great artist profits by them to appear eternally young. However, it would be a critical blunder as well as a personal folly on my part to suggest that Duse, any more than Sarah Bernhardt, neglects any art that could heighten the effect of her acting when she is impersonating young and pretty women. The truth is that in the art of being beautiful, Madame Bernhardt is a child beside her. The French artist's stock of attitudes and facial effects could be catalogued as easily as her stock of dramatic ideas : the counting would hardly go beyond the fingers of both hands. Duse produces the illusion of being infinite in variety of beautiful pose and motion. Every idea, every shade of thought and mood, expresses itself delicately but vividly to the eye ; and yet, in an apparent million of changes and inflexions, it is impossible to catch any line at an awkward angle, or any strain interfering with the perfect abandonment of all the limbs to what appears to be their natural gravitation towards the finest grace. She is ambidextrous and supple, like a gymnast or a panther ; only the multitude of ideas which find physical expression in her movements are all of that high quality which marks off humanity from the animals, and, I fear I must add, from a good many gymnasts. When it is remembered that the majority of tragic actors excel only in explosions of those passions which are common to man and brute, there will be no difficulty in understanding the indescribable distinction which Duse's acting acquires from the fact that behind every stroke of it is a distinctively human idea. In nothing is this more apparent than in the vigilance in her of that high human instinct which seeks to awaken the deepest responsive feeling without giving pain. In *La Dame aux Camélias*, for instance, it is easy for an intense actress to harrow us with her sorrows and paroxysms of phthisis, leaving us with a liberal pennyworth of sensation, not fundamentally distinguishable from that offered by a public execution, or any other evil in which we still take a hideous delight. As different from this as light from darkness is the method of the actress who shews us how human sorrow can express itself only in its appeal for the sympathy it needs, whilst striving by strong endurance to shield others from the infection of its torment. That is the charm of Duse's interpretation of the stage poem of Marguerite Gautier. It is unspeakably touching because it is exquisitely considerate : that is, exquisitely sympathetic. No physical charm is noble as well as beautiful unless it is the expression of a moral charm ; and it is because Duse's range includes these moral high notes, if I may so express myself, that her compass, extending from the depths of a mere predatory creature like Claude's wife up to Marguerite Gautier at her kindest or Magda at her bravest, so immeasurably dwarfs the poor little octave and a half on which Sarah Bernhardt plays such pretty canzonets and stirring marches.

Obvious as the disparity of the two famous artists has been to many of us since we first saw Duse, I doubt whether any of us realized, after Madame Bernhardt's very clever performance as Magda on Monday night, that there was room in the nature of things for its annihilation within forty-eight hours by so comparatively quiet a talent as Duse's. And yet annihilation is the only word for it. Sarah was very charming, very jolly when the sun shone, very petulant when the clouds covered it, and positively angry when they wanted to take her child away from her. And she did not trouble us with any fuss about the main theme of Sudermann's play, the revolt of the modern woman against that ideal of home which exacts the sacrifice of her whole life to its care, not by her grace, and as its own sole help and refuge, but as a right which it has to the services of all females as abject slaves. In fact, there is not the slightest reason to suspect Madame Bernhardt of having discovered any such theme in the play ; though Duse, with one look at Schwartz, the father, nailed it to the stage as the subject of the impending dramatic struggle before she had been five minutes on the scene. Before long, there came a stroke of acting which will probably never be forgotten by those who saw it, and which explained at once why those artifices of the dressing-table which help Madame Bernhardt would hinder Duse almost as much as a screen placed in front of her. I should explain, first, that the real name of the play is not Magda but

Home. Magda is a daughter who has been turned out of doors for defying her father, one of those outrageous persons who mistake their desire to have everything their own way in the house for a sacred principle of home life. She has a hard time of it, but at last makes a success as an opera singer, though not until her lonely struggles have thrown her for sympathy on a fellow student, who in due time goes his way, and leaves her to face motherhood as best she can. In the fullness of her fame she returns to her native town, and in an attack of homesickness makes advances to her father, who consents to receive her again. No sooner is she installed in the house than she finds that one of the most intimate friends of the family is the father of her child. In the third act of the play she is on the stage when he is announced as a visitor. It must be admitted that Sarah Bernhardt played this scene very lightly and pleasantly : there was genuine good fellowship in the way in which she reassured the embarrassed gallant and made him understand that she was not going to play off the sorrows of Gretchen on him after all those years, and that she felt that she owed him the priceless experience of maternity, even if she did not particularly respect him for it. Her self-possession at this point was immense : the peach-bloom never altered by a shade. Not so with Duse. The moment she read the card handed her by the servant, you realized what it was to have to face a meeting with the man. It was interesting to watch how she got through it when he came in, and how, on the whole, she got through it pretty well. He paid his compliments and offered his flowers ; they sat down ; and she evidently felt that she had got it safely over and might allow herself to think at her ease, and to look at him to see how much he had altered. Then a terrible thing happened to her. She began to blush ; and in another moment she was conscious of it, and the blush was slowly spreading and deepening until, after a few vain efforts to avert her face or to obstruct his view of it without seeming to do so, she gave up and hid the blush in her hands. After that feat of acting I did not need to be told why Duse does not paint an inch thick. I could detect no trick in it : it seemed to me a perfectly genuine effect of the dramatic imagination. In the third act of *La Dame aux Camélias*, where she produces a touching effect by throwing herself down, and presently rises with her face changed and flushed with weeping, the flush is secured by the preliminary plunge to a stooping attitude, imagination or no imagination ; but Magda's blush did not admit of that explanation ; and I must confess to an intense professional curiosity as to whether it always comes spontaneously.

I shall make no attempt to describe the rest of that unforgettable act. To say that it left the house not only frantically applauding, but actually roaring, is to say nothing ; for had we not applauded Sarah as Gismonda and roared at Mrs. Patrick Campbell as Fédora ? But there really was something to roar at this time. There was a real play, and an actress who understood the author and was a greater artist than he. And for me, at least, there was a confirmation of my sometimes flagging faith that a dramatic critic is really the servant of a high art, and not a mere advertiser of entertainments of questionable respectability of motive.

—From " The Saturday Review," 15 June, 1895 ; and reprinted in *Our Theatres in the Nineties*. By Bernard Shaw, 1932.

C. E. MONTAGUE

(1867–1928)

ON BENSON'S *RICHARD II*

To the chief interest of Mr. Benson's Richard II, which he played at the Theatre Royal [1] on Saturday afternoon, we do not think that critical justice has ever been done. An actor faulty in some other ways, but always picturesque, romantic, and inventive, with a fine sensibility to beauty in words and situations, and a voice that gives this sensibility its due, Mr. Benson brings out admirably that half of the character which criticism seems almost always to have taken pains to obscure—the capable and faithful artist in the same skin as the incapable and unfaithful King. With a quite choice and pointed infelicity, Professor Dowden, able as he is, has called Shakspere's Richard II " an amateur in living, not an artist "; Mr. Boas, generally one of the most suggestive of recent writers on Shakspere, has called Richard's grace of fancy " puerile " and its products " pseudo-poetic." The general judgment on the play reads as if the critics felt they would be " only encouraging " kings like this Richard if they did not assure him throughout the ages that his poetry was sad stuff at the best. " It's no excuse," one seems to hear them say, and " Serve you right, you and your poetry." It is our critical way to fall thus upon the wicked or weak man in books and leave him half-dead, after taking from him even the good side that he hath. Still it is well to see what Shakspere meant us to, and we wonder whether any one who hears Mr. Benson in this part with an open mind can doubt that Shakspere meant to draw, in Richard, not only a rake and muff on a throne and falling off it, but, in the same person, an exquisite poet ; to show with one hand how kingdoms are lost and with the other how the creative imagination goes about its work ; to fill the same man

[1] Manchester, 2 Dec., 1899.

with the attributes of a feckless wastrel in high place and with the quite distinct but not incompatible attributes of a typical, a consummate artist.

" But," it will be asked by persons justly tired of sloppy talk about art, " what *is* an artist ; what, exactly, is it in a man that makes an artist of him ? " Well, first a proneness in his mind to revel and bask in its own sense of fact ; not in the use of fact—that is for the men of affairs, the Bolingbrokes ; nor in the explanation of fact—that is for the men of science ; but simply in his own quick and glowing apprehension of what is about him, of all that is done on the earth or goes on in the sky, or dying and being born, of the sun, clouds, and storms, of great deeds and failures, the changes of the seasons, and the strange events of men's lives. To mix with the day's diet of sights and sounds the man of this type seems to bring a wine of his own that lights a fire in his blood as he sits at the meal. What the finest minds of other types eschew he does, and takes pains to do. To shun the dry light, to drench all he sees with himself, his own temperament, the humours of his own moods— this is not his dread but his wish, as well as his bent. " The eye sees what the eye brings the means of seeing." " A fool sees not the same tree that a wise man sees." " You shall see the world in a grain of sand And heaven in a wild flower." This heightened and delighted personal sense of fact, a knack of seeing visions at the instance of seen things, is the basis of art.

Only the basis, though. For that art may come a man must add to it a veritable passion for arresting and defining in words, or lines and colours, or notes of music, not each or any thing that he sees, nor anybody else's sense of that thing, nor yet the greatest common measure of many trained or untrained minds' senses of it, but his own unique sense of it, the precise quality and degree of emotion that the spectacle of it breeds in him and nobody else, the net result of its contact with whatever in his own temperament he has not in common with other men. That is the truth of art, to be true less to facts without you than to yourself as stirred by facts. And truth it must be with a vengeance. To find a glove fit of words for your sense of " the glory and the freshness of a dream," to model the very form and pressure of an inward vision to the millionth of a hair's breadth—the vocabulary of mensuration ludicrously fails to describe those infinitesimal niceties of adjustment between the inward feeling and the means of its presentment. But indeed it is only half true to speak as if feeling and its expression were separable at all. In a sense the former implies the latter. The simplest feeling is itself changed by issuing in a cry. Attaining a kind of completeness, given, as it were, its rights, it is not the same feeling after the cry that it was before. It has become not merely feeling interpreted by something outside it and separable from it, but fuller feeling, a feeling with more in it, feeling pushed one stage further in definiteness and intensity, an arch of feeling crowned at last. So, too, all artistic expression, if one thinks the matter out, is seen to be not merely a transcribing of the artist's sense of fact but a perfecting of that sense itself ; and the experience which never attains expression, the experience which is loosely said to be unexpressed, is really an unfinished, imperfect experience and one which, in the mind of an artist, passionately craves for its own completion through adequate expression. "There are no beautiful thoughts," a fastidious artist has said, "without beautiful forms." The perfect expression *is* the completed emotion. So the artist is incessantly pre occupied in leading his sense of fact up to the point at which it achieves not merely expression but its own completion in the one word, phrase, line, stanza that can make it, simply as a feeling of his own, all that it has in it to be. He may be said to write or paint because there is a point beyond which the joy of tasting the world about him cannot go unless he does so ; and his life passes in a series of moments at which thought and expression, the sense of fact and the consummate presentation of that sense, rush together like Blake's "soul and body reunited," to be indistinguishably fused together in a whole in which, alone, each can attain its own perfection.

We have drawn out this tedious description of the typical artist because the further it goes the more close a description does it become of the Richard whom Mr. Benson shows us in the last three acts. In him every other feeling is mastered, except at a few passing moments, by a passion of interest in the exercise of his gift of exquisite responsiveness to the appeal made to his artistic sensibility by whatever life throws for the moment in his way. Lamb said it was worth while to have been cheated of the legacy so as not to miss " the idea of " the rogue who did it. That, on a little scale, is the kind of æsthetic disinterestedness which in Shakspere's Richard, rightly presented by Mr. Benson, passes all bounds. The " idea of " a king's fall, the " idea of " a wife and husband torn apart, the " idea of " a very crucifixion of indignities—as each new idea comes he revels in his own warmed and lighted apprehension of it as freely as in his apprehension of the majesty and mystery of the idea of kingship by divine right. He runs out to meet the thought of a lower fall or a new shame as a man might go to his door to see a sunset or a storm. It has been called the aim of artistic culture to witness things with appropriate emotions. That is this Richard's aim. Good news or bad news, the first thing with him is to put himself in the right vein for getting the fullest and most poignant sense of its contents. Is ruin the word—his mind runs to steep itself in relevant pathos with which in turn to saturate the object put before it ; he will " talk of graves and epitaphs," " talk of wills," " tell sad stories of the death of kings." Once in the vein, he rejoices like a good artist who has caught the spirit of his subject. The very sense of the loss of hope becomes " that sweet way I was in to despair." To his wife at their last meeting he bequeaths, as one imaginative writer might bequeath to another, some treasure of possibilities of tragic effect, " the lamentable tale of me."

To this intoxicating sense of the beauty or poignancy of what is next him he joins the true passion of concern for its perfect expression. At the height of that preoccupation enmities, fears, mortifications, the very presence of onlookers are as if they were not. At the climax of the agony of the abdication scene Shakspere, with a magnificent boldness of truth, makes the artist's mind, in travail with the lovely poetical figure of the mirror, snatch at the possibility of help at the birth of the beautiful thing, even from the bitterest enemy,—

> say that again ;
> The shadow of my sorrow ; ha, let's see.

And nothing in Mr. Benson's performance was finer than the king's air, during the mirror soliloquy, as of a man going about his mind's engrossing business in a solitude of its own making. He gave their full value, again, to all those passages, so enigmatic, if not ludicrous, to strictly prosaic minds, in which Richard's craving for finished expression issues in a joining of words with figurative action to point and eke them out ; as where he gives away the crown in the simile of the well, inviting his enemy, with the same artistic neutrality as in the passage of the mirror, to collaborate manually in an effort to give perfect expression to the situation. With Aumerle Richard is full of these little symbolic inventions, turning them over lovingly as a writer fondles a phrase that tells. " Would not this ill do well," he says of one of them, like a poet showing a threnody to a friend.

There was just one point—perhaps it was a mere slip—at which Mr. Benson seemed to us to fail. In the beginning of the scene at Pomfret what one may call the artistic heroism of this man, so craven in everything but art, reaches its climax. Ruined, weary, with death waiting in the next room, he is shown still toiling at the attainment of a perfect, because perfectly expressed, apprehension of such flat dregs as are left him of life, still following passionately on the old quest of the ideal word, the unique image, the one perfect way of saying the one thing.

> I cannot do it ; yet I'll hammer it out.

Everybody knows that cry of the artist wrestling with the angel in the dark for the word it will not give, of Balzac " plying the pick for dear life, like an entombed miner," of our own Stevenson, of Flaubert " sick, irritated, the prey a thousand times a day of cruel pain," but " continuing my labour like a true working man, who, with sleeves turned up, in the sweat of his brow, beats away at his anvil, whether it rain or blow, hail or thunder." That " yet I'll hammer it out " is the gem of the whole passage, yet on Saturday Mr. Benson, by some strange mischance, left the words clean out. He made amends with a beautiful little piece of insight at the close, where, after the lines

> Mount, mount, my soul ! Thy seat is up on high,
> Whilst my gross flesh sinks downward, here to die,

uttered much as any other man might utter them under the first shock of the imminence of death, he half rises from the ground with a brightened face and repeats the two last words with a sudden return of animation and interest, the eager spirit leaping up, with a last flicker before it goes quite out, to seize on this new " idea of " the death of the body. Greater love of art could no man have than this, and, if we understood him rightly, it was a brilliant thought of Mr. Benson's to end on such a note. But indeed the whole performance, but for the slip we have mentioned, was brilliant in its equal grasp of the two sides of the character, the one which everybody sees well enough and the one which nearly everybody seems to shun seeing, and in the value which it rendered to the almost continuous flow of genuine and magnificent poetry from Richard, to the descant on mortality in kings, for instance, and the exquisite greeting to English soil and the gorgeous rhetoric of the speeches on divine right in kings. Of Mr. Benson's achievements as an actor, his Richard II strikes us as decidedly the most memorable.

—From " The Manchester Guardian," 4 Dec., 1899 ; and reprinted in *The Manchester Stage*, 1880–1900.

J. T. GREIN

(1862-1935)

ON RÉJANE AS SAPHO

I

IT would be interesting to know what Léon, the son of the great Daudet, thought when he read the notorious book which his father wrote for him as a present on his twentieth birthday. I know full well what I thought when I was twenty, which time coincided with the appearance of *Sapho*. I considered it a highly moral book, a book to be a guiding star in a young man's life—a book containing a dreadful warning against wasted careers and that romanticism which is the privilege and the weakness of our youthful age. I saw merely the object lesson contained in the book, and not its real meaning, which gilds an ill-spent portion of life in such a manner that it is more alluring than deterring. *Sapho*, as a book, is like one of those erotic poems which, after saying many naughty things, suddenly ends up with an envoi not unlike the honourable flag concealing a contraband cargo. To say that *Sapho* is a moral work is to speak with the optimism of twenty, when every goose is a swan, and every Jill seems to be a mate to the Jack who is one's self. To say, at this juncture, that *Sapho* is an immoral book, is to pronounce a truism which is beyond the pale of discussion. What is it then? Well, simply an extremely clever novel written by a man who, having struggled through life, knows it to the full, and casts the eye of leniency on those weaknesses of the flesh to which, in Paris, at least, nearly every youth is heir. Nor will I do the injustice to Daudet to say that *Sapho* is entirely divorced from art. Certainly, it is lurid. It is, to use a word which says more than many sentences, lecherous. But how much is there not in it

255

which causes us to pause and to think ; which sometimes gently touches the heartstrings and which anon, when we have finished, makes us sorry that so many details of fine feeling have been wasted on an unsatisfactory entity ?

The rock on which the book splits is the abject weakness of its hero, and the inherent vulgarity of the heroine. He, Jean, has no redeeming point at all. He is the sort of man who is like dough in the hands of any woman who understands the subtle art of kneading men's weaknesses. Up to a certain point he retains a claim on our sympathy, but when he meets Irene, has a grand chance of counterbalancing a life of laziness, corruption, and opprobrium, and yet returns to the woman who had convinced him of her contempt, we fling him aside as a fruit not speckled only, but rotten to the core. And when we see him leaving the shores of France to take up a Consular appointment somewhere in the Far East, the pang of sorrow which we feel is not for him ; it is caused by the poet who knows how to describe the agony of bidding farewell to Mary Stuart's " Belle France."

As for Sapho, we cannot help feeling drawn to her because she is a victim of circumstances,—I should rather say of her birth. The kernel is good, but the surrounding flesh is so degenerate that she cannot rise to something better. Her instinct tells her at times that she is born for respectability of a certain class, but her birthright seems to hold her back, and to remind her at every moment that she is the daughter of the drink-sodden ne'er-do-well cabman. Yet this woman, light of love, with a past unfathomable, rises at one juncture to greatness. It is when the only man she loved, condemned for forgery, comes out of prison a wreck in body and in soul. Then she does not hesitate to leave the rich young lover and throw in her lot with the *débris* of the other man's life.

That is told by Daudet in beautiful simplicity, and if it had only been re-told by the adaptor, Adolf Belot, in the same pathetic manner, the play of *Sapho* would have justified its right to existence. As it now stands before us it is not a play at all. There are no inner links between the fragments of the story which lingers in the minds of those who have read the book. As I saw it the other day, I was vainly striving to disenfranchise my mind of those recollections, and I would have given much to have been able to judge the play with a mind unbiased by my intimacy with the novel, for, naturally, I could supplement all that was wanting from my storehouse. But what must be the impression on the playgoer who knows nothing of the psychology of the characters, nothing of the motives guiding their actions, nothing beyond the spasmodic episodes forced from the book for the purpose of the play ? I should say that the average man, notably the English playgoer, must feel horrified by the naked exposure of Parisian immorality as depicted in this play. The atmosphere is wholly of patchouli and of cocottes, and the sole occupation of every character concerned seems to be the veneration of Aphrodite, as if there were no other aim in life.

It would likewise be instructive to know what our average playgoer thinks of the Censor who considers the production of such a play harmless to our morals. I, for one, if discussion on the subject were not futile, would say that the play *Sapho* is a comprehensive and useful guide for the young as to " how to be happy though immoral." Yet bad as this play is in construction, in aim, and certainly in characterisation, it has a redeeming charm to which even aversion from the theme cannot blind one. It is the language. Belot may have mutilated the book. He may have been, with the consent of the author, an accessory to the destruction of that which purported to be a work of art. But being a man of letters himself, being a Frenchman, he could not annihilate that which is the priceless treasure of the Gallic nation. The form may have gone ; the depth may have gone ; but one thing remains ; style ! and, through style, a certain charm which covers any amount of defects. The language is at times beautiful. It cannot fail to be beautiful, for the ear of a polished French writer is ever conscious of melody, and that constitutes, in my estimation, one of the main reasons why the French drama still holds its sway over the world.

II

The greatest actress of modern times has come to act this play for us, for I fear no contradiction in so calling Réjane. She is certainly greater than Sarah Bernhardt, because she has more imagination, greater versatility, and because her art is more spontaneous. She is greater than Duse or Sorma, because hers is not only the art of sadness and pathos, it is also the art of gaiety. Rejane, to put it shortly, is not one-sided, she is not artificial, she is universal. When we see her in her effusions of love, we men feel that it is thus we would like to be caressed. When we see her in grief, as in the terrible scene of *La Robe Rouge*, we know that grief must be expressed with that pallor of countenance, that agony of voice. True, in her passion there is an undercurrent of vulgarity, the vulgarity of the " gamin " of Paris, that kaleidoscopic being, exuberant and uncontrollable in every sense. But we cannot reproach Réjane for that. Somehow that touch of lesser refinement belongs to her ; she is a child of the people, she has lived from early youth in Bohemia, and from her blood the Bohemian touch is ineradicable. But let no one imagine that Réjane can never rise to absolute dignity. She has shown us that she can in the transformation of Sans-Gêne the washerwoman into Sans-Gêne the Marshal's wife, who becomes the foil of Napoleon. She has shown it again with greater intensity in that most beautiful play—neglected perhaps, but not forgotten— *Georgette Lemeunier*, one of the finest essays on marital life in modern French literature. She shows it in *Sapho* at intervals. Now she is the cocotte, now the woman lost in love, now the virago defending her reputation when wagging tongues are threatening its destruction—now she is the struggler for life in whom all baser feelings are extinguished in order to do that which is her duty, ruled by destiny. In all this Réjane was superb. I have heard others say that in this play of *Sapho*, she, at times, did not seem to " touch ground," that the play appeared to weary her. I have not found it so. I found her at her greatest. Her accents of love, of passion, of hatred, ever spontaneous, linger like unforgettable echoes in my ear, and that, in particular, is why she is greater than Sarah Bernhardt. The tragédienne has no secrets from me ; I realise from the beginning what she is going to do and how she is going to do it, but in Réjane we are always confronted by the unexpected. It is always a riddle what she will do next, and when it comes it springs upon us with the power of a surprise. Réjane, in fine, is an actress who has a power of governing. She is in a measure a ruler of men, for she controls our mirth as well as our sentiment. She gives herself so entirely that the tears frequently stream from her eyes. She forces us to capitulate in unconditional admiration.

I may be forgiven if my enthusiasm for this great artist has rendered me somewhat ungracious towards the company which surrounds her. The performance is one of all-round excellence, and M. Grand as Jean, Madame Viarny as the delightful Divonne, deserve a special mention. But Réjane is the play, and to sing her praises is to repay a debt of gratitude long since overdue.

—From "The Sunday Special," 23 June, 1901 ; and reprinted in *Dramatic Criticism*. By J. T. Grein, 1902.

A. B. WALKLEY

(1855–1926)

ON BERNARD SHAW'S *THE DOCTOR'S DILEMMA*

Court Theatre.

"I'VE lost the thread of my remarks," says one of Mr. Shaw's physicians; "what was I talking about?" Mr. Shaw himself might say this, or something very like it. True, he does not helplessly lose the thread of his play. But he is continually dropping it, in order that he may start a fresh topic. This foible of discursiveness has been steadily gaining on him. *John Bull* was more discursive than *Man and Superman*. *Major Barbara* was more discursive than *John Bull*. *The Doctor's Dilemma* is more discursive than *Major Barbara*. Needless to point out that this discursiveness is not a new method, but a "throwing back" to a very old method. It was, for instance, the method of Shakespeare. A certain unity of idea does, however, underlie Mr. Shaw's new play, and that is to be found in its satire of the medical profession. Therein he has been anticipated by Brieux in his *L'Evasion*. But of course the theme belongs, as of right, to Molière. Is there not something piquant in the spectacle of Mr. Shaw applying Shakespearean treatment to a Molièrean theme? After all, there is no such thoroughgoing classicist as your professed iconoclast.

Superficially, no doubt, we seem to have travelled a long way from the buffooneries of M. Purgon and M. Diafoirus. Only superficially, however. For the old mock-Latin, for the clysters, for the instruments which modern delicacy does not permit to be named, we now have barbarous Greek—opsonin and phagocytosis—surgical saws and "nuciform sacs." *Plus ça change plus c'est la même chose.* That, by the way, is the criticism which, in effect, the oldest of Mr. Shaw's physicians, Sir Patrick Cullen, is always applying to the new-fangled

discoveries of his fellow-practitioners. He has seen all these
" novelties " before ; they have their law of periodicity—say,
one in every fifteen years—and nothing is altered but the names.
Sir Patrick, who stands for bluff cynical comment on scientific
affectation, heads a group of half-a-dozen medical types.
There is Sir Ralph Bloomfield Bonnington—familiarly known
as " old B. B."—Court physician (much liked by what he
invariably calls " the Family ") and platitudinously pompous
bungler. He is, as you see, an entirely Molièresque figure.
Good easy man, he does not know the difference between a
vaccine and an anti-toxin, and is all for stimulating the phago-
cytes. There is Sir Colenso Ridgeon—just knighted as the
curtain rises for his great " opsonin " discovery—who is all
for buttering the bacilli. There is the great surgeon, Cutler
Walpole, who in every human ill sees blood-poisoning and is
all for cutting out the " nuciform sac." Physic he bluntly
characterises as " rot " ; the physicians, in return, dismiss
surgery as mere " manual labour." There remain two types
not anticipated by Molière ; Leo Schutzmacher, who has made
a fortune in the East-end by selling advice and drugs for
sixpences, under the sign " cure guaranteed," and Dr. Blenkinsop, a hardworking general practitioner who has never succeeded
in making both ends meet and begs fashionable consultants for
their cast-off frockcoats. All these people display their several
humours in a Queen Anne-street consulting-room, whither
they have come to congratulate Sir Colenso Ridgeon on his
Birthday Honour. The irony of the thing is that Sir Colenso's
knighthood is the fruit of one of " old B. B.'s " most glaring
blunders in treating one of " the Family." The disheartened
and disgusted Ridgeon remarks, in an " aside," " Ours is not a
profession, but a conspiracy."

Why not call it, rather, a procession? For that is what it turns
out to be in the conduct of Mr. Shaw's play. Our bevy of
doctors career through the play, always together (one wonders
what becomes of their unfortunate patients), like the wedding
guests in the *Chapeau de Paille d'Italie.* From Queen Anne-
street their line of march takes them to the " Star and Garter "
at Richmond, and thence to Louis Dubedat's studio. But who
is Louis Dubedat ? It is time that he was mentioned here,

though it is a whole hour by the clock—an hour devoted to the exhibition and discussion of medical humours—before you hear of him in the theatre. Louis Dubedat is an artist with a tuberculous lung. Please keep one eye fixed on the art and the other on the lung, for these are the two separate elements out of which Mr. Shaw makes his play. Examine the lung first, for that *motif* still continues the original thesis—medical humbug. Louis Dubedat is the *corpus vile* on which the medical experiments are to be made. Jennifer Dubedat, Louis's wife, has sought out Sir Colenso Ridgeon and, with great difficulty, secured his promise to undertake the case. When Ridgeon consents it is really out of his profound (but entirely discreet) admiration for Jennifer, an idealist from Cornwall, a child of nature, to whom belief in Louis's genius is a religion. But Ridgeon's consent at once places him in a dilemma. He has only staff and accommodation for 40 cases, and all his beds are full. If he takes in Louis, he must dismiss (practically to certain death) one of the original 40 ; life for life. Nevertheless, knowing what he does of Jennifer, and knowing as yet nothing of Louis, he consents. As soon as he gets to know Louis the case is altered. Now is the time for you to remember that Louis is an artist as well as a rich man. You find that he is a particular kind of artist—the non-moral artist, a man without any sense of conduct, to whom the words " right " and " wrong," as ordinarily understood, have no meaning. Think of him as a Pierrot, or as a Faun. *Imprimis*, he belongs to Elia's great race of borrowers. Invited to meet the doctors (in a body, of course) he " touches " each of them for a loan. *Item*, he is a bigamist. *Item*, he is a blackmailer. That people should reprobate these practices is a thing he cannot even begin to understand. When the doctors assume (always in a body) to upbraid him, he sits down and quietly sketches them. He gaily declares himself to be a disciple of Bernard Shaw, a celebrity unknown to Sir Patrick Cullen, who, however, promptly finds in him a moral likeness to John Wesley.

And now Sir Colenso is in a worse dilemma than ever. For he finds that his poor *confrère*, the morally irreproachable Dr. Blenkinsop, has also a tuberculous lung. Which is he to save ? The good Blenkinsop, who is a social failure, or the bad

Dubedat, who paints good pictures? Good men are fairly common, he argues. Good pictures very rare. And he decides in favour of Dubedat. But now there is a fresh complication. Jennifer Dubedat's whole life consists in the worship of Louis. If Louis ceased to be her hero, she would commit suicide—has, indeed, already marked out a certain cliff in Cornwall for that purpose. To prolong Dubedat's life is to ensure that his wife shall sooner or later find him out, and so have her religion shattered and lose her own life into the bargain. Therefore, for Jennifer's sake (even though, to the vulgar mind, it may look like murdering a man in the hope of marrying his widow) Sir Colenso must let Louis die. " Rather hard that a lad should be killed because his wife has too high an opinion of him " is old Sir Patrick's comment ; " fortunately very few of us are in that predicament."

Killed, however, Louis is. Killed because he is handed over by Sir Colenso, the only man who could save him (with magical opsonin butter for the bacilli), to "old B. B.," who doesn't know the difference between a vaccine and an anti-toxin. Louis dies, or fades away, before our eyes, with his head on Jennifer's breast (as Duse dies on Armand's in the last act of *La Dame*), dies like one of Montaigne's Emperors " in a jest," chaffing the doctors all round and uttering his artist's *credo* with his last breath—" I believe in Michael Angelo and Rembrandt and Velasquez and the Message of Art." Incorrigible Pierrot, unregenerate Faun ! *Qualis artifex pereo*, he might have said. But instead of that he says let there be no horrible crape, let not his wife lose her beauty with tears ; he hates widows, she must promise to marry again. Also he gives a plain hint that he understands Sir Colenso's game. So does Jennifer, who coldly dismisses Sir Colenso from the death-chamber. Amateurs of the morbid will revel in this realistic death-scene. Other people will dislike it as bad taste and cheap art. Bad taste in its punctuation of solemnity by jokes (for there is a touch of the Pierrot and the Faun in Mr. Shaw himself). Cheap art in its employment of such a fact as death (realistic, not poetised death) to secure an emotional thrill ; a thrill which, from the very constitution of human nature, is bound to come without any reference to the skill of the artist. Mr.

Shaw made a like mistake in the face " bashing " scene of *Major Barbara*. But it is useless to argue with him over these things. He will do them. All we can do is to be sorry.

There is a brief, quaint, not entirely comprehensible, epilogue. Jennifer and Sir Colenso meet at Louis Dubedat's posthumous " One man show." Sir Colenso, treated with cold disdain, is driven to try and open Jennifer's eyes to the truth about her dead hero. He fails utterly. The secret of his love for her pops out. She mocks at the idea of love in this " elderly gentleman "—a new view of himself for Sir Colenso. Besides, in deference to her hero's dying injunction, she has already married again. The curtain descends while we are still wondering who is Jennifer's second husband. Can it be the well-groomed manager of the Art Gallery ?

A thoroughly " Shavian " play, this, stimulating and diverting for the most part, occasionally distressing, now and then bewildering. O philosopher ! O humorist ! you say with gratitude. And then you whisper, with a half sigh, O Pierrot ! O Faun ! But you are left in no two moods about the playing. There is no such all-round acting in London as is nowadays to be seen at the Court Theatre. Everybody in *The Doctor's Dilemma* is delightful. Where all are excellent it is needless to single out names.

—From " The Times," 21 Nov., 1906 ; and reprinted in
Drama and Life. By A. B. Walkley, 1907.

A. B. WALKLEY ON *ZAZA*

Imperial. May, 1902.

IN Paris they have an expression that may be said to speak volumes, very trashy volumes—the *littérature de concierge*. It is not difficult to conjecture the sort of literature beloved by the autocrat of the street-door. It must be sentimental at all costs, even at the cost of dwelling upon illicit passion, provided that the superior respectability of family life be vindicated in the end. It must have the glitter of the gay world ; indeed, the *concierge* will not object should it verge on the garish. As many people as possible in it must be splendidly dressed. The facile contrast of tortured hearts beating under heavily bejewelled bodices must be rigorously insisted on. No direct and original observation of life is needed ; indeed, it would be resented by the *concierge*, who prefers the conventional emotions and situations which are passed on as " common form " from one hack-writer to another. In an American version of *Zaza* by Mr. Belasco the word *concierge* has, I note, been translated, presumably in accordance with American idiom, as janitor. I thank Mr. Belasco for that word. It provides a convenient and comprehensive label for this play. *Zaza* is pre-eminently janitorious. The doorkeepers of all nations—if I may use the word in a Pickwickian and metaphorical sense—will revel in it. It shows how spangles and a career of music-hall songs are not incompatible with true love. It presents violent contrasts of households in Bohemia and " correct " homes in the most expensively respectable quarters of Paris. It toys with vice and yet pays complete, if tardy, homage to virtue. In short, it is the perfect specimen of the janitorious drama.

The play, which is in five acts (for what *concierge* does not know the orthodox number of acts required for a theatrical masterpiece ?), opens behind the scenes of a concert hall in a French country town. Zaza is the " star " and, of course, has a jealous rival. They are both petulant and vixenish and, at one moment, come to blows. Zaza dresses and " makes up " for her part in view of the audience. The company come and go. Privileged gentlemen in the glossiest evening dress present bouquets. Ah ! that life behind the scenes ! How the doorkeeping mind revels in its gay wickedness ! But Zaza, it need hardly be said, is no common " star." She has a heart—and she has lost it to one of the gentlemen in glossy evening dress, M. Bernard Dufresne, who promptly falls a victim to her wiles. The next act—each act turning a different facet of the heroine to the limelight—shows Zaza playing at simple domestic bliss with M. Dufresne in a country cottage. The *concierge* remembers the parallel case of Marguerite Gautier and Armand Duval, and is happy. But Zaza's bliss is shortlived. She learns from one of her theatrical comrades that M. Dufresne has a wife in Paris. The pair have been seen at the play together, drinking chocolate. " I'll spoil their chocolate," cries the infuriated Zaza, and starts for Paris. Now comes the opportunity for that family sentiment which the doorkeeper feels to be his due. Intent on making a disturbance in the Dufresne household, Zaza is confronted by a little girl, and in the presence of childish innocence she retires humbled and in silence. Then passion has its turn. Zaza turns upon her lover and rends him, works herself into a frenzy of hysteria, and smashes the china on the mantelshelf. A woman shouting at the top of her voice and beside herself with fury is just the sort of woman the *concierge* can understand. " Women, poor things, are like that," he reflects, being in his way a philosopher and ready to take broad views of human nature. Besides, he is well aware that in all these plays a *scène de rupture* is the proper thing. Next to noise—of which in the penultimate act the *concierge* it will have been seen gets his fill—he loves worldly success, gaudy success, symbolised by extravagant costumes, the homage of the multitude, and a smart victoria. Zaza duly provides him with all this. In order to forget her lover she has devoted herself to her profession, and is now an artist of world-wide reputation and boundless wealth. When M. Dufresne comes to seek a reconciliation she parts from him more in sorrow than in anger, bidding him go back to his child, while with dignified simplicity she orders her coachman to drive her " home." A play which ends on the word " home " is bound to captivate the guardian of every street-door in both hemispheres.

Some people, not engaged in doorkeeping, may wonder why such plays as *Zaza* are written. The answer in this case is very simple. *Zaza* was constructed by MM. Berton and Simon to encircle the talent of Mme. Réjane. It is quite certain that, if Mme. Réjane had not been Mme. Réjane, there would have been no *Zaza*. That would not have been a serious calamity. But we must take the world as we find it, and Mme. Réjane as Mme. Réjane. She must be allowed to have her fling. Where is there another actress who can be so *canaille* and frisky and sentimentally grotesque and grotesquely sentimental ? Where is there another actress who can speak so comically through her nose or blow that impudent little organ so realistically after a fit of tears ? Where is there another actress who can so cleverly reproduce the gradual *crescendo* from nervous irritation to suffocating or shrieking hysteria ? The answer is that there is no other such actress, and that therefore Mme.

Réjane must do all these things and be all these things for us in her own inimitable way, and have her fling which is like nobody else's fling. That is the explanation, though not the excuse, of such a play as *Zaza*. Surely such a combination of opposites as this play exhibits—external reality and internal falsity—never was seen before. False, its implied suggestion that the courtesan is " redeemed " by a sincere passion. False, the glamour it throws over the vulgar music-hall " star," who, purged by grief, ends as a person of lofty sentiments and elegant language. False, the sentimental excuses of Zaza for her—let us say Bohemian—life, on the score of parental neglect. False, the conversion of Zaza from a virago bent on revenge to a humbled penitent, all on account of a talk with a pert little child. False, the character of Zaza's lover—or, rather not false, but null, as this personage is a mere automaton, a mere whetstone for Zaza to grind her various axes upon. False, intolerably false, the whole atmosphere of the play, its representation of love—and such love !—as sanctifying everything, accounting for everything, indeed, constituting everything. Looked at from the point of view of a mind and the feelings, the heart and the brain, *Zaza* is a miracle of falsity.

And yet, externally, how real ! Watch the music-hall " artist " at her toilet—how she rubs in the grease-paint, unpins her false hair, dabs the powder-puff over her shoulders, putting on a pinafore the while in order not to soil her skirt. Not a detail is missed. Even when the corset is unlaced, Zaza is careful to go through the pantomime of holding her breath. All the world and his wife have been shown exactly how the " artist " dresses and undresses ; we feel that the sum of human knowledge has been appreciably augmented. But on the principle that you cannot have too much of a good thing, Zaza does it all, or nearly all, over again. Having combed her hair in Act I., she combs it once more in Act IV., and offers you a further piece of minute realism by removing the loose ends of hair from the comb and throwing them out of the window. Then she dusts the chair with her uplifted petticoats, cleans the wine-glasses by blowing into them and giving them a wipe with her dressing-gown, and performs other choice little Bohemian-domestic exploits to which only the pen of a Swift could do full justice. Or watch Zaza discovering a hole in the tablecloth, making faces at the *bonne* about it, and trying to hide it with a plate. What a " convincing " spectacle, what a marvellous application of another player's famous theory about holding the mirror up to nature ! When you have done with these mechanical details, these " fireside concerns " as Elia would have called them, you may turn to examine Zaza in an attack of nerves. See her mouth twitching, her hands clenched, listen to the shrill note gradually coming into her voice. Then sit tight in your seat for the final explosion, the total physical abandonment and degradation. It is the very thing. Coleridge had a mock apostrophe to

Inoculation ! Heavenly maid !

So Mme. Réjane—for Mme. Réjane and Zaza are one—so Mme. Réjane is the muse of hystero-epilepsy.

And when you have wallowed in the crapulous, and been dragged through the sordid, and shocked with the frantic, and fooled by the sham-sentimental for five acts, at the end of it all the question occurs—Is even Mme. Réjane " worth it " ? She does it all to the life—seems, in fact, to *live* the character. But *Zaza* is rather a heavy price to pay even for this incomparable talent.

What really saves Mme. Réjane and the play is her unfailing sense of humour. Her winks of intelligence, her droll intonations, her irrepressible playfulness do relieve the character of some of its grossness. You come back to the old position. Because Réjane is Réjane, the disagreeable play has been written ; and if, on occasion, you cannot help being pleased in spite of yourself, that also is because Réjane is Réjane.

—From *Drama and Life*.

A NEW THEATRICAL ADVENTURE STARTED WITH *KING LEAR*

Haymarket Theatre.

ADVENTURES are to the adventurous, as somebody said in one of Disraeli's novels ; a poet who commences *impresario* is presumably adventurous, and a presentation of *King Lear* in the present day is without doubt an adventure. When

King Lear was done at the Lyceum now some years ago it was perhaps something of a misadventure. On the whole it was found to create a sense of boredom—and whatever new theories the latest exegetes of Aristotle may propound as to the meaning of the tragic *katharsis*, none of them, we fancy, will pretend that it is the function of tragedy to bore. It was courageous, then—or even, as R. L. Stevenson would have said, temerarious —of Mr. Herbert Trench to start his theatrical management with *King Lear*. We may say at once, however, that in our judgment his audacity has been justified by the event. His production of the tragedy gives rise to all sorts of feelings, confused, it may be conflicting, feelings, but they do not include the feeling, the least beginning of the feeling, of boredom.

One's first feelings over the play are rather feelings of bewilderment, strangeness, vague irritation. About the early scenes there is something almost babyish ! The old man who parcels out his kingdom by the map ; the daughters who overdo their thanks with a fulsome excess that any child would see through ; the simple, obvious contrast of the daughter who cannot say " thank you " at all ; the absurd wrath of the old man over a situation that any father with any daughter could not fail to understand. Then follow undignified things, acts of schoolboy rudeness, pushings and kickings and trippings up. The people remind you of some simple South Sea Islanders in some 18th century traveller's narrative—peering through the wrong end of a telescope, expressing their emotions by uncouth dances, and filled with delight by the present of some coloured beads. How, you ask, are these primitive, rather absurd, folk going to excite in you the proper tragic emotions ?

Well, the answer is that in the event they do. Hardly have you done smiling over the trivialities of the disputes between Lear and his daughters—by how many men his " establishment" shall be cut down, or whether he cannot get on very well without any " establishment " at all—hardly have you done smiling (with some irritation) over these *menus détails*, when you find yourself caught, as it were, by the throat and filled, over-filled, with a strange distress. All those mad, half-mad, or shamming-mad people on the heath in the thunderstorm—you are oppressed with the uncanny nature of the thing. You don't follow their words very closely—there is no sense, pro-saically speaking, in their words—but the melody, the atmo-sphere, of the whole thing gets hold of you till you feel you can bear it no longer.

Then comes a moment of savagery—the blinding of Glouces-ter—and you are reminded of the South Sea Islanders once more, this time with disgust. But close upon this feeling of disgust comes the other one of immense pity and tenderness over the softer moments of Lear's madness, when his frenzy has spent its strength and he has become a pleading child. "Do not laugh at me"—well, every one knows that wonderful line; it is hackneyed, and in your dread of the hackneyed you try and steel yourself against it. But your effort is of no use; you give way, and henceforth surrender yourself to the might and to the piteousness of this tremendous tragedy.

That, at any rate, is what one had to do, willy nilly, at the Haymarket last night. Your anticipated boredom never re-curred, the thing held you as in a vice, and you came away, saying once more of Shakespeare, as the gentleman in Labiche's farce said of some one else, " Oh quel dentiste, il n'y a que lui!"

What were the main elements that combined to produce this impression in you? First of all, the simplicity and directness of the acting. There was no posturing, no sacrifice of the author to the player. The actors set themselves to understand the words they had to say, and then said them for all they were worth. Mr. Norman McKinnel, for instance, knows that the part of Lear will, as it were, play itself, if fairly allowed to do so. He never forces the note, but is content to *feel* the part, and thus to make the audience feel it in their turn. He dwells most lovingly, perhaps, on the homely features of the character, upon the little childlike things, the weakness, the pleading, the *ahurissement* of the old man. That is to say he aims at nothing colossal, nothing Michelangelesque; and in that moderation we hold that he does well. For he succeeds in making the thing profoundly affecting. So it is, too, with the others, the Kent of Mr. France, the Gloucester of Mr. Hearn, the Cornwall of Mr. Fisher White, and Mr. Hignett's Fool; they are all simple, straightforward, above all sincerely *felt* performances. Miss O'Malley is a quietly pathetic, not over-sentimentalised

Cordelia ; the Goneril and Regan of Miss Ada Ferrar and Miss Marie Polini do sufficiently well ; as also do Mr. Dawson Milward and Mr. Charles Quartermaine as Edmund and Edgar.

Along with the simplicity and directness of the acting you have the simplicity of the setting. Mr. Charles Ricketts has designed his few scenes in bold masses ; they satisfy the eye without distracting the attention. One of them, the Dover cliff scene, is a thing of perfect beauty. The barbaric costumes perhaps are more curious than beautiful.

Finally, there is the musical accompaniment of Mr. Norman O'Neill, quite charming music, but never too insistent, too obtrusive. Thus the total effect is one of wholeness, harmony, simplicity. To say that is to say, is it not ? that this time *King Lear* has been worthily and successfully presented on the modern stage. Mr. Trench, then, is to be congratulated on the outcome of his first adventure ; he has given theatrical substance and form to a great work of art in the spirit of a true artist.

—From " The Times," 4 Sept., 1909.

MAX BEERBOHM

(1872-1956)

SARAH

July 9, 1904.

IT is our instinct to revere old age. In this reverence, if we analyse it, we find two constituent emotions—the emotion of pity, and the emotion of envy. Opposite though they are, both are caused by one thing. It is sad that so brief a span remains, but it must be delightful to have accomplished so long a span. Any moment may be our last. A flash of lightning, a side-slip, a falling brick—always some improvisible chance that may precipitate us into the unknown. And how foolish we should look then—we with so little to our account ! Certainly, it is enviable to have accumulated so much as have those elders, and to know, as they know, that no power can steal it away. Romantic awe is stirred in us by the contemplation of anything that has been going on for a long time. Ruins are apt to leave us cold ; but any upstanding and habitable old building must touch and warm our imagination. Undefeated by time, any old building, however humble and obscure, becomes for us majestic. But greater, of course, and more haunting, the majesty of an old castle or cathedral. To have towered illustriously through the ages, a centre of significance and pomp, and to be towering thus even now! As with buildings, so with human beings. The romantic quality of an old person is intensified in ratio to the prominence of his or her past and present. There has been in our own time one figure that incomparably illustrated this rule. I am glad to have lived in a time when it was possible to set eyes on the aged Queen Victoria. I can conceive no more romantic thrill than I had whenever, in the last years of her reign, I saw her drive past in that old-fashioned barouche, attended not only by that

273

clattering cavalcade of material guardsmen, but also by the phantoms—not less clearly there—of Melbourne and the Duke, Louis Philippe, Palmerston, Peel, Disraeli the younger—of all those many successive sovereigns, statesmen, soldiers, who were but great misty names to us, yet had been sharp little realities to her, in the interminable pageant of her existence. Strange, to see her with my own eyes—that little old lady, in the queer barouche, on her way to Paddington Station. In Queen Victoria I saw always something of that uncanny symbolism which Mr. Pater saw in the portrait of Mona Lisa. Hers, too, surely, was the head upon which all the ends of the world were come, and the eyelids were a little weary. . . . There is no one now to give me that kind of emotion in like degree ; but, certainly, the person most nearly filling the void is Madame Sarah Bernhardt, who has played during the past fortnight at His Majesty's Theatre. Year by year, when she comes among us, my wonder and awe are intensified. Seeing her, a few nights ago, in *La Sorcière*, I was more than ever moved by the apparition. The great Sarah—pre-eminently great throughout the past four decades ! My imagination roved back to lose itself in the golden haze of the Second Empire. My imagination roved back to reel at the number of plays that had been written, the number of players whose stars had risen and set, the number of theatres that had been built and theatres that had been demolished, since Sarah's début. The theatrical history of more than forty years lay strewn in the train of that bowing and bright-eyed lady. The applause of innumerable thousands of men and women, now laid in their graves, was still echoing around her. And still she was bowing, bright-eyed, to fresh applause. The time would come when our noisy hands would be folded and immobile for ever. But, though we should be beneath the grass, Sarah would still be behind the footlights—be bowing, as graciously as ever, to audiences recruited from the ranks of those who are now babes unborn. A marvellous woman ! For all the gamut of her experience, she is still lightly triumphant over time. All this has been to her, as to Mona Lisa, but as the sound of lyres and flutes, and lives only in the delicacy with which it has moulded the changing lineaments, and tinged the hair. Hers is the head upon which all the ends of the world are come, and the eyelids are not at all weary. . . .

Such was my first impression, when Sarah reappeared to me in *La Sorcière*. But presently I had to qualify it. Superficially, it is quite true that Sarah triumphs over time. Her appearance, her voice, her movements are all as ever. But her spirit shows the inevitable signs of wear and tear. Time has succeeded in damping the sacred fire that burnt within her. Gone from her are the passion and sincerity that once held us in thrall. As Phèdre, as Fédora, as any of the characters created by her in her prime, she is as enthralling, doubtless, as in the past, forasmuch as her unimpaired energy and memory enable her to reproduce exactly the effects that she produced then. But when she plays a new part, as in *La Sorcière*, you are definitely aware that she is not feeling anything—that she is merely urging herself to the performance of certain tricks. Very perfectly she performs these time-honoured tricks. The lovely voice is always in tune and time, whether it coo or hiss, and the lovely gestures are all in their proper places, and the lovely face is as expressive as ever. But the whole performance is hollow—art without life—a dead thing galvanised. Of course, the play—a play written by the venerable M. Sardou for no purpose but to show Sarah off in the ways in which she likes to be shown off—is itself an utterly dead thing. But there was a time when Sarah could have put life into it. And for her failure to put life into it now we may console ourselves with the implicit revelation that she, too, after all, is mortal, like the rest of us.

Though her genius has been touched thus by Time, all untouched is her love of adventure ; and she has given a performance of *Pelléas et Mélisande*, with herself as Pelléas, and Mrs. Campbell as Mélisande. I did not see this performance. I love the play too well, and am loth that my memory of it as performed by Mrs. Campbell in her own language, with Mr. Martin Harvey as Pelléas, should be complicated with any memory less pleasing. I am quite willing to assume that Mrs. Campbell speaks French as exquisitely as she speaks English, and that Sarah's Pelléas is not, like her Hamlet and her Duc de Reichstadt, merely ladylike. But the two facts remain that

Sarah is a woman and that Mrs. Campbell is an Englishwoman. And by these two facts such a performance is ruled out of the sphere of art into the sphere of sensationalism. If Maeterlinck were a sensationalist, that would not matter.

> —From " The Saturday Review " ; and reprinted in *Around Theatres*. By Max Beerbohm, 1924.

MAX BEERBOHM ON HENRY IRVING

October 21, 1905.

ONE mourns not merely a great actor, who had been a great manager. Irving was so romantically remarkable a figure in modern life, having such a hold on one's imagination (partly because he left so much to it), that his death is like the loss of a legend. As an actor, and as a manager, he had his faults ; and these faults were obvious. But as a personality he was flawless—armed at all points in an impenetrable and darkly-gleaming armour of his own design. " The Knight from Nowhere " was the title of a little book of Pre-Raphaelite poems that I once read. I always thought of Irving as the Knight from Nowhere.

That he, throughout his memorable tenancy of the Lyceum Theatre, did nothing to encourage the better sort of modern playwright, is a fact for which not he himself should be blamed. It was the fault of the Lyceum Theatre. In that vast and yawning gulf the better sort of modern drama would (for that it consists in the realistic handling of a few characters in ordinary modern life) have been drowned and lost utterly. On a huge stage, facing a huge auditorium, there must be plenty of crowds, bustle, uproar. Drama that gives no scope for these things must be performed in reasonably small places. A more plausible grievance against Irving, as manager, is that in quest of bustling romances or melodramas he seemed generally to alight on hack-work. I think there can be no doubt that he was lacking in literary sense, and was content with any play that gave him scope for a great and central display of his genius in acting. He did not, of course, invent the " star " system. But he carried it as far as it could be carried. And the further he carried it, the greater his success. From an artistic standpoint, I admit that this system is indefensible. But theatres, alas ! have box-offices ; and the public cares far more, alack ! for a favourite actor than for dramatic art. Justice, then, blames rather the public than the favourite actor.

It was as a producer of Shakespeare that Irving was great in management. He was the first man to give Shakespeare a setting contrived with archaic and æsthetic care—a setting that should match the pleasure of the eye with the pleasure of the ear. That was a noble conception. Many people object, quite honestly, that the pleasure of the ear is diminished by that of the eye—that spectacle is a foe to poetry. Of course, spectacle may be overdone. Irving may sometimes have overdone it ; but he always overdid it beautifully. And there was this further excuse for him : he could not, even had the stage been as bare as a desert, have given us the true music and magic of Shakespeare's verse. He could not declaim. That was one of the defects in his art. His voice could not be attuned to the glories of rhythmic cadence. It was a strange, suggestive voice that admirably attuned itself to the subtleties of Irving's conception of whatever part he was playing. It was Irving's subtle conception, always, that we went to see. Here, again, Irving was an innovator. I gather that the actors of his day had been simple, rough-and-ready, orotund fellows who plunged into this or that play, very much as the water-horse plunges through the reeds. They were magnificent, but they had no pretensions to intellect. Irving had these pretensions, and he never failed to justify them. One missed the music of the verse, but was always arrested, stimulated, by the meanings that he made the verse yield to him. These subtle and sometimes profound meanings were not always Shakespeare's own. Now and again, the verse seemed to yield them to Irving only after an intense effort, and with a rather bad grace. All the parts that Irving played were exacting parts, but he had his revenge sometimes, exacting even more from them. This was another defect in his art : he could not impersonate. His voice, face, figure, port, were not transformable. But so fine was the personality to which they belonged that none cried shame when this or that part had to submit to be crushed by it. Intransformable, he was—multi-radiant, though. He had, in acting, a keen sense of humour—of sardonic, grotesque, fantastic humour. He had an incomparable power for eeriness—for stirring a dim sense of mystery ; and not less masterly was he in evoking a sharp sense of horror. His dignity was magnificent in purely philosophic or priestly gentleness, or in the gaunt aloofness of philosopher or king. He could be benign with a tinge of malevolence, and arrogant with an undercurrent of sweetness. As philosopher or king, poet or prelate, he was matchless. One felt that if Charles the Martyr, Dante, Wolsey, were not precisely as he was, so much the worse for Wolsey, Dante, Charles the Martyr. On the other hand, less august types, such as men of action and men of passion, were outside his range, and suffered badly when he dragged them within it. Macbeth had a philosophic side, which enabled Macbeth to come fairly well out of the ordeal. But Romeo's suicide in the vault of Capulet could only be regarded as a merciful release. Unfortunately, though I saw and can remember Irving as Romeo, I never saw him as Hamlet. This is one of the regrets of my life. I can imagine the gentleness (with a faint strain of cruelty), the aloofness, the grace and force of intellect, in virtue of which that performance must have been a very masterpiece of interpretation. I can imagine, too, the mystery with which Irving must have involved, rightly, the figure of Hamlet, making it loom through the mist mightily, as a world-type, not as a mere individual—making it loom as it loomed in the soul of Shakespeare himself—not merely causing it to strut agreeably, littly, as in the average production. Above all, I can imagine how much of sheer beauty this interpretation must have had. Though, as I have said, Irving could not do justice to the sound of blank-verse, his prime appeal was always to the sense of beauty. It was not, I admit, to a sense of obvious beauty. It was to a sense of strange, delicate, almost mystical and unearthly beauty. To those who possessed not, nor could acquire, this sense, Irving appeared always in a rather ridiculous light. " Why does he walk like this ? Why does he talk like that ? " But, for any one equipped to appreciate him, his gait and his utterance were not less dear than his face—were part of a harmony that was as fine as it was strange. And, though the cruder members of the audience could not fall under the spell of this harmony, they were never irreverent until they reached their homes. Never once at the Lyceum did I hear a titter. Irving's presence dominated even those who could not be enchanted by it. His magnetism was intense, and unceasing. What exactly magnetism is, I do not know. It may be an exhalation of the soul, or it may be a purely physical thing—an effusion of certain rays which will one day be discovered, and named after their discoverer—Professor Jenkinson, perhaps : the Jenkinson Rays. I only know that Irving possessed this gift of magnetism in a supreme degree. And I conjecture that to it, rather than to the quality of his genius, which was a thing to be really appreciated only by the few, was due the unparalleled sway that he had over the many.

In private life he was not less magnetic than on the stage. The obituarists seem hardly to do justice to the intensely interesting personality of Irving in private life. He has been depicted by them merely as a benevolent gentleman who was always doing this or that obscure person a good turn. Certainly, Irving was benevolent, and all sorts of people profited by his generosity. But these two facts are poor substitutes for the impression that Irving made on those who were brought into contact with him. He was always courteous and gracious, and everybody was fascinated by him ; but I think there were few who did not also fear him. Always in the company of his friends and acquaintances—doubtless, not in that of his most intimate friends—there was an air of sardonic reserve behind his cordiality. He seemed always to be watching, and watching from a slight altitude. As when, on the first or last night of a play, he made his speech before the curtain, and concluded by calling himself the public's " respectful—devoted—loving—servant," with special emphasis on the word " servant," he seemed always so like to some mighty cardinal stooping to wash the feet of pilgrims at the altar-steps, so, when in private life people had the honour of meeting Irving, his exquisite manner of welcome stirred fear as well as love in their hearts. Irving, I think, wished to be feared as well as loved. He was " a good fellow " ; but he was also a man of genius, who had achieved pre-eminence in his art, and, thereby, eminence in the national life ; and, naturally, he was not going to let the " good fellow " in him rob him of the respect that was his due. Also, I think, the process of making himself feared appealed to something elfish in his nature. Remember, he was a comedian, as well as a tragedian. Tragic acting on the stage is, necessarily, an assumption ; but comedy comes out of the actor's own soul. Surely, to be ever " grand seigneur," to be ever pontifically gracious in what he said and in his manner of saying it, and to watch the effect that he made, was all wine to the comedic soul of Irving. He enjoyed the dignity of his position, but enjoyed even more, I conjecture, the fun of it. I formed the theory, once and for all, one morning in the year 1895—the morning of the day appointed for various gentlemen to be knighted at Windsor Castle. I was crossing the road, opposite the Marble Arch, when a brougham passed me. It contained Irving, evidently on his way to Paddington. Irving, in his most pre-latical mood, had always a touch—a trace here and there—of the old Bohemian. But as I caught sight of him on this occasion—a great occasion, naturally, in his career ; though to me it had seemed rather a bathos, this superimposition of a smug Hanoverian knighthood on the Knight from Nowhere—he was the old Bohemian, and nothing else. His hat was tilted at more than its usual angle, and his long cigar seemed longer than ever ; and on his face was a look of such ruminant, sly fun as I have never seen equalled. I had but a moment's glimpse of him ; but that was enough to show me the soul of a comedian revelling in the part he was about to play—of a comedic philosopher revelling in a foolish world. I was sure that when he alighted on the platform of Paddington his bearing would be more than ever grave and stately, with even the usual touch of Bohemianism obliterated now in honour of the honour that was to befall him.

Apart from his genuine kindness, and his grace and magnet-ism, it was this sense that he was always playing a part—that he preserved always, for almost every one, a certain barrier of mystery—that made Irving so fascinating a figure. That day, when I saw him on his way to Windsor, and tried to imagine just what impression he would make on Queen Victoria, I found myself thinking of the impression made there by Disraeli;

and I fancied that the two impressions might be rather similar. Both men were courtiers, yet incongruous in a court. And both had a certain dandyism—the arrangement of their hair and the fashion of their clothes carefully thought out in reference to their appearance and their temperament. And both, it seemed to me, had something of dandyism in the wider, philosophic sense of the word—were men whose whole life was ordered with a certain ceremonial, as courtly functions are ordered. " Brodribb," certainly, was an English name ; but surely Irving had some strong strain of foreign blood : neither his appearance nor the quality of his genius was that of an Englishman. Possibly, like Disraeli, he had Spanish blood. Anyhow, his was an exotic mind, like Disraeli's, dominating its drab environment partly by its strength and partly by its strangeness. Both men were romantic to the core, ever conceiving large and grandiose ideas, which they executed with a fond eye to pageantry. And, above all, both men preserved in the glare of fame that quality of mystery which is not essential to genius, but which is the safest insurance against oblivion. It has been truly said that Irving would have been eminent in any walk of life. Had Disraeli the Younger drifted from literature to the footlights, and had Henry Brodribb strayed from the schoolroom into politics, I daresay that neither our political nor our theatrical history would be very different from what it is—except in the matter of dates.

—From " The Saturday Review " ; and reprinted in *Around Theatres*.

C. H. HERFORD

(1853–1931)

ON IBSEN'S *THE MASTER BUILDER*

Theatre Royal, Manchester.

THE *Master Builder*, first published in 1892, has never been
and can never be, among the plays of Ibsen which appeal
powerfully to the ordinary playgoer. It exercises its undoubted fascination upon a section only of the more elect and
qualified spirits among Ibsen's admirers, and one may take it
as a very tangible compliment to Manchester that the organ-
isers of this performance have estimated the city to contain
enough even of this mere subdivision of the elect to fill the
Theatre Royal for six nights and a matinée. There are, on the
surface at any rate, none of the obvious and familiar problems,
interwoven with the very tissue of nineteenth-century thought
and passion, which meet us again and again in the earlier social
dramas—the emancipation of wives, the responsibility of
parents, the break-up of ancient form and usage. A young
lady comes on a visit to an elderly architect, and persuades him,
after long palavers, to mount the spire of a new house he is
building ; unluckily, at the top he grows giddy, falls down,
and is killed on the spot. Stated in this bald way, the plot of
the *Master Builder* must appear exasperatingly trivial ; and in
intrinsic tragic quality, considered simply as a piece of action,
the accident to Solness, which closes the play, cannot be compared with the self-sought doom of Rosmer and Rebekka, the
horrible blank cry of Oswald, or even the banged door of Nora.
Nowhere has Ibsen turned away with more complete apparent
indifference from the stock expedients and resources of tragic
drama to play ostensibly with the gossamers of fairy legend
and the chaff and straw of daily routine. And nowhere has
his amazing faculty of making these fantastic gossamers and this

banal chaff and straw indexes of the great currents and eddies in the tides of universal human life more signally asserted itself.

No doubt the symbolic way of expression which Ibsen here so freely uses has its disadvantages, particularly for the type of hearer who calls everything unintelligible which cannot be set down in unmistakable black and white. It is possible to dispute the precise drift of many details, or even whole scenes, of the *Master Builder*. But no one can dispute the richness of the harmonic chords or the amplitude of the music which these seemingly trivial notes evoke. The fundamental situation is only a subtle variation of that impact of exuberant unspoiled vitality upon lives moulded by convention or unnerved by doubt which perennially occupied Ibsen. But we are far, here, from the trenchant simplicity with which that situation is presented in Lona Hessel and Bernick, in Hakon and Skjule, in Brand and Einar. The nearest parallel is Rebekka and Rosmer in *Rosmersholm*, but it is a parallel in which almost every common ingredient is turned to an utterly different account. Solness, like Rosmer, is a man of parts whose best years are gone by ; his ambition is vigorous as ever, and he still holds his own against all rivalry ; but his nerve, his security, and his self-confidence are only ostensibly what they were. The romance and idealism of youth still flicker and gleam in his eyes, but he can neither yield to their spell nor fall back contentedly to the sober ways of prose. Once an enthusiastic builder of churches—churches wih lofty belfries,—he had turned to build " snug and comfortable homes for men " ; but that occupation was not for him either, though his flagging will can devise only half-hearted and futile measure of escape. He speculates on the chance of a fire burning down his own antiquated house, that he may be able to build an architectural marvel that will finally establish his fame ; and when the play opens he is actually building it—a home indeed, but with an enormously tall tower and spire, idly mimicking the church belfry,—a transparent enough symbol for the futile recurrence to old ideals when their day and relevance are gone by. And while Solness is preoccupied with his hollow aspirations all sound ambitions succumb or are stifled in his *entourage* ; the two Broviks, father and son, go to the wall ; the passive

Kaja drifts helplessly under his spell, Aline, his wife, becomes a hapless thing of brooding memories and mechanical pieties, resigned to the loss of her twins ("for all is well with them now"), but moaning for her burnt "dolls." Upon this little world of abortive impulses and out-of-date renascence there bursts unheralded, one day, the radiant apparition of Hilde Wangel. Hilde is one of the most original and piquant, as she is one of the strangest, of Ibsen's company of strange women ; a figure hovering perpetually between reality and romance. With her enters the very genius of youth, ready to take the world by storm, indomitably confident of its power and of its right, getting its end by the completeness of its faith, and little heeding the disasters it occasions or inflicts on the way. In the architectural symbolism of the play Hilde has her clearly marked counterpart. Her castle is in the air, the region of soaring spires, as Aline's is the old home in the vanished past ; and she sets out, alpenstock in hand and knapsack on back, to compel it to be realised, as Aline desperately hugs her fond memories and refuses to let them die. Modern readers of a certain type are shocked, or would once have been shocked, by Hilde's "improprieties," and her little social indiscretions do indeed afford her a breezy delight. But she is fundamentally incapable of being classed by these standards—a Nietzschean creature, "beyond good and evil," with the demonic witchery of the troll, the tamelessness of the bird of prey, the robust conscience of the Valkyrie. The demeanour of the flagging but still sensitive vitality of Solness in the presence of this dangerously potent stimulus is the primary subject of the play, and no close observer can mistake the extraordinary richness and delicacy of the psychological drawing by which its operation is exhibited. As always with Ibsen, who hardly recognises such a thing as a purely beneficent social contact, this clash of unlike yet kindred spirits is tragic. All the half-extinguished romance in Solness's nature revives at her touch, but only to allure him into the airy region of the "impossible," where she securely treads, but where his doubting steps inevitably betray him to a fall. Mastered by her will and inspired by her faith, he is about to put the crowning touch to her actualised "castle in the air"—symbolised by his hanging the wreath about the vane of the new spire,—when he falters, and in his crushed body Hilde's nascent "kingdom" and his own half-recovered youth alike sink shattered to the ground. Sex, it is to be noted, has very little to do with the issues that here preoccupy Ibsen. Problems of married life, which in most hands, and in his own a dozen years before, would have loomed in the forefront, are here subordinate to the problems which arise out of the eternal disparity of old and young, of the passing and the coming generation ; problems more urgent, perhaps, and more interesting than the former to the veteran poet—himself occupied in this very play in trying whether his hand retained its cunning and could still avail to place one more crown, under the eyes of expectant Europe, upon the towering fabric of his finished work.

The playing of Ibsen is a special art which makes peculiar and even unique demands upon the whole stage company. And in England there is as yet no Ibsenian school of actors, no established tradition such as, on the Continent, a few great players like Duse have created for parts like Nora or Rebekka. To play him, again, in any other language than his own involves fresh difficulties. English society is not very like Norwegian, and Ibsen's subtly calculated phrases—bare bones of speech, full of implicit marrow—are harder than a more explicit and leisurely articulate speech to render in perfectly equivalent values. A curious example of perhaps inevitable inadequacy occurs in Mr. Archer's generally admirable translation. "Duty ! Duty ! Duty !" Hilde once exclaims in a scornful outburst. "What a short, sharp, stinging word !" The epithets do not seem especially apt. But in the original she cries out "Pligt ! Pligt ! Pligt !" and the very word stings and snaps.

Mr. Lovel and his company deserve credit for a very competent, and at points even brilliant, effort to triumph over the manifold difficulties which the production of such a play as the *Master Builder* in England involves. The greatest success was no doubt achieved by Miss Kenmore. Her Hilde was throughout very fresh and delightful, full of vivacious byplay and versatile charm, and with sufficiently accentuated light and shade. All in Hilde that is arch and gay, girlish, sportive, sentimental she rendered with captivating skill. But her conception of the character seemed to us somewhat less just to the stronger, harder, more masculine side of Hilde's complex nature, to the Hilde of the robust conscience, Hilde the " bird of prey." Mr. Lovel's Solness, a supremely difficult part, was also a piece of highly intelligent acting. With him, too, as with Miss Kenmore, it was the more positive and realistic sides of the character which received the most adequate rendering. His Solness was, to our mind, too genuinely vigorous ; the man's strength suggested too little the hidden flaw, the inner hollowness ; and his open profession of madness seemed needlessly gratuitous and irrelevant. Of the other characters, Miss Caryllon's Aline was sombre indeed, an all but unbroken monotone, as Ibsen meant this somewhat thankless part to be. Dr. Herdal, whom malicious critics have declared to be the only sane person in the play, or one whose only mark of insanity is that he thinks the rest are sane, had good medical manners, but somewhat dour and grim, in the fashion of Scotland rather than of Norway ; and his occasional genial and playful remarks seemed like intrusive bits of melody in another key. Miss Lewis as Kaja was conscientious, but too restless, hysteric, and sentimental for this meek and patient Ophelia. When all qualifications are made, however, Mr. Lovel and his company have provided an experience which no student of Ibsen will willingly forego, and may be cordially congratulated on the result.

—From " The Manchester Guardian," 23 April, 1909.

ALLAN MONKHOUSE

(1858-1936)

ON *CORIOLANUS* AND *LOVE'S LABOUR'S LOST* AT STRATFORD

Memorial Theatre.

STRATFORD is a pleasant place to revisit, and, not having seen Mr. Benson since last year's festival, one likes to play with the illusion that he has been here all the time, playing to enthusiastic audiences and constantly beating the record in the revival of plays which timid spirits dare not touch. To-night, when *Love's Labour's Lost* is to be played, is the great occasion, and it seems that scores, or hundreds, will batter at the doors in the vain desire to see it ; but *Coriolanus*, with which the festival began last evening, is perhaps a better example of what can well be done at Stratford and only doubtfully and experimentally elsewhere. It is a great play that can hardly become part of the repertory of a company which must please to live, though one may remember that Mr. Benson produced it in Manchester some eight or nine years ago. On that occasion, too, he had the assistance of Miss Geneviève Ward, who played Volumnia last night. This distinguished actress, who used to stir our young blood in the famous melodrama *Forget-Me-Not* ever so many years ago, and was a memorable Lady Macbeth and Queen Katherine, is one of the famous people who are helping Mr. Benson to make this year's festival a particularly stimulating one. Several of these brilliant outsiders, such as Sir Charles Wyndham and Mr. Alexander, seem to have faded away since the first announcements were made, but a brave show of plays and players remains. There are to be several novelties not strictly Shaksperean, but next week Mr. Lewis Waller's Othello and Mr. Bourchier's Macbeth will be seen. There is to be a costume ball in the Town Hall, and a Floral Procession, and all the materials for a fine, high-toned holiday are here.

Frankly, the critical attitude is not easily maintained at Stratford-on-Avon. We are all a little elated, and with a series of great plays and fine actors and a town gaily decorated for the occasion the impulse to cry " Splendid ! " and " Glorious ! " as the pageants unroll can hardly be resisted. And here one seems to have lost the sense of detachment that encompasses the playgoer in Manchester or London. We are all concerned in the affair, and, really, one has the feeling that it would be good to take a hand. The stage seems to come nearer to us at Stratford than elsewhere ; to face the audience would hardly be formidable in this friendly atmosphere, and one would rather like to " go on " as a Volscian lord. Certainly it would be delightful to join Mr. Weir as a citizen, for the scrimmages are immense. Perhaps we are disposed to think of joining the actors because the actors here do veritably step down from their pedestals and take their part with us. They must do a vast amount of rehearsing, but we meet them at every corner, and they seem pleasant, human creatures and, one hopes and believes, great actors, every one.

Coriolanus is a noble play, but it has not the quality of entertainment to make it a popular one. It has two great interests— the opposition of Coriolanus to the rabble and " the match of passions played out for life and death between a mother and a son." The acting version of the play is a thing of shreds and patches, and it fails to convey with real significance the depth and strength of the great opposing forces. The rabble is a rabble indeed, and Coriolanus is an isolated, arrogant figure, which rarely moves our sympathies. It is partly Shakspere's fault, no doubt, that these shallow waters should be so easily stirred, and as we see the play presented the plebs have no force of their own ; they are only pawns in the game of Brutus and Sicinius. Shakspere takes the common, persistent view that survives queerly in those who regard the Labour members of the House of Commons as successors to these treacherous, brutal Tribunes. Sicinius and Brutus were very prominent last night, and Mr. E. A. Warburton's Sicinius was one of the chief acting successes. His burly, formidable aspect was curiously modern ; he might have been one of the lower type of municipal councillors or the kind of person who builds jerry houses and neglects to provide suitable drains but is very strong on moral questions. His byplay was always significant, and at the moments of stress he acted powerfully. But the play was forced a little out of gear when the mob turned on Brutus and Sicinius and murdered them. It was a ghastly business, reeking with stage blood, and to force the scene to such prominence made anti-climax. It was, too, a little like an ugly quarrel interrupting a football match. And there is nothing of the kind in the play.

Mr. Benson's Coriolanus strikes one as a splendid rough sketch. It is immensely spirited, and if he bellows like a bull, it is one of Mr. Meredith's

> Bulls that walk the pastures with kingly-flashing coats.

His movements tell more than his words, but Mr. Benson makes the queer paradox of an imaginative actor who is careless of words. As Coriolanus he exercises his old talent for para-phrasing Shakspere's text, and yet from time to time he speaks his lines with a splendid sonority and perfect balance. The scene in which he stood for the consulship was admirably done, and yet it had curious touches of a humorous geniality that seemed provoked by some kind of irrelevant understanding with an audience eager for fun and stimulated to it by the grotesque figures of the citizens. He was petulant, intolerant, always redeemed by a purity and nobility of spirit. Corio-lanus is a great child, and the passages with his mother have the peculiar significance of a natural relation extended beyond the natural term.

Last night Miss Ward made a great impression in her scenes, and Mr. Benson bore himself finely in them. Miss Ward acted with astonishing fire and spirit ; she is a tragedy queen of the old tradition, something of what we may conceive Mrs. Siddons to have been—the simple force of classic tragedy. Other good performances were those of Mr. H. O. Nicholson as Menenius Agrippa, Mr. Weir as the First Citizen, and Miss Helen Haye as Virgilia. But all worked heartily to the common good, and the Stratford audience responded heartily. It was a brave beginning.

It would be a grievous mistake to pretend that there is much in *Love's Labour's Lost* to appeal to the average man in his everyday mood. At Stratford, however, those of us who are not students are enthusiasts, and as Shakspere Day was given over to the enthusiasts it is fair that the students should have had a special provision in the evening. The distinction cannot be maintained, and if the chief interest of the play is in its relation to Shakspere's other work, there was a vast amount of scholarly enthusiasm last night. It has rarely been acted, and the Mayor of Stratford expressed the general satisfaction in this demonstration that it could be acted, but Manchester playgoers will recall an occasion when our local Independent Theatre gave it at the old Concert Hall. Brave Philistines declare sometimes that even the familiar plays are outmoded ; *Love's Labour's Lost* seems to be written by a Shakspere who cared very little about all time. His theme is conventional, and he attacked it with a delightful gaiety, but he accepted a fashion that was ready to his hand. Perhaps he never quite recovered to a clear and assured sanity of wit. This preposterous game of ingenious, arid cross-references crops up continually in later plays, and it is only useful in laying too great a burden on any theory of verbal inspiration. *Love's Labour's Lost* is, indeed, a strange, ghostly play. The actors take up their attitudes for vivacious exchanges ; they pronounce their phrases with emphasis and apparent conviction ; but spirit and savour are bleached out of them, and what they have to say is often trivial or unintelligible. To such a play one should bring learning and all learning's sympathies. Its appeal is to the historic sense of comedy.

Here, then, is a play that was once alive, and its performance last evening was, in a sense that is rarely true of Shakspere's plays, a revival. Across its dim conventions and antiquated flippancies streamed the lights of a double enthusiasm ; the actors and the audience kindled each other into more than a show of delighted appreciation. Of course we were all committed to the venture, and failure was impossible ; failure, had it been possible, could hardly have leaked out, for one has to go to Stratford to see the kind of loyal audience which an actor wants. And yet without Mr. Benson's own memorable performance of Biron the illusion would hardly have been maintained. He made a great beginning that gave us a foretaste of success, and always he played with a magnificent gusto. His high spirits and athletic exuberance infected the others until the dry bones of the play were shaken into some kind of barbarous music. It was a *tour de force*, recalling in some points his inimitable Petruchio, but gaining in even greater measure from the actor's own indomitable spirit. The whole performance was a triumph for the actors ; it was carried through gallantly by everyone. The dialogue was spoken with an admirable semblance of conviction and the points were underlined industriously, but the main lines of the invertebrate comedy were conveyed in the action, and the words must sometimes be coaxed or compelled into relevance. As Moth says, " They have been at a great feast of languages and stolen the scraps," and these scraps have shrunk and dried in the course of the centuries. Some of the rhymed exchanges, particularly between the ladies, were spoken with charming effect, and the play was raised from its trivial level by these passages of a fine sanity in which Shakspere's blank verse gives indication of its great destiny.

Happily *Love's Labour's Lost* has an essential sanity, though its surface is so riotous. The year's probation for the gay young people is an artful corrective to the cloying feast, and even the reminder of death, which jarred a little last night, breaks up the conclusion into a medley of grave and gay that was well realised in the performance. The last scene was capitally managed, and throughout there was no touch of the perfunctory. The actors elaborated the jests with an air which compelled us as a mere affair of manners to accept the intention. Mr. E. A. Warburton's Don Adriano was a wonderful compound of burlesque picturesqueness and fantastic verbiage—a piece of boredom that compelled attention by its careful finish. Another very useful piece of work was Mr. H. O. Nicholson's Boyet, and Mr. Weir's Costard was, like all his parts, soundly comic and unobtrusive. Miss Regina Laurence's

Jaquenetta scored a success, and Miss Helen Haye, Miss Leah Hanman, and Mrs. Benson worked judiciously and unflaggingly. To the audience unstinted praise may be given. When the play grew very dull and no ingenuities of the actors could save us from what might have been critical moments, there was no impatience, but only the nervous attention of agitated friends. We all breathed freely again when Mr. Benson turned a somersault or made some other exhilarating diversion.

At the end of the performance we had speeches and congratulations, and the Mayor of Stratford appeared on the stage in his chain of office to say polite things about Shakspere and Mr. and Mrs. Benson and the visitors. As " genuine lovers of the immortal Bard," we all have our share in the glory, and Mr. Benson gave us a rousing, impassioned speech that brought us to the high-water mark of enthusiasm. And if this Stratford enthusiasm is mingled with a good deal of chatter, it is not all froth. It had a peculiar quality yesterday morning, when townsfolk and visitors thronged in procession to the Holy Trinity Church to pour their offerings of flowers on Shakspere's grave and to hear Madame Marie Brema's beautiful singing. Stratford enters on its festival with new life this year. Even the decorations show a prodigious vigour of attack upon the poet's works, and in quantity and variety they make a new departure. Yesterday the morris-dancers enlivened the street ; flags, designs, and garlands hung from the walls ; and the sun shone on green fields and the pleasant Avon. The festival is only beginning ; there is nearly three weeks of good stuff yet to come. It is a jolly thing to be a Shakspere enthusiast, and one can even perceive some merit in the Shakspere maniac, specimens of which may sometimes be met at Stratford.

—From " The Manchester Guardian," 24th and 25th April, 1909.

DESMOND MacCARTHY

(1878-1952)

ON BERNARD SHAW'S *ANDROCLES AND THE LION*

MR. SHAW has written two religious dramas, *Major Barbara* and *Blanco Posnet*, and one farce, of which religious conversion is the main theme, *Fanny's First Play*. He has now tried a new form, religious pantomime.

Androcles and the Lion is the reverse of mediæval in sentiment and doctrine, but its nearest parallel as a dramatic entertainment is one of those old miracle plays in which buffoonery and religion were mixed together. No contemporary playwright, except Bernard Shaw, could write a religious pantomime (Chesterton alone among writers might entertain such an idea), for no other dramatist believes so firmly in the virtue of laughter, is so serious, yet delights so much in knocking serious people off their perch. He wants to move you—he cares more about doing that than anything else ; but of all moods, both in himself, it seems, and in others, he distrusts the melting mood most. As a rule English audiences have not sufficient emotional mobility to follow a method in which farce alternates with pathos, philosophy with fun. Consequently his plays generally divide an audience into three sections : those who take in only the funny bits (They are the majority, so his plays are popular), those who attend chiefly to the philosophy (Some of these dislike it or are bored), and those who are irritated and puzzled by fun and philosophy being so thoroughly mixed together. Among the last are to be found most of his critics. But no one can appreciate a religious play by Bernard Shaw *as a work of art* who has not, if tears come naturally to him, cried, then laughed so soon afterwards that he has forgotten that he cried at all.

However often one may have criticised Mr. Shaw, and I have

done so many times, it is exciting to do it again. One always feels as though one was going to discover something new to say about him after seeing his last play; and the walk back from the theatre on such occasions is a fine pleasure for a critic with a taste for his profession. What I am going now to say may not be new, but after seeing *Androcles* it was borne in on me with fresh force.

Most of the critics of the play have accused him of indiscriminate satire, of mocking at martyrs, and raising a cheap laugh by treating disrespectfully what has been treated with reverence. In the more indignant of these criticisms there was something of that vulgarity and obtuseness which led the last Lord Chamberlain to ban *Blanco Posnet* as a blasphemous play. *Blanco Posnet* seemed blasphemous to the Censor because a horse-stealer, burning in the fires of conversion, did not express his feelings with conventional reverence. Now it is easy to understand a man, if he hates religion, being repelled by anyone in Posnet's state of mind, whether the zealot happened to be General Gordon, Wesley, or a horse-stealer. I can understand anyone disliking martyrs next worst to the people who make them. It is possible to loathe religious zeal, and to be an admirable man like Bradlaugh, Voltaire or Samuel Butler. But to allow good taste and convention to get between you and recognition of the very thing you profess to reverence, and indeed do reverence elsewhere, and on the top of that to call that thing " blasphemous," is vulgar and inhuman. I am not a theologian, but as far as I have been able to make out what was meant by that mysterious sin, the sin against the Holy Ghost, so severely penalised that it really might have been better defined, it was nothing else but a deep, wilful, damnable unfairness to which this kind of obtuseness is certainly akin. My discovery about Mr. Shaw after seeing *Androcles* was that his most striking merits sprang from his being extraordinarily free from all forms of spiritual snobbery. I do not mean that he sees everywhere what is most important, far from it ; in some directions he seems to me quite blind, but whatever he does admire in human nature that he will see and honour equally wherever it may be found. Often he discovers it in situations and in people where it is so buried in incongruities, or so smeared over with bad manners and bad sentiment, that his recognition of it suggests to people that he is satirising the thing itself. In this play many have apparently thought that because the meek little martyr, Androcles, is made to talk in a namby-pamby fashion, and the gross, chaotic Ferrovius to parade his inward wrestlings and bawl the phrases of a hot-gospeller, that the dramatist was satirising the religion of these men. That is a mistake—their tone, their sillinesses, yes, but not their faithfulness.

Ferrovius is explained with sympathetic insight. Lavinia says (It shocks him dreadfully at the moment) that she would like to see him " fight his way to heaven "—that is to say, to obey his instincts, use his hot temper, his masterfulness and his sword. While into the mouth of the henpecked, inconspicuous Androcles is put one of those lines which summarise a character and delight a critic. Androcles is too humbly pacific to fight for his life in the arena, too incapable of resentment, so he requests with the air of a tired man timidly asking for a seat in a full waggonette, that he may be allowed " to be the one to go to the lions with the ladies."

There are four types of religious zealots represented in the play, all of them fundamental types enough to have existed in the second century just as they exist now. Androcles is the " pure fool," the sort of little man who nowadays might go about in fibre shoes and an indiarubber coat to avoid using the skins of animals, and drink almond milk with his tea. Yet in him burns a little flame of courage that no wind of misery or torment can make even flicker. The drawing of his character is an instance of Mr. Shaw's recognition of the spirit he admires in whatever character it may happen to be found. Ferrovius, on the other hand, belongs to the " born again " type : he is the overwhelmingly manly, internally miserable, fighting parson, who sometimes gets into a scandalous mess to the horror of his flock, the amusement of the world and his own scorching remorse. His religious life, apart from taking others by the scruff of the neck and compelling them to come in, is a continual struggle to acquire the Christian virtues of charity and submission, and for himself inner freedom and peace. Born a servant of Mars and ignorant of himself, he has become a follower of Jesus of Nazareth. He, too, reveals himself in a sentence. In his terror that he may betray his Master when he finds himself in the arena and give stroke for stroke, he cries out, " When I feel a sword in my hand I could as soon throw it away as the woman I love from my arms. Oh, what have I said ? My God, what have I said ? " He quickly recovers some confidence in himself, however, by officiously exhorting the others to pray as they are hustled into the arena. But once face to face with the gladiators the glory of battle seizes him and he stretches out all six of them—to return again overwhelmed with remorse and shame. The delighted Emperor pardons all the Christians to commemorate such a feat of arms, and declares that he will insist in future upon every man in the Prætorian guard becoming a Christian. He offers Ferrovius a place in it, and Ferrovius, remembering perhaps Lavinia's words about " fighting his way to heaven," accepts. His prayers and wrestlings for the grace of Christian meekness have not been heard, and in the arena he has come to understand his own nature : " The Christian God is not yet," he mournfully concludes. " I strive for the coming of the God who is not yet," is Lavinia's response to that.

Lavinia is the third type of martyr. She is the kind who goes to the stake with nearly the smallest possible amount of confidence in the rewards of martyrdom. An after-life, a martyr's crown, mean little to her ; purgatory and hell nothing at all. She is only certain of this, that the point of being alive, the secret of satisfying happiness, lie in obeying an instinct to identify herself with the Will of the World which is thought of as divine. That instinct prevents her from submitting, even by such an act of formal recognition as dropping a pinch of incense on an altar, to any cult which stands in the way of this religion. The dialogue between her and the Captain of the Guard is one of the best serious passages in the play ; it is quite short, but there is a great deal in it. He is rather in love with her, and he uses all the arguments that have been used against martyrdom to persuade her to sacrifice to Diana. He appeals to her scepticism, to her good taste as a lady and Roman (Why make a pompous, hysterical fuss about a mere form ?), to her common-sense and self-respect (You're simply committing suicide and not even doing anything fine). And to that last argument she has a reply which makes one think with that momentary intensity which may leave a mark on one's permanent opinions : " Death is harder for us Christians than for you." She means that *she* has something which she really wants to live for.

The fourth type of zealot is Spintho, who does not know what faith is. He is lashed on by his own misery and terror, and lured by the hope of currying favour with superior powers. (Spintho turned tail and was accidentally eaten by a lion.) He is the sort of creature who swells the ranks of every persecuted cause or religion, and makes it all the harder for genuine people to fight or suffer for it. He usually attracts the almost undivided attention of persecutors who want to justify their conduct ; as the centurion says while he is cuffing and shaking him, " You're the sort as makes duty a pleasure."

Mr. Shaw has omitted two other types of martyr : the man who goes to the stake with something very like a bad conscience (He is rare, but he is interesting and, I think, lovable), and the martyr who sacrifices his life simply because he thinks certain dogmas are true. Mr. Shaw holds apparently that such men do not face death for their creed. Now, if this play were an historical drama this last omission would be a serious defect, for most of the early Christians firmly believed in the dogmas which assured them a celestial crown. But it is not an historical drama ; and I have, while discussing the thought it contains, almost forgotten that it is a Pantomime. Other critics, however, have described the fun, the amusing lion, the Emperor, and the call-boy of the Colosseum, who announces the next item in the programme in the familiar voice, " No. II. Lions and Christian women." It was the thought and feeling in this delightful entertainment that needed comment. Coming out of the theatre, I heard one man say to another : " But what's the point of the whole thing ? " " Oh," said his friend, " it's a skit on religious plays like *The Sign of the Cross* and *Quo Vadis ?* That's what it comes to." I was jammed up close against them and could not help saying : " It would be nearer the mark to say that *The Sign of the Cross* was a skit on religion."

—From " The New Statesman," 1913.

DESMOND MacCARTHY ON CHEKOV'S *UNCLE VANYA*

U NCLE VANYA is an unforgettably good play. I do not
think the Stage Society did justice to it ; yet there were
excellent passages of acting in their performance. The play is
one of those which require, just because the dialogue is so
natural, an extreme *finesse* in the actors if its values are to be
fully brought out. I thought Miss Gillian Scaife's Sonya
admirable. My respect for her increases every time I see her
act. She was excellent and touching as the secretary in Mr.
Frank Harris's *Bucket Shop* a few weeks ago, and now in a part
nine times as deep she has proved herself adequate. In this
connection that cold word implies real praise. Mr. Guy
Rathbone as Uncle Vanya was extremely good—at moments.
When, for instance, he stood at the door with the roses, and
during the last five minutes of the play, while Sonya makes her
dim little speech about the happy world beyond the grave,
where both will forget, she thinks, the stale ache of their dis-
appointments. Oh, Mr. Rathbone understood his part as he
sat there motionless, the pencil with which he had been
totting up figures still between his fingers, staring before him,
suffering only as the passive, the empty, the weak can suffer,
and soothed a little—you know the irony of that ?—by consola-
tions which do not console. . . . At any rate, those two,
uncle and niece, will be kind and patient towards each other—
that is the one shred of comfort we spectators carried away
when the curtain fell on Chekov's tragedy. It is real tragedy,
having in it both the flatness and poignancy of life. There is
no depth of reflection upon humanity at which it were in-
appropriate to discuss it—were one master of obedient words.

In the garden of a country house in Russia, remote and
ramshackle as such houses mostly are, judged by our standards,
are gathered a strange—and yet how familiar ! set of people.
There is an old lady who never has her nose out of a literary
essay or pamphlet ; a middle-aged man (Uncle Vanya, her
son), restless, sensitive, intellectual ; a doctor who has a poetic
passion for forestry, and is bored by his work (He, too, like
Vanya, feels he has run to seed) ; a quiet girl who is withering
on the stalk (Sonya) ; a queer, simple, gentle hanger-on, who

contributes a little music and any amount of hero-worship when required (He is peculiarly Russian only in this sense, that in our country he would not find it so easy to graft himself on to a family) ; a faithful old servant, and a retired professor of literature about sixty (father of Sonya by a first marriage), and his young, curiously attractive wife. These two last have a maleficent influence upon the others ; but to understand how this influence affects them you must first appreciate the spiritual atmosphere in which all of them, the Professor and his wife included, live and move and have their being.

Chekov follows in the steps of Turgenev. His favourite theme is disillusionment ; and as for the kind of beauty he creates, beneath it also might be written " desolation is a delicate thing." He is fond of the same kind of setting for his stories as Turgenev : summer woods, an old country house full of cultivated people, who talk and talk. There you will find the idealist who melts over the futility of his own idealism ; the girl who keeps a tighter clutch upon daily duties in order to forget that youth is sliding away under her feet ; the slightly stronger, clever man turned maudlin-cynical after his failure to find a purpose which can hold him—to think *he*, too, should be wasted ! and an old woman who only wants things to continue peaceably on old humdrum lines. The current of the days is slow here ; the air they breathe is sultry with undischarged energy, and only broken by unrefreshing nerve-storms. It is an atmosphere of sighs and yawns and self-reproaches, vodka, endless tea and endless discussion. These people are like those loosely agglutinated sticks and straws which revolve together in a sluggish eddy. They long to be detached and ride down the rushing stream, which near, but out of reach, they imagine sparkles for ever past them. Where it is rushing they do not know. Some day—two hundred, five hundred years hence—perhaps life *will* be life. And those blessed heirs of all the ages, will they be grateful to their poor predecessors who made them possible ? It is doubtful—another reason for self-pity. Stop ! This is ridiculous (so they argue). What *are* we doing for them ? Absolutely nothing. Indeed, what *is* there to do ? That is the atmosphere in which Chekov's intellectuals live.

It differs from that of Turgenev's generation in being a still closer air, still more unresponsive to effort and hope. There are no Bazarovs to break its spell, and bring down the violent rains of tragedy. It creeps about every man and woman of them like a warm muffling mist, narrowing the world to the garden gates. We have no right to label this atmosphere "Russian," and regard it with complacent curiosity. Have you not felt that fog in your throat on English lawns, in English houses ? Indeed, the main point of difference between this spell-bound cultivated Russian society and the English variety is not in our favour. If Chekov's intellectuals are half-dead, the other half of them is very much and very painfully alive. They suffer more consciously ; there is intensity in their lassitude. At least they torture themselves, and each other, by displaying each his or her own bankruptcy. They are not comatose and outwardly contented ; they are sensitive, self-conscious, and critical. Wordsworth's description of an English family circle in hell will not fit them.

> Is it a party in a parlour ?
> Crammed just as they on earth were crammed—
>   Some sipping punch, some sipping tea,
>   But as you by their faces see,
> All silent, and all damned !

Damned these people may be, but silent, no. They have a wail in them which is responsive not only to their own frustrations, but to the inevitable disillusionments of life. It is this quality in Chekov's work, though that work was born of a phase, a period, in Russian history, which must keep it fresh :

> Entbehren sollst du ! sollst entbehren !
> Das ist der ewige Gesang.

Indeed, when the curtain has been up a little time and we have watched the grey-haired Vanya mooning about, tortured by a tremulous passion for the professor's wife, longing to fall upon her heart, one weak wave of ecstasy, humility, and abandonment ; watched, too, the restless doctor, also attracted to the house by Elena, the zest for his work ebbing out of him, we say to ourselves : " Why, these people are suffering from an unduly protracted youth ! " In Vanya's elderly passion there is indeed something of the piteousness, humiliation and beauty of young desire that expects everything without understanding itself. All these people, except the professor and the two old women, believe that life would be wonderful, if, if, if, . . . And to feel like that is to be, as far as it goes, young. It is young to want to prop your ladder against a horn of the moon, and also young not to know that though we have immortal longings in us, there are—paradox through which the work of the world gets done—wonderfully satisfying properties in a little real bread. It is characteristic of Chekov's men and women not to know that. A word or two more about them, and then—even if I only tell the story in a few sentences—the tragedy will be before you. It is a true tragedy, lying in the persons themselves, in their passions and minds, and not in the external events.

First, then, Elena. She has already played her stake. In the professor she thought—Heaven help her !—she had found a great mind, one it would be good and thrilling always to be near. Now, she has found out her mistake. She is like a ship aground on a mudbank, and the only breezes which come to shake her sails are the passions she rouses in men, but she does not believe that those breezes will blow her to any port where she would be. Like the others, she has no sense of direction, no destination. Vanya's helpless passion merely pesters her, and between that and the exactions and pomposities of her eminent husband, who, now he has retired, only wants to watch his diseases and jaw to admirers, she is almost beside herself. (I was not satisfied with Miss Ernita Lascelles's performance in this part.) Doctor Astrov, however, who knows what he wants better than the others and despises them, does move her a little. She nearly . . . but she is afraid. This man also throws a fascination over poor, plain, dutiful Sonya. He has that attraction for women which the damaged idealist often possesses. Astrov, to Sonya, is so fine in himself ; his slackness and coarseness are to her but wounds he got beneath the devil-defended walls of his peculiar virtues. He is a person to be saved (there is joy, too, in that) and comforted as well as loved ; and then—he is handsome, his voice is beautiful and she is most affectionate. Lastly, there is the old professor. He is

an industrious and magniloquent fraud. (We know his prototypes and regret that so many should read again with so
much admiration what has often been written before.) For
years Uncle Vanya and Sonya have slaved on the estate to
provide tribute for this loquacious monster, Vanya, at first,
with the belief he was watering the roots of genius. On
retirement the Professor came to live with them, bringing his
beautiful, unhappy, baleful wife. That was event number
one in the play. Event number two—they departed. In
between their arrival and departure are nerve-storms (one of
them homicidal), and scenes of exasperated draggle-tailed disorder. Astrov seeking to renew his capacity to feel by keeping
near Elena's charms, neglects his work ; Sonya is tortured by
his continued presence ; the long-retarded tide of youth is
loosed together with a flood of bitterness in Uncle Vanya, while
upstairs the tyrannic old invalid gasses and scribbles and
groans among his medicine bottles.

Elena and Sonya had a *rapprochement* late one night, after the
men had been drinking. Elena ever so tenderly drew from
Sonya her heart's secret, and both women cried and were
happy. She undertook to sound Astrov and find out if there
was any hope for Sonya. She felt very embarrassed next day
when she had to speak to him ; it was too exciting. Did her
sensitive antennæ tell her that she and Astrov would soon
begin to talk about themselves ? Yes, no, yes—I think so ;
but of course, she thought she was only thinking of Sonya. It
ended by Astrov seizing her in his arms, and that moment
Vanya, who had been out to pick her a bunch of " *autumn*
roses " (that touch of sentiment in his departing words had
exasperated her), returned, and from the doorway saw them
in each other's arms. If a man of forty-six could squeal with
sudden misery like a child, we should have heard him. Then,
down comes the professor and summons a family conclave.
He has made up his mind : the country is intolerable ; they
must sell the estate and live together in town. This is too
much for Vanya. He explodes at the old vampire and wild
with hysteria dashes from the room, crying, " I know what
must be done ! " Everybody fled after him ; we heard a
shot. Of course, we thought he had shot himself. No : in

rushed the professor leaping like a hare, coat-tails flying, mouth open, eyes goggling, and after him Vanya, a revolver in his hand and Sonya clinging to his arm. He wrenched himself free ; fired ; missed again !

It is hard to describe the effect of this scene ; it hits one between wind and water—between laughter and tears. The futility !

During the last act we live in poor Vanya's heart, feeling his exhaustion and shame, and that dreariest of all sensations : beginning life again on the flat, when a few hours before it has run shrieking up the scale of pain till it seemed the very skies might split. If I were a painter and wanted to draw the animated features of Tragedy, I should not forget the puffy, sodden-eyed familiar who peeps from behind her with a smile, something kind if it were not so vacantly meaningless,—I should not forget to put the heavy Goddess Anticlimax in the picture. In this act Dr. Astrov tries to get from Vanya a bottle of morphia he has pocketed : " Go out into the woods and put a bullet through your head if you want to, but give me that bottle." Vanya sullenly refuses, but one touch of affection from Sonya gets it from him. He has to rouse himself to say good-bye to the professor, who, of course, is leaving at once, and gives Vanya a double salute on each cheek, perfunctory as the stropping of a razor. Everything has been overlooked ; the old man now feels quite sure of his tribute. Next, Elena and Astrov have their farewell scene, and he tells her she has been a fool. Here were woods, even a ruin ! She is sure to yield to a lover in town sooner or later, and hired rooms are not a lovely setting for a love affair. As she is going, she allows herself to kiss him passionately. Finally, Vanya and Sonya sit down together at the dusty table to work at accounts—work, that is the only chance. One after the other the other inmates of the house come into the room and settle down to their old neglected habits. " They've gone," they say, one after the other, " they've gone." Astrov has gone ; Elena has gone ; uncle and niece are left sitting side by side. It is then she comes closer to him and makes that dim little speech about the time when all tears will be wiped away, when, looking back, perhaps even the long years before them will seem beautiful. And Vanya cannot say a single word.

The technical qualities of this play are superb. Note that soliloquies (there are three or four) do not conflict in the least with the naturalism of the dialogue. Our dramatists' terror of introducing soliloquy is absurd. Mr. Granville-Barker, I implore you, put this play in your repertory.

—From " The New Statesman," 16 May, 1914.

ST. JOHN ERVINE

(b. 1883)

ON CLEMENCE DANE'S *WILL SHAKESPEARE*

Shaftesbury Theatre.

M ISS CLEMENCE DANE, whose new play, *Will Shakespeare*, was done at the Shaftesbury Theatre on Thursday night, admits in advance that her case is a trumped-up one or, as she prefers to call it, an "invention," but she defends herself from our dispraise by pleading a worthy purpose : to show by what strange and moving experiences a poet grows. Shakespeare would hardly, I imagine, thank her for her singular advocacy, but might, on the contrary, be confirmed in his belief that women are queer ones ; for Miss Dane bases her assertions on the very feminine assumption that a thing must have happened because there is nothing to prove that it didn't. Kit Marlowe was killed in a tavern by someone, and since there is no evidence to show that Shakespeare did not kill him (chiefly because no one has hitherto thought of charging him with the crime), it is permissible, in Miss Dane's opinion, to assume that he did.[1] No one can prove that Shakespeare was not tricked into marrying Anne Hathaway by a pretence that she was pregnant through him. Therefore, he was tricked. Was Jude the Obscure not similarly humbugged, and if he could be deceived, why not Shakespeare ? Why not any of us, in fact ? It is just as likely that Mary Fitton was the Dark Lady of the Sonnets as that she was not. Therefore she was. And if Keats could completely lose his head over Miss Fanny Brawne, may not Miss Dane assume that Shakespeare, with as much abandon, lost his over Mary ? We cannot believe that Shakespeare killed Marlowe without a strong motive, and so,

---

[1] This was written before Mr. Leslie Hotson had made his useful discoveries.

although her name has not before been mentioned in connection with Kit, we are entitled to assume that Mary Fitton and he had been playing fast and loose with each other, and that Shakespeare killed his friend, accidentally or deliberately, out of jealousy. We can even trace the origin of *Othello* in this misadventure, with Shakespeare as the original Moor, Marlowe as the original Desdemona, and Mary Fitton as the original Iago. And is not the fact that none of the State records show that Queen Elizabeth locked Shakespeare in her palace until he had finished *As You Like It* the clearest possible evidence that she did imprison him, especially when we remember that Sheridan was locked in a room until he had completed a play for Drury Lane? If one man of genius could be treated in that manner, why not another and particularly by a Queen? If Sir Arthur Conan Doyle sees visions, may we not conclude that Anne Hathaway saw some, too, to the extent of imagining Hamlet, Shylock, Lear, Macbeth, and the whole Shakespearean gallery long before her husband had a hint of them?

All we can do is to declare from our hearts that we do not believe a word of the " inventions," and leave the matter at that. And since we cannot rebut Miss Dane's arguments with facts, we must accept her play on its merits and not on its history. And here we find ourselves on more certain ground. This humourless fellow, whom she calls Shakespeare, is not the authentic poet. We could more readily believe in him if his name were Colley Cibber, but never in this world or any other will we accept him under the name of Will Shakespeare. Nor do we believe in Henslowe (admirably though Mr. Arthur Whitby plays him) spouting high poetical stuff, for we are acquainted with theatre managers, and whoever else may utter exalted sentiments, we know that they do not. Miss Dane trusts too much in the belief that her audience is acquainted with the particulars of Shakespeare's life, to the extent, for example, of making Henslowe casually refer to Sir Thomas Lucy as " Sir Thomas," and she has Mary Fitton on the stage for a goodish while before any hint of her identity is given to us. This is bad craftsmanship. A dramatist has no right to construct a play on the assumption that his audience will help him out of his difficulties by bringing specialised knowledge into the theatre. All the vision part of the play leaves us entirely unmoved and unconvinced, and we cannot believe that even a genius like Shakespeare could sit down and plan out his life's work in two or three minutes with the particularity with which Miss Dane makes Shakespeare do so towards the end of her play. But if Miss Dane has not understood her men, and particularly her Shakespeare, she has wonderfully and beautifully understood Queen Elizabeth. This character is the creation of the piece, a loftily-conceived woman, loftily interpreted by Miss Haidée Wright. Mr. Frederick Chamberlin has lately informed an astounded world in a vast volume that Elizabeth was more of a virgin than professional humorists are willing to believe ; and he avers that she was not so much a loose liver as a tight lacer. She suffered, seemingly, less from an expansive heart than from an impaired digestion. Mr. Chamberlin prints medical evidence of these singular assertions in his book. Nevertheless, we do not believe a word of them, and although we will not accept Miss Dane's case against Shakespeare, we will gladly accept her case for Elizabeth.

The play is very beautifully put upon the stage, but we wish that the Grand Guignol incident at the end of the scene in which Marlowe is killed had been omitted from it. There is something very revolting in the spectacle of a drunken man innocently dandling a dead man's body. The play is written in blank verse and prose, most of which, however, was uttered so rapidly that a great deal of it was unintelligible to the first-night audience. Our younger actors and actresses have not learned how to combine swiftness with clear articulation. They should listen attentively to Mr. Arthur Whitby. Miss Moyna MacGill's pathetic Anne Hathaway was a trifle shrill. Miss Dane desired that it should be so, but the shrillness need not have been all on one note. Mr. Merivale's Shakespeare began very attractively, but became immensely solemn as the play went on, and we wished that he could contract some of Marlowe's heartiness. Miss Mary Clare did not completely convince us of the irresistible charm of Mary Fitton, but possibly that is our fault, for we have difficulty in believing in the irresistible charm of anybody. There was a tender Mrs. Hathaway in Miss Mary Rorke to mother the well-meaning, frustrate Anne, and, above all, there were Mr. Whitby and Miss Haidée Wright to remind us that the great days of English acting are not yet over.

—From " The Observer," 20 Nov., 1921.

ST. JOHN ERVINE ON DRYDEN'S *ALL FOR LOVE*

Phœnix Society.

THE difference between Shakespeare's *Antony and Cleopatra* and Dryden's *All for Love*; *or The World Well Lost* is mainly that between a man who is primarily a poet and a man who is primarily a scholar : Shakespeare expressed his poetic vision emotionally, Dryden expressed his intellectually. The singular fact about the two men is that the intellectual in his effort to express an emotion which he does not feel emotionally, achieves a more sentimental, a more cloying result than the poet whose principal purpose is not with the mind but with the spirit. Dryden seems always to be wrestling with his intelligence. One imagines him saying to himself, " I really must abandon myself more. All passion, and particularly poetic passion, is a process of abandonment. The fine frenzy is achieved by the removal of mental restraints ! . . ." And so he goes on, arguing and theorising about a subject which is not fit for arguments and theories. Either you feel love or you do not feel it. Whatever else is certain about an exceedingly uncertain emotion, we may be sure of this, that it can neither be produced nor quelled nor explained by argumentation. We have lately seen the deplorable condition of mind wrought in Freud and his followers by their attempts to reduce feeling to formula ; a man cannot now dream about his grandmother without being charged with a breach of the tables of consanguinity. Shakespeare was not a scholar in the sense that Dryden was, although he was obviously a well-informed man who had picked up various information (sometimes inaccurately) by listening attentively to travellers' tales ; and he was able to express emotion with greater exactness than Dryden because he did not try to do any more than express it ; he did not start off with theories about it.

And here I propose to make a digression of rather more than usual irrelevancy. Mr. Middleton Murry has lately been saying some singular things in the " Nation " in support of Mr. J. M. Robertson's astounding argument that Marlowe, not Shakespeare, wrote *Richard the Third*. Mr. Murry, agreeing with Mr. Robertson, declares that Shakespeare could not have written *Richard the Third* because it is so dissimilar from *Richard the Second*, which is, perhaps, the funniest argument ever urged by reputable commentators. Mr. Arnold Bennett is the author of *The Card* and of *The Regent*, the latter being the sequel to the former and inferior to it. On the theory invented by Mr. Robertson and supported by Mr. Murry, Mr. Bennett cannot possibly be the author of *The Regent* because it is as different in style and sentiment from *The Card* as chalk from cheese. Mr. Wells cannot be the author of *The World Set Free* and *The Soul of a Bishop* because they are astonishingly different from *The Wheels of Chance* and *Kipps*. Mr. Shaw cannot be author of *Back to Methuselah* because the style and sentiment of it are so different from the style and sentiment of *Candida*. Mr. Granville-Barker who wrote *The Marrying of Ann Leete* cannot be the same Mr. Granville-Barker who wrote *The Madras House* ! . . . But Mr. Murry goes further and declares that Marlowe *must* have been the author of *Richard the Third* because the play contains this passage :—

> Methought I saw a thousand fearful wrecks ;
> Ten thousand men that fishes gnawed upon ;
> Wedges of gold, great anchors, heaps of pearl,
> Inestimable stones, unvalued jewels
> All scattered in the bottom of the sea.

Marlowe, it appears, had a monopoly of the words " thousand " and " inestimable," and since he had employed both of them in work acknowledged to be his, therefore, since they are employed in *Richard the Third*, Marlowe, and not Shakespeare, must have written it ! To such a state of stark stupidity does unimaginative pedagogy reduce worthy minds ! Shakespeare may not be the author of " inestimable stones, unvalued jewels " because Marlowe was the author of " inestimable drugs and precious stones " ! Shakespeare may not write of " a thousand fearful wrecks " because Marlowe wrote " Was this the face that launched [not burnt, as Mr. Murry misquotes] a thousand ships " ! Well, I am no scholar, but I have had some experience as a dramatist, and I assure Mr. Murry and Mr. Robertson that their precious theory is the most childish bunkum. How will they account to us for the fact that Blake wrote these lines :—

> Bring me my bow of burning gold !
> Bring me my arrows of desire !
> Bring me my spear ; O clouds, unfold !
> Bring me my chariot of fire !

And that Mr. Yeats wrote these :—

> Put off that mask of burning gold
> With emerald eyes.
> Oh, no, my dear, you make so bold
> To find if hearts be wild and wise,
> And yet not cold.

We cannot believe that Blake wrote Mr. Yeats's poem, nor that Mr. Yeats wrote Blake's, and we are driven to the common, sensible conclusion that Mr. Yeats remembered the words " burning gold," and either used them in the belief that he had thought of them before anyone else, or boldly used them, knowing well where they came from, because he liked the sound of them. And I suggest to Mr. Murry and to Mr. Robertson that Shakespeare probably lifted fine words and phrases from Marlowe for identical reasons, and that Marlowe probably returned the compliment. Was Shakespeare likely to be punctilious about a word when he had no scruples about a plot ? And is it not conceivable that Shakespeare read his plays to Marlowe, and that Marlowe sometimes suggested an alteration ? Of course it is. Such things happen now, and have probably always happened.

This digression has taken me a long way from Dryden's *All for Love*, which was performed by the Phœnix Society last Monday afternoon, but there is some relevancy in the digression, although it may not be immediately detectable. Dryden wrote his piece in imitation, but not servile imitation, as he was careful to protest, of Shakespeare's style, and there are passages in his play which, on the theory of Mr. Robertson and Mr. Murry, indicate (were it not for the facts of time) that Dryden really wrote *Antony and Cleopatra*, or else that Shakespeare wrote *All for Love*! Those of us, however, who strive to keep some hold on reality are not likely to entertain this precious belief any more than we are likely to agree that Marlowe must have been the author of *Richard the Third*. *All for Love*, which is excellent reading, hardly seemed so excellent in performance ; partly, I thought, because most of us quickly tire of incessant maundering about hedonistic love, but chiefly because the Phœnix production was a flat one, and actually false in some respects. I do not know who had the bright idea of using Restoration costumes for a play about Romans and Egyptians, but I suggest to the Council of the Phœnix Society that if this genius has any more bright ideas he should be persuaded to keep them to himself. The effect of this particular idea was to strip all the sincerity from the play and turn it into a piece of artifice. We could not believe in a Cleopatra so bedizened with petticoats that any period of residence on the banks of the Nile must have been a clammy one. Miss Edith Evans seemed to share our disbelief, for this remarkably able actress misinterpreted the part so completely that she appeared to be miscast. She began by telling her love for Antony as if she were the Princess Victoria telling her governess, the " dear Lehzen," that she *would* be good, and ended up with an excellent imitation of Mrs. Gummidge, " the lone, lorn creetur," thinking of the old 'un. Mr. Ion Swinley was the Antony. His excellent performance was marred by frequent prompting. I thought that Mr. Campbell Fletcher's Ventidius was insufficiently bluff and soldierly, but I am bound to record the fact that this opinion was not shared by others. Miss Ellen O'Malley, like Miss Edith Evans, was encumbered by petticoats, but she gave a sound performance, which might, perhaps, have been improved by a little fire. Mr. Felix Aylmer's Alexas was not clear enough. Alexas, who is spoken of by the others as a villainous fellow, is not a villain at all, but a most devoted, honest, faithful servant of Cleopatra ; a sort of sterilised statesman. Mr. Aylmer seemed a little divided between this conception of Alexas and the general conception of him as a villain. There are, in fact, neither heroes nor villains in the play, which is the first of those pieces in which black is not black nor white white, but both are a smudgy grey.

—From " The Observer," 26 March, 1922.

ARTHUR SYMONS

(1865-1945)

STUDIES OF ELEONORA DUSE AND
SARAH BERNHARDT

ELEONORA DUSE is a great artist, the type of the artist, and it is only by accident that she is an actress. Circumstances having made her an actress, she is the greatest of living actresses ; she would have been equally great in any other art. She is an actress through being the antithesis of the actress ; not, indeed, by mere reliance upon nature, but by controlling nature into the forms of her desire, as the sculptor controls the clay under his fingers. She is the artist of her own soul, and it is her force of will, her mastery of herself, not her abandonment to it, which make her what she is.

A great, impersonal force, rushing towards the light, looking to every form of art for help, for sustenance, for inspiration ; a soul which lives on the passionate contemplation of beauty, of all the forms of beauty, without preference for Monteverde or Rodin, for Dante or Leonardo ; an intelligence alert to arrest every wandering idea that can serve it ; Duse seems to live in every nerve and brain-cell with a life which is sleepless and unslacking. She loves art so devotedly that she hates the mockery of her own art, in which disdain forces her to be faultless ; hating the stage, wondering why someone in the audience does not rise from his seat, and leap upon the stage, and cry, " Enough of this ! " she acts half mechanically, with herself, pulling up all the rags of her own soul, as she says, and flinging them in the face of the people in a contemptuous rage. When she is not on the stage she forgets the stage ; if, in the street, some words of one of her parts come to her with a shiver, it is some passage of poetry, some vivid speech in which a soul speaks. Why she acts as she does, and how she succeeds in being so great an artist while hating her art, is her secret, she tells us ; hinting that it is sorrow, discontent, thwarted desires, that have tortured and exalted her into a kind of martyrdom of artistic mastery, on the other side of which the serenity of a pained but indomitable soul triumphs.

To those who have seen Duse only across the footlights, Duse must be impenetrable, almost the contradiction of herself. As one talks with her one begins to realise the artist through the woman. There is in her a sombre and hypnotic quietude, as she broods in meditation, her beautiful, firm hand grasping the arm of the chair without movement, but so tightly that the knuckles grow rigid ; her body droops sideways in the chair, her head rests on her other hand, the eyes are like a drowsy flame ; the whole body thinks. Her face is sad with thought, with the passing over it of all the emotions of the world, which she has felt twice over, in her own flesh, and in the creative energy of her spirit. Her stillness is the stillness of one in the act to spring. There is no transition from the energy of speech to the energy of silence. When she speaks, the words leap from her lips one after another, hurrying, but always in coloured clothes, and with beautiful movements. As she listens silently to music, she seems to remember, and to drink in nourishment for her soul, as she drinks in perfume, greedily, from flowers, as she possesses a book or a picture, almost with violence. I have never seen a woman so passionate after beauty. I have never seen a woman so devoured by the life of the soul, by the life of the mind, by the life of the body.

When she talks intently with some one whose ideas interest her, she leaves her chair, comes and sits down quite close, leans over till her face almost touches one's face, the eyes opening wider and wider until one sees an entire rim of white about the great brown pupils ; but, though she occasionally makes a gesture, she never touches one, never lays her hand on one's sleeve ; remains impersonal, though so close. Her intent eyes see nothing but the ideas behind one's forehead ; she has no sense of the human nearness of body to body, only of the intellectual closeness of soul to soul. She is a woman always, but she is a woman almost in the abstract ; the senses are asleep, or awake only to give passion and substance to the disembodied energy of the intellect. When she speaks of beautiful things her face takes light as from an inner source ; the dark and pallid cheeks curve into sensitive folds, the small, thin-lipped mouth, scarcely touched with colour, grows half tender, half ironical, as if smiling at its own abandonment to delight ; an exquisite tremor awakens in it, as if it brushed against the petal of a flower, and thrilled at the contact ; then the mouth opens, freely, and the strong white teeth glitter in a vehement smile.

I have seen her before a Rodin, a Whistler, and a Turner. As she handled the little piece of clay, in which two fingers, suggested, not expressed, embrace passionately, in a tightening quiver of the whole body which seems to thrill under one's eyesight, it seemed as if force drank in force until the soul of the woman passed into the clay, and the soul of the clay passed into the woman. As she stood before the portrait of Carlyle, which she had never seen, though a photograph of it goes with her wherever she goes, there was the quietude of content, perfect satisfaction before a piece of ardent and yet chastened perfection. As she moved about the room of the Turners, in the National Gallery, it was with little cries, with a sort of unquiet joy. "The dear madman ! " she repeated, before picture after picture, in which a Venice, so false to the Venice which she knew, so true to a Venice which had been actually thus seen, rose up like a mist of opals, all soft flame and rushing light. And, her eyes full of that intoxication, she almost ran out of the gallery, refusing to look to right or left, that she might shut down her eyelids upon their vision.

The face of Duse is a mask for the tragic passions, a mask which changes from moment to moment, as the soul models the clay of the body after its own changing image. Imagine Rodin at work on a lump of clay. The shapeless thing awakens under his fingers, a vague life creeps into it, hesitating among the forms of life ; it is desire, waiting to be born, and it may be born as pity or anguish, love or pride ; so fluid is it to the touch, so humbly does it await the accident of choice. The face of Duse is like the clay under the fingers of Rodin. But with her there can be no choice, no arresting moment of repose; but an endless flowing onward of emotion, like tide flowing after tide, moulding and effacing continually. Watch her in the scene of *La Dame aux Camélias*, where Armand's father pleads with Marguerite to give up her lover for the sake of her love. She sits there quietly beside the table, listening and saying nothing, thinking mournfully, debating with herself, conquering herself, making the great decision. The outline of the face is motionless, set hard, clenched into immobility ; but within that motionless outline every nerve seems awake, expression after expression sweeps over it, each complete for its instant, each distinct, each like the finished expression of the sculptor, rather than the uncertain forms of life, as they appear to us in passing. The art of the actor, it is supposed, is to give, above all things, this sense of the passing moment, and to give it by a vivacity in expression which shall more than compete with life itself. That is the effective thing ; but what Duse does is, after all, the right thing. We have rarely, in real life, the leisure to watch an emotion in which we are the sharers. But there are moments, in any great crisis, when the soul seems to stand back and look out of impersonal eyes, seeing things as they are. At such moments it is possible to become aware of the beauty, the actual plastic beauty, of passionate or sorrowful emotion, as it interprets itself, in all its succession of moods, upon the face. At such moments, as at the supreme moment of death, all the nobility of which a soul is capable comes transformingly into the body ; which is then, indeed, neither the handmaid, nor the accomplice, nor the impediment of the soul, but the soul's visible identity. The art of Duse is to do over again, consciously, this sculpture of the soul upon the body.

The reason why Duse is the greatest actress in the world is that she has a more subtle nature than any other actress, and that she expresses her nature more simply. All her acting seems to come from a great depth, and to be only half telling profound secrets. No play has ever been profound enough, and simple enough, for this woman to say everything she has to say in it. When she has thrilled one, or made one weep, or exalted one with beauty, she seems to be always holding back something else. Her supreme distinction comes from the kind of melancholy wisdom which remains in her face after the passions have swept over it. Other actresses seem to have heaped up into one great, fictitious moment all the scattered energies of their lives, the passions that have come to nothing, the sensations that have withered before they flowered, the thoughts that have never quite been born. The stage is their life ; they live only for those three hours of the night ; before and after are the intervals between the acts. But to Duse those three hours are the interval in an intense, consistent, strictly personal life ; and, the interval over, she returns to herself, as after an interruption.

And this unique fact makes for her the particular quality of her genius. When she is on the stage she does not appeal to us with the conscious rhetoric of the actress ; she lets us overlook her, with an unconsciousness which study has formed into a second nature. When she is on the stage she is always thinking ; at times, when the playing of her part is to her a mere piece of contemptuous mechanism, she thinks of other things, and her acting suddenly becomes acting, as in *Fédora* and all but the end of *The Second Mrs. Tanqueray*. At every moment of a play in which emotion becomes sincere, intelligent, or in which it is possible to transform an artificial thing into reality, she is profoundly true to the character she is representing by being more and more profoundly herself. Then it is Magda, or Gioconda, or Marguerite Gautier who thinks, feels, lives, endures love and anguish and shame and happiness before us ; and it is Magda, or Gioconda, or Marguerite Gautier because it is the primary emotion, the passion itself, everything in it which is most personal because it is most universal.

To act as Duse acts, with an art which is properly the antithesis of what we call acting is, no doubt, to fail in a lesser thing in order to triumph in a greater. Her greatest moments are the moments of most intense quietness ; she does not send a shudder through the whole house, as Sarah Bernhardt does, playing on one's nerves as on a violin. " Action," with her as with Rimbaud, " is a way of spoiling something." When once action has mastered thought and got loose to work its own way in the world, it is a disturbance, not an end in itself ; and the very expression of emotion, with her, is all a restraint, the quieting down of a tumult until only the pained reflection of it glimmers out of her eyes, and trembles among the hollows of her cheeks. Contrast her art with the art of Irving, to whom acting is at once a science and a tradition. To Irving acting is all that the word literally means ; it is an art of sharp, detached, yet always delicate movement ; he crosses the stage with intention, as he intentionally adopts a fine, crabbed, personal, highly conventional elocution of his own ; he is an actor, and he acts, keeping nature, or the too close semblance of nature, carefully out of his composition. He has not gone to himself to invent an art wholly personal, wholly new ; his acting is no interruption of an intense inner life, but a craftsmanship into which he has put all he has to give. It is an art wholly rhetorical, that is to say, wholly external ; his emotion moves to slow music, crystallises into an attitude, dies upon a long-drawn-out word. And it is this external, rhetorical art, this dramatised oratory, that we have always understood as acting, until Duse came upon the stage with new ideas and a new method. At once rhetoric disappeared, with all that is obvious in its loss, as well as what is somewhat less obviously gained by it. Duse's art, in this, is like the art of Verlaine in French poetry ; always suggestion, never statement, always a renunciation. It comes into the movement of all the arts, as they seek to escape from the bondage of form, by a new, finer mastery of form, wrought outwards from within, not from without inwards. And it conquers almost the last obstacle, as it turns the one wholly external art, based upon mere imitation, existing upon the commonest terms of illusion, triumphing by exaggeration, into an art wholly subtle, almost spiritual, a suggestion, an evasion, a secrecy.

I am not sure that the best moment to study an artist is not the moment of what is called decadence. The first energy of inspiration is gone ; what remains is the method, the mechanism, and it is that which alone one can study, as one can study the mechanism of the body, not the principle of life itself. What is done mechanically, after the heat of the blood has cooled, and the divine accidents have ceased to happen, is precisely all that was consciously skilful in the performance of an art. To see all this mechanism left bare, as the form of the skeleton is left bare when age thins the flesh upon it, is to learn more easily all that is to be learnt of structure, the art which not art but nature has hitherto concealed with its merciful covering.

The art of Sarah Bernhardt has always been a very conscious art, but it so spoke to us, once, that it was difficult to analyse coldly. She was Phèdre or Marguerite Gautier, she was Adrienne Lecouvreur, Fédora, La Tosca, the actual woman, and she was also that other actual woman, Sarah Bernhardt. Two magics met and united, in the artist and the woman, each alone of its kind. There was an excitement in going to the theatre ; one's pulses beat feverishly before the curtain had risen ; there was almost a kind of obscure sensation of peril, such as one feels when the lioness leaps into the cage, on the other side of the bars. And the acting was like a passionate declaration, offered to some one unknown ; it was as if the whole nervous force of the audience were sucked out of it and flung back, intensified, upon itself, as it encountered the single, insatiable, indomitable nervous force of the woman. And so, in its way, this very artificial acting seemed the mere instinctive, irresistible expression of a temperament ; it mesmerised one, awakening the senses and sending the intelligence to sleep.

After all, though Réjane skins emotions alive, and Duse serves them up to you on golden dishes, it is Sarah Bernhardt who prepares the supreme feast. In *La Dame aux Camélias*, still, she shows herself, as an actress, the greatest actress in the world. It is all sheer acting ; there is no suggestion, as with Duse, there is no *canaille* attractiveness, as with Réjane ; the thing is plastic, a modelling of emotion before you, with every vein visible ; she leaves nothing to the imagination, gives you every motion, all the physical signs of death, all the fierce abandonment to every mood, to grief, to delight, to lassitude. When she suffers, in the scene, for instance, where Armand insults her, she is like a trapped wild beast which some one is torturing, and she wakes just that harrowing pity. One's whole flesh suffers with her flesh ; her voice caresses and excites like a torch ; it has a throbbing, monotonous music, which breaks deliciously, which pauses suspended, and then resolves itself in a perfect chord. Her voice is like a thing detachable from herself, a thing which she takes in her hands like a musical instrument, playing on the stops cunningly with her fingers. Prose, when she speaks it, becomes a kind of verse, with all the rhythms, the vocal harmonies, of a kind of human poetry. Her whisper is heard across the whole theatre, every syllable distinct, and yet it is really a whisper. She comes on the stage like a miraculous painted idol, all nerves ; she runs through the gamut of the sex, and ends a child, when the approach of death brings Marguerite back to that deep infantile part of woman. She plays the part now with the accustomed ease of one who puts on and off an old shoe. It is almost a part of her ; she knows it through all her senses. And she moved me as much last night as she moved me when I first saw her play the part eleven or twelve years ago. To me, sitting where I was, not too near the stage, she might have been five-and-twenty. I saw none of the mechanism of the art, as I saw it in *L'Aiglon :* here art still concealed art. Her vitality was equal to the vitality of Réjane ; it is differently expressed, that is all. With Réjane the vitality is direct : it is the appeal of Gavroche, the sharp, impudent urchin of the streets ; Sarah Bernhardt's vitality is electrical, and shoots its currents through all manner of winding ways. In form it belongs to an older period, just as the writing of Dumas *fils* belongs to an earlier period than the writing of Meilhac. It comes to us with the tradition to which it has given life ; it does not spring into our midst, unruly as nature.

But it is in *Phèdre* that Sarah Bernhardt must be seen, if we are to realise all that her art is capable of. In writing *Phèdre,* Racine anticipated Sarah Bernhardt. If the part had been made for her by a poet of our own days, it could not have been brought more perfectly within her limits, nor could it have more perfectly filled those limits to their utmost edge. It is one of the greatest parts in poetical drama, and it is written with a sense of the stage not less sure than its sense of dramatic poetry. There was a time when Racine was looked upon as old-fashioned, as conventional, as frigid. It is realised nowadays that his verse has cadences like the cadences of Verlaine, that his language is as simple and direct as prose, and that he is one of the most passionate of poets. Of the character of Phèdre Racine tells us that it is " ce que j'ai peut-être mis de plus raisonnable sur le théâtre." The word strikes oddly on our ears, but every stage of the passion of Phèdre is indeed reasonable, logical, as only a French poet, since the Greeks themselves, could make it. The passion itself is an abnormal, an insane thing, and that passion comes to us with all its force and all its perversity ; but the words in which it is expressed are never extravagant, they are always clear, simple, temperate, perfectly precise and explicit. The art is an art exquisitely balanced between the conventional and the realistic, and the art of Sarah Bernhardt, when she plays the part, is balanced with just the same unerring skill. She seems to abandon herself wholly, at times, to her " fureurs," she tears the words with her teeth, and spits them out of her mouth, like a wild beast ravening upon prey ; but there is always dignity, restraint, a certain remoteness of soul, and there is always the verse, and her miraculous rendering of the verse, to keep Racine in the right atmosphere. Of what we call acting there is little, little change in the expression of the face. The part is a part for the voice, and it is only in *Phèdre* that one can hear that orchestra, her voice, in all its variety of beauty. In her modern plays, plays in prose, she is condemned to use only a few of the instruments of the orchestra : an actress must, in such parts, be conversational, and for how much beauty or variety is there room in modern conversation ? But here she has Racine's verse, along with Racine's psychology, and the language has nothing more to offer the voice of a tragic actress. She seems to speak her words, her lines, with a kind of joyful satisfaction ; all the artist in her delights in the task. Her nerves are in it, as well as her intelligence ; but everything is coloured by the poetry, everything is subordinate to beauty.

Well, and she seems still to be the same Phèdre that she was eleven or twelve years ago, as she is the same *Dame aux Camélias*. Is it reality, is it illusion ? Illusion, perhaps, but an illusion which makes itself into a very effectual kind of reality. She has played these pieces until she has got them, not only by heart, but by every nerve and by every vein, and now the ghost of the real thing is so like the real thing that there is hardly any telling the one from the other. It is the living on of a mastery once absolutely achieved, without so much as the need of a new effort. The test of the artist, the test which decides how far the artist is still living, as more than a force of memory, lies in the power to create a new part, to bring new material to life. Last year, in *L'Aiglon*, it seemed to me that Sarah Bernhardt showed how little she still possessed of that power, and this year, I see the same failure in *Francesca da Rimini*.

The play, it must be admitted, is hopelessly poor, common, melodramatic, without atmosphere, without nobility, subtlety, or passion ; it degrades the story which we owe to Dante and not to history (for, in itself, the story is a quite ordinary story of adultery : Dante and the flames of his hell purged it), it degrades it almost out of all recognition. These middle-aged people, who wrangle shrewishly behind the just turned back of the husband and almost in the hearing of the child, are people in whom it is impossible to be interested, apart from any fine meanings put into them in the acting. And yet, since de Max has made hardly less than a creation out of the part of Giovanni, filling it, as he has, with his own nervous force and passionately restrained art, might it not have been possible once for Sarah Bernhardt to have thrilled us even as this Francesca of Marion Crawford ? I think so ; she has taken bad plays as willingly as good plays, to turn them to her own purpose, and she has been as triumphant, if not as fine, in bad plays as in good ones. Now her Francesca is lifeless, a melodious image, making meaningless music. She says over the words, cooingly, chant-ingly, or frantically, as the expression-marks, to which she seems to act, demand. The interest is in following her expression-marks.

The first thing one notices in her acting, when one is free to watch it coolly, is the way in which she subordinates effects to effect. She has her crescendos, of course, and it is these which people are most apt to remember, but the extraordinary force of these crescendos comes from the smooth and level manner in which the main part of the speaking is done. She is not anxious to make points at every moment, to put all the possible emphasis into every separate phrase ; I have heard her glide over really significant phrases which, taken by themselves, would seem to deserve more consideration, but which she has wisely subordinated to an overpowering effect of ensemble. Sarah Bernhardt's acting reminds me of a musical performance. Her voice is itself an instrument of music, and she plays upon it as a conductor plays upon an orchestra. The movements of her body, her gestures, the expression of her face, are all harmonious, are all parts of a single harmony. It is not reality which she aims at giving us ; it is reality transposed into another atmosphere, as if seen in a mirror, in which all its outlines become more gracious. The pleasure which we get from seeing her as Francesca or as Marguerite Gautier is doubled by that other pleasure, never completely out of our minds, that she is also Sarah Bernhardt. One sometimes forgets that Réjane is acting at all ; it is the real woman of the part, Sapho, or Zaza, or Yanetta, who lives before us. Also one sometimes forgets that Duse is acting, that she is even pretending to be Magda or Silvia ; it is Duse herself who lives there, on the stage. But Sarah Bernhardt is always the actress as well as the part ; when she is at her best, she is both equally, and our consciousness of the one does not disturb our possession by the other. When she is not at her best, we see only the actress, the incomparable craftswoman openly labouring at her work.

—From *Eleonora Duse*. By Arthur Symons, 1926.

IVOR BROWN

(*b.* 1891)

NO MORE PARADES

OUT of nothing nothing comes. The mind of a dramatic critic recurs despairingly to the Lucretian tag. Night after night do we spend some two and a half hours watching the process whereby a dull young woman is transferred from wedlock with a dull man to wedlock with one still duller. And one man in his time meets many bores . . . but these people have not even stuffing enough to be true and faithful bores. The true bore is a positive, assertive, irrepressible creature, and when you are most cornered you can at least derive a melancholy pleasure from admiring his strategy of cornering. At least, you can observe the bore's technique. You can match him with other bores ; you can place him in a bores' handicap ; you can decide that if A is the best stayer at bumping and boring in the year's long-distance events, B is the best of the sprinting bores and could easily concede a stone to C in a tussle of six furlongs. Of such entertainment many modern comedies deprive us ; their characters are so frail as to be merely negative in their creation of a nuisance.

We used to rail against the antics of the actor-manager ; we decried his struttings and his roarings, his greedy hankering for prodigious situations and his usurpation of the electricity. We pictured him at rehearsals measuring the stage with a pocket-tape and marking the floor with chalk so that at no moment of import would he be six inches away from the central point of the eye's range. He carved up the play for his nightly supper and he loaded his plate with " fat." But at least, he was radio-active in his own kind of way ; he moved and made noises and pulled faces. In short, he laboured. If he was a glutton for fat, he was also a glutton for work—at least for the first few weeks of the run. This kind of acting could be a considerable nuisance. It stimulated flashiness in the writing of plays. The dramatist's job was to provide opportunities, and a champion at the game, like Sardou, could turn out gigantic chances as easily as Mr. Noel Coward turns out cynical chatter. Shakespeare was handed over to the pageant-master for repairs to be lavishly executed, and Irving would hurl the whole of his genius into such a tin-pot vessel as *The Bells*. We have altered all that. There are no more parades ; and the result is that small voices are now to be heard lamenting the good old days of the actor-manager, when plays were written in grease-paint and acted in a manner that was far larger than life.

Action breeds reaction in the arts as elsewhere. In this case there is an added reason for the revolt against the kind of acting whose highest emotional pinnacle is the lighting of a cigarette, the smoothing of a collar, or the mumbling of an epigram. If you set violent hands on the tyrannous player in order to release the play from his strangle-hold, it is just as well to be certain that the play is worthy of its freedom. Have we certainty ? Far from it. It is true that the passing of the great parts, which Duse, Bernhardt, and Mrs. Campbell handed to each other in the 'nineties, has resulted in a more intelligent kind of theatre. There was hardly room for Bernhardt and ideas on the stage together, and the movement away from the emotional parade and towards the intellectual play of ideas was a healthy kind of change. The repertory theatres have indeed been chambers of light, despite the jokes about their gloom. But nowadays the commercial theatre only too often gives us the worst of both worlds—that is to say, the play without either emotion or ideas, whose only content is a thin trickle of smartish jocularity. What can an actor do with this kind of thing ? There are some modern comedies which would extinguish a Salvini or fell a Tree.

Perhaps, after all, we still have some parades. There is the dress parade. The comedy of mannequins is a frequent substitute for the comedy of manners. In the programme more space is frequently devoted to the names of dressmakers and other tradesmen than to the names of the cast. I am not suggesting that the stage of to-day needs the old-style rumpus in all its fury, but that those dramatists who cannot supply a problem might try their hand at passion. Acting is being manicured out of existence amid the mild raffishness of our divorce-and-water comedies. The producer is reduced to the status of a valet making war on untidiness. The players' craft is bound in silken chains to the ideals of ease, neatness, and repose, and the result is often something just as flat as if the actor, as well as his nether garments, had spent the night in a trouser-press. The comedians, too, dare not essay a broad appeal ; they must have a slick way with the smart talk. With a drama that avoids fundamentals like the plague the most we can hope for is that dialogue and acting will be salted out of insipidity. There is no guffawing, no peal of laughter in the Touchstones and Trinculos of to-day ; they have a nervous titter, which is like the death-rattle of sanity, and the wisdom that flashes out in their intervals of polite clowning has no kinship with the universal humours of humanity, but is just the salt cynicism of the fashionable world and of the passing hour.

So our actors go to it gingerly. They do not step out to the half-volleys. They take no splendid risks. But a reaction is inevitable. There will be an end to these trite comedies about nothing in particular, which make no demand upon the actor except facility. And when a fresh and more vigorous convention does arise, we have the players ready to seize the opportunity, provided only that they have not been " produced " into the automata of realism before the day comes. The main point is that the raw material is ready for a dramatic reconstruction. If our theatre is chiefly drab, it is not the fault of the players, but of the players' training, of the producers' rigid discipline directed almost entirely to the crushing of flamboyance, and of the playwrights who insist on turning out the same drawing-room dilemmas of nincompoops, small plays about small people. So long as one spark will burn down these paper-houses, the actor must continue to specialise in safety. But it makes dull play-going.

It was a nice distinction of Théophile Gautier's when he classed the world into drabs and flamboyants, and Mr. A. B. Walkley made excellent play with these categories in an essay on Sir Henry Irving, done some thirty years ago. Of course, it is an easy game, this listing of mankind, and very good fun for the players. But, seriously viewed, dichotomies of this nature reveal as many truths as fallacies. Exploring the rock in jesting hazard we occasionally strike true metal with this tool. And the criterion of drabs and flamboyants—how pertinent it is to the actors' part.

Misconception, however, is easy. Drab is an ugly word with pitiful associations. Let us take it in terms of colour, not of conduct. Our distinction is not an affair of sheep and goats ; we are not sifting what is absolutely good from what is absolutely bad, but discriminating between types of possible excellence. The drab player is not, by implication, an ugly player, or a player of sordid parts. Rather does he see the world grey, where the flamboyant sees it all radiant white or glistening patent-leather black. Gissing and Dickens, both men of power who wrote about poverty, afford clear-cut examples of what is meant. Gissing was drab to the fingertips, but we do not rule him out on that account. The drab artist deals not in primary colours, but in the " fine shades." The drab actor thinks out his part in detail, puts it together jigsaw-wise, ponders and readjusts it with nice scruples. The flamboyant feels his part as a whole, and, feeling, lets drive.

Mr. Walkley called Sir Henry Irving " a flamboyant, a romantic in the grand style, drums beating and colours flying." Irving was, of course, a king of the flamboyants, but this judgment should not surely be taken to mean that a flamboyant can only play romance. The distinction between romance and realism is not the same as the distinction between the flamboyant and the drab. There is room for the flamboyant inside the confines of realism. Witness Miss Athene Seyler making comedy sparkle in any humdrum three-acter of modern life. What matters is the difference of temper, the discrepant method of approach. The same part can be tackled well in both conventions. The great flamboyant lifts the floodgates of emotion at the peril of technique (when flamboyance becomes merely a technique it is intolerable) ; while the drab works up by the safer path to the same or similar heights. Each method has its dangers. When flamboyance begins to

doubt itself and fumbles for stage-tricks of gesture and intona-
tion it sinks abysmally. Drabism, on the other hand, may dally
too long upon the lower slopes and never get to the summits.
Duse, at least, was no loiterer in the levels. If Irving and
Bernhardt were king and queen in the realm of blazing fire,
Duse was our princess of candle light. The drab style of execution was touched as by divinity, and quietism found a kingdom of its own.

The younger generation of English playgoers had only one
opportunity of seeing Duse in London ; that was in 1923 at the
New Oxford Theatre. Great critics have written of Duse in
her prime, and Mr. Shaw's article in " The Saturday Review "
of June 15, 1895, reprinted in *Dramatic Opinions*, enthroned
the actress in her sovereignty beyond any peradventure. I
saw a wraith-like figure, as grey as gracious, move with an
infinity of beauty through a simple peasant tragedy. Had my
Italian been of the soundest I doubt whether I could have understood her. She mumbled her part, but even her mumbling
had a beauty denied to many a rare mistress of speech. Her
acting, stripped clean of decorative artifice, was loveliness itself
to behold, yet terrible in its suggestion of baffled humanity.
The sufferings of a peasant moaning over her sick child became
as moving as though the woman herself was a child doomed
to incurable pain. A tragic actress who can shatter your
emotions as though she were guiding you through a children's
ward and yet by the beauty of her presence convince you that
life is glorious all the while, has touched the limit of her art.
Duse's name will live as the supreme argument for gentleness.
Her weapon was to have no weapons ; with a gesture she could
enchant or terrify ; the voice of gold was no more eloquent
than this quietude. But superlatives of praise elude her, for
her art was a protest against superlatives in acting. She had
no flourish and did not soar to conquer. With a pass of her
hands she walked into our hearts. And now the hands are as
still as Bernhardt's voice, and we, who had but a glimpse of the
two sovereigns in the fullness of their years, are left with dazzled
eyes, seeking the successors. As yet there are no heirs apparent.
But the fact that we have no Duse on the one hand, and no
more parades on the other, need not persuade us that we are

incorrigible decadents. Let us not rush to the ancestor-worship that sees no talent alive and genius unparagoned in every name that comes down to us in the essayists of long ago.

Have we not players, it is asked, worthy to be ranked with the mighty names of English theatrical tradition ? Have we not a team fit to hold candles against all that company described with such fondness by Colley Cibber and described, despite the *Dunciad*, with great liveliness and distinction ?

Of course there is no answer to this question, but a hundred thoughts spring out of it. It is a commonplace that acting must vanish with the actor and leave not a wrack behind. As Cibber more gracefully puts it, " Pity it is, that the momentary Beauties flowing from an harmonious Elocution, cannot like those of Poetry, be their own Record ! That the animated Graces of the Player can live no longer than the instant Breath and Motion that presents them ; or at its best can but faintly glimmer through the Memory or imperfect attestation of a few surviving Spectators. Could how Betterton spoke be as easily known as what he spoke, then might you see the Muse of Shakespeare in her Triumph, with all her beauties in the Best Array, rising into real Life, and charming her Beholders." Even the names of great actors live often by chance. Because Elia is immortal, his darling players share that gift of life. Elliston and Munden, Bensley and Dodd, we know their names, refashion their splendours or their antics in our mind's eye, but only because there was one among them taking notes that have defied the cold winds of time.

The matter is one of relative standards. Yorick may, after all, have been in the light of eternity a common bore, Burbage a ranter, Betterton but a shadow of the giant Cibber made him. Dryden wrote of Mrs. Barry as of a masterpiece, but what were Dryden's canons ? There was little competition in her time, one or two companies sufficing London. Perhaps Cibber's gods and goddesses were of normal clay, Lamb's heroes but reflections of that writer's passion for the play-house. There is no verdict possible now.

But this much we can say, that nine-tenths of modern acting must be smaller, paler stuff than the acting of one, two, or three centuries ago. This partly because a comedy of modern manners must be a comedy of reticence and quietude, since Englishmen of to-day (outside of farces wherein all faces are gargoyles) do not shout, flourish, or attitudinize. You cannot put the grand manner into the delicate containing vessels supplied by Mr. A. A. Milne ; broken porcelain were all that would result. For good or ill we have our naturalistic drama in which the first virtue of the actor is to let his verbal pleasantries slide from his lips as easily as the cigarette-smoke he inevitably exhales.

Nor does the " drama of ideas " offer much scope to the actor who would make a show of his own graces, gallantry, or bravura. The first duty of the players of the Galsworthian type of piece, say *Loyalties*, is rather like the duty of the Athenian women as enjoined by Pericles, not to be too much noticed. Let them be natural ; let them talk to the audience as to their families, applying to the dramatist's characters a disciplined art of counterfeit. Even in the most emotional of Ibsen's plays, *Hedda Gabler*, Hedda must remember that she is in a parlour of the day, not in a palace half as old as time. She has none of the mighty liberties of a Phædra, a Cleopatra, a Roxana. She is in bondage to the antimacassar ; she must take to her pistols as to parlour-tricks.

This may make Hedda's task harder than Phædra's ; it certainly makes it different. Modern acting, as far as one can judge, has more of simulation and less of presentation than the acting of past ages. The very shape of our picture-stage, with its suggestion of the fourth-wall, cries out for the imitation of the mime and defeats the individualism of the virtuoso. The players' elocution in the realistic play must be based on parlour speech and not upon rules of harmony and considerations of abstract beauty. Note that Cibber ascribes Mrs. Barry's early failure not to any inability to simulate, but to some defect of ear and " unskilful Dissonance in her manner of pronunciation." So, too, Mrs. Oldfield nearly failed through lack of " propriety " in diction. Standards of this kind would clear ninety per cent. of modern actresses off the stage. One would like to have Cibber's verdict on the methods of speech apparently considered elegant by some of our young favourites. His judgments would not, I think, be dull.

Modern English acting provides usually an adequate and sometimes a brilliant medium for the modern English play. It is life-size. It is deft and slick and suitable. Having few passions to tear, it cannot strew the stage with tatters. Like the drama itself, it goes about its business quietly. Within its limited range it has a well-groomed competence. If you refuse to allow it " greatness," it may answer that, if it began thus to swell, it would burst our drawing-room drama into fragments. And so it would. He who goes in search of new Bernhardts must provide them with a new kind of play or else a very old one.

—From *Masques and Phases*. By Ivor Brown, 1926.

IVOR BROWN ON *ANTONY AND CLEOPATRA* AT THE OLD VIC

BRADLEY will not place this play with the four great tragedies because, he says, " Antony and Cleopatra do not kindle pity and admiration to the full." Well, the great Bradley can spin what donnish pretext he likes to cover the blindness of his eyes. But some of us, who read Shakespeare plain, know better. If we had to lose one of the plays from our universe, any might go before *Antony* and *Hamlet*. If the choice had to be made between these two, I cannot prophesy my vote. Elsinore's world is complete. Tiber and Nile are but partial conducts of the human spirit. Yet they have more of glory. In Denmark is Shakespeare's brain ; in Egypt his heart. As a piece of writing, the last two acts of *Antony and Cleopatra* are to me an ecstasy unparagoned ; there is nothing to equal them in the English language, and one must be optimistic indeed to suppose that there ever will be, for Shakespeare here achieved the miracle of rising above his greatest and staying there. Not kindle pity and admiration to the full ! Was Bradley colour-blind and stone-deaf? I have read these acts score after score of times, and, whenever I look upon the words again, the sense aches at their leaping loveliness, their perfect fitness for the aim. And always some new beauty, sequestered long, is discoverable, shy amid its secret splendour.

The aim is to show the grandeur of devotion, however

frivolous, however fatal. The devotion is a double one, to empire and to passion. Kingdoms are rattled on the table like coppers.

> In his livery,
> Walk'd crowns and coronets ; realms and islands were
> As plates dropped from his pocket.

Antony knows all the time that he is staking beyond his means, but he is the gambler who would rather lose all with a flourish than walk away with a small win. That is what endears him to Shakespeare, who had no stomach for a prudent investor except in his own person.

There you have the eternal paradox of letters, the power of a man to write with supreme sympathy about the type which he most certainly is not. For, if the known facts of Shakespeare's life prove anything, it is that he was essentially the prudent investor who was not allowing any pole or perch of English land to slip uncounted from his pocket. Yet it was Antony's plunging that dazzled him to be most dazzling. Faithlessness in women he elsewhere scolds. But Cleopatra, by the sheer weight of her levity, becomes his lass unparallel'd. She is a gipsy-wanton, slippery, sensual, greedy, but she has pride, wit, the courage to play fast and loose, and finally the spirit to cut her losses with as much nobility as if she were Joan of Arc and the Mother of the Gracchi rolled into one.

There are sundry reasons why this is the hardest of all the tragedies to produce. There is the personal reason. If Antony and Cleopatra cannot realise what I can only call " size of spirit," the whole thing collapses. They are only a gambler and a wanton, but they transact their business on the tables of the demi-gods ; they go chambering in the courts of eternity. When Antony is about to join the Cleopatra whom he supposes to be dead, he knows that they will be the monarchs of the shades.

> Where souls do couch on flowers, we'll hand in hand
> And with our sprightly port make the ghosts gaze ;
> Dido and her Æneas shall want troops
> And all the haunt be ours.

The players must carry these flowers of vanity as to magnificence born.

The scene, furthermore, is cosmic. Tiber, Nile, Euphrates are in flood, yet all are tributary to the Thames, for the spirit is Western while the names are of the East. Kingdoms are here stage-properties, as cups and saucers elsewhere. How can the wooden O contain these immensities ? Certainly not by piling up masses of canvas. Word and look must do it, nothing else. Shakespeare has given the word. Mr. Harcourt Williams, at the Old Vic, releases it with speed, lucidity, and force. Virtually the whole thing is there, including the frequently cut but immensely significant glimpse of Ventidius, the true Roman, conquering in Parthia, while the triumvirs tipple and pack cards. The only exquisite and essential lines to vanish were Cleopatra's

> Nature wants stuff
> To vie strange forms with fancy

and that, I think, fell out by accident, Dolabella intervening too soon.

Undoubtedly the Shakespearean actors dressed such pieces in the vein of romantic masquerade. " Cut my laces, Charmian," suggests the stomacher, but Antony had his Roman armour. Mr. Granville-Barker suggests Paul Veronese as the model and Mr. Harcourt Williams and Mr. Owen Smyth have worked finely to give us the peacock-strut of a Renaissance Orient with all the archæology left out and all the romance left in. It is a beautiful as well as a brisk production ; considering that it is taken in the stride of repertory it is something of a miracle, the little flashes of crowd-work, like the scene on Pompey's galley and the mob's send-off to the reunited lovers, being as apt in design and as perfectly finished in their detail as if the whole had been planned and prepared and rehearsed for many months.

Mr. Gielgud's Antony caps his great seasons at the Vic, as it should. He is too young by far and lacks by nature the fleshy sensuality which one feels to have been the vessel of Antony's high spirit. But he is an actor and can mount the physical barrier on the wings of his conviction. So we see this garland of the war as a grizzled, bearded Elizabethan who might have sailed with Drake or sonneteered with the Mermaid boys, valiant, melting, melancholy, and yet marching as a Roman to his fall. It is a great joy to hear Mr. Gielgud's rhetoric, abundant in volume yet never pursuing music merely ; he so evidently understands, in a way rare to romantic actors, to what end of meaning he is making this lovely noise. Miss Dorothy Green is even less a natural Cleopatra than Mr. Gielgud is a natural Antony. She fails altogether in the animalism of the Queen ; the airs and graces of coquetry will not make the royal drab. But when the part changes from grossness to grandeur she is magnificent. The unsparing farm-yard metaphor

The breeze upon her like a cow in June

is belied in this performance, but the final, the unfleshed Cleopatra of fire, air, and immortal longings is superbly done. Mr. Ralph Richardson's Enobarbus is admirable, Mr. George Howe as Cæsar justifies a subtle stroke of casting, and the whole company is blessedly raised to the top of its form. This is the last production of the Old Vic in its present isolation, since on Twelfth Night Sadler's Wells is reopened with the proper play of that evening, and the two houses work together henceforward. *Antony and Cleopatra* thus ends an epoch and ends it in the high Roman way.

—From " The Week-end Review," 29 Nov., 1930.

IVOR BROWN'S TRIBUTE TO SYDNEY MORGAN

I HAVE seen but small tribute to Sydney Morgan, Irish actor, who died in London last week at the age of 47. He was not a top-liner of the troupe, to use, perhaps unfairly, the idiom of that starring system against which the Irish Players did once put up a fight. I suppose that you must be a top-liner to lay a strong posthumous grasp on the graveyard columns of the Press, whose mortuary editors must accept conventional values of space for fame. In matter of rank Morgan was second player, while Arthur Sinclair and, later, Barry Fitzgerald were first clowns. But if ever the rank was but the guinea stamp this was the case. Morgan was a first-rater. I never saw him spoil a part or impede the play for the privy delight of an unchartered flourish or uncovenanted

" laugh." Sinclair, an obvious genius, is always capable of bubbling over with that which is not in his part. I watched him so clowning in *The Shadow of a Gunman* as to destroy the end of the play. Morgan never obtruded. He may have had his personal resentments. It is the way of all art, particularly of those who are always Horatio and never Hamlet, to murmur bitterly beneath the scorpions of the world's inequity. But whatever Morgan may have felt, he always appeared the good ally on the stage. In the big O'Casey plays he was Joxer to Sinclair's Paycock and the Young Covey to Sinclair's Fluther Good, grand performances both in parts that were largely " feeds," adding to the already substantial deposits of " fat " upon his major colleague's platter.

Morgan is not often an Irish name, and one did not think of the square head on the shambling frame as essentially Irish or even Celtic. O'Donovan, with the tall skull and the long, flickering nose, was to me the typical Gael of the party as far as physiology went. Nor had Morgan the full trick of the lilting cadence and of the sentences that run up hill to their lyrical climax or their comic point, singing as they run. He had a deeper, huskier register than was common in the company, but the flow of his speech was copious, vehement, and varied. It was a liquid, gurgling voice with a head on it. " Give us a glass o' malt for God's sake " continually did cry The Covey, that thirsty hammer of the " Boorzwawzee." Sydney Morgan's voice, as he spoke of this bitter need, welled up like a pint of Guinness through a beer-engine, rich, dark, and syrupy beneath its crust of froth.

Morgan had twenty-three years of it. I remember him first as Bat Morrissey in *Birthright*. It was more than twenty years ago, and it was my first view of the Irish Players. There were things to be discovered in those days. The Manchester Gaiety Company were carrying *The Silver Box* in their luggage. The theatre was shedding its frippery and play-going had become as homelike as a wet Sunday, with the family fractious. It was a glorious change for serious young people whose appetite for drab delights had been cockered up by the Shavian slamming of the romantic theatre. Then came the Irishmen, so alien, so curious, so overwhelming in attack, now riding majestically into seas of tragedy, now turning ploughboys' banter to a madrigal. There is a fight of two brothers at the end of *Birthright*, and the combatants flew at each other as though blood were their argument in every particle of brain and body. Of course, one had heard all about conflict on the stage and seen much perfunctory brawling. Defiances and duelling were the small change of romantic drama. But here, suddenly, was the reality of rancour. Here was a loathing that made the actors' muscles ripple with flame. Here was a fight indeed. I can see it still, the very ecstasy of hate.

What was so strange about the Irish players was the speed of the accomplishment. There is one school of stage-mastery which talks ever of patience ; one reads of Stanislavsky's infinite broodings on a play, his incessant rehearsals ; the Moscow Art Theatre won by waiting, year after year. One is told, too, how Irving had played 429 parts before he really began. But the Irishmen, mostly starting as amateurs who turned drama into an evening's job, went slap into the fullness of achievement. When I first saw Sydney Morgan he had been an actor but a short time. He acted raw farmers and corner-boys to perfection ; he himself was never raw. Much was due to the Brothers Fay, who founded that school of speech and of strong, clear presentation. Sincerity alone never made an actor. The Irishmen had to learn the tricks ; but they seemed to learn, by some happy magic, the chief trick of all, which is to leave out all the wrong tricks.

Great stress was laid at first on the group spirit ; that sort of idealism is always showing its courageous head in the advanced, rebellious theatre. It usually withdraws its head under the bludgeoning of events. A little mundane success and out pop the stars. Leadership, supremacy, egotism, pride or vanity—call the emergent impulse what you will—is inevitable in the theatre, whose glamour is a natural magnet to the exhibitionist. We needs must love the highest when we see it ; isolation is the reward of merit ; the great droll cannot top the bill without the power to climb ; but we should acknowledge the men who stand on the rung below, year after year, filling the corner, composing the star-centred picture of the stage. If the Pay-cock and Fluther were the planets of the O'Casey plays, Joxer and The Covey were not satellites only ; they were mighty in themselves, and I shall remember for ever the angular slouch, the dragging walk, and the whole apparatus of a lean yet sensual squalor which moved in the broken boots of the actor who played these parts. So surely did Sydney Morgan work himself into the essence of these crapulous corner-boys that you felt that not the boots only, but the entire creature was held together by bits of string and by such welding and cohesive power as a glass of malt can exercise upon a thing of rags and patches. Sinclair's rascal-parts were the full-blown bladders of a taproom knavery ; Morgan's were the wry starvelings of the game. They dripped no fatness and larded no gutter. They were less largely droll than Sinclair's, but more actual, more terrible in their harsh and absolute rejection of the humbug which is so theatrically picturesque as to be endearing and refreshing.

His last part in London was, I think, in *The New Gossoon*, by Mr. George Shiels. The play did not last. But Sydney Morgan, now second to Barry Fitzgerald, came as near as might be to outplaying his leader ; he rarely had the showy parts, and in this case his rôle was the quiet matter of a patient suitor, too slow for action and too shy for speech. It was done with a rare beauty ; the acting had a canine, fawning, tail-wagging quietude as the faithful peasant spanieled his lady at heels and showed the strained eye of the dumb friend's adoration. Fitzgerald is a magnificent comedian, and he was carrying on the humours of roguery in the good old way. But Morgan, second player, was first in the discerning eye.

Let us now praise second players. The stage, with its bright personal triumphs, is often unkind to them. They are not the " daarlins," as Joxer would have said. But they are the pillars of the stage more often than common judgment will allow, and it is the pleasure as well as the duty of criticism to redress the balance of celebrity so absurdly tilted by the machinery of "featuring." The paycock side of the game is not for second players. The plough is their symbol, while the stars shine for others. Morgan, plodding the furrows of 150 parts, touched none which he did not fertilise. He is remembered.

—From " The Week-end Review," 12 Dec., 1931.

ASHLEY DUKES

(b. 1885)

ON SHAKESPEARE'S CLOWNS

THE first question to ask ourselves about Shakespeare's clowns is whether they really exist. Clowns, as we know, are to be found in circuses, in harlequinades, in pantomimes, or even in country inns, and the dictionaries set forth their clownish characteristics in great variety. But in Shakespeare's plays we cannot find any sort of men except the common sort, that is to say stupid and clever, base and noble, roguish and honest, cruel and kindly, simple and shrewd, selfish and generous, ribald and modest, coarse and fine.

Certainly in Shakespeare's plays we meet with no sort of man like Harlequin, who already wore his mask and parti-coloured tights, and carried his wooden sword, and played his lively tricks, upon the foreign stage of Shakespeare's time. The poet seems scarcely to have heard of him, though Harlequin was a very celebrated character in Italy and France, and must have been known to all travelled noblemen and patrons of the theatre who returned to England from their journeys. There is no Shakespearean comedy like that of the Italian school which we call the comedy of masks or Commedia dell' Arte. Only very pedantic people will try to trace a connection between the clowns of Elizabethan drama and the clowns of Italian make-believe. However much we may believe in the unity of the world theatre, we must admit that the English form of dramatic art has its own special character, like the English Church or the English climate.

Shakespeare's clowns, if we must use the word, are always persons, while the characters of the Italian comedy are always types. Harlequin himself is said to have been named after the devil Alichino in Dante's *Inferno*, and the harlequinade may be

341

regarded as a survival in another shape of the mediæval mystery play ; but Shakespeare's clowns grew out of life into the theatre and not out of the theatre into life. They grew out of the feudal history that created the Court jesters as noblemen's fools and out of the social history that made goodnatured butts of men in taverns and market-places ; but they had hardly anything to do with religious history, which created the earliest forms of drama that we know and has always had a hand in the creation of a traditional form.

Shakespeare's clowns are like Shakespeare's plots ; they are not entirely original, and if they were entirely original they would not be so satisfying. They were in the playhouse before the play began, because they were a part of the audience of the play. There is this in common between the dramatic art of Shakespeare and the theatrical art of improvised comedy, that both of them depend on the spectator for the business of laughter-making. The spectator alone can laugh and assure the outward success of the comedy ; the spectator alone can be laughable and ensure its inward justification. The clown is the link between the player and the public.

Much more than Shakespeare's heroes or heroines, those whom we call his clowns were created by the theatre in which they had their being. Much more than the tragedians of the Elizabethan stage, the comedians must have reflected the mood of the audience and the hour. If they did not actually make butts of certain spectators, like the comedians of the Commedia dell' Arte, they knew well that their listeners were delighted by horseplay and obscenity as well as by wit, and enjoyed topical allusions and puns as much as any other kind of humour. The gory taste of the playgoing apprentices is held responsible, no doubt justly, for many scenes in the tragedies of Marlowe and Webster. Their taste in buffoonery must likewise be held responsible for the scenes of Shakespearean clowning. Some of the best humorous lines as well as the worst may have been written to please them ; and some of the best as well as the worst may never have been written at all by the author, but only invented as " gags " and written down in the prompt book when their success in the theatre had been proved by repeated trial.

We should always beware of judging stage plays from their text, or stage characters from the printed page, which is what most scholars insist on doing. Most of all we should beware of judging comic characters in such a way, for their whole being depends upon those inversions and changes of key that provoke laughter unawares. But if it be possible at all to think of Shakespeare's clowns, or comic characters, apart from their performance, it may be possible also to reduce their infinite variety to two or three main groups of interest and importance. We may classify them, for example, as characters written to please the Elizabethan audience alone, characters written to please the audience and the playwright together, and characters written to please William Shakespeare, author of *Hamlet* and the Sonnets.

Begin at the bottom with the comic characters written to please the Elizabethan pit, and not otherwise particularly dear to Shakespeare's creative mind. We may almost call them the improvised characters, for every comedy of the period was obliged by convention to contain at least one such fool or clown, and most comedies contained several of them. Trinculo and Stephano of *The Tempest* come early to mind as examples of this first, or ultra-popular, class of clowns. It is true that neither is lacking in individual character, and Trinculo's original speech on the discovery of Caliban is a first-rate piece of prose writing ; but their repartee as a whole is in the nature of common theatrical back-chat. The much-quoted and much overrated Touchstone falls into the same class as these roisterers, for very different reasons. He is all too ready with his wit, like the most tiresome of the Court fools, and it is all too shallow ; but he satisfies the dull spectator's desire for clowning and proverbial philosophy.

In *As You Like It* there is another clown, likewise sententiously disposed but deeper, whose name is Monsieur Jaques ; but since the definition of clown would have to be widened by common consent in order to include him, he must be left out of the argument. Launce in the *Two Gentlemen of Verona* is an instance of a clown born above the station of popular mediocrity, but occasionally reduced to it through association with Speed, whose company inspires him less than that of his own dog. Costard of *Love's Labour's Lost* is surely another Touchstone in less pretentious vein, and Dogberry of *Much Ado*, with some good speeches in his part, remains in substance the traditional comic policeman. Every good comedian must want to play the opening scene of Launcelot Gobbo in *The Merchant of Venice*, and especially to deliver the opening speech, which is as full of the essence of Shakespearean clowning as an egg is full of meat; but it must be granted that Gobbo afterwards lives on the interest of this speech like any other small capitalist among comic characters, and his resources are pretty well exhausted before we see the last of him.

The truth may well be that the playwright found it hard to give these improvised or popular clowns enough to do with the action of the piece. They were supernumeraries who could only justify themselves by their wits. They had to be given one or two good speeches at least, preferably one good opening which should serve them like the *leitmotiv* in a musical composition. But they lacked usefulness, which is the prime test of the strength of a stage character. The plots of the comedies were too loose and perhaps too simple to offer them the scope they needed. Their conversations were too much in the nature of decorative interludes. The audience, let us hope, went home fully satisfied with the drolleries of the funny man in the play; the comedian went home sufficiently content with the laughter that had greeted his lines, whether they were strictly the author's or his own; but we can scarcely believe that the poet shared their satisfaction with the task accomplished. He knew how necessary it is that audiences should be made to laugh, how easily they can be tickled into mirth, and how hard it is truly to move them either to tears or laughter. For this moving quality depends upon character, and its appeal is essentially simple.

The simplest of all Shakespeare's clowns, Christopher Sly, is in many ways the most moving. Two or three words are enough to introduce him to us, and we never know any more about him than they tell us, nor do we want to know any more. It is impossible to imagine him firing off the crackers and squibs and set pieces of wit that are entrusted to the more sophisticated clowns of Shakespeare; he would never get the words aright. He is " fourteen pence on the score for sheer ale," and so simple that the whole comedy of *The Taming of the Shrew* is offered as a tribute to his simplicity. Here is an original whom we love at sight, if we have any heart for clowns or clowning. It is true that the situation of Sly and the practical joke played upon him are half the presentation of his character. He is the inevitable hero of the Induction in which he finds himself, and we are in no danger of looking at anybody else while he is on the stage ; but that only means that he is a dramatist's clown and not a property introduced into a comedy because clowning must be there.

The same warmth of life infuses the clowns who appear by twos and threes and groups in such comedies as *The Merry Wives* and *Twelfth Night* and *A Midsummer Night's Dream*. These rustics and topers, swaggerers and pedants were surely dearer to Shakespeare than his more classic clowns. An ounce of Shallow is worth a ton of Touchstone. Moreover, Quince and his company, Sir Andrew and Sir Toby, Shallow and Slender, Nym and Pistol and Bardolph are links with the entire world of clowning, the mad and irrepressible world that is Falstaff's. If one clown is to be chosen from the whole of Shakespeare, there is no other choice but Falstaff ; and if a dozen were to be chosen, we should still feel that he embraced all of them in one mountainous hulk. Falstaff marks, prodigiously and uproariously, the boundary between the comic characters who were written partly to please the Elizabethan audience and those who were written wholly to please the poet. He was Shakespeare's own, a character without an afterthought, a character of inmost necessity like Iago or Lear or Hamlet. Let us not be paradoxical, and clamour to include these giants too among the clowns ; but we must always be aware of the element of humour in their tragic composition. Lear, Edgar and the Fool are all one at the height of the storm. Hamlet and the Gravediggers are all one in the churchyard. The tragedy of *Troilus and Cressida* is swept by laughter. And for that matter the liveliest of the clowns—the nimblest, with wits like quicksilver and a note like a blackbird's call—is no clown, but the rogue Autolycus.

—From the " Theatre Arts Monthly," April 1929.

CHARLES MORGAN

(1894-1958)

ON SEAN O'CASEY'S *THE SILVER TASSIE*

Apollo Theatre.

MANY years may pass before Mr. O'Casey's art ceases to
produce confusion in the mind of an audience accustomed by long theatrical usage to consistency of mood. Hitherto
it has commonly been demanded of a play that it be tragic,
or that it be comic, or, if by profession a tragi-comedy, that
the contrasted elements should remain distinct, the one appearing as a "relief" to the other. This theory Mr. O'Casey
has definitely abandoned, and has substituted for it another,
still very unfamiliar in the theatre, though having its now
recognised counterpart in the novels of Mr. Aldous Huxley.
We are no longer invited to give attention to one aspect of life
and to consider it dominant for the time being. The unity of
the work of art is no longer to depend upon the consistency of
its material. Instead, as if the drama were being rolled over
and tossed in air before our eyes like a diamond, we are so to
observe its facets of tragedy, comedy, and open farce that their
flashing becomes at last one flash and perhaps, by imaginative
and symbolic transition, one spiritual light. Unity is to spring
from diversity. The elements of drama are to be compounded
—not separated, not mixed.

Mr. O'Casey's experimental practice of this theory is of
absorbing interest, and it is no less interesting because he has
not perfected it. Of even greater value is his attempt to break
free from the bonds of naturalism by the bold use of verse.
Anyone in this history of a footballer who was maimed in the
War may break into verse at any moment. A group of
soldiers, resting at night from their labours, falls into a
rhythmical chanting which has no relation with the matter or

347

manner of naturalistic speech. Another group joins them, and all, falling upon their knees, send up a bitter prayer to a gun raised against the skyline. Above them, like the figure of Death itself, crouches the solitary figure of a man, chanting—and Mr. Leonard Shepherd does it magnificently—a terrible parody of the Valley of Dry Bones. The whole scene is almost a masterpiece. Mr. Augustus John's setting is its background. Mr. Raymond Massey's direction of the stage—his assembling of the soldiers in closely packed groups and his disposition of them so that they have continuously the quality of great sculpture—marks him as a producer who is also a poet.

Mr. O'Casey's attempt to make his play take wings from naturalistic earth succeeds ; we move in a new plane of imagination. Yet the scene is not a masterpiece. The elements are not truly compounded. There appear two farcical figures of a Staff Wallah and a Visitor whose coming shatters the illusion and momentarily reduces Mr. O'Casey's irony to the level of a mean, silly, irrelevant sneer. And more important and more disastrous is the discovery, which we begin to make as the scene advances, that the greater part of its effect springs from the setting, the leaning crucifix, the shadowy gun, the grouping of men, and the rhythm of language—the rhythm of language, not the substance of it. Though the use of poetry has lifted the play from earth to dream, the poetry itself has not force enough to sustain so great a suspense. The scene is filled with a kind of wonder. It is, in the theatre, a new wonder ; it is exciting and, at intervals, moving ; but little proceeds from it. Mr. O'Casey has not been able to give a full answer to his own challenge.

The other acts are more limited in their range. They are not, as the second act is, a brilliant failure that might have been the core of a masterpiece. But in them also Mr. O'Casey is working at his proper experiment, twirling his diamond, leaping suddenly from a music-hall turn at a telephone to a transcendental dialogue between a blind man and a cripple, giving to a dance at a football club an extraordinary tragic significance, matching a poem with a waltz, wringing a new intensity from a scene in a hospital ward which does not hesitate to continue the broad and delightful fooling of Mr. Barry

Fitzgerald and Mr. Sydney Morgan. This method of compression does not and cannot yield the full, naturalistic portraits that arise from drama of a different kind. Miss Beatrix Lehmann plays with a fierce concentration admirably directed ; Miss Una O'Connor gives life to a shrewd, hard sketch ; Mr. Charles Laughton passes with remarkable skill from footballer to poet, becoming at last a pursuing conscience in a wheeled chair ; and there is a beautifully controlled study by Mr. Ian Hunter. But the method and not the drawing of character is the central interest of this play. It is rash ; it is extravagant ; it fails sometimes with a great stumbling failure. But it is a method with a future.

—From " The Times," 12 Oct., 1929.

CHARLES MORGAN ON GODFREY TEARLE'S HAMLET

Haymarket Theatre.

No Hamlet has had a warmer heart, a gentler or more winning humanity than Mr. Godfrey Tearle's. Before heaven, a very likeable man—one to choose as a friend, to honour as a prince. And to feel for Hamlet the liking, the almost unswerving affection, that we do feel at the Haymarket is implicitly to criticise Mr. Tearle's performance. See his welcome to Horatio from which the impression of friendship springs instantly ; observe with what warmth, what eagerness and good sense, he treats the players ; listen to his converse with the gravedigger, which is never twisted to an extravagant humour and is the more touching, and the more valuable as a retrospective comment, because held in so careful a simplicity. All this enables us to know—or, shall we say, to feel—a virtue in the man that more highly-strung and seemingly more sensitive performances have often obscured. The same merit is preserved even among the demerits of Mr. Tearle's soliloquies. They are clean of theatrical affectation ; they are never mouthed or ranted, but spoken always with a kind of modesty that draws us to the speaker ; and when, beside her grave, Hamlet says that he loved Ophelia, his love is plain and his grief directly communicated. A loving man, an honest, struggling, loyal man, held back from his active purpose by weaknesses in his character, but not, as some Hamlets have been, a neurosis on legs or an actor wallowing in a great part.

For all this a blessing on Mr. Tearle, but gratitude cannot conceal that the portrait he draws is incomplete. Two instances will serve. First, the soliloquies ; they are clear, reasonable arguments, but they are never what the soliloquies should be—a trickle, a flow, a torrent of apprehension passing through the mind into the soul, as rain passes into thirsty ground. Second, the scene in which Hamlet comes upon the King at prayer and abstains from killing him lest, if the body die upon its knees, the spirit be carried to heaven. This is a fiend's abstention ; this carrying of revenge into eternity is an act of devilish imagination of which Mr. Tearle's loving and honest man, so little troubled by the subtleties of the Renaissance, would have been altogether incapable. The defect is a damaging one. Not only is this particular scene, psychologically as important as any in the play, robbed of its effect, but the failure of it makes clear what Mr. Tearle's portrait lacks. He succeeded Mr. Ainley very recently in the part ; as the evenings pass his performance will certainly be enriched, perhaps beyond our criticism of it. It is already an extremely able piece of acting, full of life, particularly in the early scenes, and rich in those human attributes which more spectacular playing has often concealed.

It is not necessary to speak in more than general terms of the rest of the performance, which, except that Mr. Dennis Hoey now plays Horatio, is very close to the performance given at the Haymarket in the spring of last year. Mr. Hoey will be a good Horatio when he has had time to be at ease with his memory. Mr. Malcolm Keen brings a splendid vitality to the King. Miss Irene Vanbrugh's Queen is less fortunate ; the dignity is there, but the words sometimes lack the impulse of thought. The Polonius of Mr. Herbert Waring is firm in the tradition ; Mr. Baliol Holloway's ghost is genuinely impressive ; Mr. Hewitt, Mr. Robert Speaight, and Mr. Tristan Rawson all distinguish themselves ; and Miss Fay Compton's scene of Ophelia's madness is a superb mingling of terror and beauty—as lovely a treatment of the part as we may see in

our generation. And it may be long before those who miss this *Hamlet* have another opportunity to see so richly endowed a performance of Shakespeare within a mile of Charing Cross.
—From " The Times," 4 March, 1931.

CHARLES MORGAN ON ANDRÉ OBEY'S *LE VIOL DE LUCRÈCE*

Arts Theatre.

THOSE who admired the vigour and fantastic originality of M. Obey's *Noé*, and applauded it as an entertainment without hailing it as a great work of art, may now be glad of their reticence, for *Le Viol de Lucrèce* is to *Noé* what a tragic bronze is to a brilliant and agile toy. To liken the new play to a bronze is, indeed, fitting, M. Obey's writing and the performance of the Compagnie des Quinze having a sculptural quality that distinguishes them from all that we are accustomed to in our theatre. The action is illumined by the comments of Le Récitant and La Récitante, two figures half-masked, who, in the tradition that has been handed down to us by Hardy from the Greek Chorus, draw into themselves from the play and express to the audience the spirits of irony and pity, swerving sometimes into a variant of the Messenger's narrative so that we hear, while it is still far off, the clatter of Tarquin's horse through the night, and afterwards perceive, though he, too, is distant, the doubt, the struggle, the surrender, the stealthy approach through sleeping corridors of Tarquin himself.

Thus is the tension raised, the tragedy prepared. And when M. Aman Maistre emerges on to the stage, where the great bed of Lucrèce stands curtained, such is his power that the bed, though by measure within reach of his arm, becomes for us, as for him, a thing imagined and desired, a remote thing still divided from him by doors and darkness, towards which he moves, creating walls by the trembling extension of his hands, filling the little stage with long, winding corridors by the slow, tentative movements of his feet. Scenery is abolished and the theatre built, painted, and lighted by the mind.

And when at last the invisible door has been forced by

Tarquin's knee, and the curtains of the bed are thrown open, and Lucrèce is awake in her fear, Le Récitant and La Récitante, who have been watching in silence, leap to the tragic climax. They have been forgotten ; every thought is with Lucrèce, Mlle. Dasté having beautifully conveyed her pride and agony ; when her despair and Tarquin's triumph are given their final expression in two cries that clash like cruel music, the emotional summit seems to have been reached Then the observant figures speak. They cry aloud beneath their masks. The timing and the tone are masterly. The four short cries move upon one another like the syllables of a simple word. They have the distinctness of separate comments but a word's unity, and the word strikes to the heart. The same brilliance of composition shines throughout the play. What life in the soldiers ! What splendour in M. Bovério's rhetoric ! With how charming and moving a simplicity are the domestic details of Lucrèce's household suggested ! And when Mlle. Dasté falls in death, what a fall it is—like the last movement of a dance.

—From " The Times," 18 June, 1931.

R. CROMPTON RHODES

(1887-1935)

ON *ŒDIPUS TYRANNUS*—PRODUCED BY THE O.U.D.S.

MAGDALEN GROVE on an evening in June. On the lawn, a few long rows of chairs for the audience ; behind them, a dark scaffolding with three amber lights trained upon a simple stage ; before them, a long, grey, many-windowed façade of Magdalen College. Its single central doorway, hung with a black curtain, has become the *skene* of an improvised theatre, leading to a flight of steps covered with cloth of a rich warm brown ; the two windows on either flank are hidden by draperies, as yellow as ripe corn, and beyond them are the *paraskenia*, the simple wings of grey canvas. In an upper window an extraneous crimson curtain flutters gently, but the evening light mellows it with all the paler hues into one gracious harmony.

The audience has gathered, talking with a quiet restraint that would not be unseemly in a cathedral. But every sound ceases at the entrance of the long-robed chorus of Theban elders, murmuring among themselves in an alien tongue, and taking their places before the little altar of Zeus. Then from his palace, golden-helmeted, handsome, stately, comes Œdipus the King, and demands in clear tones, deep and mellifluous :

> Why sit ye here, my children, sons of ancient Cadmus.

With accents as rich and dignified, the priest tells of the sorrows that have befallen the state, and in the lovely sorrowful melody of Greek verse the tragedy of *Œdipus Tyrannus* unfolds itself. The audience listens in deep silence—young Oxford, with pipes and cigars and cigarettes that presently go out, and are lighted no more ; middle-aged Oxford, placing clerical hats under the seat, till the gnats grow too inquisitive, and following the play

353

with one eye upon the stage and the other on the Greek text : venerable Oxford, nodding appreciatively at the felicities of diction, and looking as if it knew the whole text of Sophocles by heart. A foreign gentleman, with ear-rings and a sweeping of long hair, his cloak closely buttoned to his throat, listens impassively. There are as many women, young and old, as men, and two out of three have on their knees the Greek text, interleaved, neatly annotated and scored.

We are not, however, all Grecians. An undergraduate, stirred by a familiar word, nudges his neighbour, and whispers " ' Ai ai, Io, io '—that's the full extent of my Greek " ; at which the other smiles indulgently, while the barbarian calmly and unaffectedly seeks first-aid from the synopsis, which it seems so unfashionable to consult. Oxford itself, city and university, orchestrates with its evening sounds the age-old tragedy—in the trees behind, two blackbirds engage in rapid recrimination, a clock chimes nine, and faint and far-away there are here bugle-calls and there the cheerful strumming of a piano. Every now and then, from somewhere unseen, as plaintive and silver-soft as a harp, come a few strains from a *celeste*, the prelude to the chorus of Elders, their clear eyes and smooth faces belying their coal-black beards, solemnly speaking their incantations, strophe and antistrophe.

Creon, the stalwart brother of Jocasta, old Tiresias, the blind prophet, led by a fair-haired youth, Jocasta herself—they come and go. Œdipus the King recites how he was son to Polybus of Corinth and Merope of Doris, and how the oracle foretold that he should slay his own father and marry his own mother. Jocasta the Queen, his wife, tells him how it was prophesied, too, that her son, who died long ago, should kill his own father. Then comes the message that old Polybus is dead, and just as Œdipus is exulting that the prophecy is falsified, by slow steps and implacable the tragedy moves to the discovery : the old shepherd who was told to slay the son of Jocasta and Laius preserved his life, and he is no other than the King. The oracle had spoken truly. With a cry Œdipus rushes into the palace, and presently comes the messenger to say that Jocasta has died by her own hand, while Œdipus, her son-husband, has torn out his eyes.

Now the twilight has deepened, the amber floods have been changed to green, and shadows that fall upon the text-books are green. The long façade is a darker grey, and from two or three windows undergraduates in dinner-jackets are peering down at the stage. The light from the scaffolding plays strange tricks with the stone and colours the ridges with high lights of luminous green, while the windows above the *skene* are turned to mauve ; and even the sky, which elsewhere is fading blue, is lighted to a delicate and glowing heliotrope. Œdipus the King, with the fresh blood drying beneath his eye-sockets, is caught alone in a shaft of a golden light, like a strange sunset that he cannot see. It flashes on the scales of his breastplate as he says farewell to his little daughters, Antigone and Ismene ; it gleams as he listens to Creon pronouncing his banishment ; it glints for a moment longer as he moves away, stumbling into the darkness that will be his for evermore. The Theban elders watch him into the distance, like a ship passing beyond the horizon. Then they, too, turning their backs, depart into their city, chanting the despairing philosophy of Sophocles— " Count no man happy until he is dead."

The silence of the audience is broken by applause sincere and prolonged. In the darkness the president, Mr. Hugh Hunt, makes a brief appearance to summon the producer, Mr. Alan Kerr, of New College, who shuffles modestly up and down the steps and stares at his boots while he tells, half-shyly, that the university by statute demands that the society shall give a play in Greek every fourth year, but it unfortunately does not include a clause to conscript an audience. " Therefore, if you have a friend who understands this barbarous language "— " barbarous," accented humorously, lovingly. . . .

Austerely we depart, crossing the smooth lawns of Magdalen, praising that fine actor Mr. W. G. Devlin, of Merton, for his noble impersonation of Œdipus ; the Græco-Cretan costumes of Mr. Edward Scott-Snell, of Christ Church ; the quiet beauty of the setting. " What a perfect language," says a clergyman, half to himself, as he puts away his Sophocles ; " nothing can approach its music, not even Italian or Russian." In the lane beside Magdalen the headlights of waiting motors throw their long beams, and the purr of an aeroplane is heard overhead. For a moment the Twentieth Century returns with a rush, but in the sky a solitary star gleams. We recall that Œdipus has said how wistfully he looked at the stars that hung over Corinth's towers—but Corinth, or Thebes, or Athens, could they have been more beautiful than this Oxford by moonlight?

—From " The Birmingham Post," June 1932.

JAMES AGATE

(1877-1947)

ON JOHN BARRYMORE'S HAMLET

Haymarket Theatre, 19 *Feb.,* 1925.

MOODS may be of many kinds, and Hamlet undoubtedly had his fair-weather ones. *Au fond,* this young man was of an amiable, lively, and even sunny disposition. How, else, could Ophelia have drawn up that shining catalogue ? Or how, if his Prince's heart had been otherwise, could the frank and manly Horatio have won to it ? But Shakespeare, who never hit the nail except on the head, has already settled this beyond any argument in that one-line epitaph. " Noble " and " sweet " are Horatio's adjectives, nothing being said about melancholy. Is not the case a plain one of transfusion, the dejection being Shakespeare's ? Put it the other way round. Is there a single line of the Sonnets which might not have been penned by Hamlet in one or other of his moods ?

This is only to reiterate the old statement that Hamlet is Shakespeare himself—a commonplace, doubtless, but one to be borne in mind whenever an actor reissues the old, magnificent challenge. It is the familiar affair of dual superlatives—the glorious morning obscured by basest clouds, " heavenly alchemy," and " ugly wrack." Can the actor essaying Hamlet give us both aspects—the sky of bluest blue and the sweeping storms of darkest pessimism ? Can he compass the tenderness of the " heart's core " speech, the filial piety, the polished courtesy and badinage, the sinister preoccupation, the nosing after corruption, the ranting and mouthing ? Can he, in a word, pour into this part all the treasures of the richest of human minds ? Has he the physical perfections, the romantic riches, to pour ? But Hamlet's mind has ugliness also, and your actor must in his person exhibit these as well. Mr. Barrymore's

Hamlet draws fewer tears than Forbes-Robertson's, but it is nearer to Shakespeare's whole creation than any other I have seen. In fact, this *is* Hamlet, since you have but to scratch the god and the demon instantly appears.

What are Mr. Barrymore's qualifications? Well, first a handsome face, intellectual as to the brow, a trifle womanish in the lower part, after the manner of the paintings of Angelica Kauffmann. Next an agreeable voice, touching nobility here and there, but lacking the organ-note and in emotion running too easily to the head-notes of the tenor. Add the purest diction, perfect enunciation, and unexampled clarity. Now note a slim figure and the general illusion of princeliness and youth. All these are informed—and here is the key—by intellectual capacity of a rare order and analytical power of extreme cogency.

How, with such gifts, does Shakespeare's poetry fare? A trifle ill is the answer. Mr. Barrymore has the finest possible sense of values in the case of single words. Take such a line as " How weary, stale, flat, and unprofitable . . . " and note how it is built up of successive images which come into the mind before the word is coined to represent them. The actor never gabbles. But this good quality may have its corresponding defect, by which I do not mean want of pace alone, but of power to sweep the listener off his feet. Mr. Barrymore builds lines out of words, but he does not always weld the lines into the whole which a great speech must be. The first and third soliloquies are ratiocinative, the second—" O, what a rogue and peasant slave am I ! " —belongs surely to the domain of pure emotion. It is a cadenza, a piece of virtuosity, an exercise in what musicians call *rubato*.

This is the speech in which Hamlet is to prepare the spectator for his " Get-thee-to-a-nunnery " tirade, and Ophelia's " blasted with ecstasy." Mr. Barrymore blasted it with pure reason. You felt that he saw himself first as a rogue, then as a slave, who, moreover, must take on the attributes of a *peasant* slave. He made note one by one of all the aspects of a player who should simulate grief—the tears, distraction, and broken voice. But Hamlet is at white heat, or working up to it, and the debating method does not carry us away. It is possible that this achievement is not within this actor's scope, but I submit that a declamatory failure would here be better than expository success. The sails of the actor's voice having no knack of bellying, Mr. Barrymore attempts to get power by sudden gusts, choosing a single word for an explosion. Sometimes the choice is quite arbitrary, as in his refusal to take the King when he is " fit and seasoned for his passage." Passage is the word chosen here, and the violence is without meaning. Certain it is that Mr. Barrymore cannot cope with such words as " this majestical roof fretted with golden fire." His Hamlet has too much the *indoor* look, as the essayist remarked of Raphael's figures, and will find his images in his own brain. Such a one would not rack the heavens for a comparison. Sun and stars are not his concern, and the words, being perfunctory, are robbed of their just splendour.

But I have given too much space to fault-finding. The play-scene was immensely fine, its climax being a miracle of virtuosity, and the closet-scene was perfection. Much of the latter was spoken on Gertrude's breast, and the pathos was extraordinary. And from here right on to the end I thought the performance magnificent. It gathered power, coherence, and cumulative effect ; in short, we knew ourselves to be in the presence of a fine and powerful mind. But surely the savagery and tang of the end are lost unless the quarrel with Laertes takes place where Shakespeare explicitly directs that it shall take place. At the words, " This is I, Hamlet the Dane ! " Hamlet *must* leap into the grave. This is a giant's conception, and the vaunt in " the Dane " is to prepare us for the vault. The actor made amends with a duel in which he was half impish and half " fey." At the realisation of Laertes' treachery we saw him gather up decision ; he spitted the King with gusto, and in his own dying found felicity. The whole performance had a hundred little perceptivities and touches, and no perversities of ingenuity. Only once was Mr. Barrymore naughty, when, at the words " crawling between heaven and earth," he indicated that the former was situated in Ophelia's hair. To sum up, this was a great though not an overwhelming performance. The magnanimity of genius was not present, and at times mere conscientiousness threatened her pale wing. But all that intellect could do was done.

The cast was brilliant almost throughout. Perfection is not too complete a word for Miss Constance Collier's Queen, admirably " lived " yet low in key. Would Mr. Augustus John paint another " Tragic Muse " ? Here is his subject and his colour. Miss Fay Compton's Ophelia was fragrant, wistful, and had a child's importunacy, unmatched in my time. Mr. Courtenay Thorpe's anguishing Ghost was authentically from another world, and spoke a music rare in this. Mr. Malcolm Keen made a good King, Mr. Waring a fair Polonius, Mr. Ben Field a creditable grave-digger, and Mr. Shayle Gardner a cherubic Fortinbras. A word is due to the Osric of Mr. Frederick Cooper and the Bernardo of Mr. Roy Travers, a tiny part excellently played.

But few lines are left for the setting of the American Mr. Robert Edmond Jones. I declare this to be the most beautiful thing I have ever seen on any stage. The vast arch at the back served as the battlements, and was hung with curtains for the indoor scenes, played on two platforms intersecting a flight of steps. Up these Ophelia had to make a final exit of great peril, achieved by Miss Compton with immense skill and nerve. But should not the churchyard scene of Mr. Norman Wilkinson have the melancholy of summer afternoons ? The dark and the cold may be accurate, but the mind is thereby frozen with horror, when it should melt with pity.

—From " The Sunday Times," 22 Feb., 1925 ; and reprinted in *The Contemporary Theatre*, 1925. By James Agate, 1926.

JAMES AGATE ON C. B. COCHRAN'S PRODUCTION OF *HELEN!*

Adelphi, 30 January, 1932.

HELEN, thy beauty has meant all sorts of things to all sorts of writers ! It has inspired the full orchestra of world-poets booming and banging and sawing away in what Mr. Robey has called " the halls of classic consonance." It has also served as peg for two French vaudevillists and a German melodist driving an honest trade in quips and tunes. The glory that was Greece ? " Quelle blague ! " we can imagine Meilhac saying to Halévy, and Halévy agreeing.

Though the second and wittier of the collaborators died less than fifteen years ago, few playgoers can have any recollection of the first night of the famous operette. But we can be sure of this: that Helen's time and place were definitely the 'fifties and some bandbox theatre of the boulevards—was it perhaps the Bouffes Parisiens in the Passage Choiseul?—while that which drew the applause of the now soundless clapping host was all that the librettists and their confrère could pack into the piece of French wit, French verve, French bedazzlement, and music so French that it needed a German Jew to write it. We may be sure that the heels of Helen's French shoes were as high as Ilium's towers were topless.

Mr. Cochran's problem was to furbish up the old sparkle and avoid substituting a new one, to stick to the operette and to keep the thing French. Who should do it for him? In the matter of libretto Meilhac and Halévy's day was obviously over; what about Mr. A. P. Herbert, the most English of our wits? But French poetry, even when it is grave, presents the English interpreter with difficulties; France's tragic dramatists are Restoration before the Monarchy has fallen.

Those repetitioners, Racine and Corneille, indulge in terrific mouthings about lovers slain by passion when to the English mind " smitten " would put the case high enough: French opéra-bouffe is a transposition into the key of mischief of something which, for all the noise it makes, has never, to the English sense, been really serious. Hence a French operette about Helen and Paris, Menelaus, Agamemnon, Nestor, and all the Alexandrine crowd can only be parody at two removes, and how exactly Mr. Herbert has realised this is shown in the little verse in which the contending armies agree on the pragmatical if not the moral issue:

> No wife will take
> Young men to bed
> If when they wake
> They find they're dead.

Mr. Herbert is reasonably witty throughout. To be honest, I ought to say that whenever the ear is not listening to the buzz and *frou-frou* of Mr. Oliver Messel's marvellous colourings, or desists from accompanying the composer on some haunting excursion, when the eye can momentarily forget Herr Reinhardt's marshallings and M. Massine's deployings, and shut out that inventory of beauty which is Miss Evelyn Laye—what I am getting at is that when the mind has a moment free for Mr. Herbert it always finds him bright. One says boldly that no other adaptor could have been wittier after that event of eighty years ago.

Perhaps one could not expect Mr. Herbert to maintain throughout the level of his best lyric, which begins : " Is *that* the face that launched a thousand ships ? " and then picks Homer's brains. But this is legitimate in one whose private thunder is good enough, and I shall quote in support Mercury's warning to Paris before the Judgment : " You will see three turtle-doves when you begin the business, and two hell-cats when you've done." But the fate of every librettist is to take the kicks whilst composer, producer, wardrobe-mistress, electrician, call-boy, and even the actors get the kudos, which I take to be the Greek for ha'pence. Let it be recorded that the new third act, which ascends the brightest heaven of Mr. Cochran's invention, is Mr. Herbert's own.

Professor Korngold is not going to be blamed by me because he has done for Offenbach what Mozart did for Handel. Thanks to musical comedy, the theatre ear is grosser than it was ; Professor Korngold, compelled to augment the score to the size of the theatre and the scale of production, has given volume to delicacy without encroaching on it. And how fresh in these brazen days, is Offenbach's pure lilt ! This brings me to the production, and I shall not offend if I say that Herr Reinhardt is one of the best actors in the piece. It is incomprehensible that he should have restored and redecorated and re-enacted the old thing, and made a colossal show of it without losing one jot of its boudoir, jewel-case charm.

But we must remember that Herr Reinhardt has had his henchmen, kittle cattle among whom to attempt discrimination. Let the Orgy—which will be the dream of London as it must have been the nightmare of the Censor—be put down to the credit of M. Massine, since this leaves one free to say that Mr. Messel's decorations are a triumph of wit, fantasy, and ravishment. " The centuries kiss and commingle," and so do these centurions wearing the costumes of ancient Troy as they were the courtiers of Louis Quatorze. The battle scene is something which old Poussin might have designed for the walls of a modern night club. Those amazing white plumes splashed with red may be baroque ; I prefer to say that they look as though Jupiter's nose has bled. If this show is not Mr. Messel's, whose is it ?

Miss Laye's porcelain quality is known the world over, and the blue of her eyelids and trailing robe is pure Wedgwood. Now to Naiad airs she brings competence in the hard business of acting. Her singing is the nearest possible approach to the real thing ; her breathing of " Shepherd, have done," comes o'er us like the sweet south, stealing and giving odour. Mr. Bruce Carfax will never again be so well served by a rôle as he is in the case of Paris, nor will he better fulfil any future rôle. His eyes, slanting up into his head, give him a faun-like quality happily equidistant from Russian dancer and Oxford blue, and this permits him to look like a love-god and abjure mawkishness. In addition Mr. Carfax acts and sings as well as we would have him.

As Menelaus, Mr. Robey is the cynosure of every eye off the stage, though on the stage nobody marks him, whence it will be realised that his performance is a miracle of accommodation like that of a trombone-player obliging with a pianissimo. The old-time roars have taken on a sucking-dove quality, and Robeyism, here more honoured in the breach than in the observance, is now an overtone. The gorgeous rhetoric of the halls has been subdued to the poet's " Nicean barks," and the performance is irresistibly comic throughout. As Calchas, Mr. W. H. Berry achieves a feat similar to Mr. Robey's. His part, if not very long, is very good, and I do not think a better artist could have been chosen for it. Calchas is alive throughout.

The tiny part of the Messenger is perfectly played by Mr. Hay Petrie, which may suggest to our Dull Young Things that Shakespeare is still something if only as a training-ground ! Mention must be made of Mr. Leslie Jones's Agamemnon, Miss Désirée Ellinger's Orestes, and the remarkable convolutions of

Eve. The chorus has an enormous rôle ; whether rapt and static or orgifying and corybantic, it acts as one person. The casting throughout has been a feat of jugglery combined with vision, a masterpiece of, shall I say, sleight-of-mind.

Mr. Cochran's share in all this ? I take it to have been that of the connoisseur in beauty as distinct from spectacle, of the onlooker who has seen most of the game. Sole arbiter among many claimants to our attention, he has been utterly purposed that none shall be heard more than the others. Determined, too, that the production shall prevail as a work of art, a whole greater than its parts and standing up to their sum. In this latest and finest example of his superb taste Mr. Cochran has recognised old tradition and discovered new glamour.

—From " The Sunday Times," 31 Jan., 1932.

INDEX

The Names of the Dramatic Critics whose writings have been represented are printed below in heavier type. The names of the players mentioned by the critics (often by surnames only) are given in full wherever possible. All play-titles appear in italics.